TEACHER'S EDITION

Vocabulary
for Achievement
SECOND COURSE

Margaret Ann Richek

Arlin T. McRae

Susan K. Weiler

GREAT SOURCE

WILMINGTON, MA

AUTHORS

Margaret Ann Richek
Professor of Education, Northeastern Illinois University; consultant in reading and vocabulary study; author of The World of Words *(Houghton Mifflin)*

Arlin T. McRae
Supervisor of English, Evansville-Vanderburgh School Corporation, Evansville, Indiana; Adjunct Instructor in English, University of Evansville

Susan K. Weiler
Instructor of Art History at John Carroll University in Cleveland, Ohio; former teacher of Latin, Beaumont School for Girls, Cleveland Heights, Ohio

CONSULTANT

Larry S. Krieger
Social Studies Supervisor, Montgomery Township Public Schools, New Jersey; author of World History *and* U.S. History *(D.C. Heath), co-author of* Mastering the Verbal SAT 1/PSAT *(Great Source)*

CLASSROOM CONSULTANTS

Jack Pelletier
Teacher of English, Mira Loma High School, Sacramento, California

Valerie M. Webster
Teacher of English, Walnut Hill School, Natick, Massachusetts

ACKNOWLEDGMENTS

Definitions for the three hundred words taught in this textbook are based on Houghton Mifflin dictionaries—in particular, the *Houghton Mifflin Student Dictionary*—but have been abbreviated and adapted for instructional purposes. In the skill lessons, dictionary entries from the *Houghton Mifflin Student Dictionary,* copyright © 1986, appear on pages 20 and 40; dictionary entries from the *Houghton Mifflin College Dictionary,* copyright © 1986, appear on pages 19–20, 39–40, and 59–60. Some of the entries have been abridged. The pronunciation key on the inside front cover is adapted from *The American Heritage Dictionary of the English Language, Third Edition,* copyright © 1992.

CREDITS

Production: LaurelTech

Illustrations: Alex Bloch: pages 185, 197; Dick Cole: pages 65, 77, 145, 151, 177; Simon Galkin: pages 31, 57, 117, 125; Charles Scogins: pages 11, 45, 71, 171

Printed in the United States of America

International Standard Book Number: 0-669-46486-4

7 8 9 10 11 12-HS-08 07 06 05

CONTENTS

Why Study Vocabulary Systematically?

Teachers generally agree on the importance of vocabulary development in the refining of language skills. The greater the store of words we have at our disposal, the better equipped we are to comprehend what we read and to express what we think.

A systematic approach to vocabulary building helps students

- understand and use words effectively
- recognize, retain, and apply new words
- unlock meanings of new words
- learn independently for lifelong vocabulary acquisition
- improve reading comprehension across the curriculum
- improve performance on standardized tests
- select and use words forcefully in speaking and writing
- continually assimilate new words into their vocabularies

A systematic program ensures the development of the large storehouse of words that is important to achievement, both in and out of the classroom.

How Were the Vocabulary Words Selected?

The criteria for vocabulary word selection for *Vocabulary for Achievement* were three.

- The principle source for the word lists was recent Scholastic Assessment Tests (SATs), published by the College Entrance Examination Board.
- The authors and editors also consulted numerous scholarly works, including the American Heritage *Word Frequency Book*, *The Living Word Vocabulary*, and many standard thesauruses.
- Most importantly, the words were chosen for their usefulness, appropriateness to grade level, and applicability to the lesson themes or topics.

Over 80% of the *Vocabulary for Achievement* words are on a so-called "hit parade" of SAT words. The "hit parade" is a group of words representative of the difficulty level of words frequently used in analogy and sentence-completion test items in the verbal section of the SAT. Further, almost one quarter of these "hit parade" words is taught in

Vocabulary for Achievement's Fourth Course or earlier, providing students with ample time to incorporate them into their vocabularies before encountering them on the SAT.

Vocabulary for Achievement ensures success, not only on the SAT but in lifelong vocabulary acquisition, by offering students early help with challenging new vocabulary.

A Tour of the Program

Vocabulary for Achievement is a systematic program of vocabulary development that provides comprehensive instruction and practice. In devising the seven-book program for grades 6 through 12, the authors have followed four major principles:

- Structured lessons teach best.
- Application aids retention.
- Special vocabulary-acquisition skills promote independent learning.
- Vocabulary materials must be readily accessible and easily adaptable to classroom needs.

These four principles are reflected throughout the program, which provides the structure necessary for students to learn new words; apply them in a variety of practice formats to ensure ownership; and to use dictionary, test-taking, and reading strategies to build and incorporate their growing pool of words independently. The authors' guiding principles also make the structure of the program teacher- and student-friendly.

Teacher-Friendly Elements

The consistent structure of *Vocabulary for Achievement* makes it ideal for classroom instruction or for independent use, allowing you to direct a sound and successful vocabulary program.

- **Lessons**: provide complete presentation, abundant practice (with answers), numerous examples of context, and opportunities for application.
- **Skill Features**: furnish practical strategies for ongoing vocabulary acquisition.
- **Flash Cards (in student book only)**: include all vocabulary words, with the word on one side, phonetic spelling and definition on the other. An effective tool for learning and review.

- **Tests**: 10 reproducible multiple-choice tests (with answers), each covering 3 consecutive lessons.
- **Bonuses**: 7–15 reproducible bonus activities (with answers), each covering 2–5 consecutive lessons, offer students "lighter" opportunities for reinforcement and enrichment in the forms of crossword puzzles, word searches, scrambled words, etc.
- **Teaching Suggestions**: provide concrete ideas to help you adapt the materials for special classroom needs and to extend their range and usefulness.

The Lessons

- 30 six-page lessons per level
- 10 words per lesson, theme- or root-centered
- pronunciations, part-of-speech labels, multiple definitions, etymologies, related words, usage notes, and example sentences provided dictionary-style from Houghton Mifflin dictionaries

- 4 follow-up exercises for practice in identifying definitions, using words correctly, choosing the best word, and using different forms of a word
- a reading comprehension passage, incorporating the 10 words in context, followed by a comprehension exercise. The reading passages cover all areas of the curriculum, from history, science and nature, and the arts, to myths and legends, technology, and careers.
- a writing assignment related to the theme or topic, in which students apply their newly acquired words in an effective piece of writing
- analogy exercises for practice in identifying vocabulary words in the context of word relationships
- vocabulary enrichment and activity for interesting and unusual word histories, helpful in unlocking meanings of unfamiliar words

The Anatomy of a Lesson

Lessons are **theme-centered** or **root-centered** to provide a context in which students can learn new words.

Introductions are motivational.

Pronunciations, definitions, and **etymologies** are from Houghton Mifflin dictionaries.

Word entries are presented **dictionary-style.**

Related words were chosen for their usefulness and appropriateness to grade level.

The **Word List** is a convenient reference for both students and teachers.

Writing new words on word blanks reinforces correct **spelling.**

Example sentences illustrate the primary definition of each word.

Usage notes or **memory cues** provide tips for using the words correctly or for remembering them.

A variety of **exercise formats** provides practice and aids in **recognition, recall,** and **application** of the words.

Reading passages incorporating the vocabulary words reinforce the important link between vocabulary and reading comprehension.

EXERCISE 1 COMPLETING DEFINITIONS

On the answer line, write the word from the vocabulary list that best completes each definition.

1. To be sturdy, strong, and healthy is to be ____.
2. To endure or to resist something successfully is to ____ it.
3. The closing off of an area to prevent movement in or out is a ____.
4. A person who displays great courage or boldness is considered ____.
5. Behavior that is warlike or military in style is ____.
6. Firmness of character or resistance to change is ____.
7. A position that can be easily attacked is ____.
8. When something cannot be ruined or eliminated, it is ____.
9. A person or thing that is firm, strong, and loyal is ____.
10. To have unlimited power is to be ____.

1. robust
2. withstand
3. blockade
4. valiant
5. martial
6. stability
7. vulnerable
8. indestructible
9. staunch
10. omnipotent

EXERCISE 2 USING WORDS CORRECTLY

Each of the following questions contains an italicized vocabulary word. Decide the answer to the question, and write *Yes* or *No* on the answer line.

1. Would a *martial* nation be known for its peace-loving nature?
2. Would a *valiant* person face danger in order to help a friend?
3. Is a sleeping deer *vulnerable* prey for a hungry wolf?
4. Would a weak, foolish king be an *omnipotent* ruler?
5. Would a *robust* person have difficulty walking one mile?
6. Would a *staunch* friend refuse to talk about you behind your back?
7. In the event of a naval *blockade*, would ships be allowed to pass freely in and out of a harbor?
8. Can penguins *withstand* the cold air and water of Antarctica?
9. Would a tool shed made of flattened tin cans and plywood be *indestructible* during a tornado?
10. Does a bridge that rocks back and forth when you walk on it have *stability*?

1. No
2. Yes
3. Yes
4. No
5. No
6. Yes
7. No
8. Yes
9. No
10. No

EXERCISE 3 CHOOSING THE BEST WORD

Decide which vocabulary word or related form best completes the sentence, and write the letter of your choice on the answer line.

1. The ship was able to ____ the strong winds and heavy rain.
   a. blockade   **b.** stabilize   **c.** staunch   **d.** withstand

1. d

Strength and Defense **49**

READING COMPREHENSION

Each numbered sentence in the following passage contains an italicized vocabulary word or related form. After you have read the passage, you will complete an exercise.

THE SPANISH ARMADA

Conflict had existed between Spain and England since the 1570s. England wanted a share of the wealth that Spain had been taking from the lands it had claimed in the Americas. (1) Elizabeth I, Queen of England, encouraged her *staunch* admiral of the navy, Sir Francis Drake, to raid Spanish ships and towns. (2) Though these raids were on a small scale, Drake achieved dramatic success, adding gold and silver to England's treasury and diminishing Spain's *omnipotence*.

Religious differences also caused conflict between the two countries. Whereas Spain was Roman Catholic, most of England had become Protestant. King Philip II of Spain wanted to claim the throne and make England a Catholic country again. To satisfy his ambition and also to retaliate against England's theft of his gold and silver, King Philip began to build his fleet of warships, the Armada, in January 1586.

(3) Philip intended his fleet to be *indestructible*. (4) In addition to building new warships, he marshaled 130 sailing vessels of all types and recruited more than 19,000 *robust* soldiers and 8,000 sailors. (5) Although some of his ships lacked guns and others lacked ammunition, Philip was convinced that his Armada could *withstand* any battle with England.

(6) The *martial* Armada set sail from Lisbon, Portugal, on May 9, 1588, but bad weather forced it back to port. (7) The voyage resumed on July 22 after the weather had become *stable*.

The Spanish fleet met the smaller, faster, and more maneuverable English ships in battle off the coast of Plymouth, England, first on July 31 and again on August 2. (8) The two battles left Spain *vulnerable*, costing it several ships and depleting its ammunition.

On August 7, while the Armada lay at anchor on the French side of the Strait of Dover, England sent eight burning ships into the midst of the Spanish fleet to set it on fire. (9) *Blockaded* on one side, the Spanish ships could only drift away, their crews in panic and disorder. Before the Armada could regroup, the English attacked again on August 8.

(10) Although the Spaniards made a *valiant* effort to fight back, the fleet suffered extensive damage. During the eight hours of battle, the Armada drifted perilously close to the rocky coastline. At the moment when it seemed that the Spanish ships would be driven onto the English shore, the wind shifted, and the Armada drifted out into the North Sea. The Spaniards recognized the superiority of the English fleet and returned home, defeated.

READING COMPREHENSION EXERCISE

Each of the following statements corresponds to a numbered sentence in the passage. Each statement contains a blank and is followed by four answer choices. Decide which choice fits best in the blank. The word or phrase that you choose must express roughly the same meaning as the italicized word in the passage. Write the letter of your choice on the answer line.

1. Elizabeth I encouraged her ____ admiral of the navy to raid Spanish ships and towns.
   a. wise   **b.** crafty   **c.** loyal   **d.** precise

1. c

Strength and Defense **51**

A **follow-up exercise** on the passage tests student understanding of the vocabulary words in context.

A **Writing Assignment**, related to the lesson theme or passage topic, lets students apply new words. Assignments are designed to stimulate interest, enthusiasm, and creativity.

Vocabulary Enrichment provides interesting and unusual word histories.

The **Activity** encourages students to investigate the origins of several related words.

A **Practice with Analogies** exercise helps students use the vocabulary words in a different context. Students learn various ways to complete analogies, to identify the different types of analogies, and to understand relationships between words.

---

2. Drake added wealth to the treasury and diminished Spain's _____.
   a. unlimited power   c. reputation
   b. unrestricted growth   d. territory

   2. _____a_____

3. Philip intended his fleet to be _____.
   a. respected   c. incapable of being copied
   b. incapable of being eliminated   d. special

   3. _____b_____

4. Philip recruited many _____ soldiers and sailors.
   a. warlike   b. strong   c. accomplished   d. creative

   4. _____b_____

5. Philip was convinced that the Armada could _____ any battle with England.
   a. engage   b. arrange   c. break   d. endure

   5. _____d_____

6. The _____ Armada set sail on May 9, 1588.
   a. complete   b. warlike   c. independent   d. luxurious

   6. _____b_____

7. The voyage resumed after the weather became more _____.
   a. reliable   b. idle   c. serious   d. restless

   7. _____a_____

8. The two battles left the Spanish fleet _____.
   a. open to change   c. open to attack
   b. triumphant   d. hopeful

   8. _____c_____

9. The Armada was _____ on one side.
   a. closed off   b. damaged   c. dependable   d. alone

   9. _____a_____

10. The Spaniards made a _____ attempt to fight back.
    a. slight   b. ridiculous   c. huge   d. courageous

    10. _____d_____

WRITING ASSIGNMENT

Write a letter to your local or school newspaper in which you take a position on an issue of importance in your school or community. For example, you might write a letter defending the quality of the food served in the school cafeteria. Use at least five of the words from this lesson and underline them.

VOCABULARY ENRICHMENT

The word *martial* comes from the name of a Roman god, Mars. Mars was originally the Roman god of agriculture, and the early Romans paid tribute to him for good harvests.

After the Romans captured Greece, they adopted the Greek gods and myths into their own culture. Because the Greeks believed that a goddess was responsible for growing crops, the Romans removed this function from Mars. Instead, they gave him the characteristics and responsibilities of Ares, the Greek god of war. Thus, the word *martial*, derived from the name of Mars, describes military activities.

Activity Other words besides *martial* come from the names of gods or goddesses. Use your dictionary and an encyclopedia to find the origin of each of the words that follow. Write a definition of each word as well as a brief description of the origin.

1. jovial   2. titanic   3. iridescent   4. psyche   5. narcissistic

The **Bonus activity** for Lessons 7 and 8 is on page T8.

52   Strength and Defense

Copyright © Great Source

READING COMPREHENSION EXERCISE

Each of the following statements corresponds to a numbered sentence in the passage. Each statement contains a blank and is followed by four answer choices. Decide which choice fits best in the blank. The word or phrase that you choose must express roughly the same meaning as the italicized word in the passage. Write the letter of your choice on the answer line.

1. The game show announcer introduces three _____ of the McCormack family.
   a. close relatives   c. next-door neighbors
   b. different stages of descent   d. men who are related

   1. _____b_____

2. Grandpa Horace is the _____ of the family.
   a. scholar   b. devoted grandfather   c. male leader   d. financial advisor

   2. _____c_____

3. Grandma Amelia thinks that her family's answers will be recorded for _____.
   a. future generations   c. television cameras
   b. her grandchildren   d. good friends

   3. _____a_____

4. The annnouncer warns about the conflict between _____.
   a. family   b. mothers and daughters   c. friends   d. sisters

   4. _____d_____

5. He points out that Queen Victoria was a great _____.
   a. wife and mother   c. antique collector
   b. female leader   d. devoted grandmother

   5. _____b_____

6. Furthermore, Queen Victoria also had a strong _____ side.
   a. motherly   b. historical   c. intellectual   d. fatherly

   6. _____a_____

7. Grandma Amelia talks about her own impressive _____.
   a. party   b. history   c. ancestry   d. society

   7. _____c_____

8. She is a(n) _____ of Henry Harold Horton III.
   a. daughter   b. admirer   c. friend   d. offspring

   8. _____d_____

9. The _____ from Henry Harold include(s) strength and discipline.
   a. characteristics passed down   c. large fortune
   b. ancient letters   d. descriptions

   9. _____a_____

10. Grandma Amelia questions Michael McCormack's _____ authority.
    a. personal   b. social   c. fatherly   d. political

    10. _____c_____

PRACTICE WITH ANALOGIES

See page 119 for some strategies to use with analogies.

An analogy compares word pairs that are related in some way. For example, in "Gold is to metal as coal is to fuel," both pairs are type of analogies.

Directions   On the answer line, write the vocabulary word or a form of it that completes each analogy.

1. Aquatic is to water as _____ is to land. *(Lesson 2)*
   1. ____terrestrial____

2. Partner is to business as _____ is to crime. *(Lesson 3)*
   2. ____accomplice____

3. Swarm is to insects as _____ is to people. *(Lesson 3)*
   3. ____throng____

4. _____ is to muddy as precipice is to steep. *(Lesson 2)*
   4. ____Quagmire____

5. Patriarchy is to men as _____ is to women. *(Lesson 4)*
   5. ____matriarchy____

The **Bonus activity** for Lessons 3 and 4 is on page T4.

26   Families

Copyright © Great Source

Skill Features

A skill feature on dictionary use, on test taking, or on reading appears after each group of three vocabulary lessons.

- 10 special features provide students with techniques for building and using their pool of words independently.
- Clear explanation includes examples, tables of information, strategies and procedures for learning and using new words effectively.
- Accompanying exercises allow students to practice each skill.

Dictionary Skills

- Emphasis in lessons is grade-level appropriate.
- Skills range from finding the right definition, understanding parts of speech, and utilizing etymological information, to reading usage notes, differentiating among synonyms, and using a thesaurus.
- Follow-up exercises give students an opportunity to practice their new skills by using dictionary extracts and writing original sentences.

Test-Taking Skills

- Students are given pointers for successfully completing different types of tests—sentence-completion, analogy, antonym, and reading comprehension—often found on standardized tests such as the SAT and ACT English Test.
- Examples are provided so students can understand the thought processes required to eliminate inappropriate answer choices and to select the correct answer.
- Accompanying exercises give students the opportunity to put the strategies into practice by becoming alert to misleading choices, sentence clues, and shades of meaning.

Reading Skills

These features address two separate areas of vocabulary proficiency: using context clues and analyzing word parts.

- Students learn to use context clues to determine the meanings of unfamiliar words.
- Methods of reasoning are illustrated so students can see how information in a sentence can be utilized.

- Students check their understanding by comparing their "working" definitions against those in a dictionary.
- Students are acquainted with a method of determining the meanings of unfamiliar words by analyzing word parts.
- Word-attack strategies focus on learning prefixes, suffixes, and roots.

Teacher's Edition

- **Teaching Suggestions:** The activities on pages x–xiii will help you to incorporate vocabulary study into every area of the English curriculum. Ideas for exercises, assignments, and discussion topics have been provided for vocabulary review, spelling, reading, word histories, grammar and usage, literature, composition, and college-entrance examination preparation.
- **Tests:** 10 reproducible multiple-choice tests, each covering 3 consecutive lessons, are found at the back of the Teacher's Edition. Each test is divided into 2 parts. Part A tests recognition and recall of definitions; Part B emphasizes placing

words within the context of sentences or discriminating among a choice of antonyms. Answers to the tests are located on the front sides of the reproducible masters.

- **Bonuses:** 7–15 Bonus activities, each covering 2–5 consecutive lessons, give students a "lighter" form of vocabulary study. In crossword puzzles, word searches, sentence completions, scrambled words, and other word games, students review their knowledge of vocabulary words and their definitions, synonyms, antonyms, and etymologies. Answers to the Bonuses are located on the front sides of the reproducible masters.

- **Verbal Aptitude Tests (4th–6th Courses):** 2 Verbal Aptitude Tests provide practice for students taking college-entrance examinations. Each 4-page reproducible test covers antonyms, sentence completions, analogies, and reading comprehension. Answers to the tests appear on the front sides of the reproducible masters found at the back of the Teacher's Edition.

Teaching Suggestions

Review and Retention

Frequent review helps students retain the meanings of new words. Use any or all of the following practices to help students learn and apply new words.

1. Have students use the **Flash Cards,** located on pages 201–220 of the student books, for individual drill or game-style classroom practice.

2. Assign the **Bonuses** as follow-up activities for the vocabulary lessons.

3. Provide extra-credit points for those students who use new words correctly in classroom discussion or in written assignments.

4. As you cover new lessons, ask students how particular words relate to ones already studied. EXAMPLES In what situations could you use *congenial* (Lesson 5), *amicable* (Lesson 6), and *amenable* (Lesson 21) interchangeably?
How do *accomplice* (Lesson 3) and *culprit* (Lesson 17) differ?
How are *exuberant* (Lesson 6), *blithe* (Lesson 6), and *bouyant* (Lesson 7) similar, and how are they different?
Can the same behavior be described as both *staunch* (Lesson 8) and *steadfast* (Lesson 24)?

Refer to the **Complete Word List** on page xv to aid in making similarly related word groups.

5. Have students periodically review their own or others' compositions for word choice. Encourage them to replace overused words or phrases with vocabulary words. For example, in the sentence "Jack and Lou argued over the bicycle," they might rewrite the sentence as "The argument between Jack and Lou *imperiled* their friendship" (Lesson 29), "Jack and Lou reached a *stalemate* on the topic of the bicycle" (Lesson 14), or "The discussion between Jack and Lou *degenerated* into an argument" (Lesson 5).

Vocabulary and Spelling

Vocabulary study and spelling are complementary. Students cannot completely understand a word until they can say and write it as well as cite its definition. Make use of the numerous opportunities provided in *Vocabulary for Achievement* in order to reinforce spelling skills.

1. Once students have studied the definitions and examples for each vocabulary word, have them write the word in the blank provided for this purpose. Writing the word reinforces the visual-graphic patterns of letters, aids in sight recognition, and helps students to apply the word.

2. Encourage students to pay close attention to the listing of related forms and the use of these, along with the inflected forms of words, throughout the exercises. Point out to them how different endings can change the spelling of a root word.

3. Have students pay special heed to lessons based on word roots, since these show how similar word elements contribute to the similarity of meaning and spelling. In the same way, have them study the **Skill Features** treating prefixes and suffixes. Point out how the addition of a word element can change the part of speech, the meaning, and the spelling of a root word.

4. When students apply their understanding of new words by using them in the writing assignments, remind them that checking spelling and other aspects of mechanics should be the final step in the revising process.

5. Remind students that **Bonus** features highlight correct spelling. Emphasize that for crossword puzzles, word searches, scrambled words, and word-clue games to work, students must write the letters in the correct sequence.

Vocabulary and Reading

1. To help students realize how naturally they use context clues as they read, review with them

some of the more common and obvious ways that words are defined in context.

Formal definition: A *micrometer* is a device that measures minute distances, as gauged by the rotations of a finely threaded screw in a microscope.

Definition by appositive: *Lichen,* or plants consisting of a fungus in close combination with certain green or blue-green algae, covered every surface of the fallen log.

The *metric system,* that is, a decimal system of weights and measures, is widely accepted in manufacturing, international trade, and science.

The *croissant*—a crescent-shaped roll made of dough or puff pastry—was created by bakers in Vienna to commemorate their city's successful stand against an army of Turks in 1863.

Definition by example: Mosses and liverworts are examples of *Bryophyta,* one of the oldest living groups of plants on earth.

Point out to students that words like *is, that is,* and *or,* as well as typographical aids like parentheses, commas, and dashes, may signal the presence of a definition in context.

2. To show students how their awareness of the order and function of words in sentences helps them to eliminate improbable meanings of unfamiliar words, give them a passage like the following.

EXAMPLE Primitive, *kanless* insects found their *lumwat* by *nusing* tree ferns in search of *fidals* and vegetable debris. The *sopsa* was *meresuny,* but getting down proved more *pandart,* involving detours over fingered leaf formations and shoots. At some point they started to *delp* to the ground, extending their "arms" or *kranning* in order to *bing* downward. This is one *planesis* for the development of *kans.*

Have students make a number of guesses for each nonsense word. While they may not be able to determine that *kanless* is actually *wingless* and *lumwat* is actually *food,* they will be able to reduce uncertainty and to approximate the meaning by looking at the position of the nonsense word in the sentence.

Vocabulary and Word Analogies

1. To give students practice identifying word relationships, provide them with the first half of several analogies and have them work together to determine the types of analogy. You may want to draw from the following types of analogy:

degree
type of
part/whole
relative size
is used to
place where
characteristic of
antonym
definition
part of
expression of

2. Challenge students to write visual analogies. Their analogies should be written entirely with pictures or symbols instead of words. Invite pairs of students to solve their partners' analogies.

3. To help students practice their analogy-solving strategies, give them several word pairs and ask them to restate the relationship between the words in a simple sentence. For example, in the word pair "scrap/paper," a restated simple sentence could be "A scrap is a small piece of paper."

Vocabulary and Word History

To help students appreciate languages as dynamic, use the following as discussion topics or as assignment topics.

Words that have undergone changes in meaning: *cloud* (rock or hill), *guest* (stranger or enemy), *puny* (born later), *slim* (crafty, bad, or crooked), *branch* (paw or claw), *bugle* (young ox), *nice* (ignorant), *pretty* (clever), and so forth.

Shortened forms of words: *bus/omnibus, pants/pantaloons, taxicab/taxi-meter cabriolet, airlines/airplane lines, gyp/gypsy, mend/amend, extra/extra-ordinary,* and so forth.

Compound words: *salesclerk, blackbird, shortcake, lightweight, threadbare, airtight, outlaw, underdog, self-control, law-abiding, heart-to-heart, hide-and-seek,* and so forth.

Special interest words, such as those from architecture, that have been adopted for more general use: *arch, column, gable, belfry, tower, porch, spire, pendant, vault, girder, dormer, flamboyant, arcade, capital, lattice, lantern, canopy,* and so forth.

Portmanteau words, in which the sounds and meanings of two or more words are merged to form a new word: *squawk* (squall + squeak), *broasted* (broiled + roasted), *splatter* (splash + spatter), *flounder* (founder + blunder), *Eurasia* (Europe + Asia), *flabbergast* (flappy or flap + aghast), and so forth.

Words borrowed directly from other languages such as Greek: *metropolis, phenomenon, cinema, drama, electron, oasis, parenthesis, plasma, logic, cosmic, protein, chronic, criterion,* and so forth.

Vocabulary, Grammar, and Usage

1. Remind students that a word may be used as several different parts of speech. Then have them examine the multiple meanings of such words as *progress, absent, produce, project, torment, use, contest, perfect,* and so forth. Have students write sentences like the following that illustrate the different meanings.
   EXAMPLE   Jeremy got a *perfect* score on his last math test. (*adjective*)
   EXAMPLE   Monica has *perfected* her swan dive. (*verb*)

2. Have students write original sentences that both illustrate particular principles of grammar or usage and incorporate vocabulary words. For example, when covering the independent clauses, ask students to write sentences like the following.
   EXAMPLE   Rowena is difficult to be with when she is in a *refractory* mood.
   EXAMPLE   Before we left the meeting, we had reached an *amicable* settlement.

3. Give students sentences containing malapropisms, or humorously misused words. To make certain that students can distinguish the problematic word, underline the malapropism in each sentence.
   EXAMPLE   The management requested a *conjunction* against the union.
   EXAMPLE   Mayor Dale's speech made a great *oppression* on the audience.
   EXAMPLE   Sam, an honest and truthful young man, *virtually* turned in the money he found.

   Students should be able to reword the malapropism and explain the humor that results from the misuse of the word. If not, have them use the dictionary to get definitions of both the malapropism and the correct replacement.

4. When discussing usage problems, have the students examine the likelihood of confusion between pairs of homophones like the following: *coarse/course, horse/hoarse, bear/bare, foul/fowl, fair/fare, wear/ware/where, peer/pier,* and so forth. Then have them look up the definitions of each word and write a sentence for each illustrating its use.

Vocabulary and Composition

1. You can help students become more aware of word choice by emphasizing the importance of revision. Remind them that revising a rough draft gives them the opportunity to choose the appropriate words and to use concrete or figurative words, depending on the purpose of the assignment.

2. To help students distinguish between literal and figurative language, give them pairs of sentences like the following.
   EXAMPLE   The attorney presents facts as if they were rare and valuable gemstones.
   Ann's favorite gemstone is the amethyst.
   EXAMPLE   The carpenter repaired the two broken stairsteps.
   Charles treats his friends as if they are stairsteps to success.

   After students have successfully identified which sentence uses a literal noun and which uses a figurative one, give them a list of nouns and verbs and have them write their own pairs of sentences.

3. When choosing a synonym from the dictionary or thesaurus, some students may have difficulty selecting the one with connotations appropriate to the topic and purpose of their composition. To help them learn to discriminate between positive and negative connotations, give them pairs of words like the following: *house/hovel, brief/curt, firm/stubborn, reserved/aloof, relaxed/lazy, mature/old,* and so forth. If students cannot identify the word in each pair that has negative connotations, have them look up the definitions in a dictionary.

4. To help students distinguish shades of meaning, give them a list of synonyms and ask them to rank them according to intensity, degree, or amount.
   EXAMPLE   *disorderly, chaotic, disrupted, disorganized*
   EXAMPLE   *enjoyable, amusing, convivial, propitious*

5. For students who use inflated language, provide them with proverbs that have been overwritten. By extracting the ideas hidden behind the verbiage, students can gain practice in expressing simple ideas clearly.
   EXAMPLE   Individuals who perforce are constrained to be domiciled in vitreous structures of

patent frangibility should on no account employ petrous formations as projectiles. (People who live in glass houses should never throw stones.)

Vocabulary and Literature

1. In discussing literature selections, reinforce vocabulary study by pointing out authors' literary techniques. Ask students questions like the following.
EXAMPLES   Which words or phrases indicate that a certain character believes himself or herself to be superior to others?
Which words or phrases does the author use to evoke the reader's sympathy for a particular character?

2. When covering Norse tales, Celtic legends (King Arthur), or Old and Middle English poems or ballads (*Lord Randal*, *Sir Patrick Spens*, *Barbara Allen*, and so forth), provide students with both the original and the translation of the work if possible. Have students draw conclusions about the changes in vocabulary, grammar, and mechanics by comparing the earlier and later forms.

3. To help students understand the rich nature of idioms, ask them to explain the difference between "Bury the hatchet" and "Stop fighting with each other." Help students to locate and explain the literal and figurative meanings of other expressions like the following used in short stories and novels.
EXAMPLES   *According to Hoyle, know the ropes, play second fiddle, pull strings, face the music, straight from the horse's mouth,* and so forth.

4. As an alternative, have students explore proverbs as a rich source of figurative language.
EXAMPLE   Better have an egg today than a hen tomorrow. (Italian)
EXAMPLE   Without going, you can get nowhere. (Chinese)
EXAMPLE   The best cloth has uneven threads. (Spanish)
EXAMPLE   The sweetest grapes hang the highest. (English)

As a follow-up, have students look for literal expressions with figurative meanings in the total content of stories, poems, plays, novels, and essays.

A Reading Comprehension passage appears in each of the 30 vocabulary lessons in each level. The passage is an article, essay, or story that contains all ten vocabulary words of the lesson, thereby giving students an opportunity to understand the new words in a larger context. These passages also lend an entertaining variety to the abundant practice and provide students with enriching information drawn from a wide variety of subject matter. *Vocabulary for Achievement* truly offers students a chance to read across the curriculum while they incorporate newly learned words into their vocabularies. For your convenience, the following is a level-specific list of topics and passages.

Grade 8: Second Course

Lesson	Topic	Title of Passage
1	Language	Dialects in the English Language
2	History	Magellan: Portuguese Navigator
3	Service to Humanity	The Red Cross: Bringing Humanity to Inhumanity
4	Fiction	The Family Game
5	Fiction	A Nineteenth-Century Romance
6	Science and Nature	Marie Curie: Discoverer of Radium
7	Science and Nature	The Eruption of Mount Vesuvius
8	History	The Spanish Armada
9	The Arts	Casa Loma: A Canadian Castle
10	Twentieth-Century Portraits	The Centenarian of the Caucasus Mountains
11	History	Americans on the Moon
12	Fiction	The Baby Sitter
13	History	Victory at Marathon
14	Myths and Legends	The Apple of Discord
15	Twentieth-Century Portraits	The Mystery of Anastasia
16	History	Two Ancient Governments: Athens and Sparta
17	Fiction	The Case of the Counterfeit Paintings
18	Economics and Business	Tulipomania
19	History	The Royal Spendthrifts
20	Service to Humanity	Alfred Nobel: The Man and the Prize
21	Fiction	The New Girl
22	Science and Nature	The Mammalian Diving Reflex: Fact or Fiction?
23	Careers	Professional Modeling: Hard Work or Glamour?
24	Twentieth-Century Portraits	Triumph Over Disability
25	Science and Nature	Nature's Artistry: The Grand Canyon
26	Technology	The Wright Brothers: Fathers of Aviation
27	Fiction	A Rare Cache
28	Literature and Communication	Nellie Bly: Daring Woman Journalist
29	History	Elizabeth Cady Stanton: Early Women's Rights Leader
30	Service to Humanity	Albert Schweitzer: Doctor and Humanitarian

COMPLETE WORD LIST FOR SECOND COURSE

abet, 81
abide, 133
abode, 53
abrupt, 181
accent, 1
accessible, 173
accompanist, 13
accomplice, 13
acquit, 107
administer, 141
admonish, 187
adversary, 87
aggression, 87
alienate, 187
alloy, 41
altruistic, 193
amenable, 133
amicable, 33
amiss, 113
anarchy, 101
anguish, 33
animate, 141
annex, 53
antiquated, 61
aqueduct, 73
arson, 107
articulate, 1
authoritarian, 101

belated, 67
benefactor, 193
beneficial, 193
benevolent, 193
benign, 193
bewilder, 113
bias, 133
blithe, 33
blockade, 47
blunder, 113
boisterous, 153
bountiful, 193
buoyant, 41

cache, 173
celestial, 41
censure, 187
centenarian, 61
chaos, 153
claimant, 93
clamor, 93
coagulate, 41
coalition, 13
combustible, 41
communal, 13
compel, 167
complacent, 153
complement, 13
comport, 147
compulsion, 167
concoct, 141
conduct, 73
conduit, 73
confines, 161
conflagration, 41
congenial, 27

congregate, 13
consensus, 13
conservative, 101
conspicuous, 173
contemporary, 61
contradict, 87
controversy, 87
corrupt, 107
counterfeit, 107
culprit, 107

declaim, 93
deduce, 73
defiant, 33
degenerate, 27
delegate, 101
delineate, 161
deliverance, 81
demarcation, 161
denounce, 187
deport, 147
descendant, 21
desolate, 33
despondent, 33
detriment, 187
devise, 141
dialect, 1
diction, 1
disclaim, 93
disclosure, 173
discord, 87
discrimination, 133
disgruntled, 33
disillusion, 33
disport, 147
disrupt, 181
dissection, 41
distend, 161
distill, 41
distinct, 161
distress, 33
dominion, 101
duration, 67
dynamic, 153

edifice, 53
embellish, 121
embody, 161
embroil, 87
eminent, 127
endeavor, 141
ennoble, 81
enunciate, 1
erroneous, 113
eruption, 181
evocative, 93
excavate, 53
exceed, 121
execute, 141
expedite, 81
expire, 67
exuberant, 33

fallible, 113
faux pas, 113

felony, 107
fledgling, 61
fluster, 113
forbearance, 133
foregone, 67
fractious, 181
fragment, 181
frail, 61
fundamental, 1

gender, 27
genealogy, 27
generation, 21
generic, 27
genesis, 27
gentry, 27
gerontology, 61
glut, 121
gratify, 193

haggle, 87
hijack, 107
humanitarian, 193

immoderate, 121
impeach, 101
impel, 167
imperil, 187
implement, 141
impulsive, 167
inaugurate, 101
incapacitate, 187
incessant, 67
incriminate, 107
indestructible, 47
indispensable, 127
induce, 73
inductee, 13
induction, 73
indulge, 193
infraction, 181
infringe, 181
inheritance, 21
injurious, 187
insular, 7
insupportable, 147
intelligible, 1
intense, 121
inter, 173
intercede, 81
intrigue, 173
invoke, 93

latitude, 7
lavish, 121
liberal, 101
lineage, 21
longevity, 61
longitude, 7
luxurious, 121

malign, 187
marginal, 161
martial, 47

mason, 53
maternal, 21
matriarch, 21
medieval, 67
meridian, 7
meteorology, 41
miscalculate, 113
miscellaneous, 13
misinterpret, 113
momentous, 127
monotonous, 153

nascent, 61

objective, 133
obscure, 173
offset, 81
omnipotent, 47
omnipresent, 161
outrageous, 121
overestimate, 113

pacify, 81
panorama, 7
paramount, 127
parental, 21
partisan, 133
patriarch, 21
peal, 167
peer, 1
penetration, 161
peninsula, 7
petty, 127
philanthropic, 193
portable, 147
portage, 147
porter, 147
portfolio, 147
posterity, 21
precipice, 7
preconceived, 133
prefabricate, 53
prejudice, 133
premature, 67
prestige, 127
primogeniture, 27
priority, 127
productivity, 73
profuse, 121
progeny, 27
prominence, 127
propulsion, 167
puerile, 61
pulsate, 167
purport, 147

quagmire, 7

reactivate, 141
reclaim, 93
reduction, 73
refractory, 181
refurbish, 81
regenerate, 27

reinforce, 81
render, 141
repeal, 167
repellent, 167
repent, 107
repulse, 167
respite, 67
restive, 153
revoke, 93
robust, 47
rotunda, 53
rout, 181
rupture, 181

sanctuary, 81
saturate, 41
scoff, 187
secluded, 173
sibling, 21
simultaneous, 67
skirmish, 87
solar, 53
Spartan, 101
spendthrift, 121
sportive, 147
stability, 47
stalemate, 87
static, 153
status, 1
staunch, 47
steadfast, 153
stress, 1
strife, 87
subdue, 73
subsequent, 67
substantial, 161
superficial, 127
swindle, 107

terrestrial, 7
throng, 13
tolerance, 133
topography, 7
tranquil, 153
trellis, 53
trivial, 127
turret, 53
tyrant, 101

unavailable, 173
undertaking, 141
unearth, 173

valiant, 47
velocity, 153
venerable, 61
viaduct, 73
vocation, 93
vouch, 93
vulnerable, 47

withstand, 47

SCOPE AND SEQUENCE OF SKILLS

Level	Dictionary Skills	Test-Taking Skills	Reading Skills
Sixth	Using a Dictionary and a Thesaurus to Find Synonyms (pp. 19–20)	ACT Reading-Comprehension Tests (pp. 39–40); Tests of Standard Written English (pp. 59–60)	Context Clues and the Reading of Primary Sources (pp. 79–80); Context Clues and the Reading of British Literature (pp. 99–100); The Prefixes bi-, semi- (pp. 119–120); Prefixes Indicating Number (pp. 139–140); The Prefixes conter-, contra-, anti- (pp. 159–160); The Prefixes circum-, peri- (pp. 179–180); The Prefixes extra-, super-, ultra- (pp. 199–200)
Fifth	Using a Thesaurus (pp. 19–20)	Antonym Test Items (pp. 39–40); SAT Sentence-Completion Test Items (pp. 59–60); SAT Analogy Test Items (pp. 79–80); SAT Reading-Comprehension Test Items (pp. 99–100)	Context Clues and the Reading of American History (pp. 119–120); Context Clues and the Reading of American Literature (pp. 139–140); The Prefixes bene-, mal- (pp. 159–160); The Prefixes inter-, intra-, intro- (pp. 179–180); The Prefixes ante-, post- (pp. 199–200)
Fourth	Synonym Paragraphs (pp. 19–20)	Antonym Test Items (pp. 39–40); Sentence-Completion Test Items (pp. 59–60); Analogy Test Items (pp. 79–80); Reading-Comprehension Test Items (pp. 99–100)	Context Clues: Examples and Appositives (pp. 119–120); Context Clues: Contrast (pp. 139–140); The Prefix ad- (pp. 159–160); Com- and Related Prefixes (pp. 179–180); Five Adjective Suffixes (pp. 199–200)
Third	Finding the Appropriate Definition (pp. 19–20); Usage Notes (pp. 39–40)	Antonym Tests (pp. 59–60); Analogy Tests (pp. 79–80); Reading-Comprehension Tests (pp. 99–100)	Context Clues: Substitution (pp. 119–120); The Prefixes ex-, e- (pp. 139–140); The Prefixes ab-, a-, abs- (pp. 159–160); The Suffixes -ful, -ous (pp. 179–180); Four Verb Suffixes (pp. 199–200)
Second	Finding the Appropriate Definition (pp. 19–20); Inflected Forms of Words (pp. 39–40); Biographical and Geographical Entries (pp. 59–60)	Sentence-Completion Tests (pp. 79–80); Synonym Tests (pp. 99–100); Analogy Tests (pp. 119–120)	Context Clues: Synonyms (pp. 139–140); The Prefix pre- (pp. 159–160); The Prefix in- (pp. 179–180); The Suffixes -ion, -ness (pp. 199–200)
First	Finding the Appropriate Definition (pp. 19–20); Part-of-Speech Labels (pp. 39–40); Understanding Etymologies (pp. 59–60)	Sentence-Completion Tests (pp. 79–80)	Context Clues: Definition in the Sentence (pp. 99–100); The Prefix dis- (pp. 119–120); The Prefix re- (pp. 139–140); The Prefix sub- (pp. 159–160); The Suffixes -ance, -ence, -ancy (pp. 179–180); The Suffix -able (pp. 199–200)
Introductory	Parts of a Dictionary Entry (pp. 19–20); Finding the Right Definition (pp. 39–40)	Synonym Tests (pp. 59–60); Antonym Tests (pp. 79–80)	Context Clues (pp. 99–100); Dividing Words into Parts (pp. 119–120); The Prefixes non-, un- (pp. 139–140); The Prefix trans- (pp. 159–160); The Prefix de- (pp. 179–180); The Suffixes -ity, -hood (pp. 199–200)

Vocabulary for Achievement

SECOND COURSE

Margaret Ann Richek

Arlin T. McRae

Susan K. Weiler

GREAT SOURCE
WILMINGTON, MA

AUTHORS

Margaret Ann Richek
Professor of Education, Northeastern Illinois University; consultant in reading and vocabulary study; author of The World of Words *(Houghton Mifflin)*

Arlin T. McRae
Supervisor of English, Evansville-Vanderburgh School Corporation, Evansville, Indiana; Adjunct Instructor in English, University of Evansville

Susan K. Weiler
Instructor of Art History at John Carroll University in Cleveland, Ohio; former teacher of Latin, Beaumont School for Girls, Cleveland Heights, Ohio

CONSULTANT

Larry S. Krieger
Social Studies Supervisor, Montgomery Township Public Schools, New Jersey; author of World History *and* U.S. History *(D.C. Heath), co-author of* Mastering the Verbal SAT 1/PSAT *(Great Source)*

CLASSROOM CONSULTANTS

Jack Pelletier
Teacher of English, Mira Loma High School, Sacramento, California

Valerie M. Webster
Teacher of English, Walnut Hill School, Natick, Massachusetts

ACKNOWLEDGMENTS

Definitions for the three hundred words taught in this textbook are based on Houghton Mifflin dictionaries—in particular, the *Houghton Mifflin Student Dictionary*—but have been abbreviated and adapted for instructional purposes. In the skills lessons, dictionary entries from the *Houghton Mifflin Student Dictionary,* copyright © 1986, appear on pages 20 and 40; dictionary entries from the *Houghton Mifflin College Dictionary,* copyright © 1986, appear on pages 19–20, 39–40, and 59–60. Some of the entries have been abridged. The pronunciation key on the inside front cover is adapted from *The American Heritage Dictionary of the English Language, Third Edition,* copyright © 1992.

CREDITS

Production: PC&F, Inc.

Illustrations: Alex Bloch: pages 185, 197; Dick Cole: pages 65, 77, 145, 151, 177; Simon Galkin: pages 31, 57, 117, 125; Charles Scogins: pages 11, 45, 71, 171

Printed in the United States of America

ISBN: 0-669-46478-3

11 12 13 14 15 HS 08 07 06 05 04

CONTENTS

COMPLETE WORD LIST

abet, 81
abide, 133
abode, 53
abrupt, 181
accent, 1
accessible, 173
accompanist, 13
accomplice, 13
acquit, 107
administer, 141
admonish, 187
adversary, 87
aggression, 87
alienate, 187
alloy, 41
altruistic, 193
amenable, 133
amicable, 33
amiss, 113
anarchy, 101
anguish, 33
animate, 141
annex, 53
antiquated, 61
aqueduct, 73
arson, 107
articulate, 1
authoritarian, 101

belated, 67
benefactor, 193
beneficial, 193
benevolent, 193
benign, 193
bewilder, 113
bias, 133
blithe, 33
blockade, 47
blunder, 113
boisterous, 153
bountiful, 193
buoyant, 41

cache, 173
celestial, 41
censure, 187
centenarian, 61
chaos, 153
claimant, 93
clamor, 93
coagulate, 41
coalition, 13
combustible, 41
communal, 13
compel, 167
complacent, 153
complement, 13
comport, 147
compulsion, 167
concoct, 141
conduct, 73
conduit, 73
confines, 161
conflagration, 41

congenial, 27
congregate, 13
consensus, 13
conservative, 101
conspicuous, 173
contemporary, 61
contradict, 87
controversy, 87
corrupt, 107
counterfeit, 107
culprit, 107

declaim, 93
deduce, 73
defiant, 33
degenerate, 27
delegate, 101
delineate, 161
deliverance, 81
demarcation, 161
denounce, 187
deportment, 147
descendant, 21
desolate, 33
despondent, 33
detriment, 187
devise, 141
dialect, 1
diction, 1
disclaim, 93
disclosure, 173
discord, 87
discrimination, 133
disgruntled, 33
disillusion, 33
disport, 147
disrupt, 181
dissection, 41
distend, 161
distill, 41
distinct, 161
distress, 33
dominion, 101
duration, 67
dynamic, 153

edifice, 53
embellish, 121
embody, 161
embroil, 87
eminent, 127
endeavor, 141
ennoble, 81
enunciate, 1
erroneous, 113
eruption, 181
evocative, 93
excavate, 53
exceed, 121
execute, 141
expedite, 81
expire, 67
exuberant, 33

fallible, 113
faux pas, 113
felony, 107
fledgling, 61
fluster, 113
forbearance, 133
foregone, 67
fractious, 181
fragment, 181
frail, 61
fundamental, 1

gender, 27
genealogy, 27
generation, 21
generic, 27
genesis, 27
gentry, 27
gerontology, 61
glut, 121
gratify, 193

haggle, 87
hijack, 107
humanitarian, 193

immoderate, 121
impeach, 101
impel, 167
imperil, 187
implement, 141
impulsive, 167
inaugurate, 101
incapacitate, 187
incessant, 67
incriminate, 107
indestructible, 47
indispensable, 127
induce, 73
inductee, 13
induction, 73
indulge, 193
infraction, 181
infringe, 181
inheritance, 21
injurious, 187
insular, 7
insupportable, 147
intelligible, 1
intense, 121
inter, 173
intercede, 81
intrigue, 173
invoke, 93

latitude, 7
lavish, 121
liberal, 101
lineage, 21
longevity, 61
longitude, 7
luxurious, 121

malign, 187
marginal, 161
martial, 47
mason, 53
maternal, 21
matriarch, 21
medieval, 67
meridian, 7
meteorology, 41
miscalculate, 113
miscellaneous, 13
misinterpret, 113
momentous, 127
monotonous, 153

nascent, 61

objective, 133
obscure, 173
offset, 81
omnipotent, 47
omnipresent, 161
outrageous, 121
overestimate, 113

pacify, 81
panorama, 7
paramount, 127
parental, 21
partisan, 133
patriarch, 21
peal, 167
peer, 1
penetration, 161
peninsula, 7
petty, 127
philanthropic, 193
portable, 147
portage, 147
porter, 147
portfolio, 147
posterity, 21
precipice, 7
preconceived, 133
prefabricate, 53
prejudice, 133
premature, 67
prestige, 127
primogeniture, 27
priority, 127
productivity, 73
profuse, 121
progeny, 27
prominence, 127
propulsion, 167
puerile, 61
pulsate, 167
purport 147

quagmire, 7

reactivate, 141
reclaim, 93
reduction, 73

refractory, 181
refurbish, 81
regenerate, 27
reinforce, 81
render, 141
repeal, 167
repellent, 167
repent, 107
repulse, 167
respite, 67
restive, 153
revoke, 93
robust, 47
rotunda, 53
rout, 181
rupture, 181

sanctuary, 81
saturate, 41
scoff, 187
secluded, 173
sibling, 21
simultaneous, 67
skirmish, 87
solar, 53
Spartan, 101
spendthrift, 121
sportive, 147
stability, 47
stalemate, 87
static, 153
status, 1
staunch, 47
steadfast, 153
stress, 1
strife, 87
subdue, 73
subsequent, 67
substantial, 161
superficial, 127
swindle, 107

terrestrial, 7
throng, 13
tolerance, 133
topography, 7
tranquil, 153
trellis, 53
trivial, 127
turret, 53
tyrant, 101

unavailable, 173
undertaking, 141
unearth, 173

valiant, 47
velocity, 153
venerable, 61
viaduct, 73
vocation, 93
vouch, 93
vulnerable, 47

withstand, 47

Suppose that someone said, "My car stalled, so I raised the *bonnet* and looked at the engine." This sentence would make perfect sense to a person who had grown up in England. Someone raised in the United States, however, would express the same thought by saying, "My car stalled, so I raised the *hood* and looked at the engine." Americans use the word *hood*, but the English say *bonnet* because of differences in the dialects of the English language.

Dialects are systematic variations in the pronunciation, vocabulary, and grammar of a language that distinguish one group from another. This lesson contains words that are used to discuss dialects and the variety of ways in which people talk to one another.

DEFINITIONS

After you have studied the definitions and example for each vocabulary word, write the word on the line to the right.

1. **accent** (ăk′sĕnt′) *noun*   A style of speech or pronunciation that is characteristic of a certain region or country.   *verb*   To emphasize in speech or in music. (From the Latin *ad-*, meaning "to," and *cantus*, meaning "song")

   Related Word   accentuate *verb*
   Example   When Hans speaks English, he has a slight German *accent*.

   1. _____

2. **articulate** (är-tĭk′yə-lĭt) *adjective*   **a.** Expressed in a clear and effective manner.   **b.** Able to speak effectively.   *verb* (är-tĭk′yə-lāt′) To express in words.

   Related Words   articulately *adverb*; articulation *noun*
   Example   In an *articulate* speech, the student council president talked about the exciting opportunities open to the graduates.

   2. _____

3. **dialect** (dī′ə-lĕkt′) *noun* The form or version of a language that is spoken in a country or region or by a particular social group; a dialect has characteristic differences in pronunciation, vocabulary, and grammar. (From the Greek word *dialektos*, meaning "language")

   Related Word   dialectal *adjective*
   Example   In the United States, people who speak northern *dialects* refer to "corn on the cob"; those who speak southern *dialects* refer to "roasting ears."

   3. _____

4. **diction** (dĭk'shən) *noun* **a.** The choice and use of words in speaking or writing. **b.** Distinctness of pronunciation. (From the Latin word *dicere*, meaning "to say")

    Example   The *diction* of an encyclopedia article is more difficult than that of a comic book.

4. _____

5. **enunciate** (ĭ-nŭn'sē-āt') *verb* **a.** To pronounce, especially in a clear manner. **b.** To state or set forth clearly. (From the Latin *ex-*, meaning "out," and *nuntiare*, meaning "to announce")

    Related Word   **enunciation** *noun*
    Example   The candidate carefully *enunciated* his words so that the huge audience would understand him.

5. _____

6. **fundamental** (fŭn'də-měn'tl) *adjective* **a.** Basic; primary; essential. **b.** Of major significance. *noun* A basic or necessary part: *the fundamentals of science.* (From the Latin word *fundamentum*, meaning "foundation")

    Related Word   **fundamentally** *adverb*
    Example   Plumbers must master the *fundamental* techniques of their trade.

6. _____

7. **intelligible** (ĭn-tĕl'ĭ-jə-bəl) *adjective* Able to be understood. (From the Latin word *intellegere*, meaning "to perceive")

    Related Words   **intelligibility** *noun;* **intelligibly** *adverb*
    Example   The telegram written in code was not *intelligible* to Eleanor.

7. _____

8. **peer** (pîr) *noun* **a.** A person who is equal to another in age, class, or rank. **b.** A member of the British nobility. (From the Latin word *par*, meaning "equal")

    Example   Five-year-old Scott avoided his *peers* because he preferred to play with older children.

8. _____

9. **status** (stăt'əs) *noun* **a.** Position in society; condition. **b.** A stage of progress or development. (From the Latin word *status*, meaning "position" or "standing")

    Example   Owning a carriage was once considered a symbol of high social *status*.

9. _____

10. **stress** (strĕs) *verb* To emphasize, particularly when speaking. *noun* **a.** Emphasis, particularly when speaking. **b.** Importance; significance.

    Example   People learning some foreign languages may *stress* the wrong syllables in words.

10. _____

Word History: fundamental

Latin: *fundamentum<fundare*–to lay foundation of*<fundus*=bottom

The word *fundamental*, meaning "basic, primary, or essential," comes from the Latin root *fundus*, meaning "bottom." Any word containing this root, which occurs in English as *found-* or *fund-*, conveys the idea of bottom or basic level. Consider such examples as *founder*, "one who establishes the basis of an institution, business, or city"; *foundation*, "the basis upon which a building stands"; or *profound*, "coming from the very bottom."

EXERCISE 1 MATCHING WORDS AND DEFINITIONS

Match the definition in Column B with the word in Column A. Write the letter
of the correct definition on the answer line.

Column A

1. enunciate
2. peer
3. stress
4. fundamental
5. intelligible
6. articulate
7. status
8. dialect
9. accent
10. diction

Column B

a. To pronounce, especially in a clear manner

b. Choice of words in speaking or writing

c. Expressed in a clear and effective way

d. A person who is equal to another

e. A form of a language spoken in a region or by a group

f. Position in society; stage of progress

g. A style of speech or pronunciation that is characteristic of a certain region

h. To emphasize, particularly when speaking

i. Able to be understood

j. Basic or essential; of major significance

1. _____a_____
2. _____d_____
3. _____h_____
4. _____j_____
5. _____i_____
6. _____c_____
7. _____f_____
8. _____e_____
9. _____g_____
10. _____b_____

EXERCISE 2 USING WORDS CORRECTLY

Decide whether the italicized vocabulary word has been used correctly in the
sentence. On the answer line, write *Correct* for correct use and *Incorrect* for
incorrect use.

1. The Franklin family has enjoyed high *status* in this city for many years.

2. People should *enunciate* clearly when writing letters.

3. The director told the actors and actresses to work on perfecting their English *accents*.

4. People stopped listening to the speech because it was so *articulate*.

5. Army officers and their *peers,* the enlisted men, must cooperate on the battlefield.

6. If your teacher *stresses* a certain subject, you would be wise to study that subject carefully.

7. The *dialect* is an important part of the telephone.

8. Drivers today need a *fundamental* understanding of automobiles in case their cars break down.

9. Dana could not figure out what the note said because it was *intelligible.*

10. People can improve their *diction* by using electronic calculators.

1. _____Correct_____
2. _____Incorrect_____
3. _____Correct_____
4. _____Incorrect_____
5. _____Incorrect_____
6. _____Correct_____
7. _____Incorrect_____
8. _____Correct_____
9. _____Incorrect_____
10. _____Incorrect_____

Decide which vocabulary word or related form best completes the sentence, and write the letter of your choice on the answer line.

1. Paula, who grew up in Maine, still speaks with a New England _____.
   a. status   **b.** accent   **c.** fundamental   **d.** peer

   1. _____ b

2. The actors' _____ improved so that they could be heard in the last row of the auditorium.
   a. peer   **b.** status   **c.** dialect   **d.** enunciation

   2. _____ d

3. My brother muttered a comment that was barely _____.
   a. intelligible   **b.** fundamental   **c.** dialect   **d.** diction

   3. _____ a

4. Buddy enjoyed his _____ as class president.
   a. diction   **b.** dialect   **c.** status   **d.** stress

   4. _____ c

5. The politician's remarks were so _____ that the crowd cheered.
   a. articulate   **b.** accented   **c.** dialectal   **d.** enunciated

   5. _____ a

6. Instead of always pleasing their _____, people should also please themselves.
   a. status   **b.** diction   **c.** dialects   **d.** peers

   6. _____ d

7. Computer skills are _____ to the modern office worker.
   a. accented   **b.** fundamental   **c.** intelligible   **d.** status

   7. _____ b

8. Because of their clear _____, we could understand every word of the choir's song.
   a. dialect   **b.** status   **c.** diction   **d.** accent

   8. _____ c

9. The _____ of the magazine article was on the importance of exercising regularly.
   a. enunciation   **b.** stress   **c.** peer   **d.** fundamental

   9. _____ b

10. When Roger spoke, his _____ indicated that he had grown up in our part of the country.
    a. fundamental   **b.** status   **c.** peer   **d.** dialect

    10. _____ d

Decide which form of the vocabulary word in parentheses best completes the sentence. The form given may be correct. Write your answer on the answer line.

1. The board of directors was _____ opposed to major advertising expenditures. *(fundamental)*

   1. _____ fundamentally

2. The comedian is a master of many foreign _____. *(accent)*

   2. _____ accents

3. Gloria seemed much older than her _____ in high school. *(peer)*

   3. _____ peers

4. Yesterday Mr. Chang _____ that the final examination would cover ten chapters. *(stress)*

   4. _____ stressed

5. The coach of the debate team spent an hour discussing _____. *(enunciate)*

   5. _____ enunciation

6. If you do not speak _____, people may misunderstand you. *(intelligible)*

   6. _____ intelligibly

7. I could not determine where Joni lived from hearing her _____ . *(dialect)*

8. The poem's _____ was both formal and ornate. *(diction)*

9. Some people are better than others at _____ their feelings. *(articulate)*

10. Each committee member reported on the _____ of his or her project. *(status)*

7. __dialect__

8. __diction__

9. __articulating__

10. __status__

READING COMPREHENSION

Each numbered sentence in the following passage contains an italicized vocabulary word or related form. After you read the passage, you will complete an exercise.

DIALECTS OF THE ENGLISH LANGUAGE

(1) When people from British Canada, the United States, Great Britain, and Australia gather in the same room, they speak with a wide variety of *accents.* (2) In spite of this variety, however, they are able to make themselves *intelligible* to one another. (3) This is because they all speak *dialects* of the English language.

A dialect is a version of a language that distinguishes one group of speakers from another. (4) People learn the dialects they speak from their families and from adults and *peers* in the areas in which they grow up. (5) Usually there is not a *fundamental* difference between the dialect of one region or country and that of another. There are minor differences, though, in pronunciation, vocabulary, and grammar.

The first difference that most people notice between dialects is in pronunciation. For example, when Americans say *garage,* they emphasize the second syllable.

(6) In Britain, though, people put the *stress* on the first syllable.

Even within a country, there are regional differences in pronunciation. To take just one example, when many Americans say the word *aunt,* they pronounce it in the same way that they pronounce *ant.* Many others, though, pronounce the word so that it rhymes with *font.*

(7) Another major difference among dialects is in *diction.* In the United States, people say *gasoline* and *truck.* In Britain they say *petrol* and *lorry.* In some parts of the United States, people refer to the *basement;* in other areas, *cellar* is the more common word.

(8) No dialect in itself is better than another; a person speaking one dialect can be just as *articulate* as a person speaking another. (9) Dialect, however, may indicate a person's social *status.* This fact was the basis of the Irish playwright George Bernard Shaw's play *Pygmalion,*

which was later adapted for the successful musical *My Fair Lady.*

In both the play and the musical, the main character is a young Englishwoman, Eliza Doolittle, who speaks the dialect of one of London's poor districts. Professor Henry Higgins teaches her to speak—and act—like a woman of the nobility. (10) In one famous scene, Eliza practices *enunciating* the sentence "The rain in Spain stays mainly in the plain." Once she does so successfully, she rapidly acquires the dialect that Higgins has been attempting to teach her.

The best way to learn about dialects is to listen closely to other people. Do they pronounce words differently? Do they use expressions with which you are not familiar? Do they use some grammatical constructions that are different from the ones that you use? By listening closely, you will add to your understanding of the English language.

Each of the following statements corresponds to a numbered sentence in the passage. Each statement contains a blank and is followed by four answer choices. Decide which choice fits best in the blank. The word or phrase that you choose must express roughly the same meaning as the italicized word in the passage. Write the letter of your choice on the answer line.

1. People from British Canada, the United States, Britain, and Australia display a variety of _____.
   a. ways of spelling words   c. fashions in dressing
   b. ways of behaving   d. ways of pronouncing words

   1. _____ d _____

2. People from these countries make themselves _____.
   a. suspicious   b. understood   c. helpful   d. at home

   2. _____ b _____

3. The people from these countries speak _____ of English.
   a. well   b. versions   c. fondly   d. the rules

   3. _____ b _____

4. People learn dialects from their families and _____.
   a. people their age   c. television announcers
   b. teachers   d. language records

   4. _____ a _____

5. Usually no _____ differences in dialect exist between regions.
   a. noticeable   b. minor   c. special   d. basic

   5. _____ d _____

6. The British _____ the first syllable in *garage*.
   a. drop   b. almost drop   c. emphasize   d. mispronounce

   6. _____ c _____

7. Another difference among dialects is in _____.
   a. spelling   c. word choices
   b. handwriting methods   d. dictionaries

   7. _____ c _____

8. A person speaking one dialect can be as _____ as a person speaking another dialect.
   a. confusing   b. clear   c. fancy   d. artistic

   8. _____ b _____

9. Dialect may indicate one's _____.
   a. profession   c. popularity
   b. self-confidence   d. social position

   9. _____ d _____

10. In one scene of *Pygmalion*, Eliza Doolittle practices _____ a particular sentence.
    a. pronouncing clearly   c. memorizing
    b. singing   d. explaining briefly

    10. _____ a _____

WRITING ASSIGNMENT

This lesson refers to differences among the English dialects spoken in Britain, the United States, Canada, and Australia. Find a book or an encyclopedia article in the library about the English language, and read about the differences between the English spoken in the United States and that spoken in one of the other countries. Then write a report in which you explain to other students what some of those differences are. In your report use at least five of the words from this lesson and underline them.

The study of geography is far more than just learning the names and locations of countries. Geography, or "earth description," is the investigation of facts about the earth's surface, which differs from place to place. This study includes both natural features and those that result from human occupation of an area. The geographer, who is also interested in climate, vegetation, population, and degree of use of land by animals and people, brings together information from many sciences—physical, biological, and social. In this lesson you will learn words that will aid you in your study of this complex science.

WORD LIST

insular
latitude
longitude
meridian
panorama
peninsula
precipice
quagmire
terrestrial
topography

DEFINITIONS

After you have studied the definitions and example for each vocabulary word, write the word on the line to the right.

1. **insular** (ĭn'sə-lər) *adjective*   **a.** Relating to an island.   **b.** Characteristic of the isolated life of an island people.   **c.** Narrow-minded. (From the Latin word *insula*, meaning "island")

   Related Word   **insularity** *noun*
   Example   The *insular* life of Nantucket Island is relaxed except during the summer tourist season.

1. _____

2. **latitude** (lăt'ĭ-tood') *noun*   **a.** The distance north or south of the equator, measured in degrees.   **b.** Freedom from usual restraint. (From the Latin word *latitude*, meaning "width" or "breadth")

   Related Word   **latitudinal** *adjective*
   Example   *Latitude* is indicated on a map by horizontal lines.

2. _____

3. **longitude** (lŏn'jĭ-tood') *noun*   The distance east or west of Greenwich (pronounced GRENN-itch), England, and measured in degrees. (From the Latin word *longitude*, meaning "length")

   Related Word   **longitudinal** *adjective*
   Example   *Longitude* is indicated on a map by vertical lines.

3. _____

4. **meridian** (mə-rĭd'ē-ən) *noun*   Any of the imaginary circles around the earth that pass through the North Pole and South Pole. (From the Latin word *meridies*, meaning "midday")

   Example   Although a *meridian* is an imaginary line, navigators use it to determine location.

4. _____

5. **panorama** (păn´ə-răm´ə) *noun*   **a.** A wide-ranging view over a large area. **b.** A comprehensive picture of a specific subject; an overview. (From the Greek *pan-*, meaning "all," and *horama*, meaning "sight")

5. _____

Related Word	**panoramic** *adjective*
Example	From the hills of Los Angeles, one sees a spectacular *panorama* of the coast to the downtown area.

6. **peninsula** (pə-nĭn´syə-lə) *noun*   A strip of land with water on three sides. (From the Latin words *paene*, meaning "almost," and *insula*, meaning "island")

6. _____

Related Word	**peninsular** *adjective*
Example	The scout troop camped out on a small *peninsula* that jutted into the ocean.

7. **precipice** (prĕs´ə-pĭs) *noun*   A steep cliff or overhanging rock. (From the Latin word *praeceps*, meaning "headlong")

7. _____

Related Word	**precipitous** *adjective*
Example	The horse stumbled and nearly fell from the *precipice*.

8. **quagmire** (kwăg´mīr´) *noun*   **a.** Muddy land into which one can easily sink.   **b.** A difficult situation in which one can get caught; entanglement.

8. _____

Example	David and Christina got caught in a *quagmire* while photographing ducks.

9. **terrestrial** (tə-rĕs´trē-əl) *adjective*   **a.** Having to do with the earth.   **b.** Of or consisting of land in contrast to water or air. (From the Latin word *terra*, meaning "earth")

9. _____

Example	*Terrestrial* upheavals such as earthquakes and volcanoes can endanger people living nearby.

10. **topography** (tə-pŏg´rə-fē) *noun*   The physical features of a region, such as mountains, plains, and rivers. (From the Greek words *topos*, meaning "place," and *graphein*, meaning "to write")

10. _____

MEMORY CUE:
Topography refers to the *top* of the land—the features that are visible.

Related Word	**topographical** *adjective*
Example	The *topography* of Switzerland is mountainous.

Word History: terrestrial

Latin: *terra*=earth or land

   Terrestrial comes from the Latin word *terra*, meaning "earth" or "land," and describes earth as well as land phenomena. Many words referring to the earth or the land contain the Latin root *terra-* or *ter-*. A *subterranean* cave lies under the "earth"; to *inter* a body is to bury it in the "earth"; the *territory* of Texas refers to the "land" it includes. If you combine the Latin prefix *extra-*, meaning "beyond," with the root *terr-*, you will form the word *extraterrestrial* or "creature coming from beyond the earth."

EXERCISE 1 WRITING CORRECT WORDS

On the answer line, write the word from the vocabulary list that fits each definition.

1. Relating to the earth

2. A steep cliff or overhanging rock

3. The distance east and west of Greenwich, England, measured in degrees

4. Any of the imaginary circles around the earth that pass through the poles

5. An area of land with water on three sides

6. The physical features of a region

7. Pertaining to an island

8. Wet, soft ground in which one can get caught

9. The distance north or south of the equator, measured in degrees

10. A wide-ranging view over an area; an overview

1. ____terrestrial____

2. ____precipice____

3. ____longitude____

4. ____meridian____

5. ____peninsula____

6. ____topography____

7. ____insular____

8. ____quagmire____

9. ____latitude____

10. ____panorama____

EXERCISE 2 USING WORDS CORRECTLY

Decide whether the italicized vocabulary word or related form has been used correctly in the sentence. On the answer line, write *Correct* for correct use and *Incorrect* for incorrect use.

1. Someone with a fear of heights would be comfortable walking near a *precipice*.

2. Marblehead Neck in Massachusetts is a *peninsula* because it is surrounded on three sides by water.

3. A *meridian* is parallel to the equator.

4. The inhabitants of the island of Barbados are *insular* people.

5. You can figure out the *latitude* of an island by measuring east of Greenwich.

6. When geographers examine the *topography* of a region, they are studying the elements in the earth's core.

7. Whales are *terrestrial* mammals.

8. In geography class Christopher found the *longitude* of Vancouver by measuring west of the meridian at Greenwich, England.

9. When his mother learned that he had lied to her, Joseph found himself in a *quagmire*.

10. A convict in a cell with a small window near the ceiling would probably have a *panoramic* view of the outside.

1. ____Incorrect____

2. ____Correct____

3. ____Incorrect____

4. ____Correct____

5. ____Incorrect____

6. ____Incorrect____

7. ____Incorrect____

8. ____Correct____

9. ____Correct____

10. ____Incorrect____

EXERCISE 3 CHOOSING THE BEST WORD

Decide which vocabulary word or related form best completes the sentence, and write the letter of your choice on the answer line.

1. As the chair lift reached the peak, we saw a spectacular _____ of the snow-covered landscape.
   a. meridian   **b.** quagmire   **c.** peninsula   **d.** panorama

   1. _____ d _____

2. Dogs and cats are _____ animals, but fish are aquatic and live in the sea.
   a. precipitous   **b.** insular   **c.** terrestrial   **d.** topographical

   2. _____ c _____

3. Some _____ native tribes living in South American rain forests have never seen an automobile or a telephone.
   a. insular   **b.** quagmire   **c.** peninsula   **d.** terrestrial

   3. _____ a _____

4. When the Calkins drove through Manitoba, they noticed that the _____ was very flat.
   a. quagmire   **b.** topography   **c.** peninsula   **d.** longitude

   4. _____ b _____

5. Sir Francis Drake determined the _____ of his ship to find out how far he was from the equator.
   a. topography   **b.** meridian   **c.** latitude   **d.** panorama

   5. _____ c _____

6. Fred could not pull his boot free when it got stuck in the _____.
   a. precipice   **b.** peninsula   **c.** panorama   **d.** quagmire

   6. _____ d _____

7. At 112° _____ east of Greenwich, the captain of the steamship noticed some huge rocks that were not shown on the charts.
   a. panorama   **b.** longitude   **c.** latitude   **d.** meridian

   7. _____ b _____

8. The Pritzlaffs' house on the _____ has a beautiful view of the water to the east, north, and west.
   a. panorama   **b.** meridian   **c.** quagmire   **d.** peninsula

   8. _____ d _____

9. The imaginary lines we call _____ allow us to determine how far east or west we are.
   a. latitudes   **b.** precipices   **c.** meridians   **d.** peninsulas

   9. _____ c _____

10. Our guide warned us not to get too close to the dangerous _____ because we might lose our balance and fall off.
    a. precipice   **b.** panorama   **c.** quagmire   **d.** peninsula

    10. _____ a _____

EXERCISE 4 USING DIFFERENT FORMS OF WORDS

Decide which form of the vocabulary word in parentheses best completes the sentence. The form given may be correct. Write your answer on the answer line.

1. _____ navigation involves the use of a map and compass. *(terrestrial)*

   1. _____ Terrestrial _____

2. The _____ position of the lighthouse is 14°E. *(longitude)*

   2. _____ longitudinal _____

3. The _____ form of the jetty protects the harbor from high seas and rough weather. *(peninsula)*

   3. _____ peninsular _____

4. It is hard for Hawaiians to get some goods from the mainland because of their _____. *(insular)*

   4. _____ insularity _____

5. The book provides a _____ history of the sports and games people have played since the earliest times. (*panorama*)

6. The geologists checked the _____ map to determine the shape of the mesa. (*topography*)

7. Mrs. Gunn asked the class to determine the _____ distance between Miami and Minneapolis. (*latitude*)

8. The novice skier found himself at the top of a _____ expert slope. (*precipice*)

9. Denise plotted several _____ on the map of the world. (*meridian*)

10. Can you tell me if a fen and a marsh and a bog and a _____ are different? (*quagmire*)

5. ___panoramic___

6. ___topographical___

7. ___latitudinal___

8. ___precipitous___

9. ___meridians___

10. ___quagmire___

READING COMPREHENSION

Each numbered sentence in the following passage contains an italicized vocabulary word. After you read the passage, you will complete an exercise.

MAGELLAN: PORTUGESE NAVIGATOR

(1) In the sixteenth century, an age of great marine and *terrestrial* exploration, Ferdinand Magellan led the first expedition to sail around the world. (2) As a young Portuguese noble, he served the king of Portugal, but he became involved in the *quagmire* of political intrigue at court and lost the king's favor. After he was dismissed from service to the king of Portugal, he offered to serve the future Emperor Charles V of Spain.

(3) A papal decree of 1493 had assigned all land in the New World west of 50° W *longitude* to Spain and all the land east of that line to Portugal. Magellan offered to prove that the East Indies fell under Spanish authority.

On September 29, 1519, Magellan set sail from Spain with five ships. (4) More than a year later, one of these ships was exploring the *topography* of South America in search of a water route across the continent. (5) This ship sank, but the remaining four ships searched along the southern *peninsula* of South America. (6) Finally, they found the passage they sought near a *latitude* of 50° S. Magellan named this passage the Strait of All Saints, but today we know it as the Strait of Magellan.

(7) One ship deserted while in this passage and returned to Spain, so fewer sailors were privileged to gaze at that first *panorama* of the Pacific Ocean. (8) Those who survived crossed the *meridian* we now call the International Date Line in the early spring of 1521 after ninety-eight days on the Pacific Ocean. During those long days at sea, many of Magellan's men died of starvation and disease.

(9) Later Magellan became involved in an *insular* conflict in the Philippines and was killed in a tribal battle. (10) Only one ship and seventeen sailors under the command of the Basque navigator Elcano survived to complete the westward journey to Spain and thus proved once and for all that the world is round, with no *precipice* at the edge.

Each of the following statements corresponds to a numbered sentence in the passage. Each statement contains a blank and is followed by four answer choices. Decide which choice fits best in the blank. The word or phrase that you choose must express roughly the same meaning as the italicized word in the passage. Write the letter of your choice on the answer line.

1. The sixteenth century was an age of great _____ exploration.
   a. cosmic   **b.** land   **c.** scientific   **d.** seafaring

   1. _____ b

2. Magellan lost the favor of the king of Portugal when he became involved in a political _____.
   a. entanglement   **c.** discussion
   b. assassination   **d.** negotiation

   2. _____ a

3. The Pope divided New World lands between Spain and Portugal according to their location on one side or the other of an imaginary geographical line 50° west of Greenwich that extends in a _____ direction.
   a. north-and-south   **c.** easterly
   b. crosswise   **d.** westerly

   3. _____ a

4. One of Magellan's ships explored the _____ of South America for a passage across the continent.
   a. coastline   **c.** mountain range
   b. horizon   **d.** physical features

   4. _____ d

5. Four of the ships sought a passage along a southern _____.
   a. coast   **c.** body of land with water on three sides
   b. island   **d.** body of land surrounded by water

   5. _____ c

6. The passage was found near 50° S of _____.
   a. Greenwich   **b.** Spain   **c.** Portugal   **d.** the equator

   6. _____ d

7. Few sailors gazed at the _____ of the Pacific.
   a. view   **b.** horizon   **c.** ocean   **d.** picture

   7. _____ a

8. In the spring of 1521, the ships crossed the _____ that is now called the International Date Line.
   a. ocean   **c.** imaginary circle passing through the poles
   b. area   **d.** imaginary line parallel to the equator

   8. _____ c

9. Magellan was killed in a(n) _____ conflict.
   a. violent   **b.** island   **c.** Spanish   **d.** naval

   9. _____ b

10. There is no _____ at the edge of the world.
   a. sea monster   **b.** tortoise   **c.** cliff   **d.** water

   10. _____ c

WRITING ASSIGNMENT

Using a map, select a place such as a country, state, or city. Consult an encyclopedia for additional information about that place. Then, using five words from this lesson and underlining them, give its location and tell about its natural features. Assume that you are preparing this assignment as a presentation to be given to your classmates as a geography lesson.

The **Bonus activity** for Lessons 1 and 2 is on page T1.

Members of the Elmsville High School Drama Club spent more time debating than they did acting.

"We've got four weeks to put on a production, and we still haven't decided on a play," Ron, the drama club president, informed the group.

"I'm not finding costumes for anything written in another century," Emily announced.

"That's not fair. I want to play a historical role!" John insisted.

"I want to do a musical!" Susan demanded.

"This is getting us nowhere," Ron concluded.

When you work in a group like a drama club, it is very important for group members to cooperate with one another. Individuals must respect and work with others who have different points of view. In this lesson, you will learn words that refer to people working in groups.

WORD LIST

accompanist
accomplice
coalition
communal
complement
congregate
consensus
inductee
miscellaneous
throng

DEFINITIONS

After you have studied the definitions and example for each vocabulary word, write the word on the line to the right.

1. **accompanist** (ə-kŭm′pə-nĭst) *noun* A musician, such as a pianist, who plays along with a performer or performers. (From the Old French word *compaignon*, meaning "companion")

   Related Words accompaniment *noun;* accompany *verb*
   Example The opera singer asked Alan to be her *accompanist* on the piano.

1. _____

2. **accomplice** (ə-kŏm′plĭs) *noun* One who knowingly aids or helps another person break a law but is not necessarily present at the time of the crime. (From the Middle English word *complice*, meaning "companion")

   Example Bobby was Cindy's willing *accomplice* in the plot to raid the refrigerator.

2. _____

3. **coalition** (kō′ə-lĭsh′ən) *noun* An alliance, usually temporary, of a group of people with a common cause. (From the Latin word *coalescere*, meaning "to grow together")

   Example A *coalition* of groups favored increased support for national parks.

3. _____

4. **communal** (kə-myōō′nəl) *adjective* Belonging to a community, group, or society; public. (From the Latin word *communis*, meaning "common")

   Related Words communally *adverb;* commune *noun*
   Example The *communal* recreation room was a popular feature provided by the company.

4. _____

5. **complement** (kŏm′plə-mənt) *noun*   Something that completes, makes up a whole, or brings to perfection.   *verb*   To make complete; add to the effect of. (From the Latin word *complere*, meaning "to fill out")

   Related Word   **complementary** *adjective*
   Example   An attractive table setting is a *complement* to a well-prepared meal.

5. _____
USAGE NOTE: Do not confuse *complement*, which refers to that which completes something, with *compliment*, an expression of praise.

6. **congregate** (kŏng′grĭ-gāt′) *verb*   To bring or come together in a crowd or assembly. (From the Latin *com-*, meaning "together," and *gregare*, meaning "to assemble")

   Related Words   **congregation** *noun;* **congregational** *adjective*
   Example   The geese *congregated* in a large group in front of the pond.

6. _____

7. **consensus** (kən-sĕn′səs) *noun*   General agreement among a group of people. (From the Latin *com-*, meaning "together," and *sentire*, meaning "to feel")

   Example   The board of directors reached a *consensus* that the company should have a new headquarters constructed.

7. _____

8. **inductee** (in′dŭk-tē′) *noun*   A new member of a club or organization; a person being placed formally in an office, a society, or the armed forces. (From the Latin *in-*, meaning "in," and *ducere*, meaning "to lead")

   Related Words   **induct** *verb;* **induction** *noun*
   Example   The army *inductees* were outfitted in uniforms for their first field exercise.

8. _____

9. **miscellaneous** (mĭs′ə-lā′nē-əs) *adjective*   **a.** Made up of a variety of different elements or ingredients.   **b.** Not falling into a particular category. (From the Latin word *miscere*, meaning "to mix")

   Related Word   **miscellany** *noun*
   Example   In the cluttered attic, Meg found old toys, books, and other *miscellaneous* objects.

9. _____

10. **throng** (thrông) *noun*   A large group of people or things gathered or packed closely together; a crowd.   *verb*   **a.** To crowd into; gather.   **b.** To move in a throng.

    Example   *Throngs* of shoppers filled the aisles of the department store.

10. _____

EXERCISE 1 MATCHING WORDS AND DEFINITIONS

Match the definition in Column B with the word in Column A. Write the letter of the correct definition on the answer line.

Column A

1. inductee
2. congregate
3. communal
4. coalition
5. accompanist
6. complement
7. miscellaneous
8. consensus
9. accomplice
10. throng

Column B

a. A person who helps another to commit a crime

b. A crowd of people packed tightly together

c. Someone who plays music in support of a singer or other musician

d. Belonging to a community; public

e. A new member of an organization

f. To assemble in a large group

g. General agreement or opinion

h. Temporary alliance of people sharing a common cause

i. Something that completes a whole

j. Made up of a variety of items

1. ____e____
2. ____f____
3. ____d____
4. ____h____
5. ____c____
6. ____i____
7. ____j____
8. ____g____
9. ____a____
10. ____b____

EXERCISE 2 USING WORDS CORRECTLY

Decide whether the italicized vocabulary word has been used correctly in the sentence. On the answer line, write *Correct* for correct use and *Incorrect* for incorrect use.

1. Everyone applauded the *accompanist's* solo performance.

2. A *consensus* in favor of the proposal was reached when five of the thirty club members voted for it.

3. An *accomplice* watched for security guards while the criminal opened the bank safe.

4. Many people feel that peanut butter is a perfect *complement* to jelly in a sandwich.

5. A new arrival at a school dance is an *inductee*.

6. A group of politicians formed a *coalition* for educational reform.

7. Every family in the neighborhood shared in the costs of repairing the *communal* swimming pool.

8. A *throng* of people left the crowded stadium.

9. Tanya *congregated* alone outside the building.

10. Seventeen new television sets could be referred to as a collection of *miscellaneous* items.

1. ____Incorrect____
2. ____Incorrect____
3. ____Correct____
4. ____Correct____
5. ____Incorrect____
6. ____Correct____
7. ____Correct____
8. ____Correct____
9. ____Incorrect____
10. ____Incorrect____

Decide which vocabulary word or related form best expresses the meaning of the italicized word or phrase in the sentence. On the answer line, write the letter of that word.

1. Many children *gathered* around the ice-cream truck.
   a. inducted   **b.** were accompanists   **c.** congregated   **d.** were accomplices

1. _____ c _____

2. A *new member of the army* must complete a basic training program.
   a. accomplice   **b.** accompanist   **c.** throng   **d.** inductee

2. _____ d _____

3. The *person who aided the criminal* forged company records.
   a. accompanist   **b.** inductee   **c.** throng   **d.** accomplice

3. _____ d _____

4. Hiking clothes, shoes, and a walking stick are *related parts that work together to make up a whole.*
   a. complements   **b.** congregations   **c.** miscellanies   **d.** accomplices

4. _____ a _____

5. A *closely packed group* of spectators admired the museum exhibit.
   a. coalition   **b.** commune   **c.** throng   **d.** consensus

5. _____ c _____

6. The *musician who played along with the singer* also took a bow.
   a. consensus   **b.** accomplice   **c.** accompanist   **d.** inductee

6. _____ c _____

7. The class reached a *general agreement* and voted to visit the aquarium.
   a. consensus   **b.** throng   **c.** congregation   **d.** accomplice

7. _____ a _____

8. The factory workers formed a *temporary alliance* on the issue of safety.
   a. induction   **b.** throng   **c.** coalition   **d.** complement

8. _____ c _____

9. The neighborhood pool is a *public* facility.
   a. congregational   **b.** miscellaneous   **c.** complementary   **d.** communal

9. _____ d _____

10. While looking through the back of the catalogue, Jenny discovered *various* items.
    a. communal   **b.** accomplice   **c.** congregational   **d.** miscellaneous

10. _____ d _____

Decide which form of the vocabulary word in parentheses best completes the sentence. The form given may be correct. Write your answer on the answer line.

1. The pastor gave a sermon before a large _____. (*congregate*)

1. _____ congregation _____

2. Janet was an _____ in the prank played on her little brother. (*accomplice*)

2. _____ accomplice _____

3. Mr. Newhall accumulated _____ in his barn. (*miscellaneous*)

3. _____ miscellany _____

4. Roger _____ Violet on the long walk home. (*accompanist*)

4. _____ accompanied _____

5. After hours of debate, the Senate committee reached a _____. (*consensus*)

5. _____ consensus _____

6. We worked _____ to clean up the school playground. (*communal*)

6. _____ communally _____

7. The _____ of new club members took place at a special ceremony. (*inductee*)

7. _____ induction _____

8. The cover nicely _____ the contents of the yearbook. (*complement*)

8. _____ complements _____

9. A _____ of people filled the convention center. (*throng*)

9. _____ throng _____

10. At least three _____ are working for improved social services. (*coalition*)

10. _____ coalitions _____

READING COMPREHENSION

Each numbered sentence in the following passage contains an italicized vocabulary word or related form. After you read the passage, you will complete an exercise.

THE RED CROSS: BRINGING HUMANITY TO INHUMANITY

The year was 1859. Jean-Henri Dunant, a Swiss citizen watching French and Austrian soldiers battle at Solferino, Italy, was horrified by the human cost of warfare. When the fighting was over, wounded soldiers lay helpless, without medical aid. Shocked by what he saw, he organized efforts to bring them medical attention. Five years later, with the help of his widely read book *Memory of Solferino,* Dunant was on his way to building an organization that today has international influence.

Dunant wanted a group of neutral civilians, unattached to any army, that would assist the wounded and organize emergency aid services. Assistance was to be offered regardless of which side soldiers had fought on. For, as he wrote in his book, "They are all brothers." Someone suggested that workers wear armbands bearing a red cross so that they could be easily identified. The organization became known as "The Red Cross." Today, headquartered in Geneva, Switzerland, it is the International Committee of the Red Cross, or I.C.R.C.

To make warfare more humane, Dunant proposed international agreements that countries would honor during fighting. (1) In 1864, twelve countries reached *consensus* when they signed the first Geneva Convention, which made hospitals, ambulances, and medical staff neutral. It also established the fact that soldiers on both sides of combat were entitled to the same medical treatment. (2) The I.C.R.C. felt that it was wrong to establish villains, or to try to determine which soldiers were *accomplices* of wrongdoers.

The I.C.R.C extended its efforts into guidelines for treatment of prisoners of war. Today, I.C.R.C. volunteers go into prisoner-of-war camps, monitoring conditions, and registering prisoners. (3) Captured soldiers *throng* I.C.R.C. workers, who hand out yellow registration cards. The Red Cross has also helped thousands of families by finding missing soldiers. (4) It has delivered millions of cards, letters, and packages of *miscellaneous* items to prisoners of war. It has also supervised exchanges of prisoners of war.

The I.C.R.C. has also taken a leadership role in assuring civilian safety. It has championed safe areas for civilians. (5) Civilians who are in danger in their homes can *congregate* in these areas. (6) Although they often must live in *communal* tents, they are to be safe and free from attack.

The I.C.R.C. has adapted its message about humane warfare to the many local cultures it serves. In one country, it runs theater groups. (7) It has hired singers and *accompanists* to make recordings about humane warfare. It has reprinted the ancient wisdom of traditional books that urge warriors to treat wounded soldiers and civilians with respect.

The I.C.R.C. remains a volunteer organization, with staff from around the world. (8) *Inductees* receive training, including how to deal with danger such as minefields and rocket attacks. Yet they must remain unarmed, even in the middle of dangerous conflict. (9) The *coalition* of dedicated people who form the I.C.R.C. volunteers are brave people indeed.

(10) Today, there are many organizations that provide relief in war, *complementing* the efforts of the I.C.R.C. Yet the International Committee of the Red Cross remains the first, and one of the most important, organizations. The bloodshed that Jean-Henri Dunant saw almost a century and a half ago has resulted in humane treatment for hundreds of thousands of human beings.

Each of the following statements corresponds to a numbered sentence in the passage. Each statement contains a blank and is followed by four answer choices. Decide which choice fits best in the blank. The word or phrase that you choose must express roughly the same meaning as the italicized word in the passage. Write the letter of your choice on the answer line.

1. In 1864, twelve countries reached _____ when they signed the first Geneva Convention.
   a. a victory **b.** an alliance **c.** an end **d.** an agreement

   1. ____d____

2. The I.C.R.C. felt it was wrong to establish villains or to try to determine which soldiers were _____ of wrongdoers.
   a. partners **b.** preventers **c.** recorders **d.** witnesses

   2. ____a____

3. Captured soldiers _____ I.C.R.C. workers, who hand out yellow registration cards.
   a. avoid **b.** amuse **c.** enjoy **d.** crowd

   3. ____d____

4. It has delivered millions of cards, letters, and packages of _____ items to prisoners of war.
   a. large **b.** special **c.** interesting **d.** varied

   4. ____d____

5. Civilians who are in danger in their homes can _____ in these areas.
   a. eat **b.** work **c.** gather **d.** exist

   5. ____c____

6. Although they often must live in _____ tents, they are to be safe and free from attack.
   a. uncomfortable **b.** crowded **c.** shared **d.** hot

   6. ____c____

7. It has hired singers and _____ to make recordings about humane warfare.
   a. people to play instruments **c.** people to write words
   b. people to compose songs **d.** people to produce songs

   7. ____a____

8. _____ receive training, including how to deal with danger such as minefields and rocket attacks.
   a. new members **c.** special workers
   b. leading members **d.** workers in danger

   8. ____a____

9. The _____ of dedicated people who form the I.C.R.C. volunteers are brave people indeed.
   a. series **b.** supporters **c.** alliance **d.** nurses

   9. ____c____

10. Today there are many organizations that provide relief in war, _____ the efforts of the I.C.R.C.
    a. adding to **b.** unlike **c.** similar to **d.** negating

   10. ____a____

Imagine that you are a reporter for a local television station. Your assignment is to cover a town meeting that promises to be controversial. Invent and write a news story that explains what went on at the meeting. Follow news-writing format by making sure that your story answers the questions who, what, where, when, why, and how. Use five words from the lesson and underline each one.

The **Test** for Lessons 1, 2, and 3 is on page T2.

A B C

DICTIONARY SKILLS

FINDING THE APPROPRIATE DEFINITION

Most dictionary words have more than one definition. When you look up a word, you must decide which definition is most appropriate—that is, which one best fits the way the word is used. To do so, use the following strategies.

STRATEGIES

1. *Read all of the definitions in a dictionary entry.* Suppose that the italicized word in the following example sentence is unfamiliar to you. You would look up *contingent* in the dictionary and read the seven definitions.

    The launching of the space shuttle is *contingent* on the weather.

    > **con•tin•gent** (kən-tĭn′jənt) *adj.* [ME < Lat. *contingens,* pr. part. of *contingere,* to touch. — see CONTACT.] **1.** Likely but not certain to occur: POSSIBLE. **2.** Dependent on conditions or events not yet established: CONDITIONAL. **3.** Happening by accident or chance: FORTUITOUS. **4.** *Logic.* Possessing a truth value derived from facts apart from the proposition itself: not necessarily true or false. —*n.* **1.** A contingent event: CONTINGENCY. **2.** A share or quota, as of troops, contributed to a general effort. **3.** A representative group forming part of an assemblage. **—con•tin′gent•ly** *adv.*

2. *If the word can be more than one part of speech, decide which part of speech the word is in the sentence. Then concentrate on the definitions for that part of speech.* In a dictionary entry, the part-of-speech label is italicized and comes before the definitions. In the sentence above, *contingent* is an adjective modifying the noun *launching.* Of the four adjective definitions in the entry, only one is appropriate.

3. *Read the sentence to yourself, substituting each correct-part-of-speech definition for the word. Decide which one best fits the sentence.* The appropriate definition of *contingent* as it is used in the sentence is the second:

    The launching of the space shuttle is *dependent on conditions not yet established* (the weather).

4. *If there is more than one entry for a word, read each entry completely.* Some words are **homographs**—they are spelled alike but have different origins and meanings. For example, the words *fly* meaning "to move through the air" and *fly* meaning "an insect" are homographs. Homographs are given separate entries in the dictionary. Be sure to choose the correct one.

EXERCISE FINDING THE APPROPRIATE DEFINITION

Using the dictionary entries provided, find the appropriate definition of the italicized word in each of the following sentences. *Step 1:* Write the appropriate dictionary definition. *Step 2:* Write a sentence of your own using the word with this definition.

1. Desperate to get a laugh, Steven *resorted* to slapstick comedy.

   Definition To turn for help or as a means of achieving something

   Sentence Their food gone, the stranded explorers resorted to eating roots, berries, and nuts.

2. The aircraft carrier was accompanied by seven destroyer *escorts*.

   Definition A ship accompanying another to provide protection

   Sentence The Coast Guard escort stayed close to the disabled sailboat.

3. Before the ceremony an usher *escorted* the bride's mother to her seat.

   Definition To accompany as an escort

   Sentence I escorted Ms. Duarte to the auditorium stage.

4. The potter painted a design on the jar before applying the *glaze*.

   Definition A coating of material applied to ceramics before firing

   Sentence This glaze is very hard and resists chipping.

5. Last summer my parents were finally able to take a vacation at a *resort* in Wisconsin.

   Definition A place where people go for relaxation or recreation

   Sentence I have a summer job this year at a lake resort.

6. The workers removed a panel from the door and *glazed* the opening.

   Definition To furnish or fit with glass

   Sentence I did not have enough material to glaze all the windows.

---

es•cort (ĕs′kôrt′) *n.* **1.** One or more persons accompanying another to give protection or guidance or to pay honor. **2.** One or more planes, ships, etc., accompanying another or others to provide protection. **3.** A man who acts as the companion of a woman in public. —*v.* (ĭ-skôrt′) To accompany as an escort: *Police escorted the President during the parade. I escorted her home.*

glaze (glāz) *n.* [ME *glasen < glas, glass <* OE *glæs.*] **1.** A smooth, thin, shiny coating. **2.** A thin, glassy ice coating. **3. a.** A coating of colored, opaque, or transparent material applied to ceramics before firing. **b.** A coating, as of syrup, applied to food. **c.** A transparent coating applied to the surface of a painting to modify color tones. **4.** A glassy film, as over the eyes.

—*v.* **glazed, glaz•ing, glaz•es.** **1.** To furnish or fit with glass <*glaze* the broken windows> **2.** To apply a *glaze* to <*glazing* a dozen doughnuts> <*glaze* a set of pottery dishes> **3.** To give a smooth, lustrous surface to. **4.** To be or become glazed or glassy <eyes *glazing* over with fatigue> **5.** To form a glaze. —**glaz′er** *n.*

re•sort (rĭ-zôrt′) *v.* To go or turn for help or as a means of achieving something: *resort to violence.* —*n.* **1.** A place where people go for relaxation or recreation: *a ski resort.* **2.** A person or thing to which one turns for help: *I would ask him only as a last resort.* **3.** The act of turning for help in a certain situation: *raising money without resorting to borrowing.*

Years ago, families were much larger than they are today. There were more children in the average family, and grandparents often lived with their children and grandchildren. Other relatives sometimes lived with the family or in the same neighborhood. This was known as the "extended family."

Today we speak of the modern family as a "nuclear family" because a typical household now usually contains only the nucleus of parents and children. It is also common for families to be separated geographically from grandparents and other relatives. In this lesson you will learn words that refer to the family.

WORD LIST

descendant
generation
inheritance
lineage
maternal
matriarch
parental
patriarch
posterity
sibling

DEFINITIONS

After you have studied the definitions and example for each vocabulary word, write the word on the line to the right.

1. **descendant** (dĭ-sĕn′dənt) *noun*   An individual or animal coming from a specific ancestor; offspring of a certain family or group. (From the Latin *de-*, meaning "down," and *scandere,* meaning "to climb")

   Related Words descend *verb*; **descent** *noun*
   Example   John claims to be a *descendant* of George Washington.

   1. _____

2. **generation** (jĕn′ə-rā′shən) *noun*   **a.** All of the offspring that are at the same stage of descent from a common ancestor.   **b.** A group of people who grow up at the same time and are thought to have similar ideas. (From the Latin word *genus,* meaning "birth")

   Related Words generate *verb*; **generational** *adjective*
   Example   Three *generations* of McCleary women were represented at the party—Alice, Alice's mother, and Alice's grandmother.

   2. _____

3. **inheritance** (ĭn-hĕr′ĭ-təns) *noun*   **a.** The act of receiving property or money after the death of a relative or friend.   **b.** the property or money received at such a time.   **c.** A characteristic, such as red hair, that is received genetically from a parent, grandparent, etc. (From the Latin *in-*, meaning "in," and *heres,* meaning "heir")

   Related Words inherit *verb*; **inheritor** *noun*
   Example   Esther received a large *inheritance* after her grandmother's death.

   3. _____

4. **lineage** (lĭn'ē-ĭj) *noun*   **a.** Direct descent from a particular ancestor; ancestry.   **b.** All of the descendants of a common ancestor. (From the Old French word *ligne*, meaning "line")

   Related Word   **lineal** *adjective*
   Example   The horse had an impressive *lineage*, which began with the thoroughbred champion Thunder.

4. _____

5. **maternal** (mə-tûr'nəl) *adjective*   **a.** Referring to a mother or motherhood: *maternal concern.*   **b.** Inherited from one's mother: *maternal trait.*   **c.** Related to one's mother. (From the Latin word *mater*, meaning "mother")

   Related Word   **maternally** *adverb*
   Example   Baby-sitting brought out the *maternal* side of Joan's personality.

5. _____

6. **matriarch** (mā'trē-ärk') *noun*   A woman who rules a family or clan. (From the Latin word *mater*, meaning "mother," and the Greek word *arkhos*, meaning "ruler")

   Related Words   **matriarchal** *adjective*; **matriarchy** *noun*
   Example   Because she is a strong leader, Grandma Jessie is the *matriarch* of the Hobart family.

6. _____

7. **parental** (pə-rĕn'tl) *adjective*   Characteristic of a mother or father. (From the Latin word *parere*, meaning "to give birth")

   Related Words   **parent** *noun;* **parentally** *adverb*
   Example   Small children require a great deal of *parental* guidance.

7. _____

8. **patriarch** (pā'trē-ärk') *noun*   **a.** The male leader of a a family or clan.   **b.** A very old and respected man. (From the Greek word *pater*, meaning "father," and *arkhos*, meaning "ruler")

   Related Words   **patriarchal** *adjective;* **patriarchy** *noun*
   Example   At family reunions, Uncle Charlie is the acknowledged *patriarch.*

8. _____

9. **posterity** (pŏ-stĕr'ĭ-tē) *noun*   **a.** Future generations.   **b.** All of a person's descendants. (From the Latin word *posterus*, meaning "coming after")

   Example   The famous artist will leave many paintings to *posterity.*

9. _____

10. **sibling** (sĭb'lĭng) *noun*   One of two or more children of the same parents; a brother or a sister. (From the Old English word *sibb*, meaning "kinsman")

   Example   *Siblings* often resemble one another physically.

10. _____

EXERCISE 1 COMPLETING DEFINITIONS

On the answer line, write the word from the vocabulary list that best completes each definition.

1. Something that relates to a mother or father is _____.

2. The male ruler of a clan or family is called a(n) _____.

3. If something is left to future generations, it is given to _____.

4. Something that refers to a mother or motherhood is _____.

5. The offspring of a specific ancestor is a(n) _____.

6. Property or a characteristic received from a parent or ancestor is a(n) _____.

7. A _____ consists of people who are at the same stage of descent.

8. Two or more individuals having the same parents are _____.

9. A female ruler of a clan or family is a(n) _____.

10. One's _____ is one's descent from a particular ancestor.

1. ___parental___
2. ___patriarch___
3. ___posterity___
4. ___maternal___
5. ___descendant___
6. ___inheritance___
7. ___generation___
8. ___siblings___
9. ___matriarch___
10. ___lineage___

EXERCISE 2 USING WORDS CORRECTLY

Each of the following questions contains an italicized vocabulary word. Decide the answer to the question, and write *Yes* or *No* on the answer line.

1. Would a *matriarch* lack power within a family?

2. Are you a member of the same *generation* as your grandfather?

3. Is an older brother a *sibling?*

4. Would a male ruler of a Scottish clan be a *patriarch?*

5. If a poet destroyed his or her work, could it still be left to *posterity?*

6. Would a direct ancestor of a king be of royal *lineage?*

7. Would your father's uncle be a *maternal* relative?

8. Would a *descendant* be born before an ancestor?

9. Is a five-dollar loan an *inheritance?*

10. Might a father sign a *parental* permission form?

1. ___No___
2. ___No___
3. ___Yes___
4. ___Yes___
5. ___No___
6. ___Yes___
7. ___No___
8. ___No___
9. ___No___
10. ___Yes___

EXERCISE 3 CHOOSING THE BEST WORD

Decide which vocabulary word or related form best completes the sentence, and write the letter of your choice on the answer line.

1. The devoted mother of five has strong _____ instincts.
   a. descendant   **b.** patriarchal   **c.** lineage   **d.** maternal

2. As the great-granddaughter of homesteaders, Judy is proud of her _____.
   a. lineage   **b.** posterity   **c.** sibling   **d.** generation

1. ___d___
2. ___a___

3. "Introduce your younger _____," Mrs. Henderson instructed Lynn, the older of the two sisters.
   a. generation   **b.** patriarch   **c.** sibling   **d.** matriarch

3. _____ c _____

4. The graduates of the class of 1980 are members of the same _____.
   a. inheritance   **b.** patriarch   **c.** matriarch   **d.** generation

4. _____ d _____

5. City officials left a time capsule for _____.
   a. posterity   **b.** lineage   **c.** siblings   **d.** descendants

5. _____ a _____

6. A beautiful gold watch and cufflinks were part of the _____ I received from my grandfather.
   a. posterity   **b.** inheritance   **c.** sibling   **d.** decendant

6. _____ b _____

7. Lady Agatha Ashcroft is a powerful _____ who controls a large family.
   a. patriarch   **b.** descendant   **c.** sibling   **d.** matriarch

7. _____ d _____

8. "_____ intervention is sometimes unavoidable," the counselor told the mothers and fathers.
   a. Descendant   **b.** Posterity   **c.** Parental   **d.** Lineal

8. _____ c _____

9. Lisa thinks that she is a _____ of the poet Henry Wadsworth Longfellow.
   a. matriarch   **b.** descendant   **c.** sibling   **d.** patriarch

9. _____ b _____

10. The members of the village looked to their _____ for advice because he was a great leader.
    a. patriarch   **b.** descendant   **c.** lineage   **d.** matriarch

10. _____ a _____

EXERCISE 4 USING DIFFERENT FORMS OF WORDS

Each sentence contains an italicized vocabulary word in a form that does not fit the sentence. On the answer line, write the form of that word that does fit the sentence.

1. Donald *inheritance* eight thousand dollars.

1. _____ inherited _____

2. Before going on a class field trip, Steve had to get permission from his *parental*.

2. _____ parents _____

3. Blair discovered that she was *descendant* from Thomas Jefferson.

3. _____ descended _____

4. The explorers found a *matriarch* family group while exploring the islands.

4. _____ matriarchal _____

5. Gerald's *lineage* history includes famous painters and writers.

5. _____ lineal _____

6. Although they do not look alike, Martha and Rachel are *sibling*.

6. _____ siblings _____

7. In early Scottish history, clans ruled the land through a *patriarch* system.

7. _____ patriarchal _____

8. The park system was created not just for present residents of the city but also for *posterity*.

8. _____ posterity _____

9. Claude wrote a composition about the *generation* differences between his views and those of his grandparents.

9. _____ generational _____

10. The young girl cradled the doll *maternal* in her arms.

10. _____ maternally _____

READING COMPREHENSION

Each numbered sentence in the following passage contains an italicized vocabulary word. After you read the passage, you will complete an exercise.

THE FAMILY GAME

ANNOUNCER: Welcome to another round of the Family Game. I'm your announcer and host, Eddie Hull. Now let's meet our competing families, the McCormacks and the Westovers. (1) To my right, we have Team One, which includes three *generations* of McCormack men. Audience, say hello to Grandpa Horace, son Michael, and grandson Robby. *(There is a pause.)* Folks, Robby told me that Grandpa Horace was the one who insisted that the family audition for the show.

GRANDPA HORACE: That's right, Ed. The rules in our family are simple. After everyone voices an opinion, I make the final decision. (2) You might call me the *patriarch* of the family.

GRANDMA AMELIA WESTOVER: Say, Ed, aren't you forgetting about the Westovers? (3) My girls and I are sure to give answers that will be recorded for *posterity.*

ANNOUNCER: Team number one, say hello to Team Two, the Westovers: Grandma Amelia, daughter Rebecca, and granddaughter Tracey.

AMY: Hey, how about me?

ANNOUNCER: Whoops! Tracey, please introduce your sister.

TRACEY: Do I have to?

ANNOUNCER: (4) Now, now, don't let *sibling* rivalry get in the way.

TRACEY: This is my sister, Amy, everyone.

ANNOUNCER: Very nice. Now let's play the Family Game! Remember the rules. I'll begin by asking Team One a question about a well-known head of a family. You McCormack men will have thirty seconds to give the right answer. If you can't answer the question in time, Team Two, the Westovers, will have a chance. Get ready, McCormacks! Here's your question. (5) Queen Victoria was considered one of the greatest *matriarchs* in the history of England. (6) In addition to being an impressive leader, Queen Victoria raised many children and had a strong *maternal* side. For one hundred dollars and a chance for our jackpot, whom was Queen Victoria married to?

GRANDPA HORACE: That's easy. I'll let Robby tell you.

ROBBY: Queen Victoria's husband was—

GRANDMA AMELIA *(interrupting Robby):* (7) You know, Ed, Queen Victoria is not the only one with an impressive *lineage.* (8) It just so happens that I am a direct *descendant* of Henry Harold Horton III.

ROBBY *(in a loud voice):* Queen Victoria's husband was—

ANNOUNCER *(interrupting Robby):* Tell me more about your fascinating family history, Amelia. Charting family trees is my favorite hobby. *(joking)* It's no accident that I'm the host of the Family Game.

GRANDMA AMELIA: And a wonderful one at that. Now, where was I? (9) Oh, yes, from Henry Harold's line our family has received its *inheritance* of strength and discipline. Henry Harold was one of the original settlers who came over on the *Mayflower.*

ANNOUNCER: Imagine that! *(He checks the clock.)* Oops! Time's running out, McCormacks!

ROBBY *(angry):* Well, if you and Mrs. Westover would quit interrupting, I could answer the question.

GRANDPA AMELIA: Interrupting! How dare you? Mr. McCormack, I demand that you do something about your son's bad manners. (10) Where is your *parental* authority?

ANNOUNCER: Time's up! Do you have an answer, Westovers?

GRANDMA AMELIA: Well, Ed, everyone knows Queen Victoria was married to—

ROBBY *(interrupting):* Prince Albert!

(For once, Grandma Amelia is speechless.)

ANNOUNCER: You are right, Robby! You are absolutely right for one hundred dollars and a chance to compete against another family for our super jackpot! Time's up, but thanks for a terrific Family Game.

Each of the following statements corresponds to a numbered sentence in the passage. Each statement contains a blank and is followed by four answer choices. Decide which choice fits best in the blank. The word or phrase that you choose must express roughly the same meaning as the italicized word in the passage. Write the letter of your choice on the answer line.

1. The game show announcer introduces three _____ of the McCormack family.
   a. close relatives
   b. different stages of descent
   c. next-door neighbors
   d. men who are related

   1. _____ b

2. Grandpa Horace is the _____ of the family.
   a. scholar   b. devoted grandfather   c. male leader   d. financial advisor

   2. _____ c

3. Grandma Amelia thinks that her family's answers will be recorded for _____ .
   a. future generations
   b. her grandchildren
   c. television cameras
   d. good friends

   3. _____ a

4. The annnouncer warns about the conflict between _____ .
   a. family   b. mothers and daughters   c. friends   d. sisters

   4. _____ d

5. He points out that Queen Victoria was a great _____ .
   a. wife and mother
   b. female leader
   c. antique collector
   d. devoted grandmother

   5. _____ b

6. Furthermore, Queen Victoria also had a strong _____ side.
   a. motherly   b. historical   c. intellectual   d. fatherly

   6. _____ a

7. Grandma Amelia talks about her own impressive _____ .
   a. party   b. history   c. ancestry   d. society

   7. _____ c

8. She is a(n) _____ of Henry Harold Horton III.
   a. daughter   b. admirer   c. friend   d. offspring

   8. _____ d

9. The _____ from Henry Harold include(s) strength and discipline.
   a. characteristics passed down
   b. ancient letters
   c. large fortune
   d. descriptions

   9. _____ a

10. Grandma Amelia questions Michael McCormack's _____ authority.
    a. personal   b. social   c. fatherly   d. political

    10. _____ c

An analogy compares word pairs that are related in some way. For example, in "Gold is to metal as coal is to fuel," both pairs are type of analogies.

See page 119 for some strategies to use with analogies.

Directions   On the answer line, write the vocabulary word or a form of it that completes each analogy.

1. Aquatic is to water as _____ is to land. (*Lesson 2*)

   1. _____ terrestrial

2. Partner is to business as _____ is to crime. (*Lesson 3*)

   2. _____ accomplice

3. Swarm is to insects as _____ is to people. (*Lesson 3*)

   3. _____ throng

4. _____ is to muddy as precipice is to steep. (*Lesson 2*)

   4. _____ Quagmire

   The **Bonus activity** for Lessons 3 and 4 is on page T4.

5. Patriarchy is to men as _____ is to women. (*Lesson 4*)

   5. _____ matriarchy

LESSON 5 THE ROOT -GEN-

The root -gen- has ancient origins and can be found in various forms in many Indo-European languages. As you will learn in this lesson, -gen- conveys many meanings, such as kind, type, class, family, race, origin, birth, or source. When it is combined with prefixes and/or suffixes, it produces many words that you will find useful when speaking or writing about the origins of things or about their classifications and types.

WORD LIST

congenial
degenerate
gender
genealogy
generic
genesis
gentry
primogeniture
progeny
regenerate

DEFINITIONS

After you have studied the definitions and example for each vocabulary word, write the word on the line to the right.

1. **congenial** (kən-jēn′yəl) *adjective* **a.** Having the same tastes, habits: *congenial friends.* **b.** Sociable; agreeable; amiable. (From the Latin *com-*, meaning "together," and *genialis*, meaning "festive")

   Related Word congeniality *noun*
   Example Adrian and Anastasia are very *congenial* and spend most of their spare time together.

   1. _____

2. **degenerate** (dĭ-jĕn′ə-rāt) *verb* To sink into a much worse or lower condition; deteriorate. *adjective* (dĭ-jĕn′ər-ĭt) Having deteriorated from a previous state. (From the Latin *de-*, meaning "down," and *genus*, meaning "family" or "ancestry")

   Related Words degeneration *noun*; **degenerative** *adjective*
   Example Houses often *degenerate* after decades of exposure to the elements.

   2. _____

3. **gender** (jĕn′dər) *noun* One of the categories—masculine, feminine, or neuter—into which words and the people, animals, or objects they denote are divided.

   Example A deer, rabbit, or kangaroo of the female *gender* is called a doe.

   3. _____

4. **genealogy** (jē′nē-ŏl′ə-jē) *noun*   **a.** A record of the descent of a family or person from an ancestor or ancestors.   **b.** Direct descent from an ancestor; lineage.   **c.** The study of ancestry and family histories. (From the Greek words *genea*, meaning "family," and *logos*, meaning "speech")

    Related Words   **genealogical** *adjective*; **genealogist** *noun*
    Example   David traced his *genealogy* back to Charlemagne, the ninth-century Frankish ruler.

4. _____

5. **generic** (jə-nĕr′ĭk) *adjective*   **a.** Of, including, or indicating an entire group, class, category; general rather than specific.   **b.** Not protected by a trademark: *generic aspirin*. (From the Latin word *genera*, meaning "kinds")

    Related Word   **generically** *adverb*
    Example   The word "cats" is a *generic* term for tigers, jaguars, and house cats.

5. _____

6. **genesis** (jĕn′ĭ-sĭs) *noun*   The coming into being of anything; origin. (From the Greek word *genesis*, meaning "birth")

    Example   The *genesis* of Paul's short story was an experience that he had when he was ten.

6. _____

7. **gentry** (jĕn′trē) *noun*   **a.** Well-bred people of good family and high social standing.   **b.** A social class ranking next below the nobility. (From the Latin word *gens*, meaning "race" or "clan")

    Example   In that country the *gentry* has large holdings of private property

7. _____

8. **primogeniture** (prī′mō-jĕn′ĭ-chŏŏr′) *noun*   **a.** The condition of being the first-born child in a family.   **b.** In law, the right of the eldest child—especially the eldest son—to inherit all of his parents' estate. (From the Latin words *primus*, meaning "first," and *genitura*, meaning "birth")

    Example   Because of Jonathan's *primogeniture*, he assumed many responsibilities for his younger brothers.

8. _____

9. **progeny** (prŏj′ə-nē) *noun*   Children; descendants; offspring. (From the Latin *pro-*, meaning "forward," and *gignere*, meaning "to beget")

    Related Word   **progenitor** *noun*
    Example   Several of the *progeny* of the great composer Johann Sebastian Bach were also composers.

9. _____

10. **regenerate** (rĭ-jĕn′ə-rāt′) *verb*   **a.** To give new life to; revive.   **b.** To reform spiritually or morally.   **c.** To replace (a damaged or lost part or organ) by growing new tissue. (From the Latin *re-*, meaning "again," and *generare*, meaning "produce")

    Related Words   **regeneration** *noun*; **regenerative** *adjective*
    Example   The astonishing success of the Alamo High School football team has *regenerated* interest in the game.

10. _____

EXERCISE 1 WRITING CORRECT WORDS

On the answer line, write the word from the vocabulary list that fits each definition.

1. Agreeable; sociable; having the same tastes

2. Classification as male or female

3. To create anew or revive

4. Descendants; offspring

5. General; relating to an entire class or group

6. Origin, source, or birth

7. To deteriorate or decline

8. People of high social position and good breeding

9. A record of ancestry

10. The condition of being first-born; the custom or law by which the eldest child receives property or inheritance

1. _____congenial_____

2. _____gender_____

3. _____regenerate_____

4. _____progeny_____

5. _____generic_____

6. _____genesis_____

7. _____degenerate_____

8. _____gentry_____

9. _____genealogy_____

10. _____primogeniture_____

EXERCISE 2 USING WORDS CORRECTLY

Decide whether the italicized vocabulary word or related form has been used correctly in the sentence. On the answer line, write *Correct* for correct use and *Incorrect* for incorrect use.

1. My grandmother's *progeny* include her sisters, Mary and Martha, and her cousin Simeon.

2. Most plant life *degenerates* during a drought.

3. The Earl of Wessex, following the law of *primogeniture,* left his estate to his eldest son.

4. Christina looked in the family *genealogy* and learned that her great-grandfather had nine brothers and sisters.

5. The *gender* of a cardinal is red.

6. The *genesis* of a novel may lie in the author's imagination.

7. Our *congenial* neighbor offered to help me with the heavy suitcases.

8. In the supermarket the paper towels with specific brand names are *generic.*

9. Weakened muscles can be *regenerated* through exercise.

10. A story about the *gentry* would be about poor people with no education.

1. _____Incorrect_____

2. _____Correct_____

3. _____Correct_____

4. _____Correct_____

5. _____Incorrect_____

6. _____Correct_____

7. _____Correct_____

8. _____Incorrect_____

9. _____Correct_____

10. _____Incorrect_____

Decide which vocabulary word or related form best expresses the meaning of the italicized word or phrase in the sentence. On the answer line, write the letter of that word.

1. Some scientists think that the *origin* of nuclear theory lay in the philosophy of Aristotle.
   a. progeny   **b.** degeneration   **c.** genesis   **d.** primogeniture

   1. _____c_____

2. The diplomats believe that relations will *deteriorate* between the two countries.
   a. gender   **b.** degenerate   **c.** regenerate   **d.** gentry

   2. _____b_____

3. Some people do not consider the *classification as male or female* of the President to be an important issue.
   a. gender   **b.** progeny   **c.** genealogy   **d.** primogeniture

   3. _____a_____

4. The *descendants* of the famous author helped to restore his estate.
   a. primogeniture   **b.** regeneration   **c.** gender   **d.** progeny

   4. _____d_____

5. As a result of his *moral reformation,* my friend Tyrone has become very thoughtful.
   a. congeniality   **b.** regeneration   **c.** genealogy   **d.** degeneration

   5. _____b_____

6. Some of the *well-bred, upper-middle class* maintain estates in Virginia.
   a. primogeniture   **b.** progeny   **c.** gender   **d.** gentry

   6. _____d_____

7. While looking at our *record of ancestry,* I discovered names like Ezekiel and Ebenezer.
   a. genealogy   **b.** primogeniture   **c.** progeny   **d.** gentry

   7. _____a_____

8. When the king died, his throne was to be taken over by his eldest son according to the law of *inheritance by the eldest child.*
   a. genesis   **b.** regeneration   **c.** primogeniture   **d.** gender

   8. _____c_____

9. The *unnamed, general type of* canned tomatoes are cheaper.
   a. degenerate   **b.** generic   **c.** regenerative   **d.** congenial

   9. _____b_____

10. My friend James is so *sociable and friendly* that most people like him.
    a. generic   **b.** degenerate   **c.** regenerative   **d.** congenial

    10. _____d_____

Decide which form of the vocabulary word in parentheses best completes the sentence. The form given may be correct. Write your answer on the line.

1. Only peafowl of the male _____ have beautiful tail feathers. (*gender*)

   1. _____gender_____

2. The healing of a wound is an example of the _____ power of the human body. (*regenerate*)

   2. _____regenerative_____

3. The biologist gave a lecture on the _____ of amphibians. (*genesis*)

   3. _____genesis_____

4. The term *gentrification,* which refers to the upgrading of urban neighborhoods, comes from the word _____. (*gentry*)

   4. _____gentry_____

5. *Cheaper by the Dozen* tells the story of the crusty but lovable _____ of twelve children. (*progeny*)

   5. _____progenitor_____

6. Our neighbors were known for their _____. (*congenial*)

   6. _____congeniality_____

7. Carmen is a _____ and is an authority on the ancestry of early settlers in Arizona. (*genealogy*)

8. Mr. Van Allen was concerned about the _____ of the muscles in his right arm. (*degenerate*)

9. By right of _____, the title of Prince of Wales falls to the eldest son of the British sovereign. (*primogeniture*)

10. In ancient Greece, the _____ term for people who did not speak Greek was *barbarians*. (*generic*)

7. _____ genealogist

8. _____ degeneration

9. _____ primogeniture

10. _____ generic

READING COMPREHENSION

Each numbered sentence in the following passage contains an italicized vocabulary word or related form. After you read the passage, you will complete an exercise.

A NINETEENTH-CENTURY ROMANCE

Imagine for a moment what life must have been like for a younger son of the gentry in nineteenth-century England. The future must not have seemed bright. Even his chances for marriage could have been affected by the laws of primogeniture, as you will see in the following fictional letter.

My dear Cecily,

I wish to thank you for your kind and sympathetic words when last we met. (1) You, more than anyone, dear cousin, are aware of the *genesis* of my current difficulties. I love Emily deeply and genuinely, and she loves me, yet I think it unlikely that we shall be wed. (2) I shan't inherit any property because by *primogeniture* my eldest brother, Sir Stephen, will inherit everything.

Emily likewise has little of her own. (3) Her father, Lord Plumsole, is a *congenial* fellow, but he has managed his estates neither wisely nor well. (4) He has allowed Plumsole Abbey to *degenerate* to such a point that it

is no longer fit habitation for such as Emily and me. 'Tis more the pity, for it was once the fairest house in the eastern part of northwest central Shropshire.

(5) The Plumsole *genealogy* is distinguished, to be sure. (6) It is nonetheless unlikely that any present members of the Plumsole family will witness the *regeneration* of its glorious past. (7) The Plumsoles suffer from that *generic* problem of the lower nobility, an inability to organize their lives properly.

At present, Cecily, I am saddened. (8) Emily and I ask

only to be simple members of the local *gentry*, free to ride to the hounds, read novels, and play the pianoforte. (9) Is this asking too much for ourselves and our *progeny*?

(10) Whatever *gender* our children turn out to be, are they not entitled to lives even happier than ours?

These questions I leave to you, dear Cecily, to consider. I have at present neither joy nor contentment save for your kind and comforting words.

Your loving cousin,
Reginald

Each of the following statements corresponds to a numbered sentence in the passage. Each statement contains a blank and is followed by four answer choices. Decide which choice fits best in the blank. The word or phrase that you choose must express roughly the same meaning as the italicized word in the passage. Write the letter of your choice on the answer line.

1. Cecily knows something about the _____ of Reginald's difficulties.
   a. reason **b.** quality **c.** origin **d.** importance

   1. ___c___

2. Reginald will not inherit anything because of the law of inheritance by the _____.
   a. richest **b.** noblest **c.** eldest **d.** nicest

   2. ___c___

3. Lord Plumsole is _____.
   a. plump **b.** likable **c.** stingy **d.** thoughtful

   3. ___b___

4. He has allowed Plumsole Abbey to _____.
   a. deteriorate **b.** prosper **c.** be sold **d.** be painted

   4. ___a___

5. The Plumsole record of _____ is distinguished.
   a. land holdings **b.** ancestors **c.** diplomas **d.** birthdays

   5. ___b___

6. No Plumsole living is likely to see the _____ of the glorious past.
   a. record **b.** honor **c.** glory **d.** revival

   6. ___d___

7. The lower nobility has a _____ problem.
   a. minor **b.** serious **c.** general **d.** difficult

   7. ___c___

8. Reginald wishes only to be a member of _____.
   a. the nobility
   b. the well-bred upper-middle class
   c. the downtrodden lower-middle class
   d. no class at all

   8. ___b___

9. Does Reginald ask too much for his _____?
   a. offspring **b.** ancestors **c.** fiancée **d.** parents

   9. ___a___

10. Reginald wants his children to be happy, whether they are _____.
    a. rich or poor **c.** English or Scottish
    b. male or female **d.** friendly or shy

    10. ___b___

Everyone has ancestors, and some people are familiar with the lives of their parents, grandparents, and even great-grandparents. For presentation to members of a genealogical society, write a paragraph about an ancestor, real or imaginary. Use at least five words from this lesson and underline each one.

When you are happy, you feel pleasure and joy. When you are sad, you feel just the opposite. Perhaps completing a difficult task makes you happy while the illness of a close friend makes you sad. Every individual is unique in his or her experience of joy and sorrow. In this lesson you will learn words that refer to happiness and unhappiness.

WORD LIST

amicable
anguish
blithe
defiant
desolate
despondent
disgruntled
disillusion
distress
exuberant

DEFINITIONS

After you have studied the definitions and example for each vocabulary word, write the word on the line to the right.

1. **amicable** (ăm′ĭ-kə-bəl) *adjective*   Friendly in tone: *an amicable discussion.* (From the Latin word *amicus,* meaning "friend")

   Related Words **amicability** *noun;* **amicably** *adverb*
   Example   The carefree members of the soccer team are an *amicable* group.

   1. _____

2. **anguish** (ăng′gwĭsh) *noun*   Great physical or mental pain; torment; torture. *verb*   To suffer greatly. (From the Latin word *angustia,* meaning "narrowness")

   Related Word **anguished** *adjective*
   Example   Paul suffered *anguish* when his grandfather died.

   2. _____
   See *distress.*

3. **blithe** (blīth) *adjective*   Cheerful; carefree; lighthearted.

   Related Word **blithely** *adverb*
   Example   That *blithe* fellow can't keep from smiling as he walks down the street.

   3. _____

4. **defiant** (dĭ-fī′ənt) *adjective*   Openly or boldly resisting authority. (From the Old French word *desfier,* meaning "to challenge")

   Related Words **defiance** *noun;* **defiantly** *adverb;* **defy** *verb*
   Example   The *defiant* workers refused to return to the factory until they received fairer treatment.

   4. _____

5. **desolate** (dĕs′ə-lĭt) *adjective* **a.** Lonely and sad; wretched; forlorn.
b. Having little or no vegetation; barren. **c.** Having few or no
inhabitants; deserted. *verb* (dĕs′ə-lāt′) To make desolate. (From the Latin
word *desolare*, meaning "to leave all alone")

    Related Word   **desolation** *noun*
    Example   The earthquake left many people homeless and *desolate*.

5. _____

6. **despondent** (dĭ-spŏn′dənt) *adjective* In low spirits; depressed; dejected.
(From the Latin word *despondere*, meaning "to give up")

    Related Words **despondency** *noun;* **despondently** *adverb*
    Example   The artist Vincent van Gogh became *despondent* when
                          people rejected his paintings.

6. _____

7. **disgruntled** (dĭs-grŭn′tld) *adjective* Discontented or cross.

    Example   The *disgruntled* worker quit when a person who did less
                          work than he did got promoted.

7. _____

8. **disillusion** (dĭs′ĭ-lōō′zhən) *verb* To free or deprive of an idea or belief
that proves false or in error; disenchant.

    Related Word   **disillusionment** *noun*
    Example   If you expect the people you admire to be perfect, you
                          will soon become *disillusioned*.

8. _____

9. **distress** (dĭ-strĕs′) *noun* Anxiety, discomfort, or suffering; worry.
verb To cause suffering or discomfort. (From the Latin *dis-*, meaning
"apart," and *stringere*, meaning "to draw tight")

    Related Word   **distressingly** *adverb*
    Example   Our cat's sudden disappearance caused our family
                          much *distress*.

9. _____
Distress is physical or
mental discomfort.
Anguish is physical or
mental torment.

10. **exuberant** (ĭg-zōō′bər-ənt) *adjective* Lively and joyous; enthusiastic;
high-spirited. (From the Latin word *exuberare*, meaning "to abound")

    Related Words **exuberance** *noun;* **exuberantly** *adverb*
    Example   *Exuberant* at seeing his mother after ten years, Dean
                          grabbed her and lifted her into the air.

10. _____

EXERCISE 1 WRITING CORRECT WORDS

On the answer line, write the word from the vocabulary list that fits
each definition.

1. Challenging authority

2. High-spirited; joyous; lively

3. Dejected; depressed

4. Great pain; to suffer greatly

5. Worry; discomfort; anxiety; to cause suffering

6. Cross or discontented

7. Friendly

8. Carefree or cheerful

9. To disenchant or deprive of a false idea

10. Forlorn; sad and lonely

1. ____defiant____

2. ____exuberant____

3. ____despondent____

4. ____anguish____

5. ____distress____

6. ____disgruntled____

7. ____amicable____

8. ____blithe____

9. ____disillusion____

10. ____desolate____

EXERCISE 2 USING WORDS CORRECTLY

Each of the following questions contains an italicized vocabulary word.
Decide the answer to the question, and write *Yes* or *No* on the answer line.

1. Might an actor's fans become *disillusioned* upon learning that their idol is
very conceited?

2. Would a *despondent* laborer look forward to her work each day?

3. Would a *blithe* person tend to complain constantly?

4. Would the death of a greatly loved pet be likely to *distress* someone?

5. Is *anguish* a pleasant feeling?

6. Would a gardener be *disgruntled* to find that someone had ridden a
bicycle through the flower beds?

7. Would an *amicable* person make a new student feel welcome at a school?

8. Would *exuberant* basketball fans cheer loudly at a game?

9. Would a *defiant* person be likely to obey rules happily?

10. Might a person feel *desolate* after her closest friend had moved far away?

1. ____Yes____

2. ____No____

3. ____No____

4. ____Yes____

5. ____No____

6. ____Yes____

7. ____Yes____

8. ____Yes____

9. ____No____

10. ____Yes____

EXERCISE 3 CHOOSING THE BEST WORD

Decide which vocabulary word or related form best completes the sentence,
and write the letter of your choice on the answer line.

1. Peggy felt _____ after receiving a low grade on the test.
   a. amicable   **b.** despondent   **c.** exuberant   **d.** blithe

1. ____b____

2. Although Constantine was quite _____ as a teenager, in adulthood he became fairly obedient.
   a. exuberant   b. amicable   c. desolate   d. defiant

2. _____d_____

3. Gail felt great _____ because she lost the fifty dollars her father had entrusted to her.
   a. distress   b. exuberance   c. defiance   d. amicability

3. _____a_____

4. Having received a scholarship to his favorite college, Jim was _____.
   a. disillusioned   b. disgruntled   c. amicable   d. exuberant

4. _____d_____

5. After visiting her hometown, Ellen was _____ because it was so dull.
   a. amicable   b. blithe   c. disillusioned   d. defiant

5. _____c_____

6. Our new neighbors were so _____ that I felt at ease immediately.
   a. disgruntled   b. amicable   c. despondent   d. desolate

6. _____b_____

7. Juliana felt _____ when she moved to New York City, where she knew no one.
   a. desolate   b. disillusioned   c. blithe   d. exuberant

7. _____a_____

8. George becomes _____ whenever he makes a typing error.
   a. exuberant   b. desolate   c. disgruntled   d. blithe

8. _____c_____

9. In contrast to nasty Captain Hook, Peter Pan is _____.
   a. disillusioned   b. despondent   c. desolate   d. blithe

9. _____d_____

10. Have you ever experienced the _____ of a broken bone?
    a. disillusionment   c. defiance
    b. anguish   d. exuberance

10. _____b_____

EXERCISE 4 USING DIFFERENT FORMS OF WORDS

Decide which form of the vocabulary word in parentheses best completes the sentence. The form given may be correct. Write your answer on the answer line.

1. Sally skipped _____ into the room. (blithe)

1. _____blithely_____

2. A pang of _____ struck Miguel as he watched his son drive away. (desolate)

2. _____desolation_____

3. Filled with _____ after winning the race, Terry leaped into the air. (exuberant)

3. _____exuberance_____

4. Irwin was _____ when he found that he had made several careless errors on his exam. (disgruntled)

4. _____disgruntled_____

5. Mrs. Rutherford _____ invited my sister and me to dinner when our parents had to go out. (amicable)

5. _____amicably_____

6. Leonora watched _____ as her best friend moved to another city. (despondent)

6. _____despondently_____

7. Katherine strode _____ out of the room. (defiant)

7. _____defiantly_____

8. "It _____ me to see you so unhappy," Carol told Monique. (distress)

8. _____distresses_____

9. For three hours the Robinsons suffered the _____ of not knowing whether their pet had survived the auto accident. (anguish)

9. _____anguish_____

10. A sense of _____ overwhelmed young Sidney when he discovered that there was no tooth fairy. (disillusion)

10. _____disillusionment_____

READING COMPREHENSION

Each numbered sentence in the following passage contains an italicized vocabulary word or related form. After you read the passage, you will complete an exercise.

MARIE CURIE: DISCOVERER OF RADIUM

Marie Curie was one of the most accomplished scientists in history. Together with her husband, Pierre, she discovered radium, an element widely used for treating cancer, and studied uranium and other radioactive substances. (1) Pierre and Marie's *amicable* collaboration later helped to unlock the secrets of the atom.

Marie was born in 1867 in Warsaw, Poland, where her father was a professor of physics. (2) At an early age, she displayed a brilliant mind and a *blithe* personality. (3) Her great *exuberance* for learning prompted her to continue with her studies after high school. (4) She became *disgruntled,* however, when she learned that the university in Warsaw was closed to women. (5) Determined to receive a higher education, she *defiantly* left Poland and in 1891 entered the Sorbonne, a French university, where she earned her master's degree and doctorate in physics.

Marie was fortunate to have studied at the Sorbonne with some of the greatest scientists of her day, one of whom was Pierre Curie. Marie and Pierre were married in 1895 and spent many productive years working together in the physics laboratory. In 1906, a short time after they discovered radium, Pierre was killed by a horse-drawn wagon. (6) Marie was stunned by this horrible misfortune and endured heartbreaking *anguish.* (7) *Despondently* she recalled their close relationship and the joy that they had shared in scientific research. (8) The fact that she had two young daughters to raise by herself greatly increased her *distress.*

(9) Curie's feeling of *desolation* finally began to fade when she was asked to succeed her husband as a physics professor at the Sorbonne. She was the first woman to be given a professorship at the world-famous university. In 1911 she received the Nobel Prize in chemistry for isolating radium. (10) Although Marie Curie eventually suffered a fatal illness from her long exposure to radium, she never became *disillusioned* about her work. Regardless of the consequences, she had dedicated herself to science and to revealing the mysteries of the physical world.

READING COMPREHENSION EXERCISE

Each of the following statements corresponds to a numbered sentence in the passage. Each statement contains a blank and is followed by four answer choices. Decide which choice fits best in the blank. The word or phrase that you choose must express roughly the same meaning as the italicized word in the passage. Write the letter of your choice on the answer line.

1. The Curies' _____ collaboration helped to unlock the secrets of the atom.   1. _____d_____
   a. competitive b. courteous c. cold d. friendly

2. Marie had a bright mind and a _____ personality.   2. _____a_____
   a. lighthearted b. humorous c. strong d. depressed

3. Her _____ for learning did not end with her high school education.   3. _____a_____
   a. enthusiasm b. aptitude c. desire d. talent

    Happiness and Unhappiness   **37**

4. When she learned that she could not attend the university in Warsaw, she felt _____.

    a. hopeless   **b.** sad   **c.** annoyed   **d.** depressed

4. _____ c _____

5. Marie _____ by leaving Poland and traveling to France to enter the Sorbonne.

    a. challenged authority   **c.** showed intelligence

    b. made a mistake   **d.** behaved well

5. _____ a _____

6. Marie's _____ over Pierre's accidental death was great.

    a. pity   **b.** emptiness   **c.** pain   **d.** loneliness

6. _____ c _____

7. _____ she remembered their joy together.

    a. Joyously   **b.** Dejectedly   **c.** Worriedly   **d.** Tearfully

7. _____ b _____

8. Her _____ increased because she had two children to raise all alone.

    a. anxiety   **b.** loss   **c.** work   **d.** problem

8. _____ a _____

9. Her _____ began to fade when she returned to the Sorbonne to succeed her husband.

    a. misfortune   **b.** bad luck   **c.** wretchedness   **d.** anger

9. _____ c _____

10. Even though she became fatally ill from working with radium, Marie was never _____.

    a. troubled   **b.** worried   **c.** bored   **d.** disenchanted

10. _____ d _____

WRITING ASSIGNMENT

Jane is a wonderful athlete and has been involved in gymnastics since she was very young. Often Jane participates in competitions. Sometimes she wins, and other times she loses. Write a story for a sports magazine that tells about Jane's most recent competition. If necessary, research the topic at the library before writing your story. Use at least five words from this lesson and underline each one.

VOCABULARY ENRICHMENT

In French the word for "friend" is *ami*. In Spanish it is *amigo*; in Italian, *amico*. All three are derived from *amicus*, the Latin word for "friend." Although the English word *friend* does not come from *amicus*, there are many English words concerning friends and friendship that are derived from *amicus*.

In this lesson you learned the word *amicable*, meaning "friendly." There is also the word *amiable* (without a *c*), which means "likable" or "good-natured." In other words, *amiable* implies having the qualities one would wish for in a friend. The word *amity*, a noun, means friendship in the special sense of peaceful relations between nations.

Activity The word *amicus* also has a negative form in Latin, *inimicus*, which means "not friendly." The English word *enemy* is derived from *inimicus*, as are the two words that follow. Using a dictionary, look up these two words, write a definition for each one, and use each in a sentence.

1. enmity   2. inimical

The **Bonus activity** for Lessons 5 and 6 is on page T5. The **Test** for Lessons 4, 5, and 6 is on page T6.

A B C

DICTIONARY SKILLS
INFLECTED FORMS OF WORDS

The spelling of words changes to indicate things such as number, tense, and degree. Dictionaries include these different forms of words, called **inflected forms.** This lesson explains the way in which inflected forms are listed in dictionaries.

1. *Noun plurals.* Some noun plurals present a spelling problem or are formed in irregular ways. For example, the dictionary entry for *penny* gives the plural (often abbreviated *pl.*), *pennies.*

2. *Verb forms.* Irregular forms of a verb or forms that involve a spelling change are also given in dictionary entries. The forms are usually listed in this order: past tense, past participle, present participle, third-person singular present tense. *Show* is an example of a verb entry that lists each of these inflected forms. Notice that *show* has both regular *(showed, showing, shows)* and irregular *(shown)* forms. All the inflected forms of a verb may be given if any one is irregular.

   show (shō) *v.* **showed, shown** (shōn) or
      showed, show•ing, shows.

3. *Comparatives and superlatives of modifiers.* Dictionary entries give both regular and irregular comparison forms of modifiers. The following entries show the inflected forms of a regular adjective, *slow,* and an irregular adjective, *good.*

   slow (slō) *adj.* **slow•er, slow•est.**

   good (good) *adj.* **bet•ter** (bĕt'ər), **best** (bĕst).

   A dictionary will not show comparatives and superlatives when they are formed with *more* and *most,* as for example, *more pitiful* and *most pitiful.*

EXERCISE FINDING INFLECTED FORMS OF WORDS

Using the dictionary entries at the end of this exercise, write the inflected form asked for in each item. Then write a sentence of your own in which you use this form.

1. Write the present participle form of *delete.* _deleting_____
   Sentence _Rodney is deleting the incorrect figures from the club minutes.____

2. Write the comparative form of *oily.* _oilier_____
   Sentence _My hair is oilier than yours._____

3. Write the plural form of *parenthesis*. parentheses

   Sentence Michael put parentheses around the shopping list items that he couldn't find.

4. Write the superlative form of *expressive*. most expressive

   Sentence She has the most expressive face I've ever seen.

5. Write the past tense form of *throw*. threw

   Sentence Before we moved to Brownsville, we threw away everything that was no longer usable.

6. Write the past participle form of *throw*. thrown

   Sentence Although my sister has ridden a horse almost all her life, she has never been thrown.

7. Write the plural form of *bacterium*. bacteria

   Sentence Canned food is cooked at high temperatures to kill bacteria.

8. Write the third-person singular present form of *belie*. belies

   Sentence His enormous size belies a gentle spirit.

9. Write the past tense form of *delete*. deleted

   Sentence The student deleted the unnecessary words from her rough draft.

10. Write the superlative form of *oily*. oiliest

    Sentence This is the oiliest salad dressing that I have ever used.

---

bac•te•ri•um (băk•tŭr′ē•əm) *n. pl.* **-ri•a** (ē-ə) [NLat. < Gk. *baktērion,* little rod, dim. of *baktron,* rod.] Any of numerous unicellular microorganisms of the class Schizomycetes, occurring in many forms, existing either as free-living organisms or as parasites, and having a broad range of biochemical, often pathogenic properties. —**bac•te′ri•al** *adj.* —**bac•te′ri•al•ly** *adv.*

be•lie (bĭ-lī′) *v.* **be•lied, be•ly•ing, be•lies.** **1.** To give a wrong or false idea of: *His cheerful tone belied his feelings of anger and frustration.* **2.** To be inconsistent with; contradict: *Nineteenth-century America went on a pleasure-seeking binge that belied its puritanical past.*

de•lete (dĭ-lēt′) *v.* **de•let•ed, de•let•ing.** To strike out; remove; eliminate: *delete a name from a list; delete the last sentence of a paragraph.*

ex•pres•sive (ĭk-sprĕs′ĭv) *adj.* **1.** Of, relating to, or marked by expression. **2.** Serving to indicate or express <a tone of voice *expressive* of anger> **3.** Full of expression: SIGNIFICANT <an *expressive* smile> —**ex•pres′sive•ly** *adv.* —**ex•pres′sive•ness** *n.*

oil•y (oi′lē) *adj.* **oil•i•er, oil•i•est.** **1.** Of or like oil: *an oily liquid.* **2.** Covered with, soaked with, or containing much oil: *oily rags; an oily complexion.* **3.** Unpleasantly smooth, as in manner or behavior: *his oily, insincere compliments.* —**oil′i•ness)** *n.*

pa•ren•the•sis (pə-rĕn′thĭ-sĭs) *n., pl.* **pa•ren•the•ses** (pə-rĕn′thĭ-sēz′) **1.** Either or both of the upright curved lines, ( ), used to mark off additional remarks in printing or writing. **2.** An additional phrase, explanation, etc., enclosed within such marks. **3.** A qualifying phrase placed within a sentence in such a way that the sentence is grammatically complete without it. **4.** Any comment departing from the main topic.

throw (thrō) *v.* **threw** (thro͞o), **thrown** (thrōn), **throw•ing.** **1.** To propel through the air with a swift motion of the arm; fling: *throw a ball.* **2.** To hurl with great force, as in anger: *He threw himself at his opponent.* **3.** To cast: *throw a glance at the window displays; throw a shadow.* **4.** To put on or off casually: *hurriedly throwing a cape over her shoulders.* **5.** To hurl to the ground or floor: *The wrestler threw his opponent with a swift blow.* **6.** *Informal.* To arrange or give: *throw a party.* **7.** *Informal.* To lose (a fight, race, etc.) purposely. **8.** To put into a specified condition: *new regulations that threw the players into confusion.* **9.** To actuate (a switch or control lever). —*n.* **1.** The act of throwing; a cast. **2.** The distance, height, or direction of something thrown. **3.** A scarf, shawl, or light coverlet. **4.** the distance or region through which a mechanical part moves. —**throw′ er** *n.*

Throughout history, scientific research has led to new inventions. For example, Ben Franklin's kite experiments helped later scientists to harness electricity. Today bionicists study anatomy in order to create devices such as artificial hearts. Many technical developments like these have altered and enriched our lives.

The words in this lesson will help you to understand some of the vocabulary used by scientists and technologists. Studying these words may also help you to understand how scientific knowledge leads to technological progress.

WORD LIST

alloy
buoyant
celestial
coagulate
combustible
conflagration
dissection
distill
meteorology
saturate

DEFINITIONS

After you have studied the definitions and example for each vocabulary word, write the word on the line to the right.

1. **alloy** (ăl'oi') *noun* A metal that is formed by mixing two or more other metals, or by combining a metal and a nonmetal. *verb* (ə-loi') To combine metals to form an alloy. (From the Latin word *alligare*, meaning "to bind to")

   Example Candlesticks are frequently made of brass, which is an *alloy* of zinc and copper.

   1. _____

2. **buoyant** (boi'ənt) *adjective* **a.** Capable of floating; able to keep other things afloat. **b.** Not easily depressed; cheerful.

   Related Word **buoyancy** *noun*
   Example The *buoyant* raft bounced over the swirling rapids.

   2. _____

3. **celestial** (sə-lĕs'chəl) *adjective* **a.** Of or related to the sky or heavens. **b.** Heavenly or divine. (From the Latin word *caelum*, meaning "sky")

   Example The astronomers tracked the *celestial* object carefully with their high-powered telescopes.

   3. _____

4. **coagulate** (kō-ăg'yə-lāt') *verb* **a.** To change a liquid into a solid or nearly solid mass; clot. **b.** To become coagulated. (From the Latin *com-*, meaning "together," and *agere*, meaning "to bring")

   Example Egg whites *coagulate* when they are cooked.

   4. _____

5. **combustible** (kəm-bŭs′tə-bəl) *adjective*   **a.** Capable of catching fire and burning; inflammable.   **b.** Easily excited; quick to anger. (From the Latin word *combustus*, meaning "burnt up")

> **Related Word**   **combustion** *noun*
> **Example**   Rags that have been soaked in turpentine are highly *combustible*.

5. _____

6. **conflagration** (kŏn′flə-grā′shən) *noun*   A large and destructive fire. (From the Latin word *conflagrare*, meaning "to burn up")

> **Example**   In 1906 many blocks of buildings were destroyed by the *conflagration* that followed the San Francisco earthquake.

6. _____

7. **dissection** (dĭ-sĕk′shən) *noun*   **a.** The process of cutting apart a dead animal or plant to examine its internal structure.   **b.** A detailed analysis or examination. (From the Latin *dis-*, meaning "apart," and *secare*, meaning "to cut")

> **Related Word**   **dissect** *verb*
> **Example**   We noted the strong leg muscles of the frog we *dissected* in biology class.

7. _____

8. **distill** (dĭ-stĭl′) *verb*   To treat or purify a liquid by heating it until it forms a vapor and then cooling it so that it returns to liquid form. (From the Latin *de-*, meaning "down," and *stillare*, meaning "to drip")

> **Related Word**   **distillation** *noun*
> **Example**   The engineers *distilled* gasoline from crude oil in their small laboratory.

8. _____

9. **meteorology** (mē′tē-ə-rŏl′ə-jē) *noun*   The science dealing with atmospheric conditions, especially weather conditions. (From the Greek word *meteōron*, meaning "astronomical phenomenon," and *logos*, meaning "speech")

> **Related Words**   **meteorological** *adjective;* **meteorologist** *noun*
> **Example**   People who do research in *meteorology* believe that volcanic eruptions affect the weather.

9. _____

10. **saturate** (săch′ə-rāt′) *verb*   To cause to be thoroughly soaked; fill to capacity. (From the Latin word *satur*, meaning "full")

> **Related Words**   **saturated** *adjective;* **saturation** *noun*
> **Example**   Rain had *saturated* the garden and killed all of the seedlings.

10. _____

EXERCISE 1 WRITING CORRECT WORDS

On the answer line, write the word from the vocabulary list that fits each definition.

1. Tending to float in a liquid; not easily depressed
2. Located in the sky or heavens
3. To treat or purify a liquid
4. The study of atmospheric conditions
5. To soak thoroughly or fill to capacity
6. A large, destructive fire
7. A mixture of two or more metals
8. To change a liquid into a solid mass; clot
9. The process of cutting apart to examine and study
10. Inflammable; easily excited

1. buoyant
2. celestial
3. distill
4. meteorology
5. saturate
6. conflagration
7. alloy
8. coagulate
9. dissection
10. combustible

EXERCISE 2 USING WORDS CORRECTLY

Decide whether the italicized vocabulary word has been used correctly in the sentence. On the answer line, write *Correct* for correct use and *Incorrect* for incorrect use.

1. Doug was fascinated by the *celestial* creatures of the sea.
2. *Dissection* of the maps in geography class made them easier to study.
3. The towel was *saturated* before I had dried all the dishes.
4. In order to gain a better understanding of *meteorology*, Betty read a book on weaving.
5. A handshake confirmed the *alloy* between the boys.
6. The children were upset that their toy boat was not *buoyant*.
7. Grandfather *distills* tap water to make it purer for cleaning his contact lenses.
8. If *combustible* materials collect in a storage area, they may become a fire hazard.
9. Lucinda's *conflagration* was interrupted by her brother's singing.
10. The sauce has to be stirred constantly so that it will not *coagulate*.

1. Incorrect
2. Incorrect
3. Correct
4. Incorrect
5. Incorrect
6. Correct
7. Correct
8. Correct
9. Incorrect
10. Correct

EXERCISE 3 CHOOSING THE BEST DEFINITION

For each italicized vocabulary word in the following sentences, write the letter of the best definition on the answer line.

1. The insurance agent photographed what remained of the beach houses after the *conflagration*.
   a. storm   **b.** large fire   **c.** loud party   **d.** earthquake

1. b

2. The jewelry designer displayed necklaces made of a new *alloy*.
   a. synthetic material   **c.** mixture of liquids
   b. mineral   **d.** mixture of metals

2. _____ d

3. Roger is looking forward to the frog *dissection* scheduled for the final week of biology class.
   a. test   **c.** cutting and examining
   b. sketching and labeling   **d.** review

3. _____ c

4. Margot's interest in *meteorology* began when a heat wave damaged her lettuce crop.
   a. agricultural study   **c.** weather study
   b. vegetable study   **d.** insect study

4. _____ c

5. Jon has worked hard to control his *combustible* personality.
   a. easily angered   **c.** unpopular
   b. complex   **d.** easily influenced

5. _____ a

6. As part of the experiment, the scientist tested the rate at which blood *coagulates.*
   a. flows   **b.** clots   **c.** burns   **d.** is created

6. _____ b

7. Our spirits were *buoyant* despite the terrible weather.
   a. cheerful   **b.** soaked   **c.** confused   **d.** depressed

7. _____ a

8. My family spent the evening discussing *celestial* phenomena.
   a. strange   **c.** ancient
   b. occurring on the earth   **d.** occurring in the sky

8. _____ d

9. Rochelle *saturated* the sponge with soapy water before washing her car.
   a. dampened   **b.** covered   **c.** soaked   **d.** cleaned

9. _____ c

10. The scientist could not obtain accurate results without *distilling* the liquids.
    a. purifying   **b.** removing   **c.** combining   **d.** stirring

10. _____ a

EXERCISE 4 USING DIFFERENT FORMS OF WORDS

Decide which form of the vocabulary word in parentheses best completes the sentence. The form given may be correct. Write your answer on the answer line.

1. In 1871 a major _____ leveled much of the city of Chicago. *(conflagration)*

1. _____ conflagration

2. Many students will _____ snakes and frogs in biology class. *(dissection)*

2. _____ dissect

3. Greg's gelatin failed to _____ because he added too much water. *(coagulate)*

3. _____ coagulate

4. To cultivate flowers, the Dutch use fresh water that has been _____ from sea water. *(distill)*

4. _____ distilled

5. My ring is not pure gold; it is made from an _____. *(alloy)*

5. _____ alloy

6. The room seemed to be _____ with the spicy aromas of cinnamon and cloves. *(saturate)*

6. _____ saturated

7. In a planetarium one can learn about ＿＿ occurrences. (*celestial*)

8. Under certain conditions ＿＿ takes place spontaneously—that is, it starts without a match or other external source. (*combustible*)

9. Janine is reading about unusual ＿＿ events. (*meteorology*)

10. When Helda scuba-dives in salt water, she adds ten pounds of weight to control her ＿＿. (*buoyant*)

7. ___celestial___

8. ___combustion___

9. ___meteorological___

10. ___buoyancy___

READING COMPREHENSION

Each numbered sentence in the following passage contains an italicized vocabulary word or related form. After you read the passage, you will complete an exercise.

THE ERUPTION OF MOUNT VESUVIUS

Mount Vesuvius, a volcano located between the ancient Italian cities of Pompeii and Herculaneum, has received much attention because of its frequent and destructive eruptions. The most famous of these eruptions occurred in A.D. 79.

The volcano had been inactive for centuries. (1) There was little warning of the coming eruption, although one account unearthed by archaeologists says that a hard rain and a strong wind had disturbed the *celestial* calm during the preceding night. (2) Early the next morning, the volcano poured a huge river of molten rock down upon Herculaneum, completely burying the city and filling in the harbor with *coagulated* lava.

Meanwhile, on the other side of the mountain, cinders, stone, and ash rained down on Pompeii. (3) Sparks from the burning ash ignited the *combustible* rooftops quickly. (4) Large portions of the city were destroyed in the *conflagration.* Fire, however, was not the only cause of destruction. (5) Poisonous sulphuric gases

saturated the air. (6) These heavy gases were not *buoyant* in the atmosphere and therefore sank toward the earth and suffocated people.

Over the years, excavations of Pompeii and Herculaneum have revealed a great deal about the behavior of the volcano. (7) By analyzing data, much as a zoologist *dissects* a specimen animal, scientists have concluded that the eruption changed large portions of the area's geography. For instance, it turned the Sarno River from its course and raised

the level of the beach along the Bay of Naples. (8) *Meteorologists* studying these events have also concluded that Vesuvius caused a huge tidal wave that affected the world's climate.

(9) In addition to making these investigations, archaeologists have been able to study the skeletons of victims by using *distilled* water to wash away the volcanic ash. By strengthening the brittle bones with acrylic paint, scientists have been able to examine the skeletons and draw conclusions about the diet and habits of the residents. (10) Finally, the excavations at both Pompeii and Herculaneum have yielded many examples of classical art, such as jewelry made of bronze, which is an *alloy* of copper and tin.

The eruption of Mount Vesuvius and its tragic consequences have provided us with a wealth of data about the effects that volcanoes can have on the surrounding area. Today volcanologists can locate and predict eruptions, saving lives and preventing the destruction of cities and cultures.

Each of the following statements corresponds to a numbered sentence in the passage. Each statement contains a blank and is followed by four answer choices. Decide which choice fits best in the blank. The word or phrase that you choose must express roughly the same meaning as the italicized word in the passage. Write the letter of your choice on the answer line.

1. The night before the earthquake a storm disturbed the _____ calm.
   a. heavenly   b. uneasy   c. residents'   d. ocean's

2. Herculaneum and its harbor were buried under _____ lava.
   a. liquid   b. solid   c. hot   d. flowing

3. Sparks from burning ash ignited the _____ rooftops.
   a. peaked   b. wooden   c. inflammable   d. flat

4. A _____ destroyed major portions of the city.
   a. burning ash   b. strong wind   c. large fire   d. hot coal

5. Poisonous gases _____ the air.
   a. half-filled   b. removed   c. diminished   d. filled

6. The poisonous gases were not _____ in the air.
   a. able to float   c. present
   b. visible   d. able to evaporate

7. Scientists analyzed data about Vesuvius in the same way that a zoologist _____ a specimen.
   a. describes in detail   c. photographs
   b. studies by cutting apart   d. x-rays

8. _____ have concluded that the volcanic eruption caused a tidal wave.
   a. Scientists who study bones and teeth
   b. Scientists who study oceans
   c. Scientists who study atmospheric conditions
   d. Scientists who study metals

9. Scientists have used _____ water to wash away volcanic ash from the skeletons of victims.
   a. warm   b. bottled   c. volcanic   d. purified

10. Archaeologists have found jewelry made of bronze, which is a(n) _____ of copper and tin.
    a. layering   b. ore   c. mixture   d. design

1. _____a_____
2. _____b_____
3. _____c_____
4. _____c_____
5. _____d_____
6. _____a_____
7. _____b_____
8. _____c_____
9. _____d_____
10. _____c_____

See page 119 for some strategies to use with analogies.

Directions   On the answer line, write the vocabulary word or a form of it that completes each analogy.

1. Terror is to fear as _____ is to pain. (Lesson 6)

2. Barren is to vegetation as _____ is to inhabitants. (Lesson 6)

3. Despondent is to sad as _____ is to happy. (Lesson 6)

4. Inflexible is to bend as _____ is to sink. (Lesson 7)

5. Terrestrial is to land as _____ is to sky. (Lesson 7)

1. _____anguish_____
2. _____desolate_____
3. _____exuberant_____
4. _____buoyant_____
5. _____celestial_____

LESSON 8 STRENGTH AND DEFENSE

In addition to requiring food, clothing, and shelter, people need to feel secure as they carry out their daily activities. Consequently, societies around the world establish and maintain armies and navies that they hope will prevent attack. The words in this lesson are used in describing different aspects of strength and defense. By studying these words, you will better understand how individuals and groups try to insure their own safety.

WORD LIST

blockade
indestructible
martial
omnipotent
robust
stability
staunch
valiant
vulnerable
withstand

DEFINITIONS

After you have studied the definitions and example for each vocabulary word, write the word on the line to the right.

1. **blockade** (blŏ-kād′) *noun*   The closing off of an area to prevent entrance or exit; an obstruction that prevents passage or progress.   *verb*   To set up a blockade against.

   Example   The *blockade* of the harbor kept all ships from entering or leaving the port.

   1. _____

2. **indestructible** (ĭn′dĭ-strŭk′tə-bəl) *adjective*   Not capable of being ruined or eliminated. (From the Latin *in-*, meaning "not," and *destruere*, meaning "to destroy")

   Related Word   **indestructibility** *noun*
   Example   The massive stone pillars used as supports for the front of the building seemed *indestructible*.

   2. _____

3. **martial** (mär′shəl) *adjective*   **a.** Inclined or disposed toward war; warlike. **b.** Military in style. (From the Latin word *martialis*, meaning "of Mars")

   Example   The army band was well known for its performances of *martial* music.

   3. _____
   MEMORY CUE: *Martial* comes from the word *Mars*. Mars was the god of war in Roman mythology.

4. **omnipotent** (ŏm-nĭp′ə-tənt) *adjective*   Having unlimited power, authority, or force. (From the Latin words *omnis*, meaning "all," and *potens*, meaning "having power")

   Related Words   **omnipotence** *noun*; **omnipotently** *adverb*
   Example   Ancient Romans considered their emperors *omnipotent*.

   4. _____

5. **robust** (rō-bŭst′) *adjective*   Full of strength and health; sturdy; powerfully built. (From the Latin word *robustus*, meaning "of oak")

   Related Words   **robustly** *adverb*; **robustness** *noun*
   Example   People who climb the mountains of Tibet must have bodies *robust* enough to tolerate great cold.

5. _____
MEMORY CUE: The adjective *robust* comes from the Latin word for *oak*, an extremely strong and hard wood.

6. **stability** (stə-bĭl′ĭ-tē) *noun*   **a.** Firmness of character or purpose. **b.** Resistance to change; changelessness.   **c.** Reliability and dependability. (From the Latin word *stabilis*, meaning "standing firm")

   Related Words   **stablilize** *verb*; **stable** *adjective*
   Example   After decreasing for many years, the African elephant population is achieving *stability*.

6. _____

7. **staunch** (stônch) *adjective*   **a.** Characterized by firmness, steadfastness, or loyalty.   **b.** Strong and substantial.

   Related Words   **staunchly** *adverb*; **staunchness** *noun*
   Example   The judge was a *staunch* defender of equal rights.

7. _____
USAGE NOTE: The verb *staunch* (or *stanch*) means "to check the flow of (blood)"—by pressing firmly.

8. **valiant** (văl′yənt) *adjective*   Displaying bravery, courage, and boldness. (From the Latin word *valere*, meaning "to be strong")

   Related Words   **valiantly** *adverb*; **valor** *noun*
   Example   The soldier was rewarded for his *valiant* actions in battle.

8. _____

9. **vulnerable** (vŭl′nər-ə-bəl) *adjective*   Capable of being wounded or hurt; open to attack or difficult to defend. (From the Latin word *vulnerare*, meaning "to wound")

   Related Words   **vulnerability** *noun*; **vulnerably** *adverb*
   Example   In football, running backs are particularly *vulnerable* to injury.

9. _____

10. **withstand** (wĭth-stănd′) *verb*   To resist something successfully by using force; endure. (From the Old English words *with*, meaning "against," and *standan*, meaning "to stand")

    Example   The sand castle could not *withstand* the force of the powerful waves.

10. _____

EXERCISE 1   COMPLETING DEFINITIONS

On the answer line, write the word from the vocabulary list that best completes each definition.

1. To be sturdy, strong, and healthy is to be _____.

2. To endure or to resist something successfully is to _____ it.

3. The closing off of an area to prevent movement in or out is a _____.

4. A person who displays great courage or boldness is considered _____.

5. Behavior that is warlike or military in style is _____.

6. Firmness of character or resistance to change is _____.

7. A position that can be easily attacked is _____.

8. When something cannot be ruined or eliminated, it is _____.

9. A person or thing that is firm, strong, and loyal is _____.

10. To have unlimited power is to be _____.

1. ____robust____
2. ____withstand____
3. ____blockade____
4. ____valiant____
5. ____martial____
6. ____stability____
7. ____vulnerable____
8. ____indestructible____
9. ____staunch____
10. ____omnipotent____

EXERCISE 2   USING WORDS CORRECTLY

Each of the following questions contains an italicized vocabulary word. Decide the answer to the question, and write *Yes* or *No* on the answer line.

1. Would a *martial* nation be known for its peace-loving nature?

2. Would a *valiant* person face danger in order to help a friend?

3. Is a sleeping deer *vulnerable* prey for a hungry wolf?

4. Would a weak, foolish king be an *omnipotent* ruler?

5. Would a *robust* person have difficulty walking one mile?

6. Would a *staunch* friend refuse to talk about you behind your back?

7. In the event of a naval *blockade*, would ships be allowed to pass freely in and out of a harbor?

8. Can penguins *withstand* the cold air and water of Antarctica?

9. Would a tool shed made of flattened tin cans and plywood be *indestructible* during a tornado?

10. Does a bridge that rocks back and forth when you walk on it have *stability?*

1. ____No____
2. ____Yes____
3. ____Yes____
4. ____No____
5. ____No____
6. ____Yes____
7. ____No____
8. ____Yes____
9. ____No____
10. ____No____

EXERCISE 3   CHOOSING THE BEST WORD

Decide which vocabulary word or related form best completes the sentence, and write the letter of your choice on the answer line.

1. The ship was able to _____ the strong winds and heavy rain.
   a. blockade   **b.** stabilize   **c.** staunch   **d.** withstand

1. ____d____

2. A table with four legs has greater _____ than one with only three legs.   2. _____**b**_____
   a. valor   **b.** stability   **c.** vulnerability   **d.** omnipotence

3. _____ seafaring people called Vikings invaded many countries in northern   3. _____**a**_____
   and western Europe.
   a. Martial   **b.** Stable   **c.** Blockading   **d.** Vulnerable

4. The _____ camper chopped wood for a campfire.   4. _____**d**_____
   a. martial   **b.** valiant   **c.** vulnerable   **d.** robust

5. The trainer said that the boxer was _____ because he had won every fight.   5. _____**a**_____
   a. indestructible   **b.** vulnerable   **c.** martial   **d.** blockaded

6. Kate received a standing ovation for her _____ attempts to win the   6. _____**c**_____
   basketball game.
   a. vulnerable   **b.** stable   **c.** valiant   **d.** martial

7. No one could leave or enter the town because of the enemy's _____.   7. _____**c**_____
   a. stability   **b.** staunchness   **c.** blockade   **d.** vulnerability

8. Carlisle has several _____ friends who support her effort to become an   8. _____**b**_____
   artist.
   a. omnipotent   **b.** staunch   **c.** robust   **d.** martial

9. The old house was _____ to the winds that blew off the ocean.   9. _____**d**_____
   a. valiant   **b.** robust   **c.** staunch   **d.** vulnerable

10. As ruler of the Roman Empire, Julius Caesar was very nearly _____.   10. _____**a**_____
    a. omnipotent   **b.** vulnerable   **c.** stable   **d.** withstanding

EXERCISE 4 USING DIFFERENT FORMS OF WORDS

Decide which form of the vocabulary word in parentheses best completes
the sentence. The form given may be correct. Write your answer on the
answer line.

1. Hannah _____ risked her life to save the kittens from the burning house.   1. _____**valiantly**_____
   (*valiant*)

2. The old barn could not _____ the hurricane's winds. (*withstand*)   2. _____**withstand**_____

3. The falcon could sense the mouse's _____. (*vulnerable*)   3. _____**vulnerability**_____

4. The police are _____ the avenue so that the ambassadors can leave their   4. _____**blockading**_____
   meeting safely. (*blockade*)

5. The _____ of the sea wall assured the residents that large waves would   5. _____**indestructibility**_____
   not destroy their houses. (*indestructible*)

6. Lynn's family _____ supported her decision to go to law school. (*staunch*)   6. _____**staunchly**_____

7. _____ is an essential quality in a furniture mover. (*Robust*)   7. _____**Robustness**_____

8. Before the painter climbed the ladder, he made sure that it was _____.   8. _____**stable**_____
   (*stability*)

9. The army doctor received a medal for his _____ at the front. (*valiant*)   9. _____**valor**_____

10. In Greek mythology, Zeus ruled _____ over all other gods and goddesses.   10. _____**omnipotently**_____
    (*omnipotent*)

READING COMPREHENSION

Each numbered sentence in the following passage contains an italicized vocabulary word or related form. After you have read the passage, you will complete an exercise.

THE SPANISH ARMADA

Conflict had existed between Spain and England since the 1570s. England wanted a share of the wealth that Spain had been taking from the lands it had claimed in the Americas. (1) Elizabeth I, Queen of England, encouraged her *staunch* admiral of the navy, Sir Francis Drake, to raid Spanish ships and towns. (2) Though these raids were on a small scale, Drake achieved dramatic success, adding gold and silver to England's treasury and diminishing Spain's *omnipotence.*

Religious differences also caused conflict between the two countries. Whereas Spain was Roman Catholic, most of England had become Protestant. King Philip II of Spain wanted to claim the throne and make England a Catholic country again. To satisfy his ambition and also to retaliate against England's theft of his gold and silver, King Philip began to build his fleet of warships, the Armada, in January 1586.

(3) Philip intended his fleet to be *indestructible.* (4) In addition to building new warships, he marshaled 130 sailing vessels of all types and recruited more than 19,000 *robust* soldiers and 8,000 sailors. (5) Although some of his ships lacked guns and others lacked ammunition, Philip was convinced that his Armada could *withstand* any battle with England.

(6) The *martial* Armada set sail from Lisbon, Portugal, on May 9, 1588, but bad weather forced it back to port. (7) The voyage resumed on July 22 after the weather had become *stable.*

The Spanish fleet met the smaller, faster, and more maneuverable English ships in battle off the coast of Plymouth, England, first on July 31 and again on August 2. (8) The two battles left Spain *vulnerable,* costing it several ships and depleting its ammunition.

On August 7, while the Armada lay at anchor on the French side of the Strait of Dover, England sent eight burning ships into the midst of the Spanish fleet to set it on fire. (9) *Blockaded* on one side, the Spanish ships could only drift away, their crews in panic and disorder. Before the Armada could regroup, the English attacked again on August 8.

(10) Although the Spaniards made a *valiant* effort to fight back, the fleet suffered extensive damage. During the eight hours of battle, the Armada drifted perilously close to the rocky coastline. At the moment when it seemed that the Spanish ships would be driven onto the English shore, the wind shifted, and the Armada drifted out into the North Sea. The Spaniards recognized the superiority of the English fleet and returned home, defeated.

READING COMPREHENSION EXERCISE

Each of the following statements corresponds to a numbered sentence in the passage. Each statement contains a blank and is followed by four answer choices. Decide which choice fits best in the blank. The word or phrase that you choose must express roughly the same meaning as the italicized word in the passage. Write the letter of your choice on the answer line.

1. Elizabeth I encouraged her _____ admiral of the navy to raid Spanish ships and towns.

   a. wise   **b.** crafty   **c.** loyal   **d.** precise

1. _____c_____

2. Drake added wealth to the treasury and diminished Spain's _____.
   a. unlimited power   c. reputation
   b. unrestricted growth d. territory

2. _____ a _____

3. Philip intended his fleet to be _____.
   a. respected   c. incapable of being copied
   b. incapable of being eliminated d. special

3. _____ b _____

4. Philip recruited many _____ soldiers and sailors.
   a. warlike   b. strong   c. accomplished   d. creative

4. _____ b _____

5. Philip was convinced that the Armada could _____ any battle with England.
   a. engage   b. arrange   c. break   d. endure

5. _____ d _____

6. The _____ Armada set sail on May 9, 1588.
   a. complete   b. warlike   c. independent   d. luxurious

6. _____ b _____

7. The voyage resumed after the weather became more _____.
   a. reliable   b. idle   c. serious   d. restless

7. _____ a _____

8. The two battles left the Spanish fleet _____.
   a. open to change   c. open to attack
   b. triumphant   d. hopeful

8. _____ c _____

9. The Armada was _____ on one side.
   a. closed off   b. damaged   c. dependable   d. alone

9. _____ a _____

10. The Spaniards made a _____ attempt to fight back.
    a. slight   b. ridiculous   c. huge   d. courageous

10. _____ d _____

WRITING ASSIGNMENT

Write a letter to your local or school newspaper in which you take a position on an issue of importance in your school or community. For example, you might write a letter defending the quality of the food served in the school cafeteria. Use at least five of the words from this lesson and underline them.

VOCABULARY ENRICHMENT

The word *martial* comes from the name of a Roman god, Mars. Mars was originally the Roman god of agriculture, and the early Romans paid tribute to him for good harvests.

   After the Romans captured Greece, they adopted the Greek gods and myths into their own culture. Because the Greeks believed that a goddess was responsible for growing crops, the Romans removed this function from Mars. Instead, they gave him the characteristics and responsibilities of Ares, the Greek god of war. Thus, the word *martial*, derived from the name of Mars, describes military activities.

Activity   Other words besides *martial* come from the names of gods or goddesses. Use your dictionary and an encyclopedia to find the origin of each of the words that follow. Write a definition of each word as well as a brief description of the origin.

1. jovial   2. titanic   3. iridescent   4. psyche   5. narcissistic

The **Bonus activity** for Lessons 7 and 8 is on page T8.

LESSON 9 BUILDINGS AND STRUCTURES

9

Architecture is one of the oldest art forms. Unlike other creative arts, such as painting, sculpture, and music, architecture must satisfy practical considerations. Someone may design an office building that looks beautiful, but if people cannot work comfortably and efficiently in it, the building does not serve its purpose. The words in this lesson will introduce you to some of the terminology used by architects to describe aspects of buildings and other structures.

WORD LIST

abode
annex
edifice
excavate
mason
prefabricate
rotunda
solar
trellis
turret

DEFINITIONS

After you have studied the definitions and example for each vocabulary word, write the word on the line to the right.

1. **abode** (ə-bōd′) *noun* A dwelling place or home. (From the Old English word *abidan,* meaning "to wait")

    Example   Mt. Olympus was the *abode* of the ancient Greek gods and goddesses.

1. _____
USAGE NOTE: One meaning of the related verb *abide* is "to dwell." One *abides* in an *abode.*

2. **annex** (ăn′ĕks′) *noun* A wing or building added to or located close to a larger building and used for the same purpose. *verb* (ə-nĕks′) To join or attach. (From the Latin *ad-,* meaning "to," and *nectere,* meaning "to bind")

    Related Word   **annexation** *noun*
    Example   The Library of Congress has an *annex* to house additional books.

2. _____
MEMORY CUE: An *annex* is usually *next* to the original structure.

3. **edifice** (ĕd′ə-fĭs) *noun* A building, especially one of great size or elegant appearance. (From the Latin words *aedis,* meaning "a building," and *facere,* meaning "to make")

    Example   The Doge's Palace in Venice is a colorful marble *edifice* perched on the side of a canal.

3. _____

4. **excavate** (ĕk′skə-vāt′) *verb* **a.** To dig or hollow out. **b.** To expose or uncover by digging. (From the Latin *ex-,* meaning "out," and *cavere,* meaning "to hollow")

    Related Word   **excavation** *noun*
    Example   The construction crew *excavated* the basement of the building in three days.

4. _____

© Great Source DO NOT COPY

Buildings and Structures **53**

5. **mason** (mā′sən) *noun*   A person who works with stone and brick.

  Related Word   **masonry** *noun*
  Example   The Ghilardis hired a *mason* to build their patio.

5. _____
USAGE NOTE: *Masonry* means "the trade of a mason" and also the finished product: "stone- or brickwork."

6. **prefabricate** (prē-făb′rĭ-kāt′) *verb*   To produce or build in advance; make in sections that can be shipped easily and assembled quickly. (From the Latin *prae-*, meaning "before," and *fabricari,* meaning "to make")

  Related Word   **prefabrication** *noun*
  Example   Today, many companies *prefabricate* houses.

6. _____

7. **rotunda** (rō-tŭn′də) *noun*   A circular building or room, especially one with a domed ceiling. (From the Latin word *rotunda,* meaning "round")

  Example   Tourists who visit the Capitol are fascinated by the high ceiling of the *rotunda.*

7. _____

8. **solar** (sō′lər) *adjective*   Having to do with the sun; using energy from the sun. (From the Latin word *sol,* meaning "sun")

  Example   Our *solar* heating system has helped to decrease our electricity bill.

8. _____

9. **trellis** (trĕl′ĭs) *noun*   A framework of crossed strips of wood on which vines or climbing plants are trained to grow. (From the Latin word *trilix,* meaning "woven with three threads")

  Example   Masses of pink roses covered the *trellis* on the side of the house.

9. _____

10. **turret** (tûr′ĭt) *noun*   **a.** A small ornamental tower projecting from a building, usually at a corner.   **b.** A dome or tower, usually rotating, that contains the mounted guns of a tank, warship, or warplane. (From the Latin word *turris,* meaning "tower")

  Example   We stood in the castle's *turret* and looked down at the drawbridge and moat.

10. _____

EXERCISE 1 WRITING CORRECT WORDS

On the answer line, write the word from the vocabulary list that fits
each definition.

1. To uncover by digging; hollow out or remove

2. A round building or room

3. A person who works with stone or brick

4. An addition to a building; to join or attach

5. A framework for climbing plants

6. To construct in advance; make in sections that can be shipped and
   assembled

7. Relating to the sun; using energy from the sun

8. A building, often of great size or elegant appearance

9. A small tower on the roof of a building; a rotating dome that contains the
   mounted guns of a tank or warship

10. A dwelling place

1. _____excavate_____
2. _____rotunda_____
3. _____mason_____
4. _____annex_____
5. _____trellis_____
6. _____prefabricate_____

7. _____solar_____
8. _____edifice_____
9. _____turret_____

10. _____abode_____

EXERCISE 2 USING WORDS CORRECTLY

Decide whether the italicized vocabulary word or related form has been used
correctly in the sentence. On the answer line, write *Correct* for correct use and
Incorrect for incorrect use.

1. Daily use of an *edifice* will keep your teeth healthy.

2. A greenhouse can use *solar* energy on bright winter days.

3. *Masons* must know the qualities of different types of stone used in
   construction.

4. Donna looked for an appropriate *trellis* to wear for the wedding.

5. If you do not like your *abode,* you can buy another at a hardware store.

6. A *rotunda* has four corners.

7. If a business wishes to expand, it may add an *annex* to its original store.

8. The company will send a *turret* repairperson to fix the washing machine.

9. Workers might have to *excavate* part of a lawn to build a fishpond.

10. Builders can put up a structure quickly with *prefabricated* parts.

1. _____Incorrect_____
2. _____Correct_____
3. _____Correct_____

4. _____Incorrect_____
5. _____Incorrect_____
6. _____Incorrect_____
7. _____Correct_____
8. _____Incorrect_____
9. _____Correct_____
10. _____Correct_____

For each italicized vocabulary word in the following sentences, write the letter of the best definition on the answer line.

1. When Diane could not find what she wanted in the main store, she walked over to the *annex.*
   a. addition   **b.** station   **c.** shed   **d.** basement

   1. _____a_____

2. It was easy to put together the doghouse once we had the *prefabricated* parts.
   a. separate   **c.** constructed in advance
   b. produced by machine   **d.** necessary

   2. _____c_____

3. The stairway to the *turret* was blocked during the renovation of the castle.
   a. prison   **b.** cellar   **c.** attic   **d.** tower

   3. _____d_____

4. Firefighters put out the blaze before it severely damaged the *edifice.*
   a. large building   **b.** thatched roof   **c.** window   **d.** addition

   4. _____a_____

5. Many buildings have large windows facing south to collect *solar* energy.
   a. atomic   **b.** from the sun   **c.** isolated   **d.** from the south

   5. _____b_____

6. Miners began to *excavate* the area, hoping to find valuable minerals.
   a. survey   **b.** dig out   **c.** claim   **d.** map out

   6. _____b_____

7. The dome of the *rotunda* provided a landmark for travelers several miles from the city.
   a. rotating building   **c.** arena
   b. state capitol   **d.** round building

   7. _____d_____

8. The Geralds sold their mansion and built a new *abode* by the sea.
   a. apartment   **b.** garage   **c.** home   **d.** castle

   8. _____c_____

9. The *mason* repaired the wall quickly and skillfully.
   a. stoneworker   **b.** bulldozer   **c.** painter   **d.** carpenter

   9. _____a_____

10. Covered with dried vines and a few brown leaves, the *trellis* looked dismal in the winter.
    a. porch   **b.** wooden frame   **c.** garden   **d.** view

    10. _____b_____

Decide which form of the vocabulary word in parentheses best completes the sentence. The form given may be correct. Write your answer on the answer line.

1. At the beach, the children built a _____ of sand. *(rotunda)*

   1. _____rotunda_____

2. When the store next to them became vacant, the Corderos _____ it. *(annex)*

   2. _____annexed_____

3. The _____ of parts makes the assembly of a jungle gym quite simple. *(prefabricate)*

   3. ___prefabrication___

4. The children recognized the castle and its many _____ from the photograph. *(turret)*

   4. _____turrets_____

5. During the archaeological _____, scientists uncovered a number of ancient relics. *(excavate)*

   5. _____excavation_____

6. Lila learned _____ in order to join her father's company. (*mason*)

7. Carl settled himself at the gate and sketched the front of the _____. (*edifice*)

8. The city's _____ of several suburbs created some problems at first. (*annex*)

9. Delia moaned that she would find her missing ring only by _____ the entire field. (*excavate*)

10. The _____ was not strong enough to support the heavy vine. (*trellis*)

6. ___**masonry**___

7. ___**edifice**___

8. ___**annexation**___

9. ___**excavating**___

10. ___**trellis**___

READING COMPREHENSION

Each numbered sentence in the following passage contains an italicized vocabulary word or related form. After you read the passage, you will complete an exercise.

CASA LOMA: A CANADIAN CASTLE

(1) Some houses assembled from *prefabricated* sections look ultra-modern because of their sleek exteriors and lack of architectural detail. (2) Other *edifices,* inspired by designs of the past, are built purposely to appear old. (3) One such place, located in Toronto, Ontario, Canada, is Casa Loma, a grand *abode* that resembles a castle of the Middle Ages.

(4) The *excavation* for this ninety-eight-room castle started in 1911, and the home was completed, at a cost of three million dollars, in 1914. Its owner, Sir Henry Pellatt, a financier and industrialist, had a lifelong interest in medieval architecture. (5) Casa Loma reflects that interest with its numerous *turrets,* hidden passageways, and winding staircases.

Sir Henry spared no expense to create his architectural fantasy. (6) He hired special *masons* from Scotland to build the huge wall that surrounds the six-acre site. Other artisans worked for three years to carve the French paneling for the Oak Room. Pellatt

even imported glass, marble, and bronze from Europe and Asia for the interior of the castle.

Built to show Sir Henry's collection of massive furniture and art, the castle is dramatic and magnificent in every way. (7) The spacious *rotunda* is filled with large plants placed in front of arched Gothic windows. (8) With light streaming through the windows and stained-glass panels,

the rotunda becomes a *solar* room where orchids thrive. The large library has a marble floor and shelves for a hundred thousand books. (9) An eight-hundred-foot underground tunnel connects the house with the stable *annex.* Even the horses lived luxuriously at Casa Loma, for Spanish tiled floors and mahogany-paneled walls decorate the stalls.

A view from either of the two stable towers reveals the handsome grounds. (10) Roses climbing on *trellises,* carefully clipped hedges, sculpted flower beds, and manicured lawns contribute to the atmosphere of medieval elegance.

Unfortunately, Sir Henry Pellatt lived in his castle for only ten years. In the early 1920s he found the cost of the castle's upkeep beyond even his ample means. The castle fell into disrepair until the Kiwanis Club purchased it in 1937. Since then, Casa Loma has been a Toronto landmark and an attraction for tourists.

Each of the following statements corresponds to a numbered sentence in the passage. Each statement contains a blank and is followed by four answer choices. Decide which choice fits best in the blank. The word or phrase that you choose must express roughly the same meaning as the italicized word in the passage. Write the letter of your choice on the answer line.

1. Some modern houses are constructed from sections that are _____.
   a. fabric
   b. produced in advance
   c. recycled lumber
   d. unique

   1. _____ b

2. Many _____ are based on past designs and are built to look old.
   a. large buildings
   b. small structures
   c. churches
   d. castles

   2. _____ a

3. Casa Loma is a _____ that resembles a castle from the Middle Ages.
   a. dwelling   **b.** stable   **c.** monument   **d.** symbol

   3. _____ a

4. The _____ for the castle began in 1911.
   a. framework   **b.** plans   **c.** digging   **d.** contracts

   4. _____ c

5. The castle has many hidden passageways and _____.
   a. cannons
   b. towers
   c. rotating windows
   d. stairways

   5. _____ b

6. Scottish _____ built a huge wall to surround the castle and its grounds.
   a. architects   **b.** sculptors   **c.** researchers   **d.** stoneworkers

   6. _____ d

7. The spacious _____ has Gothic windows and many plants.
   a. circular room   **b.** arch   **c.** garden   **d.** castle

   7. _____ a

8. The rotunda becomes a(n) _____ room where orchids thrive.
   a. operating   **b.** spacious   **c.** sunny   **d.** successful

   8. _____ c

9. The stable _____ is connected to the house by an underground passage.
   a. door   **b.** addition   **c.** yard   **d.** room

   9. _____ b

10. Sculpted flower beds and _____ of climbing roses create an atmosphere of elegance.
    a. additions
    b. creations
    c. clay pots
    d. wooden frameworks

    10. _____ d

Suppose that your local newspaper is sponsoring a contest for essays about the most attractive or impressive example of architecture in your city. Winning entries will be published in the paper. For the contest you wish to nominate a skyscraper, the wing of a museum, a school, or a restored house. Write a description of your choice, and explain why it is attractive or impressive. Use at least five of the vocabulary words from this lesson in your contest entry and underline each one.

The **Test** for Lessons 7, 8 and 9 is on page T9.

A B C

DICTIONARY SKILLS

BIOGRAPHICAL AND GEOGRAPHICAL ENTRIES

Dictionaries do more than define words. Many also contain biographical entries about notable people and geographical entries about important places and geographical features. In some dictionaries the entries are contained in the body of the dictionary. In others they are grouped in special sections at the back. The entries are usually very short. The primary information that they contain is how the name is spelled, how it is divided into syllables, and how it is pronounced. They also give a few basic facts about each person or place. The following information is typical.

1. *Biographical entries give the years of a person's birth and death.* Suppose that you need to know when Grover Cleveland was born. The following entry tells you that he was born in 1837.

   Cleve•land (klĕv′lənd), **(Stephen) Grover,** 1837–1908. 22nd & 24th U.S. President (1885–89, 1893–97.)

2. *Biographical entries note the individual's historical importance.* Biographical entries briefly state the field or the accomplishment of a famous person. The entry above tells you that Grover Cleveland was President of the United States twice.

3. *Geographical entries give facts about political divisions.* The following entry lists three cities named Paris with their locations and populations. Paris, Texas, for example, is located in northeast Texas and has a population of 25,498.

   Par•is (păr′ĭs). **1.** Cap. of France in the N central part on the Seine. Pop. 2,291,554. **2.** City of NW Tenn. WNW of Nashville. Pop. 10,728. **3.** City of NE Tex. NE of Dallas. Pop. 25,498. **—Pa•ri′sian** (pə-rē′zhən, -rĭzh′ən) *adj. & n.*

4. *Geographical entries give information about natural geographical features.* Entries on oceans and seas, important lakes and waterways, mountain ranges and peaks, and deserts are included in geographical listings. The entries give such facts as the lengths of rivers and the heights of mountain peaks.

EXERCISE USING BIOGRAPHICAL AND GEOGRAPHICAL ENTRIES

Use the dictionary entries at the end of this exercise to answer each of the following questions.

1. What are the dates of Franklin Delano Roosevelt's birth and death?
   1882 and 1945

2. Who was President of the United States longer, Franklin Delano Roosevelt or Theodore Roosevelt?
Franklin Delano Roosevelt

3. What were Eleanor Roosevelt's achievements?
American diplomat, author, and wife of President Franklin Delano Roosevelt

4. What else was Theodore Roosevelt besides President of the United States?
A soldier and an author

5. What are the locations and populations of the two American cities named Miami?
Miami, Florida, pop. 346,931; and Miami, Ohio, pop. 14,237

6. In which American state is the Great Miami River located, and how long is the river?
Ohio; 160 miles long

7. Which of the following is *not* named Victoria; a waterfall, a river, a city, or a desert?
A desert

8. In which country is Victoria Island located?
Canada

9. In which country or countries is Lake Victoria located?
Uganda, Kenya, and Tanzania

10. What is the Namib?
A desert in Africa

Mi•am•i (mĭ-ăm′ē). **1.** *also* **Great Miami.** river, c. 160 mi (257 km), of W Ohio flowing c. 160 mi (257 km) into the Ohio R. **2.** City of SE Fla. on Biscayne Bay S of West Palm Beach. Pop. 346,931. **3.** City of extreme NW Ohio WSW of Joplin, Mo. Pop. 14,237.

Na•mib (nä′mĭb′). Desert of SW Africa extending c. 800 mi (1,290 km) along the coast of Namibia.

Roo•se•velt (rō′zə-vĕlt′, rōz′vĕlt′, rōō′zə-), **(Anna) Eleanor,** 1884–1962. Amer. diplomat, author, & wife of Franklin Delano Roosevelt.

Roosevelt, Franklin Delano ("FDR"). 1882–1945. 32nd U.S. President (1933–45).

Roosevelt, Theodore. 1858–1919. 26th U.S. President (1901–9; Nobel, 1906), soldier, & author.

Vic•to•ri•a (vĭk-tôr′ē-ə, -tōr′-). **1. Lake.** *also* **Victoria Ny•an•za** (nē-ăn′zə, nī-). Lake, c. 26,830 sq mi (69,490 sq km), of E central Africa in Uganda, Kenya, & Tanzania. **2.** River, c. 240 mi (386 km), of N Australia. **3.** Falls, c. 420 ft (128 m) high & 1.1 mi (1.7 km) wide, in the Zambezi R. on the Zambia-Zimbabwe border. **4.** Island of N.W.T., Canada, in the Arctic Ocean N of the mainland & S of Parry Channel. **5. Land.** Region of E Antarctica S of New Zealand, bordering the Ross Sea. **6.** Cap. of B.C., Canada, on SE Vancouver Is. & Juan de Fuca Strait. Pop. 62,551. **7.** Cap. of Hong Kong colony on the NW coast of Hong Kong Is. Pop. 1,026,870. **8.** Cap. of the Seychelles on the NE coast of Mahé Is. Pop. 15,559. **9.** city of SE Tex. SE of San Antonio. Pop. 50,695.

Nearly all children have been asked, "What do you want to be when you grow up?" For most of these children, a response is simple to make. As they grow older, however, they learn that there are many options and possibilities available that they did not consider earlier. Life grows richer and much more complex as one matures, and the experience that leads to adulthood makes one more confident and also more competent to deal with these complexities. Maturity is the triumph of experience. In this lesson you will study words concerning the process of maturing.

WORD LIST

antiquated
centenarian
contemporary
fledgling
frail
gerontology
longevity
nascent
puerile
venerable

DEFINITIONS

After you have studied the definitions and example for each vocabulary word, write the word on the line to the right.

1. **antiquated** (ăn′tĭ-kwā′tĭd) *adjective*   Old and no longer useful or suitable; outmoded.

   Related Words   **antique** *noun;* **antique** *adjective*
   Example   At the car museum, Maureen and I learned about the *antiquated* practice of starting an automobile by hand-cranking it.

1. _____
USAGE NOTE: *Antique* means "made in an earlier period." Unlike *antiquated*, *antique* suggests great value in age.

2. **centenarian** (sĕn′tə-nâr′ē-ən) *noun*   One who lives one hundred or more years. (From the Latin word *centum*, meaning "hundred")

   Related Words   **centenary** *noun;* **centenary** *adjective*
   Example   In our little town of Scarborough Falls, we are fortunate to have three *centenarians*.

2. _____
MEMORY CUE: There are one hundred years in a *century*.

3. **contemporary** (kən-tĕm′pə-rĕr′ē) *adjective*   **a.** Living or happening during the same period of time.   **b.** Current; modern: *contemporary history.*   *noun*   Someone of the same age or living at the same time as another or others. (From the Latin *con-*, meaning "together," and *tempus*, meaning "time")

   Related Word   **contemporaneous** *adjective*
   Example   Michelangelo and Leonardo were *contemporary* artists.

3. _____
USAGE NOTE: The adjective *contemporaneous* means the same as *contemporary* but applies most often to things.

4. **fledgling** (flĕj′lĭng) *noun* **a.** A young or inexperienced person. **b.** A young bird that has just grown feathers needed for flying. *adjective* Inexperienced.

> **Example** As a reporter Moses was only a *fledgling*, but he was given many different assignments.

4. _____

ETYMOLOGY NOTE: *Fledgling* probably comes from the obsolete word *fledge*, meaning "feathered."

5. **frail** (frāl) *adjective* **a.** Flimsy; not strong or substantial; fragile. **b.** Physically weak. (From the Latin word *fragilis*, meaning "fragile")

> **Related Word** frailty *noun*
> **Example** The staircase was so *frail* that is was roped off.

5. _____

6. **gerontology** (jĕr′ən-tŏl′ə-jē) *noun* The scientific study of the process and effects of aging. (From the Greek words *gerōn*, meaning "old man," and *logos*, meaning "word")

> **Related Words** gerontological *adjective*; **gerontologist** *noun*
> **Example** As the average life span increases, *gerontology* is becoming an increasingly important field of study.

6. _____

7. **longevity** (lŏn-jĕv′ĭ-tē) *noun* **a.** Length of life. **b.** Long duration, as in an occupation. (From the Latin words *longa*, meaning "long," and *aevitas*, meaning "age")

> **Example** *Longevity* is increasing because of better nutrition and medical treatment.

7. _____

8. **nascent** (nā′sənt) *adjective* Coming into existence; emerging. (From the Latin word *nasci*, meaning "to be born")

> **Example** The students' *nascent* interest in the stock market prompted the school library to buy books on investment planning.

8. _____

9. **puerile** (pyŏŏr′ĭl′) *adjective* **a.** Childish; immature; silly. **b.** Belonging to childhood; youthful. (From the Latin word *puer*, meaning "boy")

> **Related Word** puerility *noun*
> **Example** When her brother was born, Sara exhibited *puerile* behavior for several weeks.

9. _____

10. **venerable** (vĕn′ər-ə-bəl) *adjective* Worthy of respect or reverence, particularly because of position or age.

> **Related Words** venerably *adverb*; **venerate** *verb*; **veneration** *noun*
> **Example** Charles de Gaulle remained a *venerable* statesman in France even after his retirement from active political life.

10. _____

USAGE NOTE: Don't confuse *venerable* with *vulnerable*, which means "capable of being wounded or hurt."

EXERCISE 1 COMPLETING DEFINITIONS

On the answer line, write the word from the vocabulary list that best completes each definition.

1. Someone with little experience is a _____.

2. _____ refers to the length of life.

3. Something that is current or modern is _____.

4. One who is worthy of respect because of age is _____.

5. Anything useless or outmoded is _____.

6. A person who is physically weak is _____.

7. A _____ is a person who is at least one hundred years old.

8. Someone whose behavior is childish or silly can be said to be _____.

9. Something just emerging is _____.

10. _____ refers to the scientific study of aging.

1. _____fledgling_____
2. _____Longevity_____
3. _____contemporary_____
4. _____venerable_____
5. _____antiquated_____
6. _____frail_____
7. _____centenarian_____
8. _____puerile_____
9. _____nascent_____
10. _____Gerontology_____

EXERCISE 2 USING WORDS CORRECTLY

Each of the following questions contains an italicized vocabulary word. Decide the answer to the question, and write *Yes* and *No* on the answer line.

1. Is a *frail* person usually very strong?

2. Is a student likely to be a *contemporary* of another student in the same grade?

3. Is a withering flower *nascent?*

4. Is a *fledgling* old and wise?

5. Are practical jokes sometimes *puerile?*

6. Is an *antiquated* tool the most efficient one available?

7. Would people be likely to seek advice from a *venerable* leader?

8. Does a dog have greater *longevity* than a fly?

9. Would *gerontology* teach you about caring for a baby's skin?

10. Has a *centenarian* lived for a whole century?

1. _____No_____
2. _____Yes_____
3. _____No_____
4. _____No_____
5. _____Yes_____
6. _____No_____
7. _____Yes_____
8. _____Yes_____
9. _____No_____
10. _____Yes_____

EXERCISE 3 CHOOSING THE BEST WORD

Decide which vocabulary word or related form best completes the sentence, and write the letter of your choice on the answer line.

1. Born in 1885, Prince Igor became a _____ in 1985.
   a. puerility   **b.** fledgling   **c.** centenarian   **d.** frailty

2. Grandmother enjoys telling about the _____ technology of her youth.
   a. frail   **b.** nascent   **c.** puerile   **d.** centenary

1. _____c_____
2. _____b_____

3. I enjoy _____ music more than traditional music.

   a. frail   **b.** venerable   **c.** antiquated   **d.** contemporary

3. _____d_____

4. For decades we have respected the noble words of this _____ poet.

   a. nascent   **b.** fledgling   **c.** venerable   **d.** puerile

4. _____c_____

5. _____ behavior, such as pushing and shoving, will not be tolerated on the field trip.

   a. Puerile   **b.** Contemporary **c.** Frail   **d.** Antiquated

5. _____a_____

6. Dr. Crane's talk on _____ included a discussion of the effects of aging on human bones.

   a. puerility   **b.** fledglings   **c.** veneration   **d.** gerontology

6. _____d_____

7. Although she was an experienced swimmer, Anna was a _____ diver.

   a. centenary   **b.** fledgling   **c.** gerontological **d.** contemporary

7. _____b_____

8. Because the textile factory had only _____ machinery, it was less productive than its competitors.

   a. venerable   **b.** contemporary **c.** antiquated   **d.** nascent

8. _____c_____

9. Although Julio appeared _____, he was quite strong.

   a. antiquated   **b.** venerable   **c.** puerile   **d.** frail

9. _____d_____

10. Human _____ varies from nation to nation and is generally greater in Europe than in Asia.

   a. longevity   **b.** frailty   **c.** puerility   **d.** fledgling

10. _____a_____

EXERCISE 4 USING DIFFERENT FORMS OF WORDS

Decide which form of the vocabulary word in parentheses best completes the sentence. The form given may be correct. Write your answer on the answer line.

1. A flash of the dragon's eyes warned Sir Geoffrey of the beast's _____ anger. *(nascent)*

1. _____nascent_____

2. The mother bird watched as her three _____ left the nest. *(fledgling)*

2. _____fledglings_____

3. The teenagers continued to _____ their teacher years after they had graduated. *(venerable)*

3. _____venerate_____

4. The inventions of the phonograph and motion pictures were _____. *(contemporary)*

4. _____contemporaneous_____

5. Dr. Wong's specialty is _____. *(gerontology)*

5. _____gerontology_____

6. The _____ of redwood trees is amazing. *(longevity)*

6. _____longevity_____

7. Brooks and Felicia will celebrate August Partridge's _____ next month in Bedminster. *(centenarian)*

7. _____centenary_____

8. The _____ of the play offended the audience. *(puerile)*

8. _____puerility_____

9. My grandmother's house is full of fine _____ furniture that her grandparents brought from France. *(antiquated)*

9. _____antique_____

10. Mary's outward appearance of _____ was deceptive. *(frail)*

10. _____frailty_____

READING COMPREHENSION

Each numbered sentence in the following passage contains an italicized vocabulary word. After you read the passage, you will complete the exercise.

THE CENTENARIANS OF THE CAUCASUS MOUNTAINS

(1) Around the upper reaches of the Caspian Sea in the Caucasus Mountains live the Georgians, a people known for their *longevity.* (2) Many of these people are *centenarians* leading active lives. (3) There are, in fact, so many people who have lived to the age of one hundred or more that a sixty-year-old in Georgia might seem to be a mere *fledgling.*

What accounts for such long lives? (4) Research in *gerontology* has not been able to provide any definite answers. Nevertheless, the Georgians do have, and have historically had, a high level of physical activity. (5) Their society, while not *antiquated,* relies much less on labor-saving devices than many other societies do. (6) Even in *contemporary* Georgia, automobiles and tractors are less common than in western Europe. Every day presents many opportunities for vigorous exercise, and this fact may contribute to longevity. One must keep in mind, however, that other nations with high levels of physical activity do not necessarily have the same extreme longevity.

(7) One can build only a *frail* argument for the accuracy of the ages claimed by older Georgians, because the evidence is so limited. In the last century, Georgians were not issued birth certificates, and the baptismal certificates for most of them are no longer available. (8) It would be *puerile* to quibble over whether an elderly person is one hundred ten or one hundred twenty. Whatever the case, Georgians are exceptionally long-lived.

(9) A *nascent* interest in the process of aging has developed during the twentieth century into a large-scale scientific concern. The more we learn about how people age, the more likely we are to improve life expectancy among all people. (10) The *venerable* centenarians of Georgia may yet teach us much about long life.

Each of the following statements corresponds to a numbered sentence in the passage. Each statement contains a blank and is followed by four answer choices. Decide which choice fits best in the blank. The word or phrase that you choose must express roughly the same meaning as the italicized word in the passage. Write the letter of your choice on the answer line.

1. The Georgians are renowned for their _____.
   a. wisdom   **b.** health   **c.** length of life   **d.** seclusion

1. _____ c

2. Many of these people are _____.
   a. more than one hundred years old   **c.** healthy and happy
   b. fun to be with   **d.** living alone in the mountains

2. _____ a

3. A sixty-year-old in Georgia might seem to be a _____.
   a. healthy person   **c.** fortunate person
   b. young person   **d.** retired person

3. _____ b

4. Research in the _____ has provided no firm answers.
   a. field of public health   **c.** study of aging
   b. study of nutrition   **d.** usefulness of exercise

4. _____ c

5. Georgian society is not _____.
   a. valuable   **b.** civilized   **c.** out-of-date   **d.** quaint

5. _____ c

6. In _____ Georgia, automobiles are not common.
   a. unpolluted   **b.** urban   **c.** fashionable   **d.** modern

6. _____ d

7. One can build only a _____ case for the accuracy of the ages claimed by older Georgians.
   a. weak   **b.** serious   **c.** natural   **d.** reasonable

7. _____ a

8. Quibbling over ages would be _____.
   a. wise   **b.** unscientific   **c.** difficult   **d.** silly

8. _____ d

9. There is _____ interest in the process of aging.
   a. medical   **b.** emerging   **c.** valuable   **d.** scholarly

9. _____ b

10. The _____ centenarians may yet teach us much.
    a. honorable   **b.** old   **c.** clever   **d.** wise

10. _____ a

See page 119 for some strategies to use with analogies.

Directions On the answer line, write the vocabulary word or a form of it that completes each analogy.

1. Dam is to river as _____ is to road. *(Lesson 8)*

1. _____ blockade

2. Addendum is to book as _____ is to building. *(Lesson 9)*

2. _____ annex

3. Superhighway is to road as cathedral is to _____. *(Lesson 9)*

3. _____ edifice

4. Potter is to clay as _____ is to stone. *(Lesson 9)*

4. _____ mason

5. Housemate is to residence as _____ is to age. *(Lesson 10)*

5. _____ contemporary

6. Tiny is to size as _____ is to strength. *(Lesson 10)*

6. _____ frail

The **Bonus activity** for Lessons 9 and 10 is on page T11.

How big a role does time play in your life?

To find out, read the following list of time-related statements, and ask yourself which ones apply to you.

I check a clock or wristwatch every fifteen minutes.

I frequently remind myself to stop wasting time.

I constantly ask others what time it is.

I often use expressions like "Procrastination is the thief of time" or "Time waits for no one."

I create elaborate time schedules and actually stick to them.

If three or more of the statements apply to you, then time plays an important part in your life. Whether time is important to you or not, the words in this lesson will give you new ways to express yourself on this subject.

WORD LIST

belated
duration
expire
foregone
incessant
medieval
premature
respite
simultaneous
subsequent

DEFINITIONS

After you have studied the definitions and example for each vocabulary word, write the word on the line to the right.

1. **belated** (bǐ-lā′tǐd) *adjective*   Tardy; too late.

   Related Word   **belatedly** *adverb*
   Example   Lorraine sent a *belated* birthday card to a friend whose birthday had already passed.

1. _____

2. **duration** (dŏŏ-rā′shən) *noun*   The period of time during which something exists or persists. (From the Latin word *durare*, meaning "to last")

   Example   An average movie is about two hours in *duration*.

2. _____

3. **expire** (ĭk-spīr′) *verb*   **a.** To come to an end; terminate; die.   **b.** To exhale or breathe out. (From the Latin *ex-*, meaning "out," and *spirare*, meaning "to breathe")

   Related Word   **expiration** *noun*
   Example   Harold hurried to renew his magazine subscription before it *expired*.

3. _____

   USAGE NOTE: One meaning of *inspire* is "to inhale"; in that sense it is an antonym of *expire*.

4. **foregone** (fôr′gôn′) *adjective*   Having gone before; past; previous.
   foregone conclusion   An end or result regarded as inevitable.

   Related Word   **forego** *verb*
   Example   The nomination of the popular politician was considered a *foregone* conclusion.

4. _____

   USAGE NOTE: Don't confuse *forego* ("to precede in time or place") with *forgo* ("to abstain from; relinquish").

5. **incessant** (ĭn-sĕs′ənt) *adjective*   Continuing without interruption; constant. (From the Latin *in-*, meaning "not," and *cessare*, meaning "to stop")

   Related Word   **incessantly** *adverb*
   Example   The *incessant* rain upset the picnickers.

5. _____

6. **medieval** (mē′dē-ē′vəl) *adjective*   Characteristic of or referring to the Middle Ages, the period in European history from the fall of the western Roman Empire (about A.D. 476) to the rise of the Renaissance (about 1453). (From the Latin words *medius*, meaning "middle," and *aevum*, meaning "age")

   Example   Numerous castles were built during the *medieval* period of history.

6. _____

7. **premature** (prē′mə-tyo͞or′) *adjective*   Appearing or occurring before the usual time; unexpectedly early; happening too soon. (From the Latin *prae-*, meaning "before," and *maturus*, meaning "ripe")

   Related Words **prematurely** *adverb;* **prematureness** *noun*
   Example   Arthur's congratulations were *premature* because Lisa's birthday was still one week away.

7. _____

8. **respite** (rĕs′pĭt) *noun*   A short time of rest or relief; a postponement or delay. (From the Latin word *respectus*, meaning "a refuge")

   Example   A half-hour break provided a welcome *respite* from studying.

8. _____

9. **simultaneous** (sī′məl-tā′nē-əs) *adjective*   Happening, existing, or done at the same time. (From the Latin word *simul*, meaning "at the same time")

   Related Word   **simultaneously** *adverb*
   Example   Because they were *simultaneous*, we could not attend both Judy's basketball game and Ben's play.

9. _____

10. **subsequent** (sŭb′sĭ-kwĕnt′) *adjective*   Following in time or order; succeeding. (From the Latin word *subsequi*, meaning "to follow close after")

    Related Word   **subsequently** *adverb*
    Example   Heavy rains and *subsequent* floods caused a great deal of damage to the town.

10. _____

EXERCISE 1 COMPLETING DEFINITIONS

On the answer line, write the word from the vocabulary list that best completes each definition.

1. Time _____ at the end of an event.

2. We refer to events that took place in the Middle Ages as _____.

3. If an event happens before its expected or usual time, it is _____.

4. When an event is delayed or late, it is _____.

5. When events occur at the same time, they are _____.

6. An action that continues without interruption is _____.

7. The amount of time that an event lasts is its _____.

8. One event that follows another is _____ to the first event.

9. A brief period of rest or relaxation is called a _____.

10. When a conclusion is inevitable or unavoidable, it is _____.

1. ___expires___
2. ___medieval___
3. ___premature___
4. ___belated___
5. ___simultaneous___
6. ___incessant___
7. ___duration___
8. ___subsequent___
9. ___respite___
10. ___foregone___

EXERCISE 2 USING WORDS CORRECTLY

Decide whether the italicized vocabulary word has been used correctly in the sentence. On the answer line, write *Correct* for correct use and *Incorrect* for incorrect use.

1. The bus driver could not hear Peter's shouts because he was already too *foregone*.

2. The *premature* baby had to stay in the hospital for three extra weeks.

3. Ted silently forgave Marcella but still hoped for a *belated* apology.

4. *Subsequent* to its retirement, the horse won three more races.

5. A good exercise instructor is able to *expire* students to do more.

6. Vanessa plans to be an artist *respite* the fact that she knows very little about art.

7. The *medieval* castle was recently built.

8. Glen opened the *duration* of his briefcase and took out a writing pad.

9. Running neck and neck, two runners had *simultaneous* bursts of speed and tied for first place at the finish line.

10. The *incessant* noise from the party next door kept Penny awake.

1. ___Incorrect___
2. ___Correct___
3. ___Correct___
4. ___Incorrect___
5. ___Incorrect___
6. ___Incorrect___
7. ___Incorrect___
8. ___Incorrect___
9. ___Correct___
10. ___Correct___

EXERCISE 3 CHOOSING THE BEST WORD

Decide which vocabulary word or related form best completes the sentence, and write the letter of your choice on the answer line.

1. _____ to his fall from the tree, Tommy was afraid of heights.
   a. Respite   **b.** Subsequent   **c.** Belated   **d.** Foregone

1. ___b___

2. Millie received a parking ticket when the time on the meter _____.
   a. was subsequent   c. expired
   b. was foregone   d. was premature

2. _____c_____

3. Troy continued weeding the garden after a brief _____
   a. respite   b. duration   c. expiration   d. subsequent

3. _____a_____

4. To turn the machine on, you must push both buttons _____.
   a. incessantly   b. prematurely   c. belatedly   d. simultaneously

4. _____d_____

5. Gretchen was fully recovered by the time she received Terry's _____ get-well card.
   a. belated   b. premature   c. incessant   d. medieval

5. _____a_____

6. The _____ chatter of the small child annoyed the baby sitter.
   a. premature   b. subsequent   c. incessant   d. simultaneous

6. _____c_____

7. Robert's football gear resembled a _____ suit of armor.
   a. foregone   b. belated   c. medieval   d. premature

7. _____c_____

8. When they began their study, the committee's _____ conclusion was that the company should build a new main office.
   a. foregone   b. simultaneous   c. incessant   d. belated

8. _____a_____

9. Mr. Lowell assigned seats for the _____ of the semester.
   a. foregone   b. expiration   c. duration   d. respite

9. _____c_____

10. Instead of making _____ decisions, you should first weigh all the facts.
    a. medieval   b. belated   c. premature   d. simultaneous

10. _____c_____

EXERCISE 4   USING DIFFERENT FORMS OF WORDS

Decide which form of the vocabulary word in parentheses best completes the sentence. The form given may be correct. Write your answer on the answer line.

1. The Millers are angry at Rover because he barks _____. (*incessant*)

1. _____incessantly_____

2. The stories of King Arthur and the Knights of the Round Table take place in a _____ setting. (*medieval*)

2. _____medieval_____

3. I spoke _____ when I predicted that Carl would win the tennis match. (*premature*)

3. _____prematurely_____

4. The orchestra will be leaving the city upon the _____ of its contract. (*expire*)

4. _____expiration_____

5. Alan and Trudy left the movie theater; _____ they went to a restaurant. (*subsequent*)

5. _____subsequently_____

6. Because of Celeste's _____ opinion that the play was dull, she did not attend. (*foregone*)

6. _____foregone_____

7. Walter _____ warned Betty about the detour on Route 3. (*belated*)

7. _____belatedly_____

8. Jimmy spent the _____ of his vacation visiting new places. (*duration*)

8. _____duration_____

9. The actors walked onstage _____. (*simultaneous*)

9. _____simultaneously_____

10. Drinking a glass of water was a welcome _____ for the speaker. (*respite*)

10. _____respite_____

READING COMPREHENSION

Each numbered sentence in the following passage contains an italicized vocabulary word or related form. After you read the passage, you will complete an exercise.

AMERICANS ON THE MOON

For centuries people wondered about the moon. Was its surface like the earth's? Could anyone actually live there? (1) Greek, Roman, and *medieval* authors wrote that walking on the moon was an impossible dream. On July 20, 1969, though, that dream became a reality for two American astronauts.

President John F. Kennedy did much to bring this reality about when he launched the Apollo program, the United States mission to the moon, in 1961. (2) For nine years, scientists worked *incessantly* on this project. (3) When they started, the possibility of a successful moon landing was by no means a *foregone* conclusion. Flights into space were considered very dangerous.

The most depressing setback in the Apollo program occurred in 1967. (4) Scientists hoped to put a spacecraft with three astronauts into orbit, but this attempt turned out to be tragically *premature*. During a practice take-off, fire broke out inside the spacecraft, and three astronauts lost their lives. (5) Saddened by this disaster, Apollo scientists *belatedly* planned improvements in fire-prevention equipment.

Two years later, scientists launched another spacecraft, with astronauts Neil Armstrong, Edwin "Buzz" Aldrin, and Michael Collins aboard. The launch was successful.

Once their craft was in orbit around the moon, Collins remained in the command module. Meanwhile, Aldrin and Armstrong boarded the lunar module and descended to the moon's surface. (6) Via a world-wide television broadcast transmitted by satellite, millions of people watched *simultaneously* as Neil Armstrong took the first step onto the moon. Eighteen minutes later, Aldrin joined him. (7) This first moon landing was almost twenty-two hours in *duration*. (8) When the scheduled time for the excursion on the moon *expired*, Armstrong and Aldrin returned to the command module.

(9) Even after the astronauts had landed safely on Earth, there was no *respite* from duty. The men remained in isolation for almost three weeks before scientists were satisfied that the three men were free from contamination by harmful germs or chemicals.

(10) Since 1969 Americans have made *subsequent* moon landings, but the first voyage will always be remembered. As Armstrong said as he took his first step on the moon, "That's one small step for a man and one giant leap for mankind."

Each of the following statements corresponds to a numbered sentence in the passage. Each statement contains a blank and is followed by four answer choices. Decide which choice fits best in the blank. The word or phrase that you choose must express roughly the same meaning as the italicized word in the passage. Write the letter of your choice on the answer line.

1. Authors in ancient times and in _____ considered reaching the moon to be an impossible dream.
   a. the Victorian era   **c.** prehistoric times
   b. modern days   **d.** the Middle Ages

   1. _____ d _____

2. Scientists worked _____ on the Apollo moon mission.
   a. without stopping   **c.** without knowledge
   b. without success   **d.** without leadership

   2. _____ a _____

3. The possibility of a successful moon landing was not a(n) _____ conclusion.
   a. inevitable   **b.** true   **c.** negative   **d.** worrisome

   3. _____ a _____

4. The 1967 attempt to put a manned spacecraft into orbit was _____.
   a. successful   **c.** poorly executed
   b. unwise   **d.** too early

   4. _____ d _____

5. The planners of the Apollo program designed improvements _____ in fire-prevention equipment.
   a. too late   **b.** previously   **c.** efficiently   **d.** reluctantly

   5. _____ a _____

6. Television viewers _____ watched a broadcast of Armstrong's walk on the moon.
   a. breathlessly   **c.** at different times
   b. listlessly   **d.** at the same time

   6. _____ d _____

7. The first moon landing was almost twenty-two hours in _____.
   a. length   **b.** space   **c.** danger   **d.** miles

   7. _____ a _____

8. When the astronauts' time on the moon _____, they returned to the spacecraft.
   a. continued   **c.** was renewed
   b. ended   **d.** was determined

   8. _____ b _____

9. The astronauts landed safely on Earth, but there was no _____ from duty.
   a. satisfaction   **b.** reward   **c.** break   **d.** fun

   9. _____ c _____

10. Since 1969 the United States has made _____ landings on the moon.
    a. additional   **c.** energetic
    b. more spectacular   **d.** unsuccessful

    10. _____ a _____

People sometimes have trouble budgeting their time well in order to meet deadlines. In a paragraph or two of advice to younger students, tell about a situation in which you had trouble managing your time. Explain how you resolved this problem. Include five words from the lesson and underline them.

LESSON 12 THE ROOT -*DUCE*-

All of the words in this lesson are formed from the Latin root -*duce*-. This root comes from the Latin word *ducere*, meaning "to lead," and also takes the form -*duc*-, -*duct*-, -*duit*-, and -*due*-. More than fifty English words are derived from this useful root. You may already be familiar with some of them, such as *introduction*, *producer*, and *product*. Studying the vocabulary words in this lesson will increase your understanding of other words derived from -*duce*- and their related forms.

WORD LIST

aqueduct
conduct
conduit
deduce
induce
induction
productivity
reduction
subdue
viaduct

DEFINITIONS

After you have studied the definitions and example for each vocabulary word, write the word on the line to the right.

1. **aqueduct** (ăk′wĭ-dŭkt′) *noun*   **a.** A large pipe or channel made to carry water from a distant source.   **b.** A bridgelike structure designed to carry such a pipe or channel across low ground or a river. (From the Latin words *aqua*, meaning "water," and *ducere*, meaning "to lead")

   Example   The ancient Romans built *aqueducts* to transport water into Rome.

   1. _____
   See *conduit*.

2. **conduct** (kən-dŭkt′) *verb*   **a.** To lead or guide.   **b.** To direct the course of something such as an experiment.   **c.** To lead or direct musicians or a musical work.   **d.** To act as a medium through which a form of energy such as electricity can travel.   *noun* (kŏn′dŭkt) The way a person acts or behaves. (From the Latin *com-*, meaning "together," and *ducere*)

   Related Words conducive *adjective*; **conductor** *noun*
   Example   The guide *conducted* a tour of the museum.

   2. _____

3. **conduit** (kŏn′dōō-ĭt) *noun*   **a.** A channel or pipe for carrying water or other fluids.   **b.** A tube or pipe through which electrical wires or cables pass. (From the Medieval Latin word *conductus*, meaning "transportation")

   Example   The plumber installed *conduits* in the new house.

   3. _____
   USAGE NOTE: A *conduit* is a channel for fluids such as water. An *aqueduct* also carries water but is much larger.

4. **deduce** (dĭ-dōōs′) *verb*   To reach a conclusion by logical reasoning. (From the Latin *de-*, meaning "away," and *ducere*)

   Related Words **deduction** *noun;* **deductive** *adjective*
   Example   When Susan saw that the picnic table was filled with food, she *deduced* that the campers were nearby.

4. _____

5. **induce** (ĭn-dōōs′) *verb*   **a.** To persuade or influence.   **b.** To cause or bring about the occurrence of.   **c.** In reasoning, to reach a general principle from particular facts or instances. (From the Latin *in-*, meaning "in," and *ducere*)

   Related Words **inducement** *noun;* **inductive** *adjective*
   Example   The promise of better working conditions *induced* Charles to change jobs.

5. _____

6. **induction** (ĭn-dŭk′shən) *noun*   The act of being formally admitted to the armed forces or placed in office. (From the Latin *in-*, meaning "in," and *ductus*, meaning "the act of drawing or pulling")

   Related Words **induct** *verb;* **inductee** *noun*
   Example   A large crowd attended the *induction* of the newly elected public officials.

6. _____

7. **productivity** (prō′dŭk-tĭv′ĭ-tē) *noun*   **a.** The ability to produce or manufacture food or goods.   **b.** Abundance of output; output. (From the Latin *pro-*, meaning "forth," and *ducere*)

   Related Words **product** *noun;* **productive** *adjective*
   Example   Farmers increase their *productivity* by using new tractors.

7. _____

8. **reduction** (rĭ-dŭk′shən) *noun*   The act or process of making something smaller. (From the Latin *re-*, meaning "back," and *ducere*)

   Related Word   **reduce** *verb*
   Example   Price *reductions* on all merchandise attracted many people to the sale.

8. _____

9. **subdue** (səb-dōō′) *verb*   **a.** To conquer, quiet, or bring under control. **b.** To make less intense; tone down. (From the Latin *sub-*, meaning "away," and *ducere*)

   Example   With soothing words the speaker *subdued* the noisy audience.

9. _____

10. **viaduct** (vī′ə-dŭkt′) *noun*   A series of spans or arches used to carry a road or railroad over a wide valley or over other roads. (A blend of the Latin word *via*, meaning "road," and the English word *aqueduct*)

    Example   The *viaduct* enabled trains to cross the river.

10. _____

EXERCISE 1 WRITING CORRECT WORDS

On the answer line, write the word from the vocabulary list that fits each definition.

1. The ability to manufacture or produce goods

2. To conquer or to quiet

3. A bridge with arches that supports a road or a railroad

4. To guide or direct

5. The process of decreasing in size or amount

6. To come to a logical conclusion

7. A means of transporting water over long distances

8. To persuade; bring about or cause something to happen

9. A formal installation in office or admittance to the armed forces

10. A channel for transporting liquid or carrying electrical cables

1. _____productivity_____

2. _____subdue_____

3. _____viaduct_____

4. _____conduct_____

5. _____reduction_____

6. _____deduce_____

7. _____aqueduct_____

8. _____induce_____

9. _____induction_____

10. _____conduit_____

EXERCISE 2 USING WORDS CORRECTLY

Each of the following statements contains an italicized vocabulary word. Decide whether the sentence is true or false, and write *True* or *False* on the answer line.

1. The type of furniture in a farmhouse affects the farm's *productivity*.

2. To *conduct* people through the zoo, you should walk away from them.

3. Plumbers and electricians work with *conduits*.

4. People often ride underwater in a *viaduct*.

5. You could reasonably *deduce* that a person walking with the aid of a guide dog is blind.

6. *Induction* occurs when a person resigns from a public office.

7. A mother might *subdue* her son if he fell asleep at a play.

8. An *aqueduct* could make farming possible in a dry region.

9. A *reduction* in food intake helps people to lose weight.

10. Trainers *induce* seals to perform tricks by offering them fish.

1. _____False_____

2. _____False_____

3. _____True_____

4. _____False_____

5. _____True_____

6. _____False_____

7. _____False_____

8. _____True_____

9. _____True_____

10. _____True_____

EXERCISE 3 CHOOSING THE BEST WORD

Decide which vocabulary word or related form best expresses the meaning of the italicized word or phrase in the sentence. On the answer line, write the letter of the correct choice.

1. The workers needed two weeks to repair the sagging *bridge*.
   a. reduction   **b.** viaduct   **c.** deduction   **d.** induction

1. _____b_____

2. The children could not *persuade* their busy father to drive them to the beach.
   a. subdue **b.** conduct **c.** deduce **d.** induce

   2. _____d_____

3. The company's *making of goods* slowed down after many employees became ill with the flu.
   a. productivity **b.** conduit **c.** reduction **d.** induction

   3. _____a_____

4. Was John able to *conclude by reasoning* that school closed early because of the snow?
   a. conduit **b.** subdue **c.** deduce **d.** conduct

   4. _____c_____

5. The *channel for transporting water* in the area had sprung a leak.
   a. reduction **b.** induction **c.** aquaduct **d.** viaduct

   5. _____c_____

6. The *formal installation* of the president took place yesterday.
   a. conduit **b.** induction **c.** reduction **d.** productivity

   6. _____b_____

7. The politician *directed* the discussion in a loud manner.
   a. conducted **b.** subdued **c.** induced **d.** deduced

   7. _____a_____

8. Janet was delighted about the *decrease* in homework.
   a. viaduct **b.** reduction **c.** productivity **d.** conduit

   8. _____b_____

9. The baby sitter was unable to *quiet* the noisy five-year-old.
   a. induct **b.** conduct **c.** deduce **d.** subdue

   9. _____d_____

10. The *pipe for transporting water* through the park is very convenient for campers.
    a. induction **b.** viaduct **c.** conduit **d.** reduction

    10. _____c_____

EXERCISE 4 USING DIFFERENT FORMS OF WORDS

Decide which form of the vocabulary word in parentheses best completes the sentence. The form given may be correct. Write your answer on the answer line.

1. Viewing a frightening movie is not _____ to getting a good night's sleep. *(conduct)*

   1. _____conducive_____

2. During the ceremony, the club will _____ five new members. *(induction)*

   2. _____induct_____

3. The frantic robbery victim was not easily _____. *(subdue)*

   3. _____subdued_____

4. To meet deadlines, newspaper reporters must be _____. *(productivity)*

   4. _____productive_____

5. Susan built a miniature _____ for her school project. *(viaduct)*

   5. _____viaduct_____

6. The detective made a _____ concerning the crime. *(deduce)*

   6. _____deduction_____

7. The builder ordered a new supply of _____. *(conduit)*

   7. _____conduits_____

8. The Winslows hoped to _____ the amount of clutter in their cellar. *(reduction)*

   8. _____reduce_____

9. The promise of a picnic was an effective _____. *(induce)*

   9. _____inducement_____

10. The ancient _____ were of great interest to the tourists. *(aqueduct)*

    10. _____aqueducts_____

READING COMPREHENSION

Each numbered sentence in the following passage contains an italicized vocabulary word. After you read the passage, you will complete an exercise.

THE BABY SITTER

My friends tried to caution me about baby-sitting for nine-year-old Elizabeth Meyers. (1) "No matter how much money Mrs. Meyers offers to pay, don't let her *induce* you to watch Elizabeth!" they warned.

I didn't tell them that Mrs. Meyers had already offered me double my usual rate, which I had gratefully accepted. After all, how noisy and out-of-control could one nine-year-old be? (2) Plenty of times in the past, I had *subdued* several screaming children and still got my homework done.

I was ready for anything when I arrived. (3) Elizabeth opened the front door and *conducted* me into the living room. She looked like a pleasant well-behaved little girl until her critical eyes studied me from head to toe.

"Well, Amanda," she said, wearing a look of superiority, "it's pretty obvious why you took this job. (4) I can *deduce* from your appearance that you need the money for new clothes."

I was speechless as Mrs. Meyers appeared, dressed to go out. "I'm off to the library," Elizabeth's mother explained. (5) "I'm working on my master's degree, and I'm eager to increase my *productivity*. It's sometimes difficult to concentrate at home." Her eyes wandered to Elizabeth.

"Just call me if you get stuck, Mom," Elizabeth advised.

"Elizabeth is quite advanced

for her age," Mrs. Meyers whispered to me before making a hasty exit.

After Mrs. Meyers closed the door behind her, Elizabeth smiled slyly. "I've had many baby sitters," she said.

"Oh, really?"

"Mm-hm. (6) But in my opinion, most of them had experienced a severe *reduction* in intelligence somewhere along the line. I hope you're not like that."

I felt the need to defend myself. "I'm smart. I get good grades."

"If you say so." Elizabeth smiled her infuriating smile. "Well, what plans do you have to entertain me?"

"I could read you a story, but I

guess you don't read children's books. How about a game?"

"Yes, let's play something on my computer. (7) As far as I'm concerned, the computer is the best *conduit* to all kinds of interesting information. Fascinating Facts is my favorite game." Elizabeth led me to the den and turned on the computer. "Pick a field you know something about."

"History," I said, with some degree of confidence.

(8) "What year was Vice President Daniel D. Tompkins *inducted* into office?" Elizabeth asked.

"Uh, who was President that year?"

Elizabeth shook her head. "We'd better go down to the beginner's level. How did Roman engineers transport water to Rome?"

I was silent.

Elizabeth couldn't believe my ignorance. (9) "The Romans transported water through a system of *aqueducts*. (10) These structures are similar to *viaducts*, except that viaducts support roads and train tracks, not channels of water." Elizabeth sighed. "I knew this would be hopeless. What grade did you say you were in?" Elizabeth switched off her computer. "Never mind." Having totally humiliated me, she was unexpectedly sympathetic. "I'll help you with your homework until Mom comes home."

Each of the following statements corresponds to a numbered sentence in the passage. Each statement contains a blank and is followed by four answer choices. Decide which choice fits best in the blank. The word or phrase that you choose must express roughly the same meaning as the italicized word in the passage. Write the letter of your choice on the answer line.

1. Amanda's friends warned her not to be _____ to baby-sit Elizabeth.
   a. offended   **b.** limited   **c.** persuaded   **d.** expected

2. However, Amanda felt that she could _____ noisy children.
   a. control   **b.** entertain   **c.** ignore   **d.** separate

3. Elizabeth _____ the baby sitter into the living room.
   a. followed   **b.** led   **c.** helped   **d.** pushed

4. Elizabeth _____ that Amanda needed money for new clothes.
   a. disagreed   **b.** hoped   **c.** reasoned   **d.** argued

5. Mrs. Meyers went to the library to increase her work _____.
   a. knowledge   **b.** reading   **c.** interest   **d.** output

6. Elizabeth believed that most baby sitters had suffered a _____ in intelligence.
   a. decrease   **b.** increase   **c.** change   **d.** advancement

7. She felt that the computer was a(n) _____ for interesting information.
   a. example   **b.** channel   **c.** helper   **d.** storehouse

8. Elizabeth asked Amanda in what year Daniel Tompkins was _____ as Vice President.
   a. impeached   **b.** elected   **c.** installed   **d.** overruled

9. Amanda didn't know that the Romans transported water through _____.
   a. tunnels   **b.** large channels   **c.** sprinklers   **d.** dams

10. Elizabeth pointed out that _____ are similar to aqueducts in design.
    a. governments   **c.** stone sculptures
    b. irrigation systems   **d.** bridges with arches

1. _____ c _____
2. _____ a _____
3. _____ b _____
4. _____ c _____
5. _____ d _____
6. _____ a _____
7. _____ b _____
8. _____ c _____
9. _____ b _____
10. _____ d _____

See page 119 for some strategies to use with analogies.

Directions   On the answer line, write the vocabulary word or a form of it that completes each analogy.

1. _____ is to early as belated is to late. *(Lesson 11)*

2. Perpetual is to end as _____ is to stop. *(Lesson 11)*

3. Recess is to school as _____ is to work. *(Lesson 11)*

4. Pipeline is to oil as _____ is to water. *(Lesson 12)*

5. Vessel is to blood as _____ is to water. *(Lesson 12)*

6. Inaugurate is to president as _____ is to soldier. *(Lesson 12)*

1. _____ Premature _____
2. _____ incessant _____
3. _____ respite _____
4. _____ aqueduct _____
5. _____ conduit _____
6. _____ induct _____

The **Bonus activity** for Lessons 11 and 12 is on page T12. The **Test** for Lessons 10, 11, and 12 is on page T13.

TEST-TAKING SKILLS

SENTENCE-COMPLETION TESTS

Standardized tests often contain sentence-completion items. These items require you to choose a word or phrase. Use the following strategies to answer sentence-completion test items.

STRATEGIES

1. *Read the directions carefully.* You can lose credit for answers if you fail to follow the directions for answering sentence-completion items.

2. *Read the entire sentence and analyze its structure and probable meaning.* The sentence you are asked to complete will contain a key word or phrase that will guide you to the correct answer.

    The obas of the West African kingdom of Benin were _____ rulers who possessed absolute authority over their people.
    a. powerless   **b.** miscellaneous   **c.** omnivorous   **d.** omnipotent

    In this test item the key phrase is, "possessed absolute authority." Since this phrase is the definition of *omnipotent* the correct answer is *d*.

3. *Read all of the answer choices and eliminate as many wrong answers as you can.* In the test item above, you can eliminate *powerless*. A ruler with absolute authority over his people would not be powerless.

4. *Insert your choice in the blank and read the sentence to make sure your answer makes sense.* A correct answer must sound right in the sentence. Choice *b*, *miscellaneous*, means "made up of a variety of different elements or ingredients." If you insert *miscellaneous* in the blank, the sentence does not make sense.

5. *Be alert for words that look or sound much like the right answer.* Answer choice *c*, *omnivorous* (eating all types of foods), could easily be confused with the correct answer *omnipotent*. Answer choices like *c* are often used to make the question more challenging.

EXERCISE ANSWERING SENTENCE-COMPLETION TEST ITEMS

Choose the word that best completes each of the following sentences. Write the letter of your choice on the answer line. Use your dictionary as needed.

1. The desert valley was completely _____, so dry that even the hardiest plants and animals could not survive.
   a. desolate   **b.** exuberant   **c.** inattentive   **d.** remote

        1. _____ a _____

2. Skilled leaders try to build a _____ because they want everyone to agree on a common goal.
   a. deduction   **b.** dialect   **c.** conduit   **d.** consensus

        2. _____ d _____

3. Confident and optimistic by nature, Amir became even more _____ when he received a promotion and a raise.
   a. frail   **b.** tardy   **c.** subdued   **d.** exuberant

        3. _____ d _____

4. She was a woman of amazing contrasts: periods of _____ alternated with periods of great exuberance.
   a. distress   **b.** congeniality   **c.** defiance   **d.** valor

        4. _____ a _____

5. Although their philosophies differed, Martin Luther King, Jr. and Malcolm X were _____ who lived and worked during the same time period.
   a. neighbors   **c.** contemporaries
   b. accomplices   **d.** enemies

        5. _____ c _____

6. A small fire left by a careless camper sparked a _____ that destroyed the entire forest.
   a. flood   **b.** confrontation   **c.** conflagration   **d.** fight

        6. _____ c _____

7. The house featured a _____ view of the entire bay.
   a. stressful   **b.** panoramic   **c.** worthless   **d.** defiant

        7. _____ b _____

8. During the Persian Gulf War the United States led a _____ of nations united in their goal of liberating Kuwait.
   a. generation   **b.** coalition   **c.** lineage   **d.** commune

        8. _____ b _____

9. Lauren argued that the _____ attitudes of the island people prevented them from learning new ideas from other cultures.
   a. parental   **b.** congenial   **c.** generic   **d.** insular

        9. _____ d _____

10. Critics of the Vietnam War often referred to it as a _____ that entangled America in a difficult situation.
    a. quagmire   **b.** peninsula   **c.** precipice   **d.** meridian

        10. _____ a _____

People are constantly trying to improve their lives and abilities. Even as adults, many people learn to speak a new language, to cook, or to play a sport. Improvement is a lifelong process.

When people give help, they try to improve something. For example, one might help a friend with mathematics, and then that friend might get an improved score on the next math test.

The words in this lesson are about improving and helping. These words will increase your ability to communicate about ways of making things better.

WORD LIST

abet
deliverance
ennoble
expedite
intercede
offset
pacify
refurbish
reinforce
sanctuary

DEFINITIONS

After you have studied the definitions and example for each vocabulary word, write the word on the line to the right.

1. **abet** (ə-bĕt′) *verb* To encourage or assist, particularly in doing something wrong.

   Related Word **abettor, abetter** *noun*
   Example One who *abets* the criminal actions of another may also be found guilty of a crime.

   1. _____

2. **deliverance** (dĭ-lĭv′ər-əns) *noun* **a.** Rescue from danger. **b.** Liberation. (From the Latin word *liber*, meaning "free")

   Related Word **deliver** *verb*
   Example Farmers hoped for rain to bring them *deliverance* from the dry weather.

   2. _____

3. **ennoble** (ĕn-nō′bəl) *verb* To add to the honor of; make finer or more noble in nature. (From the Latin word *nobilis*, meaning "noble")

   Example Good deeds *ennoble* those who perform them.

   3. _____

4. **expedite** (ĕk′spĭ-dīt′) *verb* **a.** To speed or ease the progress of; assist. **b.** To perform quickly and efficiently. (From the Latin word *expedire*, meaning "to set free")

   Related Words **expeditious** *adjective;* **expeditiously** *adverb*
   Example We shall *expedite* the delivery of the package by sending it through a special mail service.

   4. _____

5. **intercede** (ĭn′tər-sēd′) *verb*   To ask for help for or plead for another person. (From the Latin *inter-*, meaning "between," and *cedere*, meaning "to go")

5. _____

   Related Word   **intercession** *noun*
   Example   Dominic *interceded* with his parents on behalf of his younger brother, who wanted to go to the carnival with him.

6. **offset** (ôf′sĕt′) *verb*   To make up for; compensate for; counteract.
   noun (ôf′sĕt′)   Something that balances, compensates, or counteracts.

6. _____

   Example   The runner *offset* her slow time on the first lap by speeding up the pace on the second lap.

7. **pacify** (păs′ə-fī′) *verb*   **a.** To ease the anger or agitation of; calm.   **b.** To establish peace in; end fighting or violence in. (From the Latin words *pax*, meaning "peace," and *facere*, meaning "to make")

7. _____

   Related Words   **pacification** *noun;* **pacifier** *noun*
   Example   When the singer failed to perform at the concert, the management issued refunds to *pacify* the crowd.

8. **refurbish** (rē-fûr′bĭsh) *verb*   To clean, renew, repair, or refresh.

8. _____

   Example   We wanted to *refurbish* the apartment before we moved in, so we hired someone to paint it.

9. **reinforce** (rē′ĭn-fôrs′) *verb*   To strengthen; give more effectiveness to; support.

9. _____

   Related Word   **reinforcement** *noun*
   Example   The citizens' requests for a new hospital were *reinforced* by the mayor's speech.

10. **sanctuary** (săngk′chōo-ĕr′ē) *noun*   **a.** Any place of safety or protection. **b.** A holy place; a house of worship. (From the Latin word *sanctus*, meaning "sacred")

10. _____

   Example   Many different kinds of animals roam freely in the wildlife *sanctuary*.

EXERCISE 1 MATCHING WORDS AND DEFINITIONS

Match the definition in Column B with the word in Column A. Write the letter of the correct definition on the answer line.

Column A

1. deliverance
2. refurbish
3. expedite
4. sanctuary
5. ennoble
6. reinforce
7. pacify
8. intercede
9. abet
10. offset

Column B

a. To ask for help for another person
b. To encourage in doing wrong
c. Rescue from danger
d. To calm; establish peace in
e. To clean, renew, or refresh
f. To make up for; counteract
g. To add to the honor of
h. To speed the progress of; perform efficiently
i. To strengthen; support
j. A place of safety or protection

1. _____ c _____
2. _____ e _____
3. _____ h _____
4. _____ j _____
5. _____ g _____
6. _____ i _____
7. _____ d _____
8. _____ a _____
9. _____ b _____
10. _____ f _____

EXERCISE 2 USING WORDS CORRECTLY

Each of the following statements contains an italicized vocabulary word. Decide whether the sentence is true or false, and write *True* or *False* on the answer line.

1. Sometimes only food will *pacify* a crying baby.
2. When someone *abets* a prank, that person helps another to commit it.
3. People often send important mail by special *deliverance*.
4. An employer can always *expedite* work by sending the workers on vacation.
5. In construction, steel is often used to *reinforce* concrete blocks.
6. A *sanctuary* is usually a safe place to hide.
7. Weather, time, and neglect will gradually *refurbish* the exterior of a house.
8. If you *intercede* your flower bed, you will have flowers in bloom all summer long.
9. Spending money will help *offset* one's debts.
10. Helping others can *ennoble* a person's life.

1. _____ True _____
2. _____ True _____
3. _____ False _____
4. _____ False _____
5. _____ True _____
6. _____ True _____
7. _____ False _____
8. _____ False _____

9. _____ False _____
10. _____ True _____

EXERCISE 3 CHOOSING THE BEST DEFINITION

For each italicized vocabulary word in the following sentences, write the letter of the best definition on the answer line.

1. Those who *abet* criminals are liable to be prosecuted.
   a. please   b. assist   c. defend   d. trick

2. All the students were asking for *deliverance* from the final examination.
   a. surrender   b. transfer   c. rescue   d. security

1. _____ b _____

2. _____ c _____

3. After his defeat by English forces at Culloden Moor in 1746, Bonnie
Prince Charlie found *sanctuary* in Scotland.
   a. direction
   b. a place of safety
   c. peace
   d. a new place to live

3. _____ b _____

4. Genevieve will *refurbish* her old coat by cleaning and shortening it and
adding new buttons.
   a. renew b. retain c. resell d. trade

4. _____ a _____

5. Treating his tenant farmers badly did not *ennoble* the squire.
   a. enliven
   b. enrich
   c. harm the reputation of
   d. add to the honor of

5. _____ d _____

6. The tide turned against Napoleon at the Battle of Waterloo when the
Prussians arrived to *reinforce* the British troops under Wellington.
   a. rout b. strengthen c. restrict d. lead

6. _____ b _____

7. Groups often try to *expedite* the passage of bills by lobbying members of
Congress.
   a. slow b. speed c. influence d. block

7. _____ b _____

8. To *pacify* her mother, Simone promised to write twice a week while
traveling.
   a. rouse b. help c. calm d. please

8. _____ c _____

9. The team's early losses were *offset* by wins later in the season.
   a. counteracted b. overcome c. excused d. worsened

9. _____ a _____

10. The princess *interceded* with her father to free the prisoner.
   a. argued b. conspired c. agreed d. pleaded

10. _____ d _____

EXERCISE 4 USING DIFFERENT FORMS OF WORDS

Decide which form of the vocabulary word in parentheses best completes
the sentence. The form given may be correct. Write your answer on the
answer line.

1. The most _____ sea route between the Atlantic and the Pacific is the
Panama Canal. (*expedite*)

1. _____ expeditious _____

2. In ancient times Moses _____ his people out of bondage in Egypt.
(*deliverance*)

2. _____ delivered _____

3. Archie was charged as an _____ of the criminal. (*abet*)

3. _____ abettor _____

4. Dogs can be trained through the _____ of good behavior. (*reinforce*)

4. _____ reinforcement _____

5. _____ the library was a challenging task. (*refurbish*)

5. _____ Refurbishing _____

6. Some people feel that great art _____ human character. (*ennoble*)

6. _____ ennobles _____

7. Not even the _____ of the president could save the bill from defeat.
(*intercede*)

7. _____ intercession _____

8. The diplomats brought about the _____ of the two nations involved in a
dispute. (*pacify*)

8. _____ pacification _____

9. The _____ was a quiet refuge from the noise and bustle of the city.
(*sanctuary*)

9. _____ sanctuary _____

10. The small company had to raise prices as a means of _____ its losses.
(*offset*)

10. _____ offsetting _____

READING COMPREHENSION

Each numbered sentence in the following passage contains an italicized vocabulary word or related form. After you read the passage, you will complete an exercise.

VICTORY AT MARATHON

The victory of the small Greek democracy of Athens over the mighty Persian empire in 490 B.C. is one of the most famous events in history. **(1)** Darius, king of the Persian empire, was furious because Athens had *interceded* for the other Greek city-states in revolt against Persian domination. In anger the king sent an enormous army to defeat Athens. **(2)** He thought it would take steps to *pacify* the rebellious part of the empire.

Persia was ruled by one man. In Athens, however, all citizens helped to rule. **(3)** *Ennobled* by this participation, Athenians were prepared to die for their city-state. Perhaps this was the secret of the remarkable victory at Marathon, which freed them from Persian rule.

On their way to Marathon, the Persians tried to fool some Greek city-states by claiming to have come in peace. The frightened citizens of Delos refused to believe this. **(4)** Not wanting to *abet* the conquest of Greece, they fled from their city and did not return until the Persians had left. They were wise, for the Persians next conquered the city of Etria and captured its people.

Tiny Athens stood alone against Persia. **(5)** The Athenian people went to their *sanctuaries*. **(6)** There they prayed for *deliverance*. **(7)** They asked their gods to *expedite* their victory.

(8) The Athenians *refurbished* their weapons and moved to the plain of Marathon, where their little band would meet the Persians. **(9)** At the last moment, soldiers from Plataea *reinforced* the Athenian troops.

The Athenian army attacked, and Greek citizens fought bravely. **(10)** The power of the mighty Persians was *offset* by the love that the Athenians had for their city. Athenians defeated the Persians in archery and hand combat. Greek soldiers seized Persian ships and burned them, and the Persians fled in terror. Herodotus, a famous historian, reports that 6400 Persians died, compared with only 192 Athenians.

READING COMPREHENSION EXERCISE

Each of the following statements corresponds to a numbered sentence in the passage. Each statement contains a blank and is followed by four answer choices. Decide which choice fits best in the blank. The word or phrase that you choose must express roughly the same meaning as the italicized word in the passage. Write the letter of your choice on the answer line.

1. Athens had _____ the other Greek city-states against the Persians.
   a. wanted to fight
   b. intervened on behalf of
   c. provided reasons for
   d. refused help to

   1. _____**b**_____

2. Darius took drastic steps to _____ the rebellious Athenians.
   a. weaken   b. destroy   c. calm   d. raise

   2. _____**c**_____

3. Their participation _____ to the Athenians.
   a. gave comfort
   b. gave honor
   c. gave strength
   d. gave safety

   3. _____**b**_____

4. The people of Delos did not want to _____ the conquest of Greece.
   a. end   b. encourage   c. allow   d. think about

5. The Athenian people went to their _____ and prayed.
   a. homes   b. priests   c. gatherings   d. holy places

6. They prayed for _____.
   a. rain   b. rescue   c. defeat   d. riches

7. The Athenians asked their gods to _____ their victory.
   a. join   b. encourage   c. speed   d. watch

8. The Athenians _____ their weapons and moved to the plain of Marathon.
   a. repaired   b. threw out   c. replaced   d. grabbed

9. The Athenians were _____ by some soldiers who arrived from Plataea.
   a. welcomed   b. strengthened c. held   d. awaited

10. The power of the Persians was _____ by the love that the Athenians had
    for Athens.
    a. made stronger b. increased   c. required   d. counteracted

4. _____ b
5. _____ d
6. _____ b
7. _____ c
8. _____ a
9. _____ b
10. _____ d

WRITING ASSIGNMENT

Government and businesses have often tried to improve the quality of
people's lives. Choose one example of a government agency or a business
renovating a historic building, protecting parkland, helping the disabled, or
making any similar improvement. Write a paragraph explaining the program.
Use at least five words from this lesson in your paragraph and underline them.

VOCABULARY ENRICHMENT

The term *marathon*, widely used to describe any difficult task or contest
requiring great effort and endurance, is derived from the plain of Marathon,
where the Athenians defeated the Persians. After the battle of Marathon, an
Athenian soldier ran from Marathon to Athens, a distance of approximately
twenty-six miles, to announce to the citizens of Athens the victory over the
Persians. Today races of this length are run in many cities throughout the
world and are known as *marathons.*

Activity *Marathon* is one of many words in English derived from the names
of places. Using a dictionary that includes etymologies, identify the origin of
the following words, write a definition for each word, and use each word in a
sentence.

1. cashmere 2. dollar 3. meander 4. tuxedo

Mark Twain, in his novel *Pudd'nhead Wilson,* comments, "It were not best that we should all think alike; it is difference of opinion that makes horse races." Twain seems to indicate that differences of opinion keep life interesting.

Sometimes disagreement may lead to a better understanding or a changed attitude. At other times, disagreement may result in hurt feelings or a stubborn refusal to listen to another's point of view. The words in this lesson describe different aspects and different outcomes of disputes.

WORD LIST

adversary
aggression
contradict
controversy
discord
embroil
haggle
skirmish
stalemate
strife

DEFINITIONS

After you have studied the definitions and example for each vocabulary word, write the word on the line to the right.

1. **adversary** (ăd′vər-sĕr′ē) *noun*   An opponent; enemy. (From the Latin word *adversus,* meaning "against")

   Example   The *adversaries* had a spirited debate on television.

   1. _____

2. **aggression** (ə-grĕsh′ən) *noun*   **a.** The act of beginning an invasion; a bold, unprovoked attack.   **b.** Hostile action or behavior. (From the Latin *ad-,* meaning "toward," and *gradi,* meaning "to advance")

   Related Words   **aggressive** *adjective;* **aggressively** *adverb*
   Example   The defenseless country was not prepared for the *aggression* of its warlike neighbor.

   2. _____

3. **contradict** (kŏn′trə-dĭkt′) *verb*   **a.** To express the opposite of.   **b.** To deny the statement of.   **c.** To be inconsistent with; be contrary to. (From the Latin *contra-,* meaning "against," and *dicere,* meaning "to say")

   Related Words   **contradiction** *noun;* **contradictory** *adjective*
   Example   On the radio show, the caller *contradicted* several of the guest's ideas.

   3. _____
   See *controversy.*

4. **controversy** (kŏn′trə-vûr′sē) *noun*   **a.** A public dispute between sides holding opposing views.   **b.** Argument or debate. (From the Latin *contra-,* meaning "against," and *vertere,* meaning "to turn")

   Related Word   **controversial** *adjective*
   Example   The sale of the forest preserve to commercial developers sparked *controversy* in the community.

   4. _____
   MEMORY CUE: In a *controversy,* people *contradict* one another.

5. **discord** (dĭs′kôrd′) *noun*   **a.** A lack of agreement between or among persons or groups.   **b.** A combination of harsh or unpleasant sounds or musical tones; dissonance. (From the Latin *dis-*, meaning "apart," and *cor*, meaning "heart")

> **Related Word**   **discordant** *adjective*
> **Example**   The *discord* among the committee members was noticeable as soon as the meeting began.

5. _____
See *skirmish*.

6. **embroil** (ĕm-broil′) *verb*   **a.** To involve in an argument or conflict.   **b.** To throw into confusion or disorder; entangle. (From the French word *embrouiller*, meaning "to tangle")

> **Related Word**   **embroiled** *verb*
> **Example**   The traffic accident *embroiled* the drivers of the two cars in an argument.

6. _____

7. **haggle** (hăg′əl) *verb*   **a.** To bargain, as over the price of something.   **b.** To argue in an attempt to come to terms.

> **Related Word**   **haggler** *noun*
> **Example**   Many people enjoy shopping at flea markets because they can *haggle* over prices.

7. _____

8. **skirmish** (skûr′mĭsh) *noun*   **a.** A minor battle between small groups of troops, often as part of a larger battle.   **b.** A minor or preliminary conflict or disagreement.   *verb*   To engage in a skirmish. (From the Old French word *eskermir*, meaning "to fight with a sword")

> **Example**   The first battle at Bull Run was a *skirmish* between Union and Confederate troops.

8. _____
USAGE NOTE: A *skirmish* is a fight, whereas a *discord* is lack of agreement.

9. **stalemate** (stāl′māt′) *noun*   **a.** A situation in which action or progress has come to a halt; a deadlock.   **b.** A situation in chess in which neither player can win.

> **Example**   Union and management reached a *stalemate* in their negotiations.

9. _____

10. **strife** (strīf) *noun*   **a.** Bitter conflict; heated and often violent disagreement.   **b.** A struggle between rivals.

> **Example**   Fearing for their lives, people fled the *strife* in their homeland and took refuge in a neighboring country.

10. _____

EXERCISE 1 COMPLETING DEFINITIONS

On the answer line, write the word from the vocabulary list that best completes each definition.

1. A dispute between sides holding opposing views is called a(n) _____.

2. People who like to bargain over the price of something like to _____.

3. A bold, unprovoked attack is an act of _____.

4. When progress in a situation has stopped, there is a(n) _____.

5. An opponent or enemy is a(n) _____.

6. Bitter conflict or violent disagreement is _____.

7. A minor battle or a preliminary conflict is a(n) _____.

8. To involve someone in an argument is to _____ that person.

9. If you deny or oppose an idea, you _____ it.

10. A lack of agreement between people is called _____.

1. _____controversy_____
2. _____haggle_____
3. _____aggression_____
4. _____stalemate_____
5. _____adversary_____
6. _____strife_____
7. _____skirmish_____
8. _____embroil_____
9. _____contradict_____
10. _____discord_____

EXERCISE 2 USING WORDS CORRECTLY

Decide whether the italicized vocabulary word has been used correctly in the sentence. On the answer line, write *Correct* for correct use and *Incorrect* for incorrect use.

1. Before the football season starts, the coach divides our team for practice *skirmishes*.

2. Loretta enjoys the *strife* of sleep after a hard day's work.

3. The town is *embroiled* in a disagreement about cable television.

4. Proud Dancer is the *stalemate* of the famous thoroughbred Citation.

5. Judge Smith is an *adversary* of injustice.

6. The witness *contradicted* his earlier testimony.

7. The *controversy* over who could run faster ended when Leah beat Ray.

8. "If you want to open those curtains, Jessica, pull the *discord* on the left," said Grandmother.

9. Because of his *aggressive* behavior, Marty had to sit in the penalty box during the hockey game.

10. Terry had to *haggle* behind the other hikers because of a sprained ankle.

1. _____Incorrect_____
2. _____Incorrect_____
3. _____Correct_____
4. _____Incorrect_____
5. _____Correct_____
6. _____Correct_____
7. _____Correct_____
8. _____Incorrect_____
9. _____Correct_____
10. _____Incorrect_____

EXERCISE 3 CHOOSING THE BEST WORD

Decide which vocabulary word or related form best completes the sentence, and write the letter of your choice on the answer line.

1. Emma and Josie become _____ on the tennis court.
   a. stalemates **b.** hagglers **c.** adversaries **d.** contradictions

1. _____c_____

2. My dad _____ with the dealer until he gets a good price on a car.
   a. haggles   **b.** contradicts   **c.** embroils   **d.** discords

2. _____ a _____

3. The governor expected that no one on his staff would _____ him.
   a. haggle   **b.** contradict   **c.** discord   **d.** embroil

3. _____ b _____

4. Garth's resignation ended the _____ with his boss.
   a. strife   **b.** aggression   **c.** adversary   **d.** contradiction

4. _____ a _____

5. The principal refused to state her opinion on the _____ concerning the school dance.
   a. aggression   **b.** adversary   **c.** haggle   **d.** controversy

5. _____ d _____

6. The crowd just wants to _____ you in a dispute.
   a. haggle   **b.** embroil   **c.** contradict   **d.** discord

6. _____ b _____

7. The _____ between the fans of the two teams reached a peak at last night's game.
   a. contradiction   **b.** adversary   **c.** discord   **d.** stalemate

7. _____ c _____

8. The referee warned Cindy that she would be penalized if she could not control her _____.
   a. skirmish   **b.** adversary   **c.** discord   **d.** aggression

8. _____ d _____

9. The newspaper misrepresented the _____ by calling it a battle.
   a. skirmish   **b.** adversary   **c.** contradiction   **d.** stalemate

9. _____ a _____

10. Contract negotiations between management and players reached a _____.
    a. contradiction   **b.** skirmish   **c.** stalemate   **d.** strife

10. _____ c _____

EXERCISE 4 USING DIFFERENT FORMS OF WORDS

Decide which form of the vocabulary word in parentheses best completes the sentence. The form given may be correct. Write your answer on the answer line.

1. Senator Matthews tried to ease the _____ caused by his statements. (*embroil*)

1. _____ embroilment _____

2. The teacher was concerned about the child's _____ behavior on the playground. (*aggression*)

2. _____ aggressive _____

3. The _____ between his two children caused Mr. Hooper much sorrow. (*strife*)

3. _____ strife _____

4. Professor Bevilaqua and Professor Strate have _____ political views. (*discord*)

4. _____ discordant _____

5. Jon learned to be a successful _____ by watching his boss. (*haggle*)

5. _____ haggler _____

6. The outcome of the final _____ will determine which team wins Capture-the-Flag. (*skirmish*)

6. _____ skirmish _____

7. The Senate reached a _____ on the new tax bill. (*stalemate*)

7. _____ stalemate _____

8. The Bulldogs won on a _____ call by the umpire. (*controversy*)

8. _____ controversial _____

9. Although the two attorneys were _____, they managed to work out a solution. (*adversary*)

9. _____ adversaries _____

10. Celina's _____ statements about where she had been aroused our suspicion. (*contradict*)

10. _____ contradictory _____

READING COMPREHENSION

Each numbered sentence in the following passage contains an italicized vocabulary word or related form. After you read the passage, you will complete the exercise.

THE APPLE OF DISCORD

The Trojan War is one of the most famous wars in history. It is well known for its ten-year duration, for the heroism of a number of legendary characters, and for the Trojan horse. What may not be familiar, however, is the story of how the war began.

(1) According to Greek myth, the *strife* between the Trojans and the Greeks started at the wedding of Peleus, King of Thessaly, and Thetis, a sea nymph. (2) All of the gods and goddesses had been invited to the wedding celebration in Troy except Eris, goddess of *discord.* (3) She had been omitted from the guest list because her presence always *embroiled* mortals and immortals alike in conflict.

(4) To take revenge on those who had slighted her, Eris decided to cause a *skirmish.* Into the middle of the banquet hall, she threw a golden apple marked "for the most beautiful." (5) All of the goddesses began to *haggle* over who should possess it. (6) The gods and goddesses reached a *stalemate* when the choice was narrowed to Hera, Athena, and Aphrodite. (7) Someone was needed to settle the *controversy* by picking a winner. The job eventually fell to Paris, son of King Priam of Troy, who was said to be a good judge of beauty.

Paris did not have an easy job. (8) Each goddess, eager to win the golden apple, tried *aggressively* to bribe him.

"I'll grant you vast kingdoms to rule," promised Hera.

(9) "Vast kingdoms are nothing in comparison with my gift," *contradicted* Athena. "Choose me and I'll see that you win victory and fame in war."

(10) Aphrodite outdid her *adversaries,* however. She won the golden apple by offering Helen, Zeus' daughter and the most beautiful mortal, to Paris.

Paris, anxious to claim Helen, set off for Sparta in Greece. Although Paris learned that Helen was married, he accepted the hospitality of her husband, King Menelaus of Sparta, anyway. Therefore, Menelaus was outraged for a number of reasons when Paris departed, taking Helen and much of the king's wealth back to Troy. Menelaus collected his loyal forces and set sail for Troy to begin the war to reclaim Helen.

READING COMPREHENSION EXERCISE

Each of the following statements corresponds to a numbered sentence in the passage. Each statement contains a blank and is followed by four answer choices. Decide which choice fits best in the blank. The word or phrase that you choose must express roughly the same meaning as the italicized word in the passage. Write the letter of your choice on the answer line.

1. The _____ between the Greeks and the Trojans began at a wedding.
   a. game   **b.** conflict   **c.** history   **d.** debate

   1. ____**b**____

2. Eris, the goddess of _____, was not invited to the wedding.
   a. love   **b.** war   **c.** music   **d.** disagreement

   2. ____**d**____

3. Eris was known for _____ both mortals and immortals.
   a. scheming against   **c.** keeping aloof from
   b. involving in conflict   **d.** feeling hostile toward

   3. ____**b**____

4. To get revenge, Eris caused a _____.
   a. minor battle   **b.** hurricane   **c.** problem   **d.** major mistake

   4. _____ a

5. The goddesses _____ who should win the apple.
   a. argued about   **b.** decided on   **c.** voted for   **d.** ignored

   5. _____ a

6. They reached a _____ when the choice was narrowed to three of the goddesses.
   a. decision   **b.** majority   **c.** deadlock   **d.** conclusion

   6. _____ c

7. Someone was needed to settle the _____.
   a. debt   **b.** group   **c.** dispute   **d.** problem

   7. _____ c

8. Each goddess tried _____ to bribe Paris.
   a. boldly   **b.** quietly   **c.** secretly   **d.** effectively

   8. _____ a

9. Athena _____ Hera, promising Paris victory and fame in war.
   a. denied the statement of   **c.** agreed with
   b. defeated   **d.** laughed at

   9. _____ a

10. Aphrodite outdid her _____.
    a. friends   **b.** sisters   **c.** students   **d.** opponents

    10. _____ d

WRITING ASSIGNMENT

Imagine that your class is working on a debate unit. In preparation for your debate, your teacher has asked you to write a practice dialogue between two student debaters. Choose a topic that is appropriate for a debate, such as the pros and cons of a school dress code. Show how each student would present his or her side of the issue. In your dialogue use at least four vocabulary words from this lesson and underline them.

VOCABULARY ENRICHMENT

Discord, as you have already learned, comes from the Latin *dis-,* meaning "apart," and *cor,* meaning "heart." The word *discord* has an interesting connection with the heart. People once associated the heart with certain characteristics and capabilities, such as memory, bravery, and friendliness. We have preserved this association in modern expressions such as *to learn by heart, to have heart,* and *kindhearted.*

   In *discord* the prefix *dis-* gives the major clue to the meaning of the word. If you are "apart" from the heart, you are "apart from friendliness," or ready for an argument. Consequently, for us *discord* has taken on its current meaning— "disagreement."

Activity   In a high school or college dictionary, look up the following words, all of which are derived from the root *-cor-.* Write the meaning and Latin etymology of each word. Then write an explanation of the connection between the etymology and definition.

1. concord   2. cordial   3. discourage   4. encourage   5. record

The **Bonus activity** for Lessons 13 and 14 is on page T15.

The Latin roots -*clam*- and -*voc*- are the foundations of many of our English words. In Latin the word *clamare* means "to cry or call out." Therefore, if you *proclaim* something, you call it out officially and publicly. If you *exclaim*, you cry out from surprise or emotion. A second Latin word, *vocare*, means "to call." If you *convoke* a meeting, you call together or assemble a group. If you make an *irrevocable* decision, you make a decision that cannot be called back. In this lesson you will study words that are derived from the roots -*clam*- and -*voc*- as well as from their related forms, -*claim*- and -*voke*-.

DEFINITIONS

After you have studied the definitions and example for each vocabulary word, write the word on the line to the right.

1. **claimant** (klā′mənt) *noun*   One who makes a claim or asks for something that he or she believes rightfully belongs to him or her. (From the Latin word *clamare*, meaning "to call out")

   Related Words   **claim** *verb*; **claimable** *adjective*
   Example   During the conquest of the New World, both Spain and Portugal were *claimants* to all of South America.

   1. _____

2. **clamor** (klăm′ər) *noun*   **a.** A loud, continuous noise.   **b.** A strong expression of discontent or protest; public outcry.   *verb*   To make insistent demands or complaints. (From the Latin word *clamare*)

   Related Words   **clamorous** *adjective*; **clamorously** *adverb*
   Example   The *clamor* of rush-hour traffic prevented Gary from concentrating on his book.

   2. _____

3. **declaim** (dĭ-klām′) *verb*   **a.** To speak loudly and forcefully.   **b.** To deliver a formal speech. (From the Latin word *declamare*, meaning "to make speeches")

   Related Words   **declamation** *noun*; **declamatory** *adjective*
   Example   Patrick Henry *declaimed* for liberty.

   3. _____

4. **disclaim** (dĭs-klām′) *verb*   **a.** To deny or give up any claim to or connection with; disown.   **b.** To reject as untrue. (From the Latin *dis-*, meaning "reversal of," and *clamare*)

   Related Word   **disclaimer** *noun*
   Example   The senator *disclaimed* any involvement with the scandal.

   4. _____

5. **evocative** (ĭ-vŏk′ə-tĭv) *adjective*   **a.** Tending to call to mind or memory.   **b.** Tending to create anew through the power of the memory or imagination: *an evocative poem.* (From the Latin *ex-*, meaning "out," and *vocare*, meaning "to call")

   Related Word   **evoke** *verb*
   Example   Driving down the street where she had grown up was an *evocative* experience for Sheila.

5. _____

6. **invoke** (ĭn-vōk′) *verb*   **a.** To call upon for assistance, support, or inspiration.   **b.** To use or apply: *The president invoked his veto power.* (From the Latin *in-*, meaning "in," and *vocare*)

   Related Word   **invocation** *noun*
   Example   The family *invoked* the help of their friends.

6. _____

7. **reclaim** (rē-klām′) *verb*   **a.** To ask for the return of something; recover.   **b.** To convert to something better; reform: *to reclaim land.* (From the Latin *re-*, meaning "back" or "again," and *clamare*)

   Related Words   **reclaimable** *adjective;* **reclamation** *noun*
   Example   Alicia *reclaimed* her runaway dog from the pound.

7. _____

8. **revoke** (rĭ-vōk′) *verb*   To cancel or make void by reversing, recalling, or withdrawing. (From the Latin *re-*, meaning "back" or "again," and *vocare*)

   Related Words   **revocable** *adjective;* **revocation** *noun*
   Example   Ms. Slocum *revoked* Nat's library privileges.

8. _____

9. **vocation** (vō-kā′shən) *noun*   **a.** An occupation or profession, especially one for which a person is specially suited or trained.   **b.** A strong desire to do a particular type of work, especially one of a religious nature; a calling. (From the Latin word *vocare*)

   Related Word   **vocational** *adjective*
   Example   After seven summers as a camp counselor, Anita decided that teaching was her *vocation.*

9. _____
MEMORY CUE: A *vocational* school is one that offers training in specific trades or occupations.

10. **vouch** (vouch) *verb*   **a.** To give personal assurance.   **b.** To furnish or serve as a guarantee; supply supporting evidence. (From the Old French word *voucher*, meaning "to summon to court")

   Example   Ms. Gordon *vouched* for Morgan's dependability.

10. _____
USAGE NOTE: *Vouch* is usually followed by a phrase beginning with *for* or clause beginning with *that.*

EXERCISE 1 WRITING CORRECT WORDS

On the answer line, write the word from the vocabulary list that fits each definition.

1. To deliver a formal speech; speak forcefully about a subject

2. To ask for the return of something; convert to something better

3. To give personal assurance; supply supporting evidence

4. Tending to call to mind or memory

5. To cancel by reversing or withdrawing

6. One who makes a claim or asks for something that he or she believes rightfully belongs to him or her

7. An occupation or profession for which one is specially suited or trained

8. To call upon for assistance; use or apply

9. A loud noise; a strong expression

10. To deny or give up any claim to; reject as untrue

1. __declaim__

2. __reclaim__

3. __vouch__

4. __evocative__

5. __revoke__

6. __claimant__

7. __vocation__

8. __invoke__

9. __clamor__

10. __disclaim__

EXERCISE 2 USING WORDS CORRECTLY

Decide whether the italicized vocabulary word has been used correctly in the sentence. On the answer line, write *Correct* for correct use and *Incorrect* for incorrect use.

1. Jim is a fine sculptor: his style is *evocative* of Michelangelo's style.

2. A baby kangaroo spends much time in its mother's *vouch*.

3. The *clamor* of hoofs on the cobblestones startled the innkeeper.

4. The Dutch *reclaim* much of their land from the sea.

5. Dolores spent her three weeks of *vocation* water-skiing on Lake Powell.

6. By using ropes, Edmund can *declaim* the mountain faster than anyone else.

7. Hal was the only *claimant* to the reward money.

8. Connie must learn to *revoke* direction several times to complete a perfect figure eight on ice skates.

9. Before Homer created any poetry, he *invoked* the aid of a muse, or guiding spirit.

10. Corinne *disclaimed* any knowledge of who might have broken the window.

1. __Correct__

2. __Incorrect__

3. __Correct__

4. __Correct__

5. __Incorrect__

6. __Incorrect__

7. __Correct__

8. __Incorrect__

9. __Correct__

10. __Correct__

For each italicized vocabulary word in the following sentences, write the letter of the best definition on the answer line.

1. Galileo is one of several *claimants to* the title "Father of Modern Astronomy."
   a. undeserving seekers of   **c.** designators of
   b. candidates for   **d.** originators of

1. _____**b**_____

2. For thousands of years, most astronomers had *vouched* that the earth was the center of the solar system.
   a. asserted as true **b.** hoped   **c.** guessed   **d.** required proof

2. _____**a**_____

3. Galileo *revoked* traditional assumptions of science.
   a. canceled   **b.** strengthened   **c.** proved   **d.** questioned

3. _____**a**_____

4. Galileo's ideas raised a(n) *clamor* among scientists and philosophers.
   a. eyebrow   **b.** question   **c.** plea   **d.** outcry

4. _____**d**_____

5. In *declaiming* his beliefs Galileo caused controversy.
   a. whispering   **c.** forcefully expressing
   b. nervously stuttering   **d.** guessing

5. _____**c**_____

6. Although Galileo *invoked* proof that his theory was true, he could not convince others.
   a. criticized   **b.** used   **c.** forgot   **d.** rejected

6. _____**b**_____

7. Certain leaders wanted Galileo to *disclaim* his theories.
   a. present   **b.** prove   **c.** deny   **d.** burn

7. _____**c**_____

8. These leaders wanted to *reclaim* the reputation of the traditional theories of astronomy.
   a. destroy   **b.** discover   **c.** restore   **d.** irrigate

8. _____**c**_____

9. In Germany Johannes Kepler proposed a theory of the solar system that was *evocative of* Galileo's theory.
   a. tending to call to mind   **c.** the opposite of
   b. more concentrated than   **d.** easier than

9. _____**a**_____

10. Today the study of astronomy is as acceptable to us as any other *vocation*.
    a. hobby   **b.** idea   **c.** science   **d.** occupation

10. _____**d**_____

Decide which form of the vocabulary word in parentheses best completes the sentence. The form given may be correct. Write your answer on the answer line.

1. In Greek myths mortals often made _____ to gods and goddesses. *(invoke)*

1. _____**invocations**_____

2. Rosy _____ that she had won the race. *(claimant)*

2. _____**claimed**_____

3. Joshua wanted to go to a _____ school. *(vocation)*

3. _____**vocational**_____

4. On the editorial page is a _____ stating that views expressed in letters to the editor are not necessarily those of the newspaper. *(disclaim)*

4. _____**disclaimer**_____

5. Vanessa's driver's license can be _____ if she gets another speeding ticket. *(revoke)*

5. _____**revoked**_____

6. The crowd gathered _____ on the Capitol steps. (*clamor*)

7. Each applicant must have a sponsor who will _____ for the applicant's experience. (*vouch*)

8. Uncle Jared's barn is in such a state of disrepair that it is barely _____. (*reclaim*)

9. Senator Moore's _____ did not impress the convention delegates. (*declaim*)

10. When I see Genevieve, her smile _____ the image of her grandfather. (*evocative*)

6. **clamorously**
7. **vouch**
8. **reclaimable**
9. **declamation**
10. **evokes**

READING COMPREHENSION

Each numbered sentence in the following passage contains an italicized vocabulary word. After you read the passage, you will complete an exercise.

THE MYSTERY OF ANASTASIA

One of the most intriguing stories of the Russian Revolution concerns the identity of Anastasia, the youngest daughter of Czar Nicholas II. (1) During his reign over Russia, the Czar had planned to *revoke* many of the harsh laws established by previous czars. (2) Some workers and peasants, however, *clamored* for more rapid social reform. In 1918 a group of these people, known as Bolsheviks, overthrew the government. On July 17 or 18, they murdered the Czar and what was thought to be his entire family.

(3) Although witnesses *vouched* that all the members of the Czar's family had been executed, there were rumors suggesting that Anastasia had survived. Over the years, a number of women claimed to be Grand Duchess Anastasia. (4) Perhaps the best-known *claimant* was Anastasia Tschaikovsky, who was also known as Anna Anderson.

In 1920, eighteen months after the Czar's execution, this terri-

fied young woman was rescued from drowning in a Berlin river. (5) She spent two years in a hospital, where she attempted to *reclaim* her health and shattered mind. The doctors and nurses thought that she resembled Anastasia and questioned her about her background. (6) She *disclaimed* any connection with the Czar's family.

Eight years later, though, she claimed that she *was* Anastasia. She said that she had been rescued by two Russian soldiers after the Czar and the rest of her family had been killed. Two brothers named Tschaikovsky had carried her into Romania. (7) She had married one of the brothers, who had taken her to Berlin and left her there, penniless and without a *vocation*. (8) Unable to *invoke* the aid of her mother's family in Germany, she had tried to drown herself.

During the next few years, scores of the Czar's relatives, ex-servants, and acquaintances

interviewed her. (9) Many of these people said her looks and mannerisms were *evocative* of the Anastasia that they had known. Her grandmother and other relatives denied that she was the real Anastasia, however.

Tired of being accused of fraud, Anastasia immigrated to the United States in 1928 and took the name Anna Anderson. She still wished to prove that she was Anastasia, though, and returned to Germany in 1933 to bring suit against her mother's family. (10) There she *declaimed* to the court, asserting that she was indeed Anastasia and deserved her inheritance.

In 1957, the court decided that it could neither confirm nor deny Anna Anderson's identity. Since then, the issue has been decided by genetic testing. The woman who claimed to be a part of the Russian royal family, Anastasia, was, in fact, of Polish descent.

Each of the following statements corresponds to a numbered sentence in the passage. Each statement contains a blank and is followed by four answer choices. Decide which choice fits best in the blank. The word or phrase that you choose must express roughly the same meaning as the italicized word in the passage. Write the letter of your choice on the answer line.

1. Czar Nicholas II planned to _____ the harsh laws.
   a. enforce   **b.** announce   **c.** cancel   **d.** think about

   1. _____ c

2. Some Russian peasants and workers _____ for social reform.
   a. longed   **b.** cried out   **c.** begged   **d.** worked

   2. _____ b

3. Witnesses _____ that all members of the Czar's family had been executed.
   a. gave assurance   **b.** hoped   **c.** thought   **d.** should have known

   3. _____ a

4. Anastasia Tschaikovsky was _____ the title of Grand Duchess Anastasia.
   a. one who makes a demand for   **c.** holder of
   b. a celebrator of   **d.** named after

   4. _____ a

5. Two years in a hospital helped her to _____ her health.
   a. destroy   **b.** moderate   **c.** deny   **d.** recover

   5. _____ d

6. She _____ any connection with the Czar's family.
   a. denied   **b.** stopped   **c.** whispered   **d.** noted

   6. _____ a

7. Anastasia was without _____ after her husband abandoned her.
   a. friends   **b.** an occupation   **c.** hope   **d.** a home

   7. _____ b

8. She was unable to _____ the aid of her relatives.
   a. locate   **b.** speak about   **c.** call upon   **d.** force

   8. _____ c

9. Many people said that her looks and mannerisms were _____ of Anastasia.
   a. unlike those   **c.** poor imitations
   b. signs of the insanity   **d.** suggestive

   9. _____ d

10. In court she _____, maintaining that she was Anastasia and deserved her inheritance.
    a. finally appeared   **c.** acted as a witness
    b. spoke forcefully   **d.** testified

    10. _____ b

See page 119 for some strategies to use with analogies.

Directions On the answer line, write the vocabulary word or a form of it that completes each analogy.

1. Ally is to support as _____ is to opposition. (*Lesson 14*)

   1. _____ adversary

2. Tiff is to quarrel as _____ is to battle. (*Lesson 14*)

   2. _____ skirmish

3. Reclaim is to land as _____ is to license. (*Lesson 15*)

   3. _____ revoke

4. Argue is to differences as _____ is to prices. (*Lesson 14*)

   4. _____ haggle

5. Aggressor is to hostility as _____ is to assistance. (*Lesson 13*)

   5. _____ abettor

6. Sponge is to absorb as _____ is to calm. (*Lesson 13*)

   6. _____ pacifier

The **Test** for Lessons 13, 14, and 15 is on page T16.

TEST-TAKING SKILLS
SYNONYM TESTS

Many vocabulary tests, including some standardized tests, contain sections on identifying synonyms. A **synonym** is a word close in meaning to another word. (*Synonym* is derived from a Greek term meaning "similar name.") *Sly, tricky, cunning,* and *crafty* are all synonyms.

A synonym test item asks you to identify from several choices the word or phrase *closest* in meaning to the given word. Here are four strategies for answering such test items.

STRATEGIES

1. *Read all of the choices before selecting an answer.* Do not make the mistake of choosing an answer before you have considered all of the possibilities.

2. *Do not be misled by antonym choices.* An **antonym** (a word meaning the opposite of another word) is sometimes given as a choice in synonym items. In the following example, *injure* is an antonym of *protect. Guard* is a synonym, and the correct answer (E).

   PROTECT:

   (A) rebel   (B) handle   (C) injure   (D) lose   (E) guard

3. *Watch for other deceptive choices.* The following example has misleading choices that test your ability to distinguish differences in word meanings.

   REFUGE:

   (F) immigrant   (G) heaven   (H) shelter   (J) park   (K) denial

   The correct answer is *shelter.* An *immigrant* is sometimes a *refugee,* which is a word related to *refuge. Heaven* looks similar to *haven,* a synonym for *refuge.* If you misread the given word as *refuse,* you might choose *denial* for your answer. Finally, *park* could suggest *wildlife refuge.*

4. *Pay attention to roots, prefixes, and suffixes.* By increasing your knowledge of these word parts, you will often be able to define words that you do not know. This ability can be very important when you take vocabulary tests.

Select the one word or phrase whose meaning is closest to the word given in capital letters. Write the letter of your choice on the answer line. Use your dictionary as needed.

1. EXPEND:
   (A) rely   (B) stretch   (C) use up   (D) give off
   (E) purchase

1. _____ C

2. SERENE:
   (F) hot   (G) boring   (H) lazy   (J) peaceful   (K) humid

2. _____ J

3. IRRELEVANT:
   (A) disrespectful   (B) sorrowful   (C) not applicable
   (D) unauthorized   (E) unjust

3. _____ C

4. WANE:
   (F) tell   (G) warn   (H) surprise   (J) encourage
   (K) decrease

4. _____ K

5. INTRACTABLE:
   (A) hard to control   (B) evil   (C) poisonous
   (D) complicated   (E) untraceable

5. _____ A

6. WAFT:
   (F) airship   (G) crash   (H) float   (J) refuse   (K) wade

6. _____ H

7. INDOLENT:
   (A) lazy   (B) guiltless   (C) painful   (D) romantic
   (E) suffering

7. _____ A

8. SERF:
   (F) wave   (G) shrub   (H) tribe   (J) angle   (K) slave

8. _____ K

9. JUDICIOUS:
   (A) hasty   (B) healthful   (C) justifiable   (D) ambitious
   (E) sensible

9. _____ E

10. IMPUGN:
    (F) fall   (G) condemn   (H) stifle   (J) linger   (K) kiss

10. _____ G

11. BREADTH:
    (A) width   (B) height   (C) weight   (D) break
    (E) respiration

11. _____ A

12. RAMBLE:
    (F) propel   (G) wander   (H) hasten   (J) whisper
    (K) perplex

12. _____ G

13. UNANIMOUS:
    (A) differing   (B) in opposition   (C) in agreement
    (D) varied   (E) outstanding

13. _____ C

14. DRAB:
    (F) stylish   (G) dedicated   (H) noisy   (J) uninteresting
    (K) stubborn

14. _____ J

15. SARCASM:
    (A) harmony   (B) monotony   (C) fright   (D) complaint
    (E) scorn

15. _____ E

When people think of government, they generally think of national, state, and local organizations that control public affairs. The term *government* has a much broader application, however. Whenever people attempt to work together, a form of government arises. Groups and organizations cannot operate without some structure to make decisions, carry out tasks, and regulate change. Families, businesses, and schools are only a few of the groups that use different forms of government.

Each of the words in this lesson is related to government. Studying these vocabulary words will increase your understanding of how governments developed, why they are necessary, and how they function.

WORD LIST

anarchy
authoritarian
conservative
delegate
dominion
impeach
inaugurate
liberal
Spartan
tyrant

DEFINITIONS

After you have studied the definitions and example for each vocabulary word, write the word on the line to the right.

1. **anarchy** (ăn′ər-kē) *noun*   **a.** Political and social disorder resulting from an absence of governmental control.   **b.** Chaos; confusion. (From the Greek *an-*, meaning "without," and *arkhos*, meaning "ruler")

   Related Word **anarchist** *noun*
   Example   The country was in a state of *anarchy* after its ruler died.

   1. _____

2. **authoritarian** (ə-thôr′ĭ-târ′ē-ən) *adjective*   Requiring complete obedience to the rule of one person or group.   *noun*   A person who believes in authoritarian policies.

   Related Words **authoritarianism** *noun;* **authority** *noun*
   Example   Under an *authoritarian* government, individual freedom is greatly limited.

   2. _____
   MEMORY CUE: An *authoritarian* leader wields absolute *authority.*

3. **conservative** (kən-sûr′və-tĭv) *adjective*   **a.** Favoring traditional values and existing conditions; tending to oppose change.   **b.** Traditional in style or manners.   *noun*   A person who is moderate, cautious, and restrained. (From the Latin word *conservare*, meaning "to preserve")

   Related Words **conservatism** *noun;* **conservatively** *adverb*
   Example   The *conservative* politician did not support hasty revisions in the income-tax code.

   3. _____

4. **delegate** (dĕl'ĭ-gĭt) *noun* A person chosen to speak and act as the representative of another person or of a group. *verb* (dĕl'ĭ-gāt') To commit or entrust to another: *to delegate tasks.* (From the Latin word *delegatus*, meaning "dispatched")

   Related Word **delegation** *noun*
   Example Sonya was delighted to be her school's *delegate* to the international conference.

4. _____

5. **dominion** (də-mĭn'yən) *noun* **a.** Control or power, particularly of one country over another. **b.** A territory or area of control; domain; realm. (From the Latin word *dominus*, meaning "lord")

   Example Some parts of Africa were once under French *dominion.*

5. _____

6. **impeach** (ĭm-pēch') *verb* To accuse a public official of unacceptable conduct in office. (From the Latin word *impedicare*, meaning "to entangle")

   Related Word **impeachment** *noun*
   Example Andrew Johnson was *impeached* by the House of Representatives in 1868, but the Senate did not find him guilty.

6. _____
   USAGE NOTE: To *impeach* is to accuse. An *impeached* official must then stand trial.

7. **inaugurate** (ĭn-ô'gyə-rāt') *verb* **a.** To install in office by formal ceremony. **b.** To initiate or make a formal beginning.

   Related Words **inaugural** *adjective;* **inauguration** *noun*
   Example The new officers were *inaugurated* at a banquet.

7. _____

8. **liberal** (lĭb'ər-əl) *adjective* **a.** Having political views that favor individual rights, social and economic progress, and the protection of civil liberties. **b.** Tolerant of others; broad-minded. **c.** Tending to give generously. **d.** Generous in amount: *a liberal allowance.* *noun* A person with liberal opinions. (From the Latin word *liber,* meaning "free")

   Related Words **liberalism** *noun;* **liberalize** *verb;* **liberally** *adverb*
   Example The senator supports *liberal* health-care policies.

8. _____

9. **Spartan** (spär'tn) *adjective* Resembling the Spartans of ancient Greece by living in a simple and self-disciplined way.

   Example The athlete followed a *Spartan* routine of training.

9. _____

10. **tyrant** (tī'rənt) *noun* A ruler who exercises power in a harsh, cruel manner; an oppressor.

    Related Words **tyrannical** *adjective;* **tyrannize** *verb;* **tyranny** *noun*
    Example The *tyrant* forbade all subjects to leave the country without his permission.

10. _____

EXERCISE 1 WRITING CORRECT WORDS

On the answer line, write the word from the vocabulary list that fits each definition.

1. Favoring traditional values; a moderate and cautious person
2. Disorder resulting from an absence of governmental control
3. To accuse a public official of unacceptable conduct in office
4. Requiring complete obedience
5. Living in a simple and disciplined way
6. To install a public official by formal ceremony
7. Having political views that favor individual rights, progress, and the protection of civil liberties; broad-minded
8. A harsh ruler
9. A person who represents others
10. Control or power; an area of control

1. _____ conservative _____
2. _____ anarchy _____
3. _____ impeach _____
4. _____ authoritarian _____
5. _____ Spartan _____
6. _____ inaugurate _____
7. _____ liberal _____

8. _____ tyrant _____
9. _____ delegate _____
10. _____ dominion _____

EXERCISE 2 USING WORDS CORRECTLY

Each of the following questions contains an italicized vocabulary word. Decide the answer to the question, and write *Yes* or *No* on the answer line.

1. Is a *tyrant* a ruler who grants citizens a variety of liberties?
2. Would a *conservative* dresser be likely to choose colorful plaids?
3. Does *anarchy* consist of confusion caused by the absence of government?
4. Is a *delegate* a presidential candidate?
5. If you *inaugurate* a new activity, do you begin it?
6. Is a *liberal* person narrow-minded?
7. If public officials are *impeached,* are they placed in office?
8. Does a *Spartan* lifestyle lack luxuries?
9. Would an *authoritarian* person favor independent decision-making by people under him or her?
10. When the thirteen American colonies were ruled by Britain, did they have *dominion* over Britain?

1. _____ No _____
2. _____ No _____
3. _____ Yes _____
4. _____ No _____
5. _____ Yes _____
6. _____ No _____
7. _____ No _____
8. _____ Yes _____
9. _____ No _____
10. _____ No _____

EXERCISE 3 CHOOSING THE BEST DEFINITION

For each italicized vocabulary word in the following sentences, write the letter of the best definition on the answer line.

1. England once held *dominion* over a quarter of the world's people.
   a. fear   **b.** confusion   **c.** control   **d.** discipline

1. _____ c _____

2. To prevent *anarchy,* the Constitution of the United States provides for the orderly transfer of power if a president dies.

   a. disorder   **b.** ambition   **c.** dictatorship   **d.** jealousy

2. _____ a

3. The *authoritarian* ruler jailed several political opponents.

   a. demanding complete obedience
   b. inspiring disobedience
   c. demanding sincere opinions
   d. widely respected

3. _____ a

4. During the 1930s President Franklin Roosevelt *inaugurated* several social welfare programs.

   a. stopped   **b.** designed   **c.** increased   **d.** began

4. _____ d

5. Our waitress was so efficient that we left her a *liberal* tip.

   a. light   **b.** generous   **c.** traditional   **d.** wrong

5. _____ b

6. The convention *delegates* cheered when the nominee was introduced.

   a. supporters   **b.** workers   **c.** opponents   **d.** representatives

6. _____ d

7. The builder gave us a *conservative* estimate for building an addition to our house.

   a. brief   **b.** expensive   **c.** cautious   **d.** incomplete

7. _____ c

8. Angry citizens demanded that the governor be *impeached*.

   a. informed of their objections   **c.** supported
   b. accused of wrong-doing   **d.** encouraged

8. _____ b

9. The king was a *tyrant* who cared nothing about the rights of his subjects.

   a. harsh ruler   **c.** ineffective ruler
   b. weak ruler   **d.** kind ruler

9. _____ a

10. The campers followed a *Spartan* schedule that began at 5:00 A.M.

   a. healthy   **b.** entertaining   **c.** disciplined   **d.** Greek

10. _____ c

EXERCISE 4 USING DIFFERENT FORMS OF WORDS

Decide which form of the vocabulary word in parentheses best completes the sentence. The form given may be correct. Write your answer on the answer line.

1. Some tourists avoid traveling in countries that have _____ governments. *(authoritarian)*

1. authoritarian

2. Three articles of _____ had been proposed against President Nixon before he resigned in 1974. *(impeach)*

2. impeachment

3. The president's _____ takes place on January 20. *(inaugurate)*

3. inauguration

4. Pamela tries to _____ her younger brother. *(tyrant)*

4. tyrannize

5. During the children's play period, the room seems to be in a state of _____. *(anarchy)*

5. anarchy

6. Hortense, who now dresses _____, used to wear ribbons or feathers with every outfit. *(conservative)*

6. conservatively

7. Grant's room took on a _____ appearance after he moved his furniture out. *(Spartan)*

7. Spartan

8. Our school sent a _____ of five students to the city council meeting. *(delegate)*

8. ___delegation___

9. Britain once considered its _____ over the seas to be its best defense. *(dominion)*

9. ___dominion___

10. Max sprinkled his salad _____ with lemon juice. *(liberal)*

10. ___liberally___

READING COMPREHENSION

Each numbered sentence in the following passage contains an italicized vocabulary word or related form. After you read the passage, you will complete an exercise.

TWO ANCIENT GOVERNMENTS: ATHENS AND SPARTA

Ancient Greece was for a long time made up of loosely organized tribes of people. (1) Each tribe was governed by a chieftain whose *dominion* included the army and the priesthood. Once warfare among tribes stopped and trade began to develop, the tribes united to form city-states.

Athens and Sparta were two of the largest and most important city-states. At first, both were governed by aristocrats who were concerned primarily with their own wealth and power. These wealthy landowners believed that the majority of people were not able to make good decisions and should not participate in government. This view led to the development of two very different forms of government in Athens and Sparta.

In Athens supporters of citizen participation in government finally overthrew the aristocrats. (2) Athenians called their new leaders *tyrants* because they had seized political power unlawfully. The tyrants, however, were capable individuals who actually improved conditions in Athens.

(3) By 600 B.C. Athenians had removed the tyrants from office and *inaugurated* constitutional government. The constitution established nine rulers, ten generals, a council divided into separate committees, and citizen assembly. (4) The rulers and the *delegates* to the council were chosen annually by drawing lots; the generals were the only elected officials. (5) Built into the constitution was a provision for *impeaching* ineffective leaders. If the majority of citizens voted against an official, he was banished from Athens for ten years.

The citizen assembly, which passed laws, consisted of five hundred citizens. However, the Athenian idea of citizenship was narrowly defined. Only free male Athenians had rights and privileges; non-Athenians, women, and slaves could neither vote nor participate in government.

Unlike Athens, Sparta never developed a democracy. (6) Under the *authoritarian* rule of two kings, Spartans did not participate in government. Citizenship was based on the

ability to pay high taxes. Because most people could not pay the taxes, they were slaves. (7) The aristocratic rulers of Sparta tightly controlled the lives of the people because they feared that *anarchy* would occur if the slaves revolted. From age twenty to thirty, each free male served as a cadet and policed the countryside. (8) The *Spartan* lifestyle developed and was reinforced to serve the government of the city-state.

Because other Greek city-states copied the Athenian form of democracy, Sparta felt called upon to defend its positions as the strongest city-state. Several decades of war among the city-states resulted, weakening Greece. (9) *Conservative* Sparta, having concentrated on developing military strength and personal endurance, made few contributions to culture. (10) *Liberal* Athens, though, with its devotion to democracy and its openness to new ideas, made important advances in the arts and sciences.

Each of the following statements corresponds to a numbered sentence in the passage. Each statement contains a blank and is followed by four answer choices. Decide which choice fits best in the blank. The word or phrase that you choose must express roughly the same meaning as the italicized word in the passage. Write the letter of your choice on the answer line.

1. The _____ of the chieftain included the army and the priesthood.
   a. area of popularity   c. usefulness
   b. area of control   d. changes

1. _____b_____

2. The Greek leaders who had seized power unlawfully were regarded as _____ .
   a. oppressors   b. giants   c. gods   d. weaklings

2. _____a_____

3. Constitutional government had _____ by 600 B.C.
   a. begun   c. changed
   b. been destroyed   d. been discussed

3. _____a_____

4. Council _____ were chosen by drawing lots.
   a. witnesses   b. directions   c. visitors   d. representatives

4. _____d_____

5. The constitution had a provision for _____ ineffective leaders.
   a. predicting   b. accusing   c. supporting   d. rewarding

5. _____b_____

6. Under the _____ rule of two kings, Spartans did not take part in government.
   a. weak   b. undemocratic   c. conflicting   d. liberal

6. _____b_____

7. The rulers were afraid that _____ would occur if the slaves revolted.
   a. applause   b. hunger   c. disorder   d. anger

7. _____c_____

8. The _____ lifestyle served the government of the city-state.
   a. superior   b. luxurious   c. pleasant   d. disciplined

8. _____d_____

9. _____ Sparta had little to leave behind.
   a. Cautious   b. Military   c. Ancient   d. Democratic

9. _____a_____

10. _____ Athens left us many important contributions.
    a. Fearful   b. Creative   c. Tolerant   d. Peaceful

10. _____c_____

Imagine that a group of teachers, students, and administrators has met to discuss the need for student government at your school. The members have asked you to write a proposal in which you describe a form of student government that would be fair and effective. They want you to explain why a student government is necessary, how decisions would be made in the form of government you propose, and how student representatives would be selected. Include at least five of the vocabulary words from this lesson in your proposal and underline them.

The **Bonus activity** for Lessons 15 and 16 is on page T18.

Crime and justice are important issues in modern society. To assure the rights of all people, those accused of crimes need to be treated with fairness. In the last twenty years, science has joined with criminal justice to make criminal investigations increasingly accurate and fair-minded. The advances in DNA testing now allow suspects to be identified with a high degree of accuracy using small amounts of evidence, say from hair or skin. This breakthrough has resulted in the dismissal of charges for several people, as DNA evidence has shown that they did not commit the crimes for which they were accused. At times, these mistakenly convicted people have even been released from prison. The fairness of the criminal justice system continues to improve as legal guarantees and scientific techniques continue to ensure the rights of all of us.

WORD LIST
acquit
arson
corrupt
counterfeit
culprit
felony
hijack
incriminate
repent
swindle

DEFINITIONS

After you have studied the definitions and example for each vocabulary word, write the word on the line to the right.

1. **acquit** (ə-kwĭt′) *verb* **a.** To free from a formal accusation of wrongdoing; find innocent. **b.** To release from a duty.

   Related Word **acquittal** *noun*
   Example The defendant was *acquitted* of the crime and released.

   1. _____

2. **arson** (är′sən) *noun* The crime of deliberately setting fire to buildings or other property. (From the Latin word *ardere,* meaning "to burn")

   Related Word **arsonist** *noun*
   Example The detective investigated the remains of the burned building for evidence of *arson.*

   2. _____

3. **corrupt** (kə-rŭpt′) *adjective* Immoral; dishonest; open to bribery.
   verb To destroy someone's honesty or integrity. (From the Latin word *corrumpere,* meaning "to destroy")

   Related Words **corruptible** *adjective;* **corruption** *noun;* **corruptly** *adverb*
   Example With a bribe of $100, the driver persuaded the *corrupt* police officer not to give him a speeding ticket.

   3. _____

4. **counterfeit** (koun′tər-fĭt′) *verb* **a.** To make a copy of something, such as money, for a dishonest purpose. **b.** To make a pretense of.
   noun Something counterfeited. *adjective* Made in imitation of what is genuine, in order to deceive. (From the Latin *contra-,* meaning "opposite," and *facere,* meaning "to make")

   Related Word **counterfeiter** *noun*
   Example The criminal *counterfeited* twenty-dollar bills on a special printing machine in the basement.

   4. _____

5. **culprit** (kŭl′prĭt) *noun* A person guilty or accused of being guilty of a crime or offense.

   5. _____

   Example The store detective believed she knew who was the *culprit* in the theft.

6. **felony** (fĕl′ə-nē) *noun* A serious crime such as murder or arson. (From the Medieval Latin word *fello,* meaning "villain")

   6. _____

   Related Word **felon** *noun*
   Example The thief received a ten-year prison sentence for the *felony.*

7. **hijack** (hī′jăk′) *verb* To seize or take control of a vehicle; steal goods from a vehicle.

   7. _____

   Related Word **hijacker** *noun*
   Example The outlaws hijacked the stagecoach and robbed the passengers.

8. **incriminate** (ĭn-krĭm′ə-nāt′) *verb* To charge with or involve in a crime or other wrongful act. (From the Latin *in-,* meaning "in," and *crimen,* meaning "crime")

   8. _____

   Related Word **incrimination** *noun*
   Example The testimony of three witnesses *incriminated* the embezzler.

9. **repent** (rĭ-pĕnt′) *verb* To feel or show regret for what one has done or failed to do.

   9. _____

   Related Words **repentance** *noun;* **repentant** *adjective*
   Example Tom *repented* of bragging so much about his skill in football.

10. **swindle** (swĭn′dl) *verb* **a.** To cheat or defraud someone of money or property. **b.** To obtain by practicing fraud. *noun* A dishonest act or scheme; a fraud. (From the Old High German word *swintan,* meaning "to vanish")

    10. _____

    Related Word **swindler** *noun*
    Example The bookkeeper *swindled* the firm out of thousands of dollars.

EXERCISE 1 WRITING CORRECT WORDS

On the answer line, write the word from the vocabulary list that fits each definition.

1. Deliberate burning of property
2. To cheat out of money or property
3. To accuse of or blame for a crime
4. Open to bribery; immoral
5. To make an imitation of something
6. To feel sorry for a wrongdoing
7. A serious crime
8. To capture a vehicle
9. A person accused or guilty of a crime
10. To find innocent

1. _____arson_____
2. _____swindle_____
3. _____incriminate_____
4. _____corrupt_____
5. _____counterfeit_____
6. _____repent_____
7. _____felony_____
8. _____hijack_____
9. _____culprit_____
10. _____acquit_____

EXERCISE 2 USING WORDS CORRECTLY

Decide whether the italicized vocabulary word or related form has been used correctly in the sentence. On the answer line, write *Correct* for correct use and *Incorrect* for incorrect use.

1. The *culprit* found the defendant guilty after a two-day trial.
2. An empty gasoline can led the police to suspect *arson*.
3. A salesperson *swindled* customers by selling empty lots in a swamp.
4. The *corrupt* manager took the company's funds and sailed to Australia.
5. The *repentant* criminal robbed a bank after leaving prison.
6. The jury *acquitted* the defendant because of a lack of evidence.
7. Airport security measures in the United States have made it difficult to *hijack* airplanes.
8. A person can be arrested if he or she *incriminates* someone else.
9. The dishonest artist misused his talent to *counterfeit* paintings.
10. Because the crime was only a *felony*, the judge dismissed the defendant with a warning.

1. _____Incorrect_____
2. _____Correct_____
3. _____Correct_____
4. _____Correct_____
5. _____Incorrect_____
6. _____Correct_____
7. _____Correct_____

8. _____Incorrect_____
9. _____Correct_____
10. _____Incorrect_____

EXERCISE 3 CHOOSING THE BEST DEFINITION

For each italicized vocabulary word or related form in the following sentences, write the letter of the best definition on the answer line.

1. The defendant hoped that her alibi would fully *acquit* her.
   a. save   **b.** free   **c.** relax   **d.** harm

1. _____b_____

2. A confidence game is the *swindle* of an unsuspecting person.   2. _____ c
   a. observation   **b.** flattery   **c.** cheating   **d.** rewarding

3. Criminals often leave *incriminating* evidence at the scene of a crime.   3. _____ d
   a. very little   **c.** designed to mislead others
   b. embarrassing   **d.** telltale

4. The gangsters *hijacked* a large truck.   4. _____ b
   a. repaired   **b.** robbed   **c.** surprised   **d.** detoured

5. The *culprit* in the mystery of the missing bananas was my five-year-old cousin.   5. _____ c
   a. hero   **b.** detective   **c.** guilty person   **d.** victim

6. *Arson* is sometimes suspected as the cause of forest fires.   6. _____ a
   a. The crime of deliberately setting fire
   b. The stealing of property
   c. The invasion of tourists
   d. The falsification of documents

7. Edmund Burke wrote, "Among a people generally *corrupt*, liberty cannot long exist."   7. _____ d
   a. joyous   **b.** unhappy   **c.** lazy   **d.** dishonest

8. Joel's unhappiness was obvious even though he tried to *counterfeit* a smile.   8. _____ c
   a. hide   **b.** remember   **c.** fake   **d.** hold back

9. By burglarizing a house, the criminal committed a *felony*.   9. _____ a
   a. serious crime   **c.** irrational act
   b. mild offense   **d.** accidental crime

10. The *repentant* employee apologized for making a serious mistake.   10. _____ c
    a. sobbing   **b.** shivering   **c.** regretful   **d.** happy

EXERCISE 4 USING DIFFERENT FORMS OF WORDS

Decide which form of the vocabulary word in parentheses best completes the sentence. The form given may be correct. Write your answer on the answer line.

1. "Marry in haste, _____ at leisure," wrote eighteenth-century English playwright William Congreve. (*repent*)   1. _____ repent

2. Convicted _____ face heavy prison sentences. (*felony*)   2. _____ felons

3. Despite the defendant's _____, many people still thought that he was guilty. (*acquit*)   3. _____ acquittal

4. The three _____ moved to take control of the vehicle. (*hijack*)   4. _____ hijackers

5. The mayor was indicted on charges of operating the city government _____. (*corrupt*)   5. _____ corruptly

6. In a play entitled *The Firebugs*, Max Frisch wrote about two _____. (*arson*)   6. _____ arsonists

7. _____ were severely punished under old English law. (*counterfeit*)   7. _____ Counterfeiters

8. The _____ was easy to find. (*culprit*)   8. _____ culprit

9. The lawyer read the _____ letter to the jury. (*incriminate*)   9. _____ incriminating

10. In the Old West, _____ were dealt with severely. (*swindle*)   10. _____ swindlers

READING COMPREHENSION

Each numbered sentence in the following passage contains an italicized vocabulary word or related form. After you read the passage, you will complete an exercise.

THE CASE OF THE COUNTERFEIT PAINTINGS

NARRATOR: The weekend guests of Lady Agatha Herringbone gather in the library to await the arrival of the world-famous detective, Hercules Parrot. (1) Everyone is shocked when Lady Agatha reveals that her priceless paintings are *counterfeits.* She believes that the counterfeit paintings were exchanged for the authentic ones during the weekend. (2) She also believes that one of the guests is the *culprit.* All look up anxiously as Parrot enters.

LADY AGATHA: Ah, Monsieur Parrot, I trust that your seven-course lunch was satisfactory. (3) Have you discovered any *incriminating* evidence about my guests?

PARROT: The answer to both questions is yes. You, Madame, are a poor judge of character. (4) The men and women in this room have committed *felonies.* They are perfect suspects.

LADY AGATHA: This is totally shocking! These people are my sister Emma's dearest friends. I'm only thankful that Emma is safely at the health spa in Germany. What proof do you have to make such accusations?

PARROT: Take Monsieur Jack, for example. (5) He is well known to Scotland Yard as an *arsonist.*

LADY AGATHA: Shocking news! Emma trusted you, Jack.

JACK: I'd burn those paintings, not steal them. That's all behind me now. I'm a reformed man.

PARROT: Sitting on the couch is Mademoiselle Louise. (6) She looks innocent enough, but Scotland Yard could tell you all about the time she *swindled* an elderly companion out of a great deal of money.

LADY AGATHA: Emma trusted you, Louise.

LOUISE: (7) If you'll remember, Monsieur, I was *acquitted* of that false accusation.

PARROT: There is one more case in point—that of Monsieur André. (8) Perhaps monsieur would like to tell about the time he attempted to *hijack* a vehicle and leave the country.

ANDRÉ: I apologized for the inconvenience.

LADY AGATHA: (9) Monsieur Parrot, which one of these *corrupt* villains took my paintings?

PARROT: None of them, Madame. (10) I believe them when they say they have *repented* of their crimes. What I do not believe is that your sister is at a health spa.

LADY AGATHA: Why . . . where is she, then?

PARROT: Making arrangements to sell the real paintings. You, Madame, have invited a roomful of reformed criminals, hoping to blame them for a crime that you yourself have planned from the beginning. Otherwise, why would you invite your sister's friends for a weekend when she is out of the country?

LADY AGATHA: Outrageous! Why would I steal my own paintings?

PARROT: For the insurance money, Madame, and also for the money received from the sale of the real paintings. Your ill-gotten funds will allow you to pay back taxes. I was expected to accuse the wrong suspect, but you have foolishly underestimated the cleverness of Hercules Parrot. Now, if you will excuse me, I must call Scotland Yard and prepare for my afternoon tea.

Each of the following statements corresponds to a numbered sentence in the passage. Each statement contains a blank and is followed by four answer choices. Decide which choice fits best in the blank. The word or phrase that you choose must express roughly the same meaning as the italicized word in the passage. Write the letter of your choice on the answer line.

1. Lady Agatha discovered that her paintings were _____.
   a. masterpieces   **b.** imitations   **c.** lost   **d.** expensive

   1. _____b_____

2. She thought that one of the guests was the _____.
   a. detective   **b.** murderer   **c.** hijacker   **d.** wrongdoer

   2. _____d_____

3. Lady Agatha asked whether any evidence _____ had been discovered.
   a. that proved guilt   **c.** that was permanent
   b. that was visible   **d.** that showed innocence

   3. _____a_____

4. Hercules Parrot pointed out that all the guests had committed _____.
   a. pranks   **b.** major crimes   **c.** bad deeds   **d.** minor crimes

   4. _____b_____

5. For example, Monsieur Jack had been _____.
   a. an enjoyer of life   **c.** a setter of fires
   b. a thief   **d.** a borrower of paintings

   5. _____c_____

6. Mademoiselle Louise had _____ an elderly companion.
   a. supported   **b.** injured   **c.** abandoned   **d.** cheated

   6. _____d_____

7. Mademoiselle Louise reminded Parrot that she had been _____.
   a. accused   **b.** punished   **c.** cleared   **d.** imprisoned

   7. _____c_____

8. Hercules Parrot then revealed that Monsieur André had tried to _____ a vehicle.
   a. catch   **b.** fly in   **c.** disable   **d.** seize

   8. _____d_____

9. Lady Agatha asked which _____ guest took her paintings.
   a. dishonest   **b.** desperate   **c.** foolish   **d.** carefree

   9. _____a_____

10. Hercules Parrot felt that the suspects _____ about their crimes.
    a. were glad   **c.** were relieved
    b. were sorry   **d.** were indifferent

    10. _____b_____

Imagine that you are a successful television scriptwriter. Your assignment is to create a story that deals with crime and justice. Write a summary that briefly explains the main characters, settings, and plot of your story. Include five words from this lesson and underline each one.

Alexander Pope, an eighteenth-century writer, commented in one of his poems that "to err is human." Certainly, people try to do their best, but everybody makes mistakes. Some errors are minor and are corrected easily, such as a misspelled word. Other errors may be more serious but may still have positive results. For example, Alexander Fleming made the mistake of exposing to the air a bacteria culture that he was studying. The mistake, though, led to his discovery of penicillin.

Each of the words in this lesson deals with some form of error or confusion. You will find these words useful in describing behavior typical of all of us at various times.

WORD LIST

amiss
bewilder
blunder
erroneous
fallible
faux pas
fluster
miscalculate
misinterpret
overestimate

DEFINITIONS

After you have studied the definition and example for each vocabulary word, write the word on the line to the right.

1. **amiss** (ə-mĭs′) *adjective*   Out of proper order; wrong; faulty.   *adverb*   In an improper or defective way.

   Example   Lucinda knew immediately that something in the room was *amiss;* on closer examination she saw that the furniture had been rearranged.

1. _____
USAGE NOTE: *To take amiss* is an idiom that means "to misunder-stand" or "to feel offended by."

2. **bewilder** (bĭ-wĭl′dər) *verb*   To confuse or befuddle, especially with numerous conflicting situations, objects, or statements.

   Related Word   **bewilderment** *noun*
   Example   The noise and traffic of the busy street *bewildered* the tourist.

2. _____

3. **blunder** (blŭn′dər) *noun*   A serious mistake, usually caused by ignorance or confusion.   *verb*   **a.** To botch or bungle; say stupidly or thoughtlessly   **b.** To move awkwardly or clumsily; stumble. (From the Middle English word *blunderen*, meaning "to go blindly")

   Example   Buying the worthless automobile was a *blunder* that cost Malcolm several thousand dollars.

3. _____

4. **erroneous** (ĭ-rō′nē-əs) *adjective*   Wrong; mistaken; false. (From the Latin word *errare*, meaning "to wander")

   Related Word   **erroneously** *adverb*
   Example   There were several *erroneous* conclusions in the detective's report.

4. _____
See *fallible.*

5. **fallible** (făl′ə-bəl) *adjective*   Likely to be wrong; capable of making an error. (From the Latin word *fallere*, meaning "to cause to fall" or "to deceive")

   Related Word   **fallibility** *noun*
   Example   All human beings are *fallible*; no one is perfect.

5. _____

6. **faux pas** (fō-pä′) *noun*   A minor social error that may cause embarrassment. (From the French phrase *faux pas*, meaning "false step")

   Example   Selma made a *faux pas* when she ate her salad with her dinner fork.

6. _____

7. **fluster** (flŭs′tər) *verb*   To make nervous, excited, or confused.   *noun*   A state of agitation or confusion.

   Example   Simon *flustered* Lila when he complimented her on her haircut.

7. _____

8. **miscalculate** (mĭs-kăl′kyə-lāt′) *verb*   **a.** To make a wrong estimate of; make an error in judgment.   **b.** To compute numbers incorrectly. (From the Latin *mis-*, meaning "wrong," and *calculus*, meaning "a stone used for counting")

   Related Word   **miscalculation** *noun*
   Example   The television producer *miscalculated* the appeal of the new program.

8. _____

9. **misinterpret** (mĭs′ĭn-tûr′prĭt) *verb*   To draw a wrong conclusion from; understand incorrectly.

   Related Word   **misinterpretation** *noun*
   Example   Lionel *misinterpreted* Ms. Nelson's message and drove to the airport at the wrong time to pick her up.

9. _____

10. **overestimate** (ō′vər-ĕs′tə-māt′) *verb*   To rate, value, or esteem too highly.

    Related Word   **overestimation** *noun*
    Example   Erica often feels that her coach *overestimates* her ability to make the Olympic team.

10. _____

EXERCISE 1 COMPLETING DEFINITIONS

On the answer line, write the word from the vocabulary list that best completes each definition.

1. If you value or rate something too highly, you _____ it.

2. If you compute numbers incorrectly or if you make an error in judgment, you _____.

3. If you understand something incorrectly, you _____ it.

4. To make nervous, upset, or confused is to _____.

5. Something out of proper order is _____.

6. An embarrassing social error is a _____.

7. To confuse or befuddle is to _____.

8. If someone is capable of error or likely to be wrong, the person is _____.

9. A serious mistake caused by ignorance or confusion is a _____.

10. If something is wrong, mistaken, or false, it is _____.

1. **overestimate**
2. **miscalculate**
3. **misinterpret**
4. **fluster**
5. **amiss**
6. **faux pas**
7. **bewilder**
8. **fallible**
9. **blunder**
10. **erroneous**

EXERCISE 2 USING WORDS CORRECTLY

Each of the following questions contains an italicized vocabulary word. Decide the answer to the question, and write *Yes* or *No* on the answer line.

1. Is a *faux pas* a serious mistake?

2. Is an *erroneous* answer incorrect?

3. Is a *fallible* person perfect?

4. If you compute numbers incorrectly, do you necessarily *overestimate?*

5. If you *misinterpret* a statement, do you misunderstand it?

6. If something is *amiss,* is it in its proper place?

7. Is a *blunder* a minor error in mathematics?

8. If you are *bewildered* by something, are you confused?

9. If you make an error in judgment, do you *miscalculate?*

10. If you *fluster* someone, do you make that person nervous or upset?

1. **No**
2. **Yes**
3. **No**
4. **No**
5. **Yes**
6. **No**
7. **No**
8. **Yes**
9. **Yes**
10. **Yes**

EXERCISE 3 CHOOSING THE BEST WORD

Decide which vocabulary word or related form best completes the sentence, and write the letter of your choice on the answer line.

1. The police searched the room carefully but found nothing _____.
   a. fallible   **b.** flustered   **c.** bewildered   **d.** amiss

2. People's use of erasers shows that they are _____.
   a. flustered   **b.** fallible   **c.** amiss   **d.** bewildered

1. **d**
2. **b**

3. Michael made a _____ by forgetting to introduce his mother to his friends.
   a. miscalculation b. fluster   c. faux pas   d. overestimation

   3. _____ c _____

4. Michael then exaggerated his error, saying "Oh, what a _____!"
   a. miscalculation b. blunder   c. faux pas   d. overestimation

   4. _____ b _____

5. Helga was _____ when she forgot her lines.
   a. flustered   c. overestimated
   b. erroneous   d. miscalculated

   5. _____ a _____

6. The highways in and around Los Angeles can _____ many a visitor.
   a. miscalculate   b. misinterpret c. bewilder   d. blunder

   6. _____ c _____

7. Before the time of Copernicus, most people held the _____ view that Earth was the center of the solar system.
   a. erroneous   b. overestimated c. bewildered   d. flustered

   7. _____ a _____

8. David _____ the amount of time that remained for finishing the test.
   a. bewildered   b. flustered   c. blundered   d. miscalculated

   8. _____ d _____

9. Researchers who _____ their information may draw conclusions that are false.
   a. blunder   b. misinterpret   c. bewilder   d. fluster

   9. _____ b _____

10. Jessica _____ her strength when she attempted to carry both bags of groceries at once.
    a. bewildered   b. flustered   c. overestimated d. blundered

    10. _____ c _____

EXERCISE 4 USING DIFFERENT FORMS OF WORDS

Decide which form of the vocabulary word in parentheses best completes the sentence. The form given may be correct. Write your answer on the answer line.

1. Written sentences without punctuation are often open to _____. (misinterpret)

   1. misinterpretation

2. The student took _____ the teacher's well-intentioned criticism. (amiss)

   2. amiss

3. A person who _____ is frequently compared to a bull in a china shop. (blunder)

   3. blunders

4. During an election campaign, a _____ can cost a candidate hundreds of votes. (faux pas)

   4. faux pas

5. Many animals try to _____ their enemies by making threatening gestures before an attack. (fluster)

   5. fluster

6. In 1948 some newspapers _____ reported that Thomas Dewey had defeated Harry Truman for the presidency. (erroneous)

   6. erroneously

7. Instant replays of sporting events sometimes show the _____ of the officials. (fallible)

   7. fallibility

8. To untrained people, Morse code is a _____ collection of dots and dashes. (bewilder)

   8. bewildering

9. We definitely _____ the intelligence of our dog, who could not even learn to fetch the newspaper. (overestimate)

   9. overestimated

10. _____ of timing and distance can cause a trapeze artist to fall into the safety net. (Miscalculate)

    10. Miscalculation

READING COMPREHENSION

Each numbered sentence in the following passage contains an italicized vocabulary word or related form. After you read the passage, you will complete an exercise.

TULIPOMANIA

It is difficult to believe that the tulip, one of the most popular and beautiful spring flowers, was once the cause of a national scandal and an economic disaster. *Tulpenwoede,* or tulipomania, overtook Holland between 1633 and 1637.

The Viennese ambassador to Turkey introduced the onionlike bulbs, which actually belong to the lily family, to the Western world. In 1562 the arrival at Antwerp, Belgium, of a cargo of the bulbs marked the beginning of a new flower-cultivation industry. Soon the tulip, whose name comes from the Turkish word for turban, became the most fashionable flower in Europe.

The demand for new varieties of tulips gradually exceeded the supply. Unusual flowers were particularly costly. (1) One tulip fancier in Holland *erroneously* paid too high a price for a spectacular specimen. (2) News of this costly *blunder* spread quickly to bulb sellers, and within weeks nearly everyone in Holland was trading tulips. Special markets sprang up just for buying and selling bulbs. A single bulb of a new variety became acceptable as the dowry for a bride. One person traded a flourishing factory for a tulip bulb. (3) The financial *miscalculation* that started this tulip madness caused homes and industries to be mortgaged so that

more flower bulbs could be purchased and resold at increasingly higher prices. The expectation that there was always someone willing to pay more for tulip bulbs supported tulipomania.

A story about a sailor and a shopkeeper illustrates what happened during the five years of tulip madness. One morning a sailor purchased a herring for his breakfast. Left alone while the shopkeeper went into his storeroom, the sailor noticed a delicious-looking onion, which was actually a tulip bulb. He took it and sliced it to eat with his herring. (4) The merchant

returned and noticed something was *amiss,* for his rare tulip bulb was gone. (5) Extremely *flustered,* he got the police and rushed after the sailor. (6) Imagine how *bewildered* the sailor was when he learned that his breakfast had cost him more than a thousand dollars!

People sold and resold tulip bulbs many times without the bulbs leaving the ground or the flowers being seen by their buyers. When a single bulb reached the astounding price of three thousand florins—a sum large enough to feed an entire family for a year—the tulip market crashed. (7) Suddenly, people realized that they had *overestimated* the value of the flower. Everyone began to sell tulips, and prices fell faster than they had risen.

(8) When it was all over, many people had lost fortunes by *misinterpreting* the trends in prices. (9) The few who had made money kept quiet about their good fortune, for it was considered a *faux pas* even to mention tulips.

(10) The story of tulipomania reminds us that human beings are *fallible.* No person has good judgment all the time. The Dutch continue to grow tulips and to export them, but no one since 1637 has paid a thousand dollars for one bulb.

Each of the following statements corresponds to a numbered sentence in the passage. Each statement contains a blank and is followed by four answer choices. Decide which choice fits best in the blank. The word or phrase that you choose must express roughly the same meaning as the italicized word in the passage. Write the letter of your choice on the answer line.

1. One tulip buyer _____ paid a high price for a spectacular bulb.
   a. thoughtlessly   **b.** ridiculously   **c.** quickly   **d.** mistakenly

   1. ___d___

2. News of his costly _____ spread quickly.
   a. mistake   **b.** plan   **c.** bulbs   **d.** trick

   2. ___a___

3. A financial _____ started tulip madness.
   a. greediness   **b.** error in judgment   **c.** panic   **d.** need for flowers

   3. ___b___

4. The merchant realized something was _____ when he saw that his rare bulb was gone.
   a. wrong   **b.** right   **c.** clear   **d.** moved

   4. ___a___

5. Feeling very _____, he got the police and went after the sailor.
   a. serious   **b.** wrong   **c.** upset   **d.** hungry

   5. ___c___

6. The sailor was _____ when he learned about his expensive breakfast.
   a. angry   **b.** confused   **c.** incorrect   **d.** sorry

   6. ___b___

7. People realized that they had _____ tulips.
   a. underpriced   **c.** overrated
   b. forgotten   **d.** found the right market for

   7. ___c___

8. People had _____ the trends in tulip prices.
   a. wrongly judged   **c.** changed
   b. destroyed   **d.** accurately explained

   8. ___a___

9. After tulipomania, it was a _____ even to mention the subject of tulips.
   a. serious mistake   **c.** bad judgment
   b. social error   **d.** financial loss

   9. ___b___

10. The story of tulipomania illustrates that people are _____.
    a. capable of perfection   **c.** funny
    b. able to make money   **d.** capable of error.

    10. ___d___

See page 119 for some strategies to use with analogies.

Directions   On the answer line, write the vocabulary word or a form of it that completes each analogy.

1. Ordain is to priest as _____ is to president. *(Lesson 16)*

   1. ___inaugurate___

2. Braggart is to boastful as _____ is to dishonest. *(Lesson 17)*

   2. ___swindler___

3. Fraudulent is to identity as _____ is to money. *(Lesson 17)*

   3. ___counterfeit___

4. Misinterpret is to fact as _____ is to money. *(Lesson 18)*

   4. ___miscalculate___

5. Anarchist is to order as _____ is to change. *(Lesson 16)*

   5. ___conservative___

6. Discharge is to soldier as _____ is to president. *(Lesson 16)*

   6. ___impeach___

The **Bonus activity** for Lessons 17 and 18 is on page T19. The **Test** for Lessons 16, 17, and 18 is on page T20.

TEST-TAKING SKILLS
ANALOGY TESTS

Analogy items on vocabulary tests and standardized examinations measure your ability to understand relationships between words. An *analogy* is a similarity between things that are otherwise dissimilar. A word analogy is usually given in this form: Word A is to Word B as Word C is to Word D. The following strategies will help you answer analogy test items.

STRATEGIES

1. *Determine the relationship between the given words.* In the following example, you must first understand the relationship between *scrap* and *paper* before you can answer the item.

   Scrap is to paper as
   (A) edge is to knife
   (B) wall is to brick
   (C) dust is to broom
   (D) shoe is to heel
   (E) splinter is to wood

   The relationship between *scrap* and *paper* can best be stated as, "A scrap is a small piece of paper." Note that our sentence is short and specific. Avoid long sentences. They usually mean you are off the track.

2. *Apply your sentence to each of the answer choices.*
   (A) edge is to knife   Is edge a small piece of knife? No.
   (B) wall is to brick   Is wall a small piece of brick? No.
   (C) dust is to broom   Is dust a small piece of broom? No.
   (D) shoe is to heel   Is shoe a small piece of heel? No.
   (E) splinter is to wood   Is splinter a small piece of wood? Yes.

3. *Select the answer that best matches the relationship between the original pair of words.* In this example, the answer is (E) since, "a scrap is a small piece of paper in the same way that a splinter is a small piece of wood."

EXERCISE IDENTIFYING ANALOGIES

Find the relationship between the words in the first pair of each sentence, and choose the answer that shows the same relationship or a similar one. Write the letter of your choice on the answer line. Use your dictionary as needed.

1. Peerless is to equal as
   (A) aimless is to purpose
   (B) formal is to style
   (C) contagious is to disease
   (D) temporary is to fame
   (E) analogous is to parallel

   1. ____**A**____

2. Conflagration is to fire as
   (A) flower is to seed
   (B) muscle is to bone
   (C) drought is to rain
   (D) breeze is to wind
   (E) metropolis is to city

   2. ____**E**____

3. Inauguration is to president as
   (A) demotion is to employee
   (B) divorce is to spouse
   (C) coronation is to monarch
   (D) decoration is to soldier
   (E) maturation is to teenager

   3. ____**C**____

4. Combustible is to burn as
   (A) durable is to deteriorate
   (B) eternal is to end
   (C) hefty is to bounce
   (D) perishable is to spoil
   (E) perpetual is to stop

   4. ____**D**____

5. Meteorology is to weather as
   (A) plagiarism is to ideas
   (B) drama is to costumes
   (C) etymology is to insects
   (D) religion is to churches
   (E) gerontology is to aging

   5. ____**E**____

6. Aquatic is to water as
   (A) terrestrial is to land
   (B) solar is to energy
   (C) vegetarian is to plants
   (D) isolated is to island
   (E) scientific is to experiments

   6. ____**A**____

7. Mason is to stone as
   (A) surgeon is to scalpel
   (B) carver is to wood
   (C) barber is to razor
   (D) actor is to stage
   (E) watchmaker is to time

   7. ____**B**____

8. Vulnerable is to defend as
   (A) dense is to penetrate
   (B) distinct is to see
   (C) erroneous is to criticize
   (D) practical is to use
   (E) fragrant is to smell

   8. ____**A**____

9. Valiant is to brave as
   (A) anguished is to cheerful
   (B) blithe is to dejected
   (C) omnipotent is to powerful
   (D) affable is to afraid
   (E) amicable is to hostile

   9. ____**C**____

10. Pacifist is to war as
    (A) conservative is to change
    (B) liberal is to rights
    (C) Spartan is to self-discipline
    (D) anarchist is to laws
    (E) delegate is to representation

    10. ____**D**____

At times everyone overdoes things. Which of the following extravagances can you plead guilty to?

Seeing the same movie seven times
Overeating at a holiday dinner
Monopolizing the telephone for two hours straight
Spending all your hard-earned money on an outfit that you'll wear only once
Listening to a favorite CD two hundred times

In this lesson you will study words that will help you understand and explain the tendencies that people have to overdo things.

<table>
<tr><th>WORD LIST</th></tr>
<tr><td>embellish
exceed
glut
immoderate
intense
lavish
luxurious
outrageous
profuse
spendthrift</td></tr>
</table>

DEFINITIONS

After you have studied the definitions and example for each vocabulary word, write the word on the line to the right.

1. **embellish** (ĕm-bĕl′ĭsh) *verb*   **a.** To make beautiful by decoration. **b.** To add fanciful or fictitious details to; exaggerate. (From the Latin *in-*, meaning "in," and *bellus*, meaning "beautiful")

   Related Word   **embellishment** *noun*
   Example   The students *embellished* the bulletin board by adding artwork.

   1. _____

2. **exceed** (ĭk-sēd′) *verb*   **a.** To go beyond reasonable limits; do more than. **b.** To be greater than. (From the Latin *ex-*, meaning "out," and *cedere*, meaning "to go")

   Related Word   **exceedingly** *adverb*
   Example   Cynthia's dreams greatly *exceeded* the realities of her life.

   2. _____
   See *immoderate*.

3. **glut** (glŭt) *verb*   **a.** To fill, feed, or eat beyond capacity; stuff.   **b.** To oversupply a market with goods.   *noun*   An oversupply. (From the Latin word *gluttire*, meaning "to eat greedily")

   Related Words   **glutton** *noun*; **gluttonous** *adjective*; **gluttony** *noun*
   Example   The guests *glutted* themselves with food at Thanksgiving dinner.

   3. _____

4. **immoderate** (ĭ-mŏd′ər-ĭt) *adjective*   Done to an extreme; not within reasonable limits; excessive. (From the Latin *in-,* meaning "not," and *moderatus,* meaning "moderate")

   Related Word   **immoderately** *adverb*
   Example   "Ten hours of straight television watching is an *immoderate* amount," Mrs. Wilson said sharply to Stanley.

4. _____
MEMORY CUE: If a quantity *exceeds* reasonable limits, it is *immoderate*.

5. **intense** (ĭn-tĕns′) *adjective*   **a.** Deeply felt: *an intense emotion.*   **b.** Very deep, strong, forceful, or concentrated: *an intense color or odor.* (From the Latin *in-,* meaning "into," and *tendere,* meaning "to stretch")

   Related Words   **intensify** *verb;* **intensity** *noun;* **intensive** *adjective*
   Example   Linda's tormented expression revealed her *intense* feelings about finishing last in the race.

5. _____

6. **lavish** (lăv′ĭsh) *adjective*   **a.** Extravagantly plentiful: *lavish refreshments.*   **b.** Generous or free in giving or using: *lavish praise.*   *verb*   To give or spend to excess. (From the Old French word *lavesse,* meaning "downpour")

   Related Words   **lavishly** *adverb;* **lavishness** *noun*
   Example   Bob was embarrassed by his friend's *lavish* compliments.

6. _____
See *profuse.*

7. **luxurious** (lŭg-zhŏŏr′ē-əs) *adjective*   Marked by luxury or showy, expensive magnificence. (From the Latin word *luxus,* meaning "overindulgence")

   Related Words   **luxuriantly** *adverb;* **luxuriate** *verb;* **luxury** *noun*
   Example   Helen enjoyed the *luxurious* texture of her new angora sweater.

7. _____

8. **outrageous** (out-rā′jəs) *adjective*   Going beyond all limits of what is right or proper; shocking; monstrous. (From the Old French word *outre,* meaning "beyond")

   Related Words   **outrage** *noun;* **outrageously** *adverb*
   Example   The audience laughed uproariously at the comic actor's *outrageous* stunts in the film.

8. _____

9. **profuse** (prə-fyoōs′) *adjective*   **a.** Large in quantity; abundant.   **b.** Giving or given generously. (From the Latin *pro-,* meaning "forward," and *fundere,* meaning "to pour")

   Related Words   **profusely** *adverb;* **profusion** *noun*
   Example   For the head table at the banquet, the florist created a *profuse* flower arrangement.

9. _____
USAGE NOTE: *Profuse* refers to something that is abundant. *Lavish* refers to abundance but also implies extravagance.

10. **spendthrift** (spĕnd′thrĭft′) *noun*   A person who spends money wastefully or foolishly.   *adjective*   Wasteful; extravagant.

   Example   The *spendthrift* found it impossible to save money.

10. _____
ETYMOLOGY NOTE: Although *thrift* means "frugality," *spendthrift* uses an obsolete definition of *thrift,* "accumulated wealth"; a spendthrift spends money!

© Great Source   DO NOT COPY

EXERCISE 1 WRITING CORRECT WORDS

On the answer line, write the word from the vocabulary list that fits
each definition.

1. Concentrated or strong; deeply felt

2. One who wastes money

3. Magnificent in a showy way

4. To make beautiful with decoration

5. Excessive; extreme

6. Shocking; going beyond the limit of what is proper

7. Extravagantly plentiful

8. To go beyond reasonable limits

9. Large in quantity; abundant

10. To fill, feed, or eat beyond capacity

1. _____ intense _____
2. _____ spendthrift _____
3. _____ luxurious _____
4. _____ embellish _____
5. _____ immoderate _____
6. _____ outrageous _____
7. _____ lavish _____
8. _____ exceed _____
9. _____ profuse _____
10. _____ glut _____

EXERCISE 2 USING WORDS CORRECTLY

Decide whether the italicized vocabulary word has been used correctly in the
sentence. On the answer line, write *Correct* for correct use and *Incorrect* for
incorrect use.

1. Showing bare legs in public was *outrageous* behavior in the nineteenth
   century.

2. Claude ate an *immoderate* amount for dinner because he wasn't very
   hungry.

3. The patient's *profuse* bleeding greatly concerned the doctor.

4. Jennifer *embellished* the walls by putting up several paintings.

5. Because the game was so difficult, Ken played it with *intense* concentration.

6. The hotel seemed very *luxurious* to the people who had been camping by
   the lake.

7. If someone *exceeds* the speed limit, he or she is driving too slowly.

8. The *spendthrift* found it easy to save money.

9. A trickle of water *glutted* the pipes.

10. A seven-course meal might be described as *lavish*.

1. _____ Correct _____
2. _____ Incorrect _____
3. _____ Correct _____
4. _____ Correct _____
5. _____ Correct _____
6. _____ Correct _____
7. _____ Incorrect _____
8. _____ Incorrect _____
9. _____ Incorrect _____
10. _____ Correct _____

EXERCISE 3 CHOOSING THE BEST DEFINITION

For each italicized vocabulary word or related form in the following
sentences, write the letter of the best definition on the answer line.

1. The movie star was uncomfortable under the *intense* studio lights.
   a. pale   **b.** irritating   **c.** gloomy   **d.** strong

1. _____ d _____

2. Julia's *outrageous* remarks embarrassed her mother.
   a. loud   **b.** serious   **c.** shocking   **d.** humorous

2. _____ c

3. Tom *embellished* the details of his simple vacation.
   a. invented   **b.** remembered   **c.** described   **d.** exaggerated

3. _____ d

4. *Profuse* recommendations from past employers helped Doug to find a new job.
   a. Generous   **b.** Sincere   **c.** Written   **d.** Personal

4. _____ a

5. The prices of computers fell because too many products *glutted* the market.
   a. emptied   **b.** oversupplied   **c.** broke   **d.** missed

5. _____ b

6. Esther received *luxurious* accommodations at the inn.
   a. shabby   **b.** ancient   **c.** magnificent   **d.** cramped

6. _____ c

7. Carl drives his new sports car at an *immoderate* speed.
   a. experimental   **b.** extreme   **c.** suitable   **d.** controlled

7. _____ b

8. Jack promised to stop being a *spendthrift*.
   a. money saver   **b.** banker   **c.** consumer   **d.** money waster

8. _____ d

9. The O'Neals held a *lavish* party that included a live band.
   a. extravagant   **b.** fun-filled   **c.** amusing   **d.** routine

9. _____ a

10. Tenderhearted Rebecca is *exceedingly* kind to her pets.
    a. never   **b.** occasionally   **c.** extremely   **d.** sometimes

10. _____ c

EXERCISE 4 USING DIFFERENT FORMS OF WORDS

Decide which form of the vocabulary word in parentheses best completes the sentence. The form given may be correct. Write your answer on the answer line.

1. The _____ of the heat caused the campers to back away from the fire. (*intense*)

1. _____ intensity

2. "This is an _____!" exclaimed Mr. Franz as he looked at his plumbing bill. (*outrageous*)

2. _____ outrage

3. Friends called Henry a _____ after he ordered a third dessert. (*glut*)

3. _____ glutton

4. Patricia, who is usually sensible, becomes a _____ in her favorite book store. (*spendthrift*)

4. _____ spendthrift

5. "You have _____ my wildest expectations," Mary's piano teacher told her. (*exceed*)

5. _____ exceeded

6. The _____ of the decorations impressed the Tuttles. (*lavish*)

6. _____ lavishness

7. The interior decorator hoped to add many _____ to the expensive mansion. (*embellish*)

7. _____ embellishments

8. Keeping fresh flowers in the house was Joanna's only _____. (*luxurious*)

8. _____ luxury

9. Sylvia was perspiring _____ after running ten miles. (*profuse*)

9. _____ profusely

10. Eating _____ caused Jonathan to gain ten pounds in two weeks. (*immoderate*)

10. _____ immoderately

READING COMPREHENSION

Each numbered sentence in the following passage contains an italicized vocabulary word or related form. After you read the passage, you will complete an exercise.

THE ROYAL SPENDTHRIFTS

King Louis XVI and Queen Marie Antoinette ruled France from 1774 to 1789, a time when the country was fighting bankruptcy. (1) The royal couple did not let France's insecure financial situation limit their *immoderate* spending, however. Even though the minister of finance repeatedly warned the king and queen against wasting money, they continued to spend great fortunes on their personal pleasure. (2) This *lavish* spending greatly enraged the people of France. (3) They felt that the royal couple bought its *luxurious* lifestyle at the poor people's expense.

(4) Marie Antoinette, the beautiful but *exceedingly* impractical queen, seemed uncaring about her subjects' misery. (5) While French citizens begged for lower taxes, the queen *embellished* her palace with extravagant works of art. (6) She also surrounded herself with artists, writers, and musicians, who encouraged the queen to spend money even more *profusely.*

(7) While the queens' favorites *glutted* themselves on huge feasts at the royal table, many people in France were starving.

(8) The French government taxed the citizens *outrageously.* These high taxes paid for the entertainments the queen and her court so enjoyed. (9) When the minister of finance tried to stop these royal *spendthrifts,* the queen replaced him.

(10) The *intense* hatred that the people felt for Louis XVI and Marie Antoinette kept building until it led to the French Revolution. During this time of struggle and violence (1789–1799), thousands of aristocrats, as well as the king and queen themselves, lost their lives at the guillotine. Perhaps if Louis XVI and Marie Antoinette had reined in their extravagant spending, the events that rocked France would not have occurred.

Each of the following statements corresponds to a numbered sentence in the passage. Each statement contains a blank and is followed by four answer choices. Decide which choice fits best in the blank. The word or phrase that you choose must express roughly the same meaning as the italicized word in the passage. Write the letter of your choice on the answer line.

1. King Louis XVI and Queen Marie Antoinette were warned against spending ____.
   a. for war   **b.** for charity   **c.** too much   **d.** too little

      1. _____ c _____

2. This ____ spending angered the people of France.
   a. extravagant   **b.** important   **c.** necessary   **d.** visible

      2. _____ a _____

3. The people resented the royal couple's ____ way of life.
   a. simple   **b.** enthusiastic   **c.** unhappy   **d.** expensive

      3. _____ d _____

4. Marie Antoinette was ____ impractical.
   a. moderately   **b.** extremely   **c.** understandably   **d.** never

      4. _____ b _____

5. She ____ her palace with expensive works of art.
   a. changed   **b.** decorated   **c.** destroyed   **d.** transformed

      5. _____ b _____

6. The people surrounding the queen encouraged her to spend money ____.
   a. abundantly   **b.** happily   **c.** carefully   **d.** wisely

      6. _____ a _____

7. Marie Antoinette's favorites ____ at large banquets.
   a. stayed on diets   **c.** danced and sang
   b. talked freely   **d.** stuffed themselves

      7. _____ d _____

8. Meanwhile, the poor people were taxed ____.
   a. carefully   **b.** yearly   **c.** shockingly   **d.** officially

      8. _____ c _____

9. The minister of finance tried to curb these royal ____.
   a. money wasters   **c.** enemies
   b. friends   **d.** aristocrats

      9. _____ a _____

10. The people of France felt ____ hatred for the king and queen.
   a. average   **b.** deep   **c.** little   **d.** fleeting

      10. _____ b _____

WRITING ASSIGNMENT

Think back to a time in your life when you were in danger of overdoing something. You might have eaten too much of one type of food or collected too many of one type of video or book. Create a brief, humorous incident of several paragraphs that tells about this experience in an exaggerated way. Write the incident from the first-person point of view, and begin by making clear what the problem is. By the time the story ends, you should have found an answer or resolution to this conflict. Include five words from this lesson and underline them.

LESSON 20 IMPORTANCE

Every day, people make decisions based on how important they think an action is. You may, for example, write yourself a reminder to make an important phone call. Your history teacher may ask you to rank in order of importance the causes of the Civil War. You probably remember important occasions like a friend's birthday and forget unimportant occurrences like yesterday's breakfast. Sometimes you have to decide which of two events—a dance or a concert, for example—is more important to you. The words in this lesson will help you to express the different degrees of importance that you assign to various situations.

WORD LIST

eminent
indispensable
momentous
paramount
petty
prestige
priority
prominence
superficial
trivial

DEFINITIONS

After you have studied the definitions and example for each vocabulary word, write the word on the line to the right.

1. **eminent** (ĕm'ə-nənt) *adjective* **a.** Outstanding or superior in performance or character; remarkable; noteworthy. **b.** Well-known and respected. (From the Latin word *eminens,* meaning "standing out")

   Related Words eminence *noun;* **eminently** *adverb*
   Example The *eminent* scientist was often asked to speak at conferences.

   1. _____
   USAGE NOTE: Don't confuse *eminent* with *imminent,* which means "about to occur." See *prominence.*

2. **indispensable** (ĭn'dĭ-spĕn'sə-bəl) *adjective* Required; essential; necessary.

   Related Word **indispensability** *noun*
   Example A bank card is *indispensable* when using an ATM.

   2. _____

3. **momentous** (mō-mĕn'təs) *adjective* Of great importance or outstanding significance. (From the Latin word *momentum,* meaning "movement" or "influence")

   Related Word **momentousness** *noun*
   Example Receiving her first paycheck was a *momentous* experience for Germaine.

   3. _____

4. **paramount** (păr'ə-mount') *adjective* Of chief concern; foremost; primary. (From the Old French words *par,* meaning "by," and *amont,* meaning "above")

   Example The *paramount* aim of the colonists was winning their independence from England.

   4. _____

5. **petty** (pĕt′ē) *adjective*   **a.** Small or insignificant in quantity or quality.
   b. Narrow-minded; selfish.   **c.** Mean and spiteful. (From the French
   word *petit*, meaning "small")

   Related Word   pettiness *noun*
   Example   The shopper made a *petty* complaint about the speed of
                      the store's elevator.

5. _____

6. **prestige** (prĕ-stēzh′) *noun*   High regard or status in the eyes of others.
   (From the Latin word *praestigiae*, meaning "tricks")

   Related Word   prestigious *adjective*
   Example   Because of his *prestige* as a diplomat, the ambassador was
                      often consulted about negotiating treaties.

6. _____

7. **priority** (prī-ôr′ĭ-tē) *noun*   **a.** Order of importance or urgency.
   b. Something more important than other considerations. (From the Latin
   word *prior*, meaning "previous" or "former")

   Related Word   prior *adjective*
   Example   In its list of improvements for the school, the committee
                      gave *priority* to a new science laboratory.

7. _____

8. **prominence** (prŏm′ə-nəns) *noun*   The condition of being immediately
   noticeable or widely known. (From the Latin word *prominere*, meaning "to
   jut out")

   Related Words   prominent *adjective*; prominently *adverb*
   Example   Ben's *prominence* in the community resulted from his
                       participation in volunteer activities.

8. _____

   USAGE NOTE: *Prominent*
   and *eminent* are syn-
   onyms, but *prominent* can
   also mean "immediately
   noticeable; conspicuous":
   a prominent nose.

9. **superficial** (sōō′pər-fĭsh′əl) *adjective*   **a.** On or near the surface; *a
   superficial wound.*   **b.** Concerned only with what is apparent or obvious;
   shallow; not deeply penetrating. (From the Latin *super-*, meaning "above,"
   and *facies*, meaning "face")

   Related Words   superficiality *noun*; superficially *adverb*
   Example   We did a *superficial* cleaning before our guests arrived.

9. _____

10. **trivial** (trĭv′ē-əl) *adjective*   **a.** Of little importance or significance.
    b. Ordinary; commonplace. (From the Latin *tri-*, meaning "three," and
    via, meaning "road")

    Related Words   trivia *noun*; triviality *noun*; trivialize *verb*
    Example   The topics for discussion seemed so *trivial* to Pam that
                        she left the conference.

10. _____

EXERCISE I   WRITING CORRECT WORDS

On the answer line, write the word from the vocabulary list that fits
each definition.

1. The condition of being favorably known or immediately noticeable

2. Small or insignificant; narrow-minded

3. Great status or favorable regard

4. Outstanding in performance or character; well-known and respected

5. Order of importance or urgency

6. Of greatest concern; supreme in rank or authority

7. Of or near the surface; concerned with what is apparent or obvious

8. Of little importance; ordinary

9. Required; necessary; essential

10. Of great importance

1. prominence
2. petty
3. prestige
4. eminent
5. priority
6. paramount
7. superficial
8. trivial
9. indispensable
10. momentous

EXERCISE 2   USING WORDS CORRECTLY

Each of the following statements contains an italicized vocabulary word. Decide
whether the sentence is true or false, and write *True* or *False* on the answer line.

1. No one pays attention to a person of *prominence*.

2. A *trivial* comment deserves a thoughtful, intelligent response.

3. Armstrong and Aldrin's landing on the moon in 1969 was a *momentous* achievement.

4. A bat and ball are *indispensable* to anyone who wants to play baseball.

5. A sincere person is likely to wear a *superficial* smile.

6. The president of a large corporation has a position of *prestige*.

7. Those who have been waiting in line for a long time usually have *priority* over newcomers.

8. Using reflectors is *paramount* when bicycling after dark.

9. An expert would be expected to make *petty* accusations on a television talk show.

10. *Eminent* people have poor reputations in their fields.

1. False
2. False
3. True
4. True
5. False
6. True
7. True
8. True
9. False
10. False

EXERCISE 3   CHOOSING THE BEST DEFINITION

For each italicized word or related form in the following sentences, write the
letter of the best definition on the answer line.

1. Color is a *trivial* consideration in the purchase of a lawnmower.
   a. important   **b.** required   **c.** realistic   **d.** unimportant

1. d

2. Dr. Bless had earned her *prestige* by writing numerous articles for scientific journals.
   a. salary   **b.** esteem   **c.** promotion   **d.** dislike

   2. _____ b

3. Mr. O'Sullivan explained that his daughter's word was *indispensable* to his business.
   a. active   **b.** harmful   **c.** necessary   **d.** serious

   3. _____ c

4. The directors made the *momentous* decision to sell the company.
   a. foolish   **b.** quick   **c.** certain   **d.** important

   4. _____ d

5. Walter became an *eminent* chef when he began to write a weekly food column for the magazine.
   a. well-known   **b.** creative   **c.** clumsy   **d.** powerful

   5. _____ a

6. Smoke detectors are the safety devices that have the highest *priority* in skyscrapers.
   a. order of importance   **b.** level of failure   **c.** superiority   **d.** power

   6. _____ a

7. The seriously ill woman has an appointment with a *prominent* doctor.
   a. wise   **b.** widely known   **c.** philosophical   **d.** prize-winning

   7. _____ b

8. Will and Josephine made *superficial* conversation while they waited for the bus.
   a. brief   **b.** enjoyable   **c.** unintelligent   **d.** shallow

   8. _____ d

9. The cartoonist's *petty* comments about the students' drawings brought groans from the class.
   a. humorous   **b.** positive   **c.** mean   **d.** kind

   9. _____ c

10. Saving lives is *paramount* to firefighters.
    a. unimportant   **b.** most important   **c.** enjoyable   **d.** normal

    10. _____ b

EXERCISE 4 USING DIFFERENT FORMS OF WORDS

Decide which form of the vocabulary word in parentheses best completes the sentence. The form given may be correct. Write your answer on the answer line.

1. Because of her _____, the artist received numerous requests to paint portraits of wealthy people. *(eminent)*

   1. _____ eminence

2. The headwaiter suggested that next time we call for reservations _____ to arriving at the restaurant. *(priority)*

   2. _____ prior

3. Arguments often reveal the _____ of the people involved. *(petty)*

   3. _____ pettiness

4. Daily brushing is _____ in keeping teeth healthy. *(paramount)*

   4. _____ paramount

5. The _____ of our new neighbor's friendliness was apparent to all of us. *(superficial)*

   5. _____ superficiality

6. People sometimes _____ important subjects by making jokes about them. *(trivial)*

   6. _____ trivialize

7. Carl's announcement added to the _____ of the occasion. *(momentous)*

   7. _____ momentousness

8. The giraffe's most _____ feature is its long neck. *(prominence)*

   8. _____ prominent

9. Finding his pockets empty, Tom moaned about the _____ of money. *(indispensable)*

   9. _____ indispensability

10. Cecelia won the _____ writing contest. *(prestige)*

    10. _____ prestigious

READING COMPREHENSION

Each numbered sentence in the following passage contains an italicized vocabulary word or related form. At the end of the passage, you will complete an exercise.

ALFRED NOBEL: THE MAN AND THE PRIZE

(1) Alfred Nobel (1833–1896) was an *eminent* Swedish chemist, inventor, and industrialist. His experiments with explosives led to his invention of dynamite in 1866 and to the development of devices that make the dynamite explode. (2) After an accidental explosion killed his brother, Nobel's *paramount* concern was to make the dangerous substance nitroglycerin, from which dynamite is made, into a safe and useful explosive. (3) In fact, the results of his work became *indispensable* in mining, building roads, blasting tunnels, and carrying out other types of construction.

Nobel was talented in many areas. He held 355 patents for such developments as synthetic rubber and leather, artificial silk, and torpedoes. He even wrote novels and plays. (4) His literary efforts never gained *prominence*, however.

(5) Swedish critics regarded his writing as *superficial.*

Nobel's health was not good, and in his later years, he became increasingly concerned about the future. (6) It was not a *trivial* matter to him that the substance he had created was used for warfare rather than for making peace. Wanting to make a contribution to the future of humanity, Nobel left his nine-million-dollar fortune in trust. He specified that the interest earned from the trust be used to award five annual prizes to people whose achievements further the welfare of humanity. (7) *Petty* concerns such as nationality, race, or political beliefs were to play no part in the selection process. (8) Instead, he intended the selections to be based solely on *momentous* contributions in physics, chemistry, physiology or medicine, literature, and international peace. Since 1969, a sixth award, in economics, has also been granted.

(9) The *prestigious* Nobel Prizes are presented annually at ceremonies in Stockholm, Sweden, and Oslo, Norway, on December 10, which is the anniversary of Nobel's death. Each Nobel laureate, as a winner is called, receives a diploma and a gold medal in addition to the cash award, which now totals more than one hundred thousand dollars for each recipient. Each laureate delivers a lecture at some time during the year on his or her field.

(10) We can best understand Alfred Nobel's *priority* of encouraging and rewarding worthwhile contributions by remembering some of the most famous winners. Pierre and Marie Curie, Albert Schweitzer, Rudyard Kipling, Pearl Buck, Albert Einstein, Martin Luther King, Jr., and Mother Teresa are but a few of the Nobel laureates chosen since the prizes were first awarded in 1901.

READING COMPREHENSION EXERCISE

Each of the following statements corresponds to a numbered sentence in the passage. Each statement contains a blank and is followed by four answer choices. Decide which choice fits best in the blank. The word or phrase that you choose must express roughly the same meaning as the italicized word in the passage. Write the letter of your choice on the answer line.

1. Alfred Nobel was a(n) _____ Swedish inventor and industrialist.
   a. well-known   **b.** creative   **c.** reserved   **d.** intelligent

   1. _____a_____

2. Nobel's _____ concern was to make nitroglycerin safe and useful.
   a. equal   **b.** present   **c.** secondary   **d.** primary

   2. _____d_____

3. Nobel's invention was _____ for many types of construction.
   a. useless   **b.** costly   **c.** necessary   **d.** extended

   3. _____c_____

4. Nobel's literary efforts never gained _____.
   a. importance   **b.** quality   **c.** good reviews   **d.** prizes

   4. _____a_____

5. Swedish critics said that Nobel's writing was _____.
   a. difficult   **b.** shallow   **c.** important   **d.** confusing

   5. _____b_____

6. To Nobel, it was not a(n) _____ matter that he had created a substance used for warfare.
   a. awful   **b.** practical   **c.** realistic   **d.** unimportant

   6. _____d_____

7. _____ concerns were to play no part in selecting Nobel prize winners.
   a. Monetary   **b.** National   **c.** Major   **d.** Unimportant

   7. _____d_____

8. Prizes would be awarded for _____ contributions.
   a. outstanding   **b.** small   **c.** glamorous   **d.** timely

   8. _____a_____

9. The _____ prizes are presented annually in Sweden and Norway.
   a. large   **b.** secret   **c.** esteemed   **d.** exciting

   9. _____c_____

10. Nobel's _____ was to encourage and reward worthwhile contributions.
    a. first concern   **b.** secret expectation   **c.** wish   **d.** demand

    10. _____a_____

WRITING ASSIGNMENT

You have been asked to introduce a famous person who will speak to an all-school assembly. Choose a prominent person, such as a scientist, a doctor, or an entertainer, who has made an important contribution to humanity. Write a short speech of introduction that provides background information about the person and that stresses his or her achievements. Use at least five of the vocabulary words from this lesson in your introduction and underline them.

VOCABULARY ENRICHMENT

Trivial, one of the words in this lesson, has an interesting history. The word derives from the Latin *tri-*, meaning "three," and *via*, meaning "road." At first glance, it would appear that *trivial* and its definition, "unimportant" or "ordinary," have little to do with three roads. In ancient Rome, however, the intersection of three roads became a public square, or a *trivium*. In these squares, travelers and residents gathered to exchange gossip and information about everyday matters. Because a *trivium* was the site of ordinary conversation, *trivial* has evolved to mean "ordinary" or "unimportant."

Activity   Other words have indirect connections with their original meanings. In a high-school or college dictionary, look up each of the following words, and write its Latin root and the meaning of that root. Then write a brief explanation of the connection between the root and the most common definition of the English word.

1. visa   2. voyage   3. itinerary   4. journey

The **Bonus activity** for Lessons 19 and 20 is on page T22.

Most basketball players would agree that they do not care how many fouls referees call, as long as those fouls are called fairly against all players. This desire for fairness holds true in every area of life, whether it be school, work, or friendship.

The words in this lesson refer to fair and unfair situations. Learning them may help you to understand and deal more effectively with the experiences in your own life that seem unfair.

WORD LIST

abide
amenable
bias
discrimination
forbearance
objective
partisan
preconceived
prejudice
tolerance

DEFINITIONS

After you have studied the definitions and example for each vocabulary word, write the word on the line to the right.

1. **abide** (ə-bīd') *verb*   **a.** To put up with; bear; tolerate.   **b.** To remain; stay.   **c.** To live; reside.   **d.** To wait patiently for; await.   **e.** To live up to; comply with: *abide by an agreement.* (From the Old English word *abidare,* meaning "to wait")

   Example   Robert could not *abide* his friend's annoying practical jokes.

   1. _____

2. **amenable** (ə-mē'nə-bəl) *adjective*   Willing to cooperate; agreeable. (From the Latin word *minari,* meaning "to threaten")

   Example   Therese was *amenable* to her parents' change of plans.

   2. _____
   ETYMOLOGY NOTE: *Amenable,* "not threatening" in Latin, is related to *menacing.*

3. **bias** (bī'əs) *noun*   An inclination for or against something or someone that affects the fairness of one's judgment.   *verb*   To cause to have a prejudiced view; influence unfairly.

   Example   Henry had a *bias* against foreign films because he hated reading subtitles.

   3. _____

4. **discrimination** (dĭ-skrĭm'ə-nā'shən) *noun*   **a.** One or more acts based on unfairness or injustice toward a particular group of persons.   **b.** The ability to distinguish, especially to recognize small differences or to make fine distinctions. (From the Latin *dis-,* meaning "apart," and *cernere,* meaning "to sift")

   Related Words **discriminate** *verb;* **discrimatory** *adjective*
   Example   Federal laws forbid *discrimination* on the basis of race, creed, color, sex, or age.

   4. _____

5. **forbearance** (fôr-bâr′əns) *noun* Patience, tolerance, or restraint.

   Related Word forbear *verb*
   Example Clifford showed great *forbearance* toward Sally, even after she made critical remarks about his cat, Claws.

   5. _____
   See *tolerance.*

6. **objective** (əb-jĕk′tĭv) *adjective* **a.** Not influenced by emotion or personal opinion. **b.** Real or actual: *objective facts.*

   Related Words objectively *adverb;* **objectivity** *noun*
   Example Paul had trouble remaining *objective* when his favorite team was playing baseball.

   6. _____

7. **partisan** (pär′tĭ-zən) *noun* A strong supporter of a party, cause, team, or person. *adjective* Having or showing a strong preference. (From the Italian word *partigiano,* meaning "supporter")

   Related Word partisanship *noun*
   Example Paul Revere was a *partisan* of the early independence movement in Colonial times.

   7. _____

8. **preconceived** (prē′kən-sēvd′) *adjective* Formed in the mind before full or adequate knowledge is acquired. (From the Latin *prae-,* meaning "before," and *concipere,* meaning "to take hold of")

   Related Word preconception *noun*
   Example Terence had a *preconceived* opinion about the issue before the committee.

   8. _____

9. **prejudice** (prĕj′ə-dĭs) *noun* **a.** A strong feeling or opinion that is formed before one knows the facts. **b.** Hostility toward members of other races, religions, nationalities, or other groups. *verb* To cause someone to judge before having complete information. (From the Latin *prae-,* meaning "before," and *judicium,* meaning "judgment")

   Example My *prejudice* against modern art vanished as I came to understand it better.

   9. _____

10. **tolerance** (tŏl′ər-əns) *noun* **a.** Respect for the opinions, practices, and behavior of others. **b.** The capacity to endure hardship or pain. (From the Latin word *tolerare,* meaning "to bear")

    Related Words tolerant *adjective;* **tolerate** *verb;* **toleration** *noun*
    Example My father's *tolerance* for my new CDs improved after he listened more closely to the music.

    10. _____
    USAGE NOTE: *Tolerance* refers to the acceptance of others. *Forbearance* suggests resigned acceptance.

EXERCISE 1 WRITING CORRECT WORDS

On the answer line, write the word for the vocabulary list that fits each definition.

1. An opinion held without knowledge of the facts

2. Patience and restraint, even when one does not like a situation

3. A preference that leads to unfair judgment

4. Formed in the mind before the facts are known

5. To tolerate or await patiently

6. One or more actions based on unfair, unjust attitudes toward a group

7. Respect for the attitudes of others

8. Agreeable; willing to cooperate

9. A supporter of a particular group or cause

10. Not influenced by emotion or personal opinion

1. _____ prejudice _____

2. _____ forbearance _____

3. _____ bias _____

4. _____ preconceived _____

5. _____ abide _____

6. _____ discrimination _____

7. _____ tolerance _____

8. _____ amenable _____

9. _____ partisan _____

10. _____ objective _____

EXERCISE 2 USING WORDS CORRECTLY

Each of the following questions contains an italicized vocabulary word. Decide the answer to the question, and write *Yes* or *No* on the answer line.

1. Does an *amenable* person argue constantly with people?

2. Would an *objective* employer hire only friends?

3. Do you show *tolerance* if you listen receptively to people's opinions?

4. Would a *partisan* of democracy support the right to vote?

5. Would a librarian *abide* loud talking by a group of library users?

6. Would you be showing *forbearance* if you reacted calmly to an insult?

7. Are *preconceived* ideas always correct?

8. Does *prejudice* result from studying all sides of an issue?

9. If one treats members of all groups equally, is one guilty of *discrimination?*

10. Does a *bias* against young people mean an unfair attitude toward them?

1. _____ No _____

2. _____ No _____

3. _____ Yes _____

4. _____ Yes _____

5. _____ No _____

6. _____ Yes _____

7. _____ No _____

8. _____ No _____

9. _____ No _____

10. _____ Yes _____

EXERCISE 3 CHOOSING THE BEST WORD

Decide which vocabulary word or related form best expresses the meaning of the italicized word or phrase in the sentence. On the answer line, write the letter of the correct choice.

1. Mark distinguished himself by his *ability to make fine distinctions.*
   a. partisanship   **b.** discrimination   **c.** bias   **d.** forbearance

1. _____ b _____

2. Monica had a *fixed idea* against outdoor weddings.
   a. tolerance   **b.** bias   **c.** discrimination **d.** objectivity

   2. _____ b

3. Blair had several *prematurely developed* ideas about the city.
   a. preconceived **b.** partisan   **c.** tolerant   **d.** forbearing

   3. _____ a

4. *Respect for the beliefs of others* is a requirement for effective student government.
   a. Partisanship   **b.** Prejudice   **c.** Preconception **d.** Tolerance

   4. _____ d

5. Janet was *agreeable* to her parents' plans to relocate in another city.
   a. amenable   **b.** objective   **c.** discriminating **d.** biased

   5. _____ a

6. The judges of the essay contest were *uninfluenced by personal opinion.*
   a. prejudiced   **b.** partisan   **c.** objective   **d.** tolerant

   6. _____ c

7. "I will *comply with* your decision," Simon told his mother.
   a. prejudice   **b.** abide by   **c.** discriminate **d.** bias

   7. _____ b

8. The sportswriter admitted to having a *fixed opinion made without consideration of the facts* against hockey.
   a. forbearance   **b.** partisanship **c.** objectivity   **d.** prejudice

   8. _____ d

9. Amanda showed great *restraint and patience* with her younger brother.
   a. partisanship   **b.** discrimination **c.** objectivity   **d.** forbearance

   9. _____ d

10. The *supporters* of wildlife preservation will meet tomorrow afternoon.
    a. biases   **b.** discriminations   **c.** partisans   **d.** tolerance

    10. _____ c

EXERCISE 4 USING DIFFERENT FORMS OF WORDS

Decide which form of the vocabulary word in parentheses best completes the sentence. The form given may be correct. Write your answer on the answer line.

1. Cathy had many _____ about the new season's television shows. *(preconceived)*

   1. preconceptions

2. Robert claims that the condominium rules _____ against owners of pets. *(discrimination)*

   2. discriminate

3. The instructor always evaluated the students' work _____. *(objective)*

   3. objectively

4. A good driver, Mrs. Beck _____ by the rules of the road. *(abide)*

   4. abides

5. A _____ opinion usually has no basis in fact. *(prejudice)*

   5. prejudiced

6. Are you able to _____ when teased by an older brother or sister? *(forbearance)*

   6. forbear

7. "I can no longer _____ your bad manners," Chuck told his younger brother. *(tolerance)*

   7. tolerate

8. Everyone was _____ to the idea of leaving early. *(amenable)*

   8. amenable

9. Alan was a _____ of the popular politician. *(partisan)*

   9. partisan

10. The car dealer was _____ against plans for improving mass transportation. *(bias)*

    10. biased

READING COMPREHENSION

Each numbered sentence in the following passage contains an italicized vocabulary word. After you read the passage, you will complete an exercise.

THE NEW GIRL

The cafeteria line moved slowly, and I was in a hurry to join my friends. We always ate lunch together in a special section reserved for eighth graders. (1) The younger students accused us of *discrimination,* but eighth-grade seating privileges were a time-honored tradition at Elmwood Junior High School. (2) It wasn't that we didn't have *tolerance* for the other students; it's just that they weren't eighth graders.

"Hi, Jennifer," Alicia said shyly. I hadn't noticed that she was behind me.

Alicia was new to the school. She seemed to have so much to say, only no one wanted to listen. It was usually like that when you were new. (3) People seemed to have a *bias* against you.

I knew how Alicia felt. It had been like that for me last year. (4) I didn't like thinking about it—the mornings when I could barely *abide* getting up, dreading another lonely day at school. That was all before I had found friends or, rather, Cindy and the other girls had found me. I knew how lonely Alicia was, I decided to smile back at her.

(5) "How do you have the *forbearance* to wait in these long cafeteria lines?" Alicia asked.

"Oh, you get used to it."

"I'm glad Mr. Fitzgibbons read your essay aloud in English class," Alicia told me. (6) "I'm also a *partisan* of the great out-

doors. Last summer, my parents and I camped throughout most of Europe."

"You did! How was it? I wish I could do something like that."

"It was wonderful!" She smiled at the memory. "Of course, camping can be difficult. (7) You have to be very *amenable* to the unexpected. Would you like to see a few pictures of our trip? We could have lunch and I could show you—"

"Oh, I'd like to, but —" I interrupted quickly.

"Sure, some other time." Alicia's enthusiasm died.

Cindy and the other girls in our group were busy dissecting what they considered to be the major event of the morning when I finally joined them. Alicia was sitting at the outskirts of the eighth-grade section, dangerously near some seventh graders. She read a book while she ate. I wondered if she ever turned a page. I hadn't when I'd sat alone in the cafeteria.

"Oh, I was talking to Alicia," I began, aware of five pairs of disapproving eyes turned in my direction. "Maybe we should ask her to eat lunch with us."

They all laughed, which was worse than an argument.

"I think Alicia's nice," I dared to say. "No one gives her a chance."

"Alicia talks funny. She doesn't dress in style, and it's obvious that she doesn't care about any-

thing that's really important," Cindy pointed out.

(8) I was silent. If I said anything to contradict the girls' *preconceived* ideas about Alicia, they might change their minds about including me in their group. It was unfair. (9) They weren't being *objective* about Alicia, but there wasn't anything I could do to change their opinion.

I didn't see Alicia in the cafeteria for the rest of the week. I felt guilty and relieved at the same time. Finally, on a rainy Friday, Alicia ventured cautiously in. All of the tables were filled in the eighth-grade section. Alicia hesitated and then sat at the end of a table with some noisy seventh graders.

Cindy turned to me. "Looks like Alicia found some friends."

All the girls laughed.

"Leave her alone!" I said, surprising myself.

They looked at me in shocked disbelief. I had dared to contradict Cindy. I held my ground.

"If you're so worried about Alicia, why don't you sit with her?" Cindy challenged.

"Maybe I will." (10) I gathered up my things and walked away from their table, glad that I finally had the courage to let the girls know how unfair and *prejudiced* I thought they were. Still, I'd be dishonest if I pretended that the loud laughter at their table didn't bother me.

Each of the following statements corresponds to a numbered sentence in the passage. Each statement contains a blank and is followed by four answer choices. Decide which choice fits best in the blank. The word or phrase that you choose must express roughly the same meaning as the italicized word in the passage. Write the letter of your choice on the answer line.

1. The younger students accused the eighth graders of _____.
   a. cheating   **b.** ignorance   **c.** unfairness   **d.** cruelty

   1. _____ c _____

2. It wasn't true, Jennifer jokingly said, that eighth graders lacked _____ the younger students.
   a. acceptance of   **c.** anger toward
   b. dislike for   **d.** mistreatment of

   2. _____ a _____

3. Jennifer pointed out the _____ new students.
   a. friendliness toward   **c.** competitions against
   b. unfair opinion of   **d.** mistreatment of

   3. _____ b _____

4. Jennifer remembered that she could barely _____ getting ready for school each day.
   a. endure   **b.** avoid   **c.** remember   **d.** stop

   4. _____ a _____

5. Alicia asked Jennifer how she had the _____ to wait in the cafeteria lines.
   a. nerve   **b.** ability   **c.** strength   **d.** patience

   5. _____ d _____

6. Alicia described herself as _____ outdoor activities.
   a. afraid of   **c.** a supporter of
   b. ready for   **d.** experienced in

   6. _____ c _____

7. She explained that it is necessary to be _____ in the face of unexpected events.
   a. healthy   **b.** flexible   **c.** active   **d.** emotional

   7. _____ b _____

8. Jennifer was afraid that she would be left out if she contradicted her friends' opinions, which were _____.
   a. formed prematurely   **c.** lacking in intelligence
   b. fair   **d.** negative

   8. _____ a _____

9. Jennifer knew that the girls were not _____ in their view of Alicia.
   a. daring   **b.** critical   **c.** fair   **d.** kind

   9. _____ c _____

10. Finally, Jennifer was able to let the girls know how _____ she thought they were.
    a. critical   **b.** right   **c.** logical   **d.** unfair

    10. _____ d _____

Think of a time when you were judged unfairly or when you were guilty of misjudging someone else. Choose an experience that you would like to share with a friend. Tell about this experience, explaining how you handled the problem. Include five words from this lesson and underline each one.

The **Test** for Lessons 19, 20, and 21 is on page T23.

READING SKILLS
CONTEXT CLUES: SYNONYMS

Sometimes you may be puzzled by an unfamiliar word in your reading. If you study the sentence containing the word, you may find clues to the meaning of the word. (A synonym is a word similar in meaning to another word.) Suppose that you do not know the meaning of the italicized word in this sentence:

> Three exhausted *raconteurs* left the party, but the fourth storyteller stayed to entertain us.

In the sentence, *storyteller* is a synonym of *raconteurs*. It is a context clue that suggests the meaning of the italicized word. The following strategies will help you use synonyms as context clues.

STRATEGIES

1. *Look for a word in the sentence that is the same part of speech as the unfamiliar word.* An unfamiliar word and its synonym will usually be the same part of speech. In the example above, both *raconteur* and *storyteller* are nouns.
2. *Examine the structure of the sentence.* The unfamiliar word and its synonym will often function in the same way in the sentence. Both *raconteur* and *storyteller* function as the subjects of independent clauses in the example above.
3. *Look for other words in the sentence that can serve as clues.* Both the unfamiliar word and its synonym will frequently be preceded or followed by words that are the same part of speech. For instance, *raconteurs* and *storyteller* are each preceded by an adjective (*three* and *fourth*).
4. *Check the meaning of the word in a dictionary.* Definitions based on context clues are approximate. Whenever possible, look up the unfamiliar word in the dictionary.

EXERCISE USING SYNONYMS AS CONTEXT CLUES

Each of the sentences on the following page contains a synonym of the italicized word. *Step 1:* Write the synonym of the italicized word. *Step 2:* Write the appropriate dictionary definition of the italicized word. *Step 3:* Write a sentence of your own in which you use the word with the same meaning as the dictionary definition.

1. The *stipend* was enough to live on, but the payment allowed no luxuries.

   Synonym payment

   Dictionary Definition A fixed and regular payment

   Sentence My brother's scholarship stipend covers tuition, room, and board.

2. The other meeting was dull, but our *symposium* was interesting.

   Synonym meeting

   Dictionary Definition A meeting or conference for discussing a topic

   Sentence The topic of our Geography Day symposium was "Rivers of South America."

3. Having promised not to *divulge* Anna's secret, Tim never did reveal it.

   Synonym reveal

   Dictionary Definition To make known; reveal; tell

   Sentence The witness refused to divulge the contents of the letter of the trial.

4. The team's *exuberance* was matched by the liveliness of the spectators.

   Synonym liveliness

   Dictionary Definition the condition of being lively and joyous; high spirits

   Sentence The exuberance of the cheerleaders spread to everyone at the rally.

5. Some thought his trite compliments and *banal* remarks brilliant.

   Synonym trite

   Dictionary Definition Lacking originality; meaningless and dull; trite

   Sentence Our entire family laughed at the unbelievably banal dialogue in the movie.

6. "You are *tenacious*," Bob told Sarah, "and I like persistent people."

   Synonym persistent

   Dictionary Definition Holding or tending to hold firmly; persistent

   Sentence The collie was tenacious in her refusal to let the sheep cross the highway.

7. Calvin's *duplicity* is no worse than the deception that Simone practices.

   Synonym deception

   Dictionary Definition Deliberate deception; double-dealing

   Sentence Cora's incorruptible honesty ruled out duplicity of any kind.

8. Sam managed to control the conversation and thus *monopolize* our discussion.

   Synonym control

   Dictionary Definition To gain exclusive control

   Sentence As usual, the baby sitter monopolized the television all evening long.

LESSON 22 PLANNING AND ACTION

Have you ever planned an action and carried it out? For example, suppose you are working on a science project. You wonder whether there is any scientific truth in the idea that house plants respond well when people talk nicely to them. In order to put this idea into action, you need to set up an experiment that tests the scientific accuracy of your idea. For example, you could give two plants equal amounts of sunlight, water, and fertilizer. However, you would talk encouragingly to one of the plants but not to the other. Then you would observe the plants to see whether one thrives more than the other.

In this lesson you will learn words that refer to many kinds of plans and activities.

WORD LIST

administer
animate
concoct
devise
endeavor
execute
implement
reactivate
render
undertaking

DEFINITIONS

After you have studied the definitions and example for each vocabulary word, write the word on the line to the right.

1. **administer** (ăd-mĭn′ĭ-stər) *verb*   **a.** To direct or manage: *to administer a business.*   **b.** To carry out: *to administer laws.*   **c.** To give as a remedy. (From the Latin *ad-*, meaning "to," and *ministrare*, meaning "to manage")

   Related Words administration *noun*; **administrator** *noun*
   Example   Personnel managers sometimes *administer* the training program of a company.

   1. _____

2. **animate** (ăn′ə-mat′) *verb*   **a.** To give life to; fill with life; enliven.
   b. To design so as to create the illusion of motion: *to animate a cartoon.*
   adjective (ăn′ə-mĭt)   Possessing life; living. (From the Latin word *anima*, meaning "soul")

   Related Word   animation *noun*
   Example   The hilarious comedian *animated* the party.

   2. _____

3. **concoct** (kən-kŏkt′) *verb*   **a.** To make up or invent, such as a plan or an excuse.   **b.** To make by mixing or combining ingredients. (From the Latin *com-*, meaning "together," and *coquere*, meaning "to cook")

   Related Word   concoction *noun*
   Example   The mystery writer *concocted* an exciting plot for her new book.

   3. _____

4. **devise** (dĭ-vīz′) *verb*   To form or arrange in the mind; plan or invent, as a solution to a problem.

   Example   Margaret *devised* an excellent advertising campaign for the new product.

   4. _____

5. **endeavor** (ĕn-dĕv′ər) *noun*   A major effort or attempt to accomplish something.   *verb*   To make an effort or attempt. (From the French word *devoir*, meaning "duty")

   Example   "I wish you luck in your new business *endeavor*," Mr. Chan told his former employee.

   5. _____

6. **execute** (ĕk′sĭ-kyōōt′) *verb*   **a.** To perform: *to execute a difficult gymnastic routine.*   **b.** To carry out what is required.   **c.** To put to death. (From the Latin *ex-*, meaning "out," and *sequi*, meaning "to follow")

   Related Words   **execution** *noun;* **executive** *noun;* **executive** *adjective*
   Example   The dolphin *executed* an impressive series of tricks.

   6. _____

7. **implement** (ĭm′plə-mĕnt′) *verb*   To put into effect; carry out: *to implement a plan.*   *noun* (ĭm′plə-mĕnt)   A tool, utensil, or instrument. (From the Latin word *implere,* meaning "to fill up")

   Related Word   **implementation** *noun*
   Example   The librarian plans to *implement* a new system for checking out books.

   7. _____

8. **reactivate** (re-ăk′tə-vāt′) *verb*   To make active again; restore the ability to function.

   Related Word   **reactivation** *noun*
   Example   The warm weather *reactivated* the children's interest in swimming.

   8. _____

9. **render** (rĕn′dər) *verb*   **a.** To give or make available: *to render service.*   **b.** To cause to become: *The hailstorm rendered the crop worthless.* (From the Latin *re-*, meaning "back," and *dare*, meaning "to give")

   Example   The volunteers *rendered* assistance to those who had lost their homes in the flood.

   9. _____

10. **undertaking** (ŭn′dər-tā′kĭng) *noun*   A task, assignment, or project.

    Related Word   **undertake** *verb*
    Example   The construction of the fifty-story building was an expensive *undertaking*.

    10. _____

    USAGE NOTE: Although the related noun *undertaker* also means "one who undertakes a task," it is more commonly used to mean "mortician."

EXERCISE 1 COMPLETING DEFINITIONS

On the answer line, write the word from the vocabulary list that best completes each definition.

1. To make something by combining ingredients is to _____ it.

2. A venture or task is a(n) _____.

3. If you put a plan into effect, you _____ it.

4. A person who knows how to manage an organization knows how to _____.

5. When you perform a task, you _____ it.

6. If you enliven something, you _____ it.

7. To _____ a solution is to plan or invent one.

8. To give or provide something, such as a service, is to _____ it.

9. A major attempt or effort is a(n) _____.

10. To restore something to action is to _____ it.

1. **concoct**
2. **undertaking**
3. **implement**
4. **administer**
5. **execute**
6. **animate**
7. **devise**
8. **render**
9. **endeavor**
10. **reactivate**

EXERCISE 2 USING WORDS CORRECTLY

Each of the following questions contains an italicized vocabulary word. Decide the answer to the question, and write *Yes* or *No* on the answer line.

1. Would a three-month-old puppy probably be *animated*?

2. Would the writing of a novel be a small *undertaking*?

3. Should a university president know how to *administer* a large organization?

4. Could a professional ice skater *execute* a difficult routine?

5. Is dialing a telephone an *endeavor* for most people?

6. Does a doctor *render* treatment to his or her patients?

7. Should a person *devise* a plan before tackling a difficult problem?

8. When you *implement* a plan, do you reject it?

9. Might a person *concoct* a new recipe?

10. If you *reactivate* an engine, do you turn it off?

1. **Yes**
2. **No**
3. **Yes**
4. **Yes**
5. **No**
6. **Yes**
7. **Yes**
8. **No**
9. **Yes**
10. **No**

EXERCISE 3 CHOOSING THE BEST DEFINITION

For each italicized vocabulary word in the following sentences, write the letter of the best definition on the answer line.

1. In the story the sorcerer *concocts* a sleeping potion.
   a. labels   **b.** drinks   **c.** boils   **d.** mixes

1. **d**

2. Studying to become a doctor is an *endeavor*.
   a. amusing game   c. good idea
   b. worthwhile pastime   d. major effort

2. _____d_____

3. The general contractor will *administer* the construction of the skyscraper.
   a. assist   b. direct   c. eliminate   d. describe

3. _____b_____

4. The aircraft company hoped to *reactivate* several old airplanes.
   a. destroy immediately   c. find unexpectedly
   b. change radically   d. restore to service

4. _____d_____

5. Mort will *implement* a new exercise program tomorrow.
   a. put into effect   c. seriously record
   b. try to invent   d. hope to finish

5. _____a_____

6. The climbing of Mount Everest is a serious *undertaking*.
   a. hike   b. project   c. mistake   d. crime

6. _____b_____

7. Several pedestrians *rendered* assistance to the motorist who was stuck in the snow.
   a. gave   b. withheld   c. promised   d. called for

7. _____a_____

8. Andrea was *animated* by an unexpected phone call.
   a. pleased   b. bored   c. enlivened   d. bothered

8. _____c_____

9. Sammy *devised* a more efficient way to wash dishes.
   a. borrowed   b. enjoyed   c. invented   d. ignored

9. _____c_____

10. In the last seconds, the quarterback *executed* a difficult play.
    a. invented   b. performed   c. botched   d. stopped

10. _____b_____

EXERCISE 4 USING DIFFERENT FORMS OF WORDS

Decide which form of the vocabulary word in parentheses best completes the sentence. The form given may be correct. Write your answer on the answer line.

1. The league has strict rules for the _____ of injured players. *(reactivate)*

1. __reactivation__

2. Bertha will soon _____ the swimming of the English Channel. *(undertaking)*

2. __undertake__

3. John's serve effectively _____ Larry's backhand useless. *(render)*

3. __rendered__

4. The _____ was admired for her strong leadership abilities. *(execute)*

4. __executive__

5. Student records are usually kept in the college _____ building. *(administer)*

5. __administration__

6. Parents were happy to hear about the _____ of a new reading program in the city schools. *(implement)*

6. __implementation__

7. The architect _____ to design unusual houses. *(endeavor)*

7. __endeavored__

8. The children enjoyed watching the _____ cartoons. *(animate)*

8. __animated__

9. Margaret invited everyone to taste her _____ of fresh fruit. *(concoct)*

9. __concoction__

10. Sid has _____ a way to do his homework faster. *(devise)*

10. __devised__

READING COMPREHENSION

Each numbered sentence in the following passage contains an italicized vocabulary word or related form. After you read the passage, you will complete the exercise.

THE MAMMALIAN DIVING REFLEX: FACT OR FICTION?

Could someone be submerged in freezing cold water for twenty minutes and survive? Four-year-old Jimmy Tontlewicz did. Here is his story.

(1) On a cold January day in 1984, Jimmy's father *concocted* a plan to take Jimmy sledding on a frozen section of Lake Michigan in Chicago. (2) This pleasant *undertaking* soon turned into a disaster when the ice broke and Jimmy slipped into the freezing lake.

(3) For twenty minutes Jimmy remained under water until scuba divers from the fire department *executed* a daring rescue mission. An ambulance then rushed Jimmy to the hospital, where he lay in a deathlike state. (4) Doctors surrounded Jimmy, trying to *devise* a treatment, but the case seemed hopeless. Jimmy's heart had stopped beating. His lungs were not functioning, and his temperature had dropped to eighty-five degrees.

(5) To start Jimmy's heart beating, the doctors *administered* electric shock treatment. Nothing happened. (6) They then *implemented* artificial respiration through the use of a respirator, hoping this would restore Jimmy's breathing. The respirator kept Jimmy's lungs inflated and his blood oxygenated, but there was still no sign of life. (7) All of the doctor's *endeavors* to save Jimmy appeared to have failed.

Suddenly, there was a beep on the screen of the heart monitor. Jimmy's heart had started. He was still alive! (8) His parents reacted to the news with great *animation.*

How could Jimmy have survived after his heart had stopped beating? Scientists explained that the shock of the cold water had put Jimmy into a state of hypothermia, a condition of abnormally low body temperature. The hypothermia had triggered what is known as the "mammalian diving reflex."

(9) This reflex *renders* marine mammals, such as whales and seals, able to remain under water for long periods of time without breathing. The "mammalian diving reflex" takes place as blood is forced near the heart and the brain. These organs then function very slowly while the mammal remains under water. (10) Once the mammal emerges from the water, normal heart and brain functions are *reactivated.*

It is rare that human beings exhibit the mammalian diving reflex. Luckily, Jimmy Tontlewicz is one of these people.

Each of the following statements corresponds to a numbered sentence in the passage. Each statement contains a blank and is followed by four answer choices. Decide which choice fits best in the blank. The word or phrase that you choose must express roughly the same meaning as the italicized word in the passage. Write the letter of your choice on the answer line.

1. Jimmy's father _____ a way to take his son sledding.
   a. thought of   **b.** imagined   **c.** obeyed   **d.** ignored

   1. _____a_____

2. The _____ turned into disaster when Jimmy slipped into the freezing water.
   a. holiday   **b.** venture   **c.** exercise   **d.** detour

   2. _____b_____

3. Scuba divers _____ a rescue mission that brought Jimmy to the surface.
   a. called   **b.** failed   **c.** planned   **d.** performed

   3. _____d_____

4. Doctors tried to _____ a treatment to save Jimmy's life.
   a. plan   **b.** remember   **c.** imitate   **d.** read about

   4. _____a_____

5. They _____ electric shock to Jimmy's heart.
   a. rejected   **b.** suggested   **c.** applied   **d.** questioned

   5. _____c_____

6. Doctors then _____ artificial respiration.
   a. invented   **b.** hoped for   **c.** rejected   **d.** carried out

   6. _____d_____

7. However, their _____ seemed to have failed.
   a. research   **b.** instruments   **c.** practice   **d.** attempts

   7. _____d_____

8. Jimmy's parents experienced great _____ at the change in their son's condition.
   a. puzzlement   **b.** depression   **c.** elation   **d.** uncertainty

   8. _____c_____

9. Jimmy's recovery was due, in part, to the mammalian diving reflex which _____ the ability to remain under water without breathing.
   a. tricks   **b.** provides   **c.** prevents   **d.** resembles

   9. _____b_____

10. When the mammal leaves the water, the actions of the heart and brain are _____.
    a. dead   **b.** numbed   **c.** restored   **d.** forgotten

   10. _____c_____

See page 119 for some strategies to use with analogies.

On the answer line, write the vocabulary word or a form of it that completes each analogy.

1. _____ is to wasteful as partisan is to biased. *(Lesson 19)*

   1. _____Spendthrift_____

2. Outrageous is to proper as _____ is to scarce. *(Lesson 19)*

   2. _____lavish_____

3. Superficial is to depth as _____ is to significance. *(Lesson 20)*

   3. _____trivial_____

4. Momentous is to important as _____ is to small. *(Lesson 20)*

   4. _____petty_____

5. Stew is to food as _____ is to ingredients. *(Lesson 22)*

   5. _____concoction_____

6. Accomplish is to task as _____ is to order. *(Lesson 22)*

   6. _____execute_____

The Latin root -port- is the basis of many of our English words. This root comes from the Latin word *portare*, which means "to carry." Therefore, *import* means to carry products into a location, and *export* means to carry products out of a location. *Transportation* is the means for carrying people from place to place. An *important* event carries weight. The words in this lesson come from the root -port- and refer in some way to the idea or action of carrying.

WORD LIST

comport
deportment
disport
insupportable
portable
portage
porter
portfolio
purport
sportive

DEFINITIONS

After you have studied the definitions and example for each vocabulary word, write the word on the line to the right.

1. **comport** (kəm-pôrt′) *verb*   To behave or conduct oneself in a particular way. (From the Latin *com-*, meaning "together," and *portare*, meaning "to carry")

   Related Word   comportment *noun*
   Example   The ambassadors *comported* themselves with dignity at the queens' garden party.

1. _____

USAGE NOTE: Although the verbs *comport* and *deport* mean the same thing, *deport* is more often used for its other meaning, "to expel from a country."

2. **deportment** (dǐ-pôrt′mənt) *noun*   Conduct or behavior. (From the Latin *de-*, meaning "away," and *portare*)

   Example   The speaker praised the polite *deportment* of the audience.

2. _____

See *comport*.

3. **disport** (dǐ-spôrt′) *verb*   To entertain or occupy oneself; play. (From the Latin *dis-*, meaning "apart," and *portare*)

   Example   At recess the children *disported* themselves on the playground.

3. _____

4. **insupportable** (ǐn′sə-pôr′tə-bəl) *adjective*   **a.** Unbearable or intolerable. **b.** Lacking grounds or defense; unjustifiable: *an insupportable argument.*

   Example   In the Middle Ages, living conditions for many people were almost *insupportable.*

4. _____

5. **portable** (pôr′tə-bəl) *adjective*   Easily carried; conveniently moved. *noun*   Something that is portable. (From the Latin word *portabilis*, meaning "able to be carried")

    Related Word   **portability** *noun*
    Example   I store my *portable* dishwasher in the corner of the kitchen.

5. _____

6. **portage** (pôr′tĭj) *noun*   The carrying of a boat and supplies over land between two waterways.   *verb*   To transport a boat and supplies. (From the Latin word *portare*)

    Example   We planned to learn to *portage* on our canoe trip.

6. _____

7. **porter** (pôr′tər) *noun*   **a.** A person employed to carry luggage for travelers.   **b.** An attendant who waits on passengers in a railroad car. (From the Latin word *portare*)

    Example   The *porter* put our luggage on a rack and wheeled it to the elevator.

7. _____

8. **portfolio** (pôrt-fō′lē-ō′) *noun*   **a.** A carrying case for loose papers, photographs, or drawings.   **b.** The materials collected in a carrying case, especially when they are samples of a person's work: *a photographer's portfolio.*   **c.** An itemized list of stocks, bonds, or other securities held by an investor or financial institution. (From the Latin words *folium*, meaning "leaf," and *portare*)

    Example   Janice's *portfolio* contained examples of her work in water colors.

8. _____

9. **purport** (pər-pôrt′) *verb*   To give the impression, often falsely, of being or intending; to profess.   *noun* (pûr′pôrt′)   The presented, intended, or implied meaning of something, such as a story. (From the Latin *pro-*, meaning "forth," and *portare*)

    Related Word   **purportedly** *adverb*
    Example   Kevin *purported* to be an excellent ice skater but fell flat on his face when he ventured onto the ice.

9. _____

10. **sportive** (spôr′tĭv) *adjective*   Playful; frolicsome. (From the English word *disport*, meaning "to play" or "to amuse oneself")

    Related Words **sportively** *adverb;* **sportiveness** *noun*
    Example   The *sportive* puppies got tangled in each other's legs.

10. _____

EXERCISE 1 WRITING CORRECT WORDS

On the answer line, write the word from the vocabulary list that fits each definition.

1. Easily carried; conveniently moved

2. A folder or carrying case for drawings or documents; the samples of a person's work that are collected in the carrying case

3. Frolicsome; playful

4. To conduct or behave oneself in a particular way

5. Unbearable or intolerable; lacking grounds or defense

6. The carrying of a boat and supplies over land between waterways

7. A person who carries baggage for travelers; an attendant in a railroad car

8. Conduct or behavior

9. To entertain oneself; play

10. To give an impression of being or intending; the implied meaning

1. __portable__
2. __portfolio__
3. __sportive__
4. __comport__
5. __insupportable__
6. __portage__
7. __porter__
8. __deportment__
9. __disport__
10. __purport__

EXERCISE 2 USING WORDS CORRECTLY

Each of the following statements contains an italicized vocabulary word. Decide whether the sentence is true or false, and write *True* or *False* on the answer line.

1. If Nathan has a job as a *porter,* he is employed to sell clothing.

2. People who *disport* themselves never have anything to do.

3. If Jeanine *comports* herself with sophistication, she acts silly.

4. An *insupportable* excuse is one that cannot be defended.

5. You can carry a *portable* computer onto an airplane.

6. Twelve-year-old dogs are usually more *sportive* than puppies.

7. If Hans *purports* to be studying hard, he may be pretending to study.

8. Orchestras frequently perform lengthy *deportments.*

9. If Lily and Sylvester cannot learn to *portage,* they cannot learn to carry their boat and supplies over land.

10. Max may use a *portfolio* to take his sketches to job interviews.

1. __False__
2. __False__
3. __False__
4. __True__
5. __True__
6. __False__
7. __True__
8. __False__
9. __True__
10. __True__

EXERCISE 3 CHOOSING THE BEST WORD

Decide which vocabulary word or related form best expresses the meaning of the italicized word or phrase in the sentence. On the answer line, write the letter of the correct choice.

1. Mrs. Barrett always chooses a *playful* horse when she goes riding.
   a. sportive   **b.** disported   **c.** portable   **d.** insupportable

1. __a__

2. Before meeting the king and queen of Spain, Franklin read a book telling him how to *conduct* himself with royalty.
   a. portage   **b.** disport   **c.** comport   **d.** purport

   2. _____ c _____

3. Giselle placed her manuscript in a *carrying case* and started for the publishing house.
   a. portage   **b.** portfolio   **c.** porter   **d.** deportment

   3. _____ b _____

4. When Jenny broke her toes, she suffered *unbearable* pain for several days.
   a. sportive   **b.** insupportable   **c.** portable   **d.** purported

   4. _____ b _____

5. A canal constructed through an isthmus saves boaters from having to *carry their boats across land.*
   a. disport   **b.** comport   **c.** purport   **d.** portage

   5. _____ d _____

6. We enjoy watching Tom's kitten *play* with a ball of yarn.
   a. comport   **b.** portage   **c.** purport   **d.** disport

   6. _____ d _____

7. The medical researchers *pretended* to have found a cure for the common cold.
   a. purported   **b.** comported   **c.** disported   **d.** portaged

   7. _____ a _____

8. During the interview Ms. Runyon studied the *conduct* of each job applicant.
   a. deportment   **b.** porter   **c.** portage   **d.** portfolio

   8. _____ a _____

9. Colin worked his way through college as a *luggage carrier* at an airport.
   a. portfolio   **b.** portage   **c.** comportment   **d.** porter

   9. _____ d _____

10. Jan liked the first radio that the salesperson showed her because it was *easily carried.*
    a. insupportable   **b.** sportive   **c.** portable   **d.** purported

    10. _____ c _____

EXERCISE 4   USING DIFFERENT FORMS OF WORDS

Decide which form of the vocabulary word in parentheses best completes the sentence. The form given may be correct. Write your answer on the answer line.

1. The only way to get across the sandbar that spans the lake is to _____ one's boat. *(portage)*

   1. _____ portage _____

2. During the graduation parade at West Point, General Saxon studied the _____ of the cadets. *(comport)*

   2. _____ comportment _____

3. Although Kevin liked the features of the television, he wondered about its _____. *(portable)*

   3. _____ portability _____

4. Mrs. O'Leary _____ contributed ten thousand dollars to the firefighters' fund. *(purport)*

   4. _____ purportedly _____

5. Tommy ran _____ through the cornfield. *(sportive)*

   5. _____ sportively _____

6. Proper _____ is essential to Harry Higgins. *(deportment)*

   6. _____ deportment _____

7. The witness's _____ testimony weakened the prosecutor's case. *(insupportable)*

   7. _____ insupportable _____

8. While Margaret was running to the bus, her _____ opened, spilling her drawings into the snow. *(portfolio)*

   8. _____ portfolio _____

9. Mr. Peters is an experienced _____ . *(porter)*

10. When she has a spare moment, the busy bank president always enjoys _____ with her grandchildren. *(disport)*

9. _____ porter

10. _____ disporting

Each numbered sentence in the following passage contains an italicized vocabulary word. After reading the passage, you will complete the exercise.

PROFESSIONAL MODELING: HARD WORK OR GLAMOUR?

(1) Some professional photographic models *purport* to lead glamorous and exciting lives. (2) Their *deportment* as celebrities is envied and copied. (3) Magazine and television advertisements show models *disporting* at the seashore, dining at elegant restaurants, or sitting at the wheel of the latest luxury car. Models who reach the top of their profession make large salaries, wear beautiful clothes, and enjoy varied assignments that take them all over the world.

This typical image of professional modeling is misleading, however. The work of a photographic model is harder and more demanding than it appears. Hours are long, and competition is fierce. Although the career attracts thousands of men, women, and children, only a small percentage become celebrities.

(4) Models begin their careers by assembling a *portfolio* of photographs that show them in a variety of poses with different facial expressions. (5) Advertisers select their models on the basis of how the models *comport* themselves in front of the camera. They must be well-groomed, physically attractive, and quite

thin, because photographs give the illusion of adding extra pounds. Models must also possess the special "look" that the advertiser wants, whether it be innocence or elegance. The ability to create the image that the client requires depends on the model's acting ability. (6) He or she may have to portray a college student in one picture or a *porter* in an airport in another.

The nature of assignments varies tremendously. (7) *Portable* cameras have enabled producers to shoot commercials in unusual places, such as deserts and mountain peaks. (8) One day models may find themselves *portaging* canoes up a stream for a blue-jeans sales promotion. (9) The next day they may have to participate *sportively* in an

exercise class for the filming of a commercial. (10) They must hold uncomfortable poses that can seem almost *insupportable* under hot lights. Large amounts of patience, energy, and flexibility are necessary. Because advertisers plan far in advance, models may find themselves wearing bathing suits in winter or heavy coats in summer.

Careers in modeling are usually short-lived. Although there are exceptions, the average length of a photographic model's career is about five years. "New faces" are always trying to break into the business, and modeling agencies and advertisers are looking constantly for fresh replacements. Photographic modeling is an exciting career, but also one that is demanding.

Each of the following statements corresponds to a numbered sentence in the passage. Each statement contains a blank and is followed by four answer choices. Decide which choice fits best in the blank. The word or phrase that you choose must express roughly the same meaning as the italicized word in the passage. Write the letter of your choice on the answer line.

1. Some professional models _____ to lead glamorous and exciting lives.
   a. try   **b.** wish   **c.** practice   **d.** profess

   1. _____d_____

2. People envy and copy the _____ of models.
   a. poses   **b.** behavior   **c.** careers   **d.** families

   2. _____b_____

3. Advertisements show models eating in elegant restaurants or _____ at the beach.
   a. swimming   **c.** enjoying themselves
   b. looking glamorous   **d.** posing

   3. _____c_____

4. Models first must assemble _____ .
   a. samples of their work   **c.** an autobiography
   b. a client list   **d.** a group of friends

   4. _____a_____

5. Advertisers are interested in the way models _____ in front of the camera.
   a. appear beautiful   **c.** conduct themselves
   b. smile   **d.** are nervous

   5. _____c_____

6. A model may have to portray a college student or a _____ .
   a. professor   **c.** rower
   b. luggage carrier   **d.** writer

   6. _____b_____

7. _____ cameras allow producers to shoot commercials in unusual locations.
   a. Advanced   **c.** Highly technical
   b. Large   **d.** Easily carried

   7. _____d_____

8. Models may have to _____ canoes for a sales promotion.
   a. carry   **b.** paddle   **c.** fall out of   **d.** pose in

   8. _____a_____

9. The following day they may have to participate _____ in an exercise class.
   a. athletically   **b.** playfully   **c.** seriously   **d.** silently

   9. _____b_____

10. Models must hold poses that can be almost _____ under hot lights.
    a. historical   **b.** artistic   **c.** easy   **d.** unbearable

    10. _____d_____

Imagine that you are a photographer hired by a sports magazine to take pictures of a canoe race for the magazine's next issue. To accompany your photographs, write a brief report that tells what you saw and photographed. You may want to include details about the contestants, the canoes, the setting, and the spectators. Use at least five of the vocabulary words from this lesson to describe your day's work and underline each word that you use.

What does being active mean to you? Listed below are some different ways to spend time. Which pastimes require a high degree of activity? Which ones indicate inactivity?

Reading a book
Swimming
Solving a math problem
Debating a controversial issue
Writing a poem
Planning a fund-raising project
Jogging two miles

All of the above items show a high degree of activity. Some of the activities are physical, such as jogging two miles, while some of them are intellectual, such as writing a poem. To function well, however, the body and the mind also require periods of inactivity or rest. The words in this lesson will help you to distinguish further between the states of activity and inactivity.

WORD LIST

boisterous
chaos
complacent
dynamic
monotonous
restive
static
steadfast
tranquil
velocity

DEFINITIONS

After you have studied the definitions and example for each vocabulary word, write the word on the line to the right.

1. **boisterous** (boi'stər-əs) *adjective*   **a.** Noisy and lacking restraint or discipline.   **b.** Rough and stormy; violent. (From the Middle English word *boistres*, meaning "rude")

   Related Words **boisterously** *adverb;* **boisterousness** *noun*
   Example   The *boisterous* football fans tore down a goal post.

   1. _____

2. **chaos** (kā'ŏs') *noun*   Great disorder or confusion. (From the Greek word *khaos,* meaning "a state of formlessness")

   Related Words **chaotic** *adjective;* **chaotically** *adverb*
   Example   A small group of four-year-olds created *chaos* at their friend's birthday party.

   2. _____

3. **complacent** (kəm-plā'sənt) *adjective*   Pleased or contented with oneself in an untroubled manner; self-satisfied; smug. (From the Latin word *complacere,* meaning "to please")

   Related Words **complacency** *noun;* **complacently** *adverb*
   Example   *Complacent* students sometimes do not study enough to do well in their classes.

   3. _____

4. **dynamic** (dī-năm'ĭk) *adjective*   **a.** Forceful; energetic; vigorous.
   b. Characterized by change, action, or movement. (From the Greek word *dunamikos*, meaning "powerful")

   Related Word   **dynamically** *adverb*
   Example   The class applauded enthusiastically after Gerard's *dynamic* presentation.

4. _____

5. **monotonous** (mə-nŏt'n-əs) *adjective*   **a.** Never varied or enlivened; repetitiously dull.   **b.** Uttered or sounded in one repeated tone; unvarying in pitch. (From the Greek words *monos*, meaning "one," and *tonos*, meaning "tone")

   Related Words   **monotonously** *adverb;* **monotony** *noun*
   Example   The office workers objected strongly to their *monotonous* routine.

5. _____

6. **restive** (rĕs'tĭv) *adjective*   **a.** Impatient; restless; nervous because of restrictions, pressures, or delays.   **b.** Hard to handle. (From the Latin word *restare*, meaning "to keep back")

   Related Words   **restively** *adverb;* **restiveness** *noun*
   Example   The *restive* commuters waited an extra half-hour for the delayed bus.

6. _____

USAGE NOTE: *Restive* is correctly used in place of *restless*. *Restive*, however, also suggests resistance to restraint.

7. **static** (stăt'ĭk) *adjective*   **a.** Having no motion; at rest.   **b.** Of or producing stationary electric charges; electrostatic.   *noun*   Random noise such as crackling in a radio receiver or specks on a television screen. (From the Greek word *statos*, meaning "standing")

   Related Word   **statically** *adverb*
   Example   A plot in a novel seems *static* when nothing important happens to the characters.

7. _____

8. **steadfast** (stĕd'făst') *adjective*   **a.** Fixed or unchanging; steady.
   b. Firmly loyal.

   Related Words   **steadfastly** *adverb;* **steadfastness** *noun*
   Example   Mrs. Alvarez was *steadfast* in her dedication to abandoned animals.

8. _____

9. **tranquil** (trăng'kwəl) *adjective*   Peaceful; calm; undisturbed; free from anxiety. (From the Latin word *tranquillus*, meaning "calm")

   Related Words   **tranquilize** *verb;* **tranquillity** *noun*
   Example   Barry spent a *tranquil* vacation at the uncrowded mountain resort.

9. _____

10. **velocity** (və-lŏs'ĭ-tē) *noun*   **a.** Speed.   **b.** In science, the rate per unit of time at which an object moves in a specified direction. (From the Latin word *velox*, meaning "quick")

    Example   Wind often travels at a high *velocity*.

10. _____

EXERCISE 1 COMPLETING DEFINITIONS

On the answer line, write the word from the vocabulary list that best completes each definition.

1. When an activity is repetitive and boring, it is _____.

2. A person who is self-satisfied is _____.

3. To be rude and noisy is to be _____.

4. The rate of speed at which something travels is its _____.

5. To be energetic or forceful is to be _____.

6. When someone is firmly loyal, he or she is _____.

7. If something is calm and peaceful, it is _____.

8. Anything that is without motion or at rest is _____.

9. To be restless and impatient is to be _____.

10. A state of great confusion is called _____.

1. _____monotonous_____

2. _____complacent_____

3. _____boisterous_____

4. _____velocity_____

5. _____dynamic_____

6. _____steadfast_____

7. _____tranquil_____

8. _____static_____

9. _____restive_____

10. _____chaos_____

EXERCISE 2 USING WORDS CORRECTLY

Each of the following statements contains an italicized vocabulary word. Decide whether the sentence is true or false, and write *True* or *False* on the answer line.

1. A library is an appropriate place for *boisterous* behavior.

2. A rock resting on the ground has no *velocity*.

3. If you try to improve something, you have a *complacent* attitude about it.

4. A *monotonous* speaker is likely to be popular with an audience.

5. A *restive* dog lies calmly in one place all day.

6. Quietly reading a book is a *tranquil* activity.

7. A cat who sits as still as a statue is in a *static* position.

8. Professional entertainers often have *dynamic* personalities on stage.

9. A good organizer aims for *chaos* in a project.

10. Someone with a *steadfast* opinion is quick to change his or her mind.

1. _____False_____

2. _____True_____

3. _____False_____

4. _____False_____

5. _____False_____

6. _____True_____

7. _____True_____

8. _____True_____

9. _____False_____

10. _____False_____

EXERCISE 3 CHOOSING THE BEST WORD

Decide which vocabulary word or related form best expresses the meaning of the italicized word or phrase in the sentence. On the answer line, write the letter of the correct choice.

1. There was total *confusion* after the fox entered the hen house.
   a. restiveness   **b.** chaos   **c.** tranquility   **d.** velocity

1. _____b_____

2. Lulu became *impatient* after waiting an hour in the dentist's chair.
   a. static   **b.** complacent   **c.** monotonous   **d.** restive

2. _____ d

3. For Jim early morning is the most *peaceful* part of the day.
   a. tranquil   **b.** dynamic   **c.** steadfast   **d.** boisterous

3. _____ a

4. Because of the friction caused by their high *rate of speed*, meteors burn up in the atmosphere.
   a. chaos   **b.** steadfastness   **c.** tranquility   **d.** velocity

4. _____ d

5. Margaret studied her *motionless* reflection in the still water of the lake.
   a. restive   **b.** dynamic   **c.** static   **d.** complacent

5. _____ c

6. Reggie was *smug* about his high position in the company.
   a. monotonous   **b.** dynamic   **c.** static   **d.** complacent

6. _____ d

7. Luther was so bored by the *repetitive* landscape that he fell asleep.
   a. monotonous   **b.** chaotic   **c.** restive   **d.** boisterous

7. _____ a

8. Tammy's *energetic* personality helped her to win the election.
   a. tranquil   **b.** dynamic   **c.** complacent   **d.** monotonous

8. _____ b

9. The soldiers pledged their *unchanging* allegiance to their country.
   a. restive   **b.** steadfast   **c.** boisterous   **d.** complacent

9. _____ b

10. The angry residents became *noisy and undisciplined* during the community meeting.
    a. restive   **b.** steadfast   **c.** boisterous   **d.** dynamic

10. _____ c

EXERCISE 4 USING DIFFERENT FORMS OF WORDS

Decide which form of the vocabulary word in parentheses best completes the sentence. The form given may be correct. Write your answer on the answer line.

1. Loren could not be stirred out of his _____. (*complacent*)

1. _____ complacency

2. The hockey team _____ protested their disqualification from the tournament. (*boisterous*)

2. _____ boisterously

3. Alicia works _____ to preserve island wildlife. (*dynamic*)

3. _____ dynamically

4. Brad could not explain his own _____. (*restive*)

4. _____ restiveness

5. The sudden snowstorm had a _____ effect on the region. (*chaos*)

5. _____ chaotic

6. Sophia broke the _____ of waiting for the bus by reading a book. (*monotonous*)

6. _____ monotony

7. For a rocket to escape the earth's gravity, it must travel at a high _____. (*velocity*)

7. _____ velocity

8. The _____ of the forest setting attracted many tourists to the lodge. (*tranquil*)

8. _____ tranquility

9. The hunting dog remained in a _____ position. (*static*)

9. _____ static

10. _____ is an admirable quality in a friend. (*steadfast*)

10. _____ Steadfastness

NAME _____   DATE _____

Each numbered sentence in the following passage contains an italicized vocabulary word or related form. After you read the passage, you will complete an exercise.

TRIUMPH OVER DISABILITY

(1) In 1995, French journalist Jean-Dominique Bauby had every reason to view life with *complacency*. The editor of a popular magazine, he was known for his wit, style, and joy of life. Then one day, driving his child to school, he began to feel sick. Within minutes, a stroke had overtaken him. For two years, Bauby lived in almost total paralysis.

Yet his story is one of triumph. (2) Although his body remained almost totally *static*, his active mind continued to create. Using only the movements of his left eyelid, Bauby was able to dictate a 137-page book, *The Diving Bell and the Butterfly*, the tale of what it is like to suffer from "locked-in" syndrome.

How did Bauby get this idea? Before his illness struck, he had been commissioned to write an updated version of Alexander Dumas' classic *The Count of Monte Cristo*. In this book, a paralyzed hero blinks with his eyelid to communicate. (3) When this tragedy also struck Bauby, he decided to combat the *monotony* of life without movement by using the same method.

(4) At first, Bauby's eye movements must have seemed to others random, like *chaotic* uncontrolled blinks. Soon his assistant realized that they had meaning. Each code of blinks represented one letter of the alphabet. To save time, the most-used letters had the shortest codes. To check the messages, the assistant would point to a letter, and Bauby would blink once for "yes," and twice for "no." (5) This required great *steadfastness* of purpose, for it took hundreds of thousands of blinks to finish the book.

(6) Most writers, even those who use word processors, find that their thoughts move at greater *velocity* than their fingers can type. Using Bauby's code, it takes about two minutes to blink out the average word! Even more troubling, he could not work from notes or outlines, or revise his writing. He composed and revised the passages entirely in his head.

(7) Bauby's book describes the experiences of a mind made *restive* by the inability to move the body. His body is confined in a "diving bell," but his mind can escape like a "butterfly." (8) He dreams about *dynamic* activities, like climbing mountains with cyclists or driving on a race course. (9) He remembers sensations: eating delicious meals, *boisterous* shouting. (10) He recalls the *tranquility* of family life, stroking the hair of his children and helping his elderly father.

Most of us take for granted the ability to walk, to taste our food, and to express ourselves. Bauby's story reminds us that even when we lose these things, the human spirit can still triumph.

READING COMPREHENSION EXERCISE

Each of the following statements corresponds to a numbered sentence in the passage. Each statement contains a blank and is followed by four answer choices. Decide which choice fits best in the blank. The word or phrase that you choose must express roughly the same meaning as the italicized word in the passage. Write the letter of your choice on the answer line.

1. In 1995, French journalist Jean-Dominique Bauby had every reason to view life with _____.
   a. happiness   **b.** contentment   **c.** dislike   **d.** disappointment

1. ____**b**____

© Great Source DO NOT COPY

Activity and Inactivity **157**

2. Although his body remained almost totally _____, his active mind continued to create.
   a. lazy   **b.** rested   **c.** still   **d.** helpless

   2. ___**b**___

3. When this tragedy struck Bauby, he decided to combat the _____ of life without movement by using the same method.
   a. unhappiness   **b.** stillness   **c.** hopelessness   **d.** boredom

   3. ___**d**___

4. At first, Bauby's eye movements must have seemed random, like _____ uncontrolled blinks.
   a. confused   **b.** meaningless   **c.** silly   **d.** painful

   4. ___**a**___

5. This required great _____ of purpose.
   a. steadiness   **b.** effort   **c.** amounts   **d.** motivation

   5. ___**a**___

6. Most writers, even those who use word processors, find that their thoughts move with greater _____ than their fingers can type.
   a. force   **b.** speed   **c.** direction   **d.** noise

   6. ___**b**___

7. Bauby's book describes the experiences of a mind made _____ by the inability to move the body.
   a. calm   **b.** uncertain   **c.** impatient   **d.** rested

   7. ___**c**___

8. He dreams about _____ activities.
   a. athletic   **b.** outdoor   **c.** ambitious   **d.** energetic

   8. ___**d**___

9. He remembers sensations: eating delicious meals, _____ shouting.
   a. tiring   **b.** group   **c.** bitter   **d.** noisy

   9. ___**d**___

10. He recalls the _____ of family life.
    a. happy   **b.** moody   **c.** calm   **d.** former

    10. ___**c**___

PRACTICE WITH ANALOGIES

Directions   On the answer line, write the letter of the phrase that best completes the analogy.

See page 119 for some strategies to use with analogies.

1. Boisterous is to restraint as
   (A) purposeful is to goal   (C) flexible is to bend
   (B) chaos is to order   (D) merciful is to forgiveness

   1. ___**B**___

2. Dynamic is to vigorous as
   (A) powerful is to weak   (C) energetic is to tired
   (B) monotonous is to dull   (D) pleasant is to effortless

   2. ___**B**___

3. Static is to move as
   (A) steadfast is to change   (C) debate is to argue
   (B) fire is to extinguish   (D) valuable is to steal

   3. ___**A**___

4. Speed is to velocity as
   (A) length is to capacity   (C) kilometer is to distance
   (B) height is to altitude   (D) quart is to pint

   4. ___**B**___

5. Portfolio is to papers as
   (A) curtain is to stage   (C) newspaper is to headline
   (B) statue is to marble   (D) bottle is to liquid

   5. ___**D**___

The **Bonus activity** for Lessons 23 and 24 is on page T26. The **Test** for Lessons 22, 23, and 24 is on page T27.

READING SKILLS

THE PREFIX *PRE-*

A **prefix** is a letter or group of letters that is added to the beginning of a root. (A root is the part of the word that contains its basic meaning. A root also can be a complete word. Many different words can be formed from a single root.) Like all prefixes, *pre-* changes the meaning of the roots to which it is added. If you know the meaning of the prefix, you can determine the meanings of unfamiliar words. The prefix *pre-* has one common meaning.

Prefix Meaning	Word	Definition
before; in advance	precaution	care taken before
	prefabricated	made in advance

Use the following procedure to determine the meaning of words that begin with the prefix *pre-*.

PROCEDURE

1. *Substitute the meaning of the prefix for the prefix itself.* Suppose that you do not know the meaning of the word *preconceptions*. Substituting the meaning *pre-* gives you "before" or "in advance of" *conceptions.*

2. *Think of possible definitions for the entire word.* If you know that *conceptions* means "ideas," you can combine the meanings of both prefix and root. This will give you the rough definition "ideas formed before" or "ideas formed in advance."

3. *Check your definition of the word in the dictionary.* The dictionary defines *preconceptions* as "ideas or opinions formed before full knowledge is available." This is close to your definition.

EXERCISE USING THE PREFIX *PRE-*

Step 1: Write your definition of the italicized word in each of the following sentences. *Step 2:* Write the dictionary definition of the word. Choose the definition that best fits the way the word is used in the sentence. *Step 3:* Write a sentence in which you use the word correctly.

1. There is a *prepaid* delivery charge on all orders from this catalogue.

    Your Definition _Paid in advance_____

    Dictionary Definition _Paid in advance_____

    Sentence _Our railroad tickets are prepaid._____

2. Alan and I went to the *preview* of Veronica's exhibit at the art gallery.

Your Definition An advance viewing

Dictionary Definition A private showing before presentation to the general public

Sentence Constance took her two best friends to the sneak preview of the movie.

3. Annie is excited about starting *preschool* this fall.

Your Definition A school before regular school

Dictionary Definition A nursery school

Sentence Sally's favorite activity in preschool is painting.

4. The child was afraid of the models of *prehistoric* animals at the museum.

Your Definition From a time before history

Dictionary Definition Of or belonging to the time before recorded history

Sentence Cave drawings tell us much about the lives of prehistoric human beings.

5. Katie is thinking about taking *premedical* courses at college.

Your Definition In advance of medical school

Dictionary Definition Courses taken in preparation for the study of medicine

Sentence Arthur's premedical training included chemistry and biology.

6. I think your suggestion that we begin writing our report is *premature*.

Your Definition Before the proper time; too soon

Dictionary Definition Done or happening too soon; too hasty

Sentence Since the plumber hadn't even arrived, Anne's estimate of the damage was premature.

7. I had a *premonition* that something might go wrong. (Clue: *-mon-* is a Latin root meaning "to warn.")

Your Definition Advance warning

Dictionary Definition A feeling that something is going to happen

Sentence Manny's premonition that the plane would be late turned out to be correct.

8. Heavy snow and strong winds *precluded* a trip into the mountains. (Clue: *-clud-* is a Latin root meaning "to close.")

Your Definition Closed off in advance

Dictionary Definition To make impossible by consequence

Sentence This year heavy spring rains precluded early plowing of the fields.

Geographers study the physical features of the earth—where mountains are located, for example, and how they were formed. Of particular interest to geographers are the surface and boundary changes that take place continually. These scientists study the effects of natural forces, such as ocean currents that alter a coastline. They are concerned also with the ways in which people have altered the environment. Recently, for instance, there has been considerable research into how overgrazing by livestock has contributed to the expansion of the Sahara Desert.

The words in this lesson will help you to describe the forms and boundaries of the landscape. In addition, studying these words may provide insight into the kinds of environmental changes that interest geographers.

WORD LIST

confines
delineate
demarcation
distend
distinct
embody
marginal
omnipresent
penetration
substantial

DEFINITION

After you have studied the definitions and example for each vocabulary word, write the word on the line to the right.

1. **confines** (kŏn′fīnz′) *noun*   The limits of a space or area; borders; boundaries. (From the Latin *com-*, meaning "with," and *fines*, meaning "limits")

   Related Word   **confine** *verb*
   Example   Snow-capped mountains mark the northern *confines* of the state.

1. _____

USAGE NOTE: The noun *confines* is plural and therefore takes a plural verb.

2. **delineate** (dĭ-lĭn′ē-āt′) *verb*   **a.** To draw or trace the outline of.   **b.** To establish the exact limits or extent of: *delineate duties*.   **c.** To describe in great detail. (From the Latin *de-*, meaning "from," and *linea* meaning "line")

   Related Word   **delineation** *noun*
   Example   The architect *delineated* the slant of the roof and the placement of the columns.

2. _____

3. **demarcation** (dē′mär-kā′shən) *noun*   **a.** The process of determining and marking off the boundaries of something.   **b.** A separation.

   Related Word   **demarcate** *verb*
   Example   The surveyor's map shows the lines of *demarcation* of our land.

3. _____

MEMORY CUE: The *demarcation* between countries is clearly *marked* on a map.

4. **distend** (dĭ-stĕnd') *verb*   **a.** To swell or stretch, as if by internal pressure; expand or increase.   **b.** To cause to expand. (From the Latin *dis-*, meaning "apart," and *tendere*, meaning "to stretch")

   Related Word   **distention** *noun*
   Example   The child's boil was badly *distended*.

4. _____

5. **distinct** (dĭ-stĭngkt') *adjective*   **a.** Different in nature or quality; individual.   **b.** Easily perceived by the senses or intellect; plain; clear; unmistakable. (From the Latin word *distinguere*, meaning "to separate")

   Related Words   **distinctly** *adverb*; **distinctness** *noun*
   Example   Each of their five cats has a *distinct* personality.

5. _____

MEMORY CUE:
Something is *distinct* if it can be *distinguished* easily from other, similar objects.

6. **embody** (ĕm-bŏd'ē) *verb*   **a.** To give concrete form to an idea; personify.   **b.** To make or include as part of a united whole; organize; incorporate.

   Related Word   **embodiment** *noun*
   Example   The Olympic athletes *embody* the vigor of youth.

6. _____

7. **marginal** (mär'jə-nəl) *adjective*   **a.** Located at the border or edge; geographically adjacent.   **b.** Minimal for requirements; barely acceptable.   **c.** Written in the margin of a book.

   Related Words   **margin** *noun*; **marginally** *adverb*
   Example   The beach area *marginal* to the shallow water teemed with frogs, crabs, and turtles.

7. _____

8. **omnipresent** (ŏm'nĭ-prĕz'ənt) *adjective*   Existing everywhere at the same time. (From the Latin words *omnis*, meaning "all," and *praesens*, meaning "present")

   Related Word   **omnipresence** *noun*
   Example   In the desert, the *omnipresent* sand found its way into our sleeping bags, our food, and our water supply.

8. _____

9. **penetration** (pĕn'ĭ-tra'shən) *noun*   **a.** The process of piercing, entering, or forcing a way into.   **b.** The ability to understand; insight. (From the Latin word *penitrare*, meaning "to penetrate")

   Related Word   **penetrate** *verb*
   Example   *Penetration* of the forest was nearly impossible because of dense thorn bushes.

9. _____

10. **substantial** (səb-stăn'shəl) *adjective*   **a.** Considerable in amount, importance, value, or extent.   **b.** Strong; firm; solidly built. (From the Latin *sub-*, meaning "under," and *stare*, meaning "to stand")

    Related Word   **substantially** *adverb*
    Example   The volunteers donated a *substantial* portion of their time to the hospital.

10. _____

EXERCISE 1 COMPLETING DEFINITIONS

On the answer line, write the word from the vocabulary list that fits
each definition.

1. Different in nature or quality; easily perceived by the senses or intellect

2. Existing everywhere at the same time

3. To draw the outline of; establish the limits of

4. Considerable; strong and solidly built

5. To swell or stretch; cause to expand

6. The limits of a space; boundaries

7. To give concrete form to an idea; include as part of a untied whole

8. The process of piercing, entering, or forcing a way into; the ability to understand

9. Situated at the border or edge; minimal for requirements

10. The process of determining and marking off boundaries; a separation

1. _____ distinct _____
2. _____ omnipresent _____
3. _____ delineate _____
4. _____ substantial _____
5. _____ distend _____
6. _____ confines _____
7. _____ embody _____
8. _____ penetration _____
9. _____ marginal _____
10. _____ demarcation _____

EXERCISE 2 USING WORDS CORRECTLY

Decide whether the italicized vocabulary word has been used correctly in the
sentence. On the answer line, write *Correct* for correct use and *Incorrect* for
incorrect use.

1. During our snorkeling trip, we stayed within the *confines* of the coral reef surrounding the island.

2. The port of *demarcation* for the cruise is Miami.

3. Gerald showed only *marginal* interest in the speech.

4. The *substantial* tree house was not damaged by the storm.

5. The snow sculpture *distended* in the sun to half its original size.

6. During the meeting Mr. Manfredo was at a *distinct* disadvantage because he had not received the report.

7. Ardis wanted to have her hair *delineated* by a professional hairdresser.

8. The children attempted to *embody* the basket of apples, but it was much too heavy for them.

9. The *penetration* of moonlight through the branches of the tree created strange shadows.

10. Most people are *omnipresent* because they eat both animal and vegetable substances.

1. _____ Correct _____
2. _____ Incorrect _____
3. _____ Correct _____
4. _____ Correct _____
5. _____ Incorrect _____
6. _____ Correct _____
7. _____ Incorrect _____
8. _____ Incorrect _____
9. _____ Correct _____
10. _____ Incorrect _____

For each italicized vocabulary word or related form in the following
sentences, write the letter of the best definition on the answer line.

1. Kyle's handwriting is so *distinct* that I can always recognize it.
   a. messy   **b.** unmistakable   **c.** elegant   **d.** complex

   1. _____ b

2. The spring floods destroyed a *substantial* portion of our corn crop.
   a. small   **b.** considerable   **c.** reserved   **d.** technical

   2. _____ b

3. If the ball passes beyond the *confines* of the playing floor, the referee calls
   "Out of bounds."
   a. limits   **b.** bleachers   **c.** wood   **d.** center

   3. _____ a

4. Mr. Hall will *delineate* the procedure for welding sheet metal.
   a. forget   **c.** memorize and use
   b. test   **d.** describe in detail

   4. _____ d

5. Classical Greek architecture *embodies* the principles of proportion and
   beauty.
   a. contradicts   **c.** gives concrete form to
   b. begins   **d.** prevents understanding of

   5. _____ c

6. The archaeologist made careful plans for *penetrating* the walls of the tomb.
   a. piercing   **b.** studying   **c.** walking by   **d.** uncovering

   6. _____ a

7. The homeowners argued about the line of *demarcation* between their
   properties.
   a. resemblance   **b.** difference   **c.** appearance   **d.** separation

   7. _____ d

8. The senator's new plan received *marginal* support.
   a. unanimous   **b.** local   **c.** minimal   **d.** great

   8. _____ c

9. The small child was frightened by the *distended* throat of the croaking
   bullfrog.
   a. colorful   **b.** exposed   **c.** swollen   **d.** ordinary

   9. _____ c

10. I have never played softball in the summer without being bothered by
    gnats; they seem to be *omnipresent*.
    a. everywhere   **b.** nuisances   **c.** hungry   **d.** multiplying

    10. _____ a

Decide which form of the vocabulary word in parentheses best completes the
sentence. The form given may be correct. Write your answer on the line.

1. Elaine's teacher praised her _____ of the Adirondack Mountain range on
   her map. *(delineate)*

   1. _____ delineation

2. The club's money-raising project was _____ successful. *(marginal)*

   2. _____ marginally

3. Abraham Lincoln is considered by many to be the _____ of honor and
   virtue. *(embody)*

   3. _____ embodiment

4. To score points in soccer, you must _____ your opponents' defense and
   kick the ball into their goal. *(penetration)*

   4. _____ penetrate

5. I _____ heard Mother tell us not to be late. *(distinct)*

   5. _____ distinctly

6. The students noted the _____ of chaperones at the dance. *(omnipresent)*

7. After living in Italy for three months, Ella _____ improved her ability to speak Italian. *(substantial)*

8. The _____ of the juice cans indicated that their contents had been contaminated. *(distended)*

9. This map _____ all the national parks in the southwestern United States. *(demarcation)*

10. Before being _____ to quarters, Lieutenant Bragg surrendered his weekend pass. *(confines)*

6. __omnipresence__

7. __substantially__

8. __distention__

9. __demarcates__

10. __confined__

READING COMPREHENSION

Each numbered sentence in the following passage contains an italicized vocabulary word or related form. After you read the passage, you will complete the exercise.

NATURE'S ARTISTRY: THE GRAND CANYON

My brother's desire to see the Grand Canyon during our family's trip to Arizona met with less than overwhelming enthusiasm. My parents believed that we would have enough sightseeing in our visits to American Indian reservations and desert museums. My sister and I could not imagine what appeal a deep gorge could have. Alexander was persuasive, though. He convinced all of us that we should not miss the Grand Canyon.

Alexander was right. The Grand Canyon was one of the most awe-inspiring spectacles we had ever seen. After only a brief glimpse, however, Alexander insisted that we go to the visitors' center, where we would learn about the canyon's geological history. From the exhibits in the center, we learned that the Grand Canyon is the world's most complex system of rock formations. (1) It owes its spectacular appearance to the powerful Colorado River, which cuts and shapes the canyon's *confines.* (2) Scientists believe that six million years ago the river was only a narrow stream moving across the Colorado Plateau, which forms a *substantial* portion of northwestern Arizona. Geologists have discovered a series of geological changes that forced the plateau above sea level. As the land rose, the slope along which the river ran became steeper. (3) The waters moved more rapidly and picked up sand and silt, which *distended* the river and cut a course through the rock. (4) Over thousands of years, water *penetrated* the rock to create the extraordinary peaks and valleys.

After our tour of the visitors' center, we returned to the south rim of the canyon. (5) Behind us and across the canyon, blue spruce and aspen trees served to *demarcate* the rims. (6) Below, the *margins* of the rock layers glistened in the sun. (7) Each rock layer was *delineated* by a different color. (8) *Distinct* shades of pink, green, violet, brown, and beige turned the canyon into a rainbow.

(9) We stood watching the shifting patterns of color and shadow and the seemingly *omnipresent* Colorado River churning its way toward the Gulf of Mexico. (10) Thanks to Alexander's stubbornness, we had the pleasure of learning about the Grand Canyon, a unique *embodiment* of nature's artistry.

Each of the following statements corresponds to a numbered sentence in the passage. Each statement contains a blank and is followed by four answer choices. Decide which choice fits best in the blank. The word or phrase that you choose must express roughly the same meaning as the italicized word in the passage. Write the letter of your choice on the answer line.

1. The Grand Canyon owes its appearance to the Colorado River, which cuts and shapes the canyon's _____.
   a. rocks   b. limits   c. depth   d. height

   1. _____ b

2. The river was once only a stream that crossed the Colorado Plateau, a _____ portion of northwestern Arizona.
   a. rocky   b. flat   c. small   d. considerable

   2. _____ d

3. Sand and silt _____ the river and helped it cut a course through the rock.
   a. moved   b. stopped   c. expanded   d. slowed

   3. _____ c

4. Water _____ the rock to form the canyon's peaks and valleys.
   a. forced its way through   c. poured over
   b. bounced off   d. covered

   4. _____ a

5. Blue spruce and aspen trees served to _____ the canyon rims.
   a. set the boundaries of   c. protect the fragility of
   b. shade   d. cross over

   5. _____ a

6. The _____ of the rock layers glistened in the sun.
   a. colors   b. roughness   c. center   d. edges

   6. _____ d

7. Each rock layer _____ a different color.
   a. was covered over by   c. was outlined in
   b. was created by   d. was decorated with

   7. _____ c

8. _____ shades of pink, green, violet, brown, and beige turned the Canyon into a rainbow.
   a. Pale   b. Different   c. Intense   d. Blended

   8. _____ b

9. The Colorado River seems _____.
   a. all-powerful   c. friendly
   b. to be everywhere   d. to stop suddenly

   9. _____ b

10. The Grand Canyon is a unique _____ of nature's artistry.
    a. example   b. tourist site   c. rejection   d. history

   10. _____ a

WRITING ASSIGNMENT

Write a descriptive paragraph about a scene that you find attractive or interesting. For example, you might describe a park in autumn or a skyline at sunset. Write the paragraph for a real or imaginary friend. Use at least five of the vocabulary words from this lesson in your description and underline them.

The Latin words *pellere*, meaning "to drive out, beat, or strike," and *appellare*, meaning "to summon or speak to," have both contributed the root *-pel-* to the English language. A large number of words come from this root. For example, if you are *expelled* from school, you are forced to leave. If a friend *dispels* your doubts about something, those doubts are driven from your mind. An *appeal* is an earnest or urgent request, while one's *appellation* is one's name or title.

Although their etymologies are different, all of the words in this lesson come from the root *-pel-*. As you study each word, pay close attention to its etymology.

WORD LIST

compel
compulsion
impel
impulsive
peal
propulsion
pulsate
repeal
repellent
repulse

DEFINITIONS

After you have studied the definitions and example for each vocabulary word, write the word on the line to the right.

1. **compel** (kəm-pĕl′) *verb*   **a.** To force to do something by using power or influence.   **b.** To make necessary: *compels careful money management*. (From the Latin *com-*, meaning "together," and *pellare*, meaning "to drive")

   Related Word   **compelling** *adjective*
   Example   High prices may *compel* people to save fuel.

2. **compulsion** (kəm-pŭl′shən) *noun*   **a.** An urge, often unreasonable, that is nearly impossible to control: *a compulsion to eat*.   **b.** The force or influence that makes it necessary for someone to do something. (From the Latin word *compulsus*, meaning "driven together" or "compelled")

   Related Words   **compulsive** *adjective*; **compulsory** *adjective*
   Example   Eric's *compulsion* for neatness and organization pleases his parents.

3. **impel** (ĭm-pĕl′) *verb*   **a.** To urge to action; spur.   **b.** To drive forward; propel. (From the Latin *in-*, meaning "in," and *pellare*, meaning "to drive")

   Example   Speaking in a soft, coaxing voice, Veronica *impelled* her horse to go faster.

1. _____
   See *impel*.

2. _____

3. _____
   USAGE NOTE: *Compel* and *impel* share the sense of using physical or other force. *Compel* suggests more actual force, whereas *impel* suggest inner drive.

4. **impulsive** (ĭm-pŭl'sĭv) *adjective*   Likely to act suddenly without thinking; uncalculated. (From the Latin word *impulsus*, meaning "driven into" or "impelled")

   Related Words   impulse *noun*; **impulsively** *adverb*; **impulsiveness** *noun*
   Example   The *impulsive* driver made a left turn without signaling and nearly caused an accident.

4. _____

5. **peal** (pēl) *noun*   **a.** The ringing of a set of bells.   **b.** A loud burst of noise or series of noises: *peals of laughter.*   *verb*   To sound loudly; ring. (From the Latin word *appellare*, meaning "to call upon")

   Example   The hourly *peal* of the church bells helped Candace learn to tell time.

5. _____

6. **propulsion** (prə-pŭl'shən) *noun*   The act or process of driving, moving, or pushing forward. (From the Latin *pro-*, meaning "forward," and *pulsus*, meaning "a beat" or "a stroke")

   Related Word   **propel** *verb*
   Example   Jet *propulsion* radically changed the nature of air travel.

6. _____

7. **pulsate** (pŭl'sāt') *verb*   **a.** To expand and contract rhythmically, as the heart does; throb; beat.   **b.** To move or occur in a regular, rhythmical way. (From the Latin word *pulsare*, meaning "to strike" or "to beat")

   Related Word   **pulsation** *noun*
   Example   Luke could feel the bird's heart *pulsate* in fear.

7. _____

8. **repeal** (rĭ-pēl') *verb*   To withdraw or cancel, especially by formal or official act; revoke.   *noun*   The act or process of repealing. (From the Old French *re-*, meaning "back," and *apeler*, meaning "to appeal")

   Example   The commission *repealed* the ban on watering lawns.

8. _____

9. **repellent** (rĭ-pĕl'ənt) *adjective*   **a.** Acting or tending to drive off, force back, or keep away.   **b.** Causing dislike or disgust.   **c.** Resistant to a specified substance or influence: *water-repellent cloth.*   *noun*   Something that repels. (From the Latin *re-*, meaning "back," and *pellere*, meaning "to drive")

   Related Words   repel *verb*; **repellence** *noun*
   Example   The odor from the paper mill was *repellent*.

9. _____
   See *repulse.*

10. **repulse** (rĭ-pŭls') *verb*   **a.** To drive back.   **b.** to reject or refuse firmly or suddenly. (From the Latin word *repulsus*, meaning "driven away" or "repelled")

    Related Words   repulsion *noun*; **repulsive** *adjective*
    Example   The odor of Limburger cheese *repulses* Anna.

10. _____
    USAGE NOTE: *Repel* and *repulse* share the sense of physically driving back or off. *Repulse* can also mean "to rebuff with rudeness," but *repel* connotes strong distaste or aversion.

EXERCISE 1 WRITING CORRECT WORDS

On the answer line, write the word from the vocabulary list that fits each definition.

1. An unreasonable urge

2. The act or process of driving, moving, or pushing forward

3. Tending to drive off or keep away; causing disgust

4. To make someone do something by using force or influence

5. To urge to action; drive forward

6. To drive back; reject

7. To expand and contract rhythmically

8. Likely to act suddenly without thinking

9. To withdraw or cancel

10. The ringing of a set of bells; a loud burst of noise

1. ___compulsion___

2. ___propulsion___

3. ___repellent___

4. ___compel___

5. ___impel___

6. ___repulse___

7. ___pulsate___

8. ___impulsive___

9. ___repeal___

10. ___peal___

EXERCISE 2 USING WORDS CORRECTLY

Decide whether the italicized vocabulary word has been used correctly in the sentence. On the answer line, write *Correct* for correct use and *Incorrect* for incorrect use.

1. An *impulsive* reply may be more truthful than one that has been carefully thought out.

2. Although the citizens disliked the new policy, the legislators would not *repeal* it.

3. Larry felt a *compulsion* to explore the cave.

4. A *peal* of leaves fell from the oak tree.

5. The doctor decided immediately to *repulse* my appendix.

6. The film showed blood vessels *pulsating* as blood ran through them.

7. The *propulsion* to operate a television set comes from electricity.

8. More than anything else, curiosity *impels* the research scientist.

9. Barney *compelled* the rock down the hill.

10. Researchers attracted the coyote to the enclosure with a *repellent* mixture of food.

1. ___Correct___

2. ___Correct___

3. ___Correct___

4. ___Incorrect___

5. ___Incorrect___

6. ___Correct___

7. ___Incorrect___

8. ___Correct___

9. ___Incorrect___

10. ___Incorrect___

EXERCISE 3 CHOOSING THE BEST WORD

Decide which vocabulary word or related form best expresses the meaning of the italicized word or phrase in the sentence. On the answer line, write the letter of the correct choice.

1. Brian experienced an *unreasonable urge* to dive into the icy water.
   a. repellent   b. peal   c. propulsion   d. compulsion

1. ___d___

2. *Loud bursts* of laughter filled the classroom when Lou's hamster escaped.
   a. Propulsions   **b.** Repeals   **c.** Peals   **d.** Repellents

2. _____ c

3. The odor of a skunk is certainly *disgusting*.
   a. repellent   **b.** repealing   **c.** impulsive   **d.** compulsive

3. _____ a

4. A longing to be alone *pushed* Sally to drive up the mountains.
   a. pulsated   **b.** repealed   **c.** repulsed   **d.** impelled

4. _____ d

5. The committee *canceled* the funding for plant research.
   a. impelled   **b.** repealed   **c.** compelled   **d.** pulsated

5. _____ b

6. The engine provided no *force pushing forward* and needed repair.
   a. propulsion   **b.** compulsion   **c.** repellent   **d.** peal

6. _____ a

7. Dwight's parents *force* him to do well in school.
   a. repeal   **b.** repel   **c.** compel   **d.** pulsate

7. _____ c

8. Daniel is so *likely to act without thinking* that he often invites friends for dinner without having any food in the house.
   a. repealed   **b.** impulsive   **c.** repellent   **d.** impelled

8. _____ b

9. The twins *rejected* Lee's efforts to be friendly.
   a. pulsated   **b.** repealed   **c.** repulsed   **d.** compelled

9. _____ c

10. Cesar could feel his heart *beat rhythmically* as he raced out of the burning house.
    a. compel   **b.** repeal   **c.** impel   **d.** pulsate

10. _____ d

EXERCISE 4 USING DIFFERENT FORMS OF WORDS

Decide which form of the vocabulary word in parentheses best completes the sentence. The form given may be correct. Write your answer on the answer line.

1. A _____ of thunder broke the silence. *(peal)*

1. _____ peal

2. Laws make it _____ to wear seat belts while driving in certain states. *(compulsion)*

2. _____ compulsory

3. An effective lieutenant _____ troops to fight bravely. *(impel)*

3. _____ impels

4. The naturalist used a homemade lotion to _____ insects. *(repellent)*

4. _____ repel

5. Larry studied the _____ of ships by steam turbines. *(propulsion)*

5. _____ propulsion

6. The litter laws could not be _____ for at least two years. *(repeal)*

6. _____ repealed

7. Agatha Christie's novels are _____ mysteries. *(compel)*

7. _____ compelling

8. The _____ beat of music soon had the crowd tapping their toes. *(pulsate)*

8. _____ pulsating

9. My first efforts in cooking were _____. *(repulse)*

9. _____ repulsive

10. Christopher's father worried that his son's _____ would lead him to make poor decisions. *(impulsive)*

10. _____ impulsiveness

READING COMPREHENSION

Each numbered sentence in the following passage contains an italicized vocabulary word or related form. After you read the passage, you will complete an exercise.

THE WRIGHT BROTHERS: FATHERS OF AVIATION

Many great inventions are greeted with ridicule and disbelief. The invention of the airplane was no exception. (1) Although many people who heard about the first powered flight on December 17, 1903, were excited and impressed, others reacted with *peals* of laughter. (2) The idea of flying an aircraft was *repulsive* to some people. (3) Such people called Wilbur and Orville Wright, the inventors of the first flying machine, *impulsive* fools. Negative reactions, however, did not stop the Wrights. (4) *Impelled* by their desire to succeed, they continued their experiments in aviation.

(5) Orville and Wilbur Wright had always had a *compelling* interest in aeronautics and mechanics. As young boys they earned money by making and selling kites and mechanical toys. Later, they designed a newspaper-folding machine, built a printing press, and operated a bicycle-repair shop. (6) In 1896, when they read about the death of Otto Lilienthal, the brothers' interest in flight grew into a *compulsion.*

Lilienthal, a pioneer in hang-gliding, had controlled his gliders by shifting his body in the desired direction. (7) This idea was *repellent* to the Wright brothers, however, and they searched for more efficient methods to control the

balance of airborne vehicles. In 1900 and 1901, the Wrights tested numerous gliders and developed control techniques. The brothers' inability to obtain enough lift power for the gliders almost led them to abandon their efforts.

After further study, the Wright brothers concluded that the published tables of air pressure on curved surfaces must be wrong. They set up a wind tunnel and began a series of experiments with model wings. (8) Because of their efforts, the old tables were *repealed* in time and replaced by the first reliable figures for air pressure on curved surfaces. This work, in turn, made it possible for them to design a machine that would fly.

In 1903 the Wrights built their first airplane, which cost less than

one thousand dollars. (9) They even designed and built their own source of *propulsion*—a light-weight gasoline engine. (10) When they started the engine on December 17, the airplane *pulsated* wildly before taking off. The plane managed to stay aloft for twelve seconds, however, and it flew one hundred twenty feet.

By 1905 the Wrights had perfected the first airplane that could turn, circle, and remain airborne for half an hour at a time. Others had flown in balloons or in hang gliders, but the Wright brothers were the first to build a full-size machine that could fly under its own power. As the contributors of one of the most outstanding engineering achievements in history, the Wright brothers are accurately called the fathers of aviation.

Each of the following statements corresponds to a numbered sentence in the passage. Each statement contains a blank and is followed by four answer choices. Decide which choice fits best in the blank. The word or phrase that you choose must express roughly the same meaning as the italicized word in the passage. Write the letter of your choice on the answer line.

1. Some of the people who had heard about the first airplane flight reacted with _____ of laughter.
   a. a burst   b. a lack   c. cheers   d. reports

   1. _____a_____

2. The idea of flying an aircraft was _____ to some people.
   a. boring   b. distasteful   c. encouraging   d. exciting

   2. _____b_____

3. People thought that the Wright brothers had _____.
   a. acted without thinking   c. been too cautious
   b. thought without acting   d. been negatively influenced

   3. _____a_____

4. The Wright brothers were _____ by their desire to succeed.
   a. stopped   b. exhausted   c. defeated   d. spurred on

   4. _____d_____

5. The Wrights had always had a _____ interest in aeronautics and mechanics.
   a. powerful   b. slight   c. financial   d. lively

   5. _____a_____

6. The Wrights' interest in flight grew into a _____.
   a. financial empire   c. need to act
   b. fear   d. plan

   6. _____c_____

7. Lilienthal's idea about controlling airborne vehicles was _____ the Wrights.
   a. proven wrong by   c. opposite to the ideas of
   b. researched by   d. disliked by

   7. _____d_____

8. The old tables were _____ and replaced by the first reliable figures for air pressure on curved surfaces.
   a. destroyed   b. canceled   c. decreased   d. multiplied

   8. _____b_____

9. The Wrights designed and built their own source of _____.
   a. force for moving forward   c. turning
   b. stopping   d. force for turning around

   9. _____a_____

10. As the engine started, the airplane _____ wildly.
    a. vibrated   b. stalled   c. skipped   d. ran

    10. _____a_____

WRITING ASSIGNMENT

In your science class, suppose that you are about to begin a unit on famous inventors. Your teacher has asked you to choose an invention that interests you and to do library research on the inventor. Write a paragraph that summarizes the inventor's life and include an explanation of some of the influences that led to his or her achievements. In your paragraph use at least four of the vocabulary words from this lesson and underline them.

The **Bonus activity** for Lessons 25 and 26 is on page T29.

LESSON 27 SECRECY AND OPENNESS

With the ease of modern communication using cellular phones, satellite transmission television, facsimile machines, and the World Wide Web, the concepts of secrecy and openness have become increasingly important.

For example, the increased use of the World Wide Web has resulted in more openness in communication and information. With the click of just a few buttons, people can access the information contained in several encyclopedias. Electronic mail and bulletin boards also foster ease and freedom of communication.

But this very ease of communication can be dangerous. In 1997, United States government authorities allowed new software, used to transfer money in bank accounts, to be used internationally because World Wide Web users had cracked the code of the older version, thus allowing them to view other people's financial records. In this age of open communication, it is important to be able to keep some information secret.

WORD LIST

accessible
cache
conspicuous
disclosure
inter
intrigue
obscure
secluded
unavailable
unearth

DEFINITION

After you have studied the definitions and example for each vocabulary word, write the word on the line to the right.

1. **accessible** (ăk-sĕs′ə-bəl) *adjective*   **a.** Easily obtained, approached, or reached.   **b.** Easy to communicate with.

   Related Words access *noun;* **accessibility** *noun*
   Example   The company library is *accessible* to all employees.

   1. _____

2. **cache** (kăsh) *noun*   **a.** A stockpile, reserve, or supply, usually hidden; a store of goods in a hiding place.   **b.** Such a hiding place itself. (From the French word *cacher*, meaning "to hide")

   Example   The secret panel in the library concealed a *cache* of jewels and stock certificates.

   2. _____

3. **conspicuous** (kən-spĭk′yōō-əs) *adjective*   Noticeable; obvious. (From the Latin word *conspicere*, meaning "to observe")

   Related Words **conspicuously** *adverb;* **conspicuousness** *noun*
   Example   Maurice made himself *conspicuous* by wearing funny hats.

   3. _____

4. **disclosure** (dĭ-sklō′zhər) *noun*   **a.** The act or process of making known; a revelation.   **b.** Something that is made known.

   Related Word   **disclose** *verb*
   Example   The museum intends to make a *disclosure* to the press of the amount paid for the Goya portrait.

   4. _____

5. **inter** (ĭn-tûr') *verb* To bury; place in a grave or tomb. (From the Latin *in-*, meaning "in," and *terra*, meaning "earth")

    Related Word   **interment** *noun*
    Example   Some pharaohs of ancient Egypt were *interred* in pyramids.

5. _____

6. **intrigue** (ĭn'trēg') *noun* A scheme or secret plot.   *verb* (ĭn-trēg') **a.** To devise a plot; scheme. **b.** To fascinate; arouse the interest of. (From the Latin word *intricare*, meaning "to entangle")

    Example   At least three people were involved in the *intrigue* to steal the crown jewels.

6. _____

7. **obscure** (ŏb-skyŏŏr') *adjective* **a.** Not easily seen or found; remote. **b.** Not well known; uncommon. **c.** Difficult to understand. *verb* To make unclear; darken. (From the Latin word *obscurare*, meaning "to darken")

    Related Words **obscurely** *adverb;* **obscurity** *noun*
    Example   At the end of the garden, there was an *obscure* doorway leading to a secret passage.

7. _____

8. **secluded** (sĭ-klōō'dĭd) *adjective* Isolated; set apart from others. (From the Latin word *secludere*, meaning "to shut away")

    Related Words **seclude** *verb;* **seclusion** *noun*
    Example   No roads passed near the *secluded* house.

8. _____

9. **unavailable** (ŭn'ə-vā'lə-bəl) *adjective* Not obtainable; not at hand; inaccessible.

    Related Word   **unavailability** *noun*
    Example   My ophthalmologist was *unavailable* for appointments on Tuesdays because he taught courses at the university.

9. _____

10. **unearth** (ŭn-ûrth') *verb* To dig up; bring up out of the ground.

    Example   Sometimes farmers *unearth* fossils while plowing their fields.

10. _____

EXERCISE 1 MATCHING WORDS AND DEFINITIONS

Match the definition in Column B with the word in Column A. Write the
letter of the correct definition on the answer line.

Column A	Column B
1. unearth	**a.** a store of goods hidden away
2. disclosure	**b.** a secret scheme
3. inter	**c.** easily obtained
4. secluded	**d.** to dig up
5. cache	**e.** not obvious
6. unavailable	**f.** to bury in a grave
7. accessible	**g.** a revelation
8. obscure	**h.** noticeable
9. conspicuous	**i.** not at hand
10. intrigue	**j.** isolated

1. _____ d
2. _____ g
3. _____ f
4. _____ j
5. _____ a
6. _____ i
7. _____ c
8. _____ e
9. _____ h
10. _____ b

EXERCISE 2 USING WORDS CORRECTLY

Decide whether the italicized vocabulary word has been used correctly in the
sentence. On the answer line, write *Correct* for correct use or *Incorrect* for
incorrect use.

1. I walked right past my friend because she was so *conspicuous*.

2. Shoes in Sheila's unusual size were *unavailable* at the discount store.

3. The meaning of the poem was so *obscure* that Sally found it easy to
understand.

4. Harold swiftly *unearthed* the bone that Rover had buried.

5. The professor is so *accessible* to students that it is impossible to find him
between classes.

6. Gently Wendy *interred* the flower arrangement on top of the dining room
table.

7. "*Disclosure* the door, and let in some fresh air," said Tom.

8. Mrs. Kasarda needed *cache* to buy the groceries.

9. Melvin found a *secluded* spot in the park, where he could read without
being disturbed.

10. The police force conducted a public *intrigue* in order to locate the missing
jewels.

1. _____ Incorrect
2. _____ Correct
3. _____ Incorrect
4. _____ Correct
5. _____ Incorrect
6. _____ Incorrect
7. _____ Incorrect
8. _____ Incorrect
9. _____ Correct
10. _____ Incorrect

EXERCISE 3 CHOOSING THE BEST DEFINITION

For each italicized vocabulary word in the following sentences, write the
letter of the best definition on the answer line.

1. The airport is easily *accessible* from the city.
   a. detoured   **b.** within reach   **c.** visible   **d.** crowded

1. _____ b

2. Katherine is familiar with many *obscure* varieties of plants.
   a. colorful **b.** poisonous **c.** isolated **d.** uncommon

2. _____ d _____

3. In his haste the pirate *unearthed* many worms with the treasure chest.
   a. dug up **b.** lifted **c.** buried **d.** found

3. _____ a _____

4. Ariadne was *conspicuous* because of her orange clothes.
   a. fashionable **b.** noticeable **c.** rich **d.** avoided

4. _____ b _____

5. Sylvia did not like the beach because it was so *secluded*.
   a. polluted **b.** warm **c.** isolated **d.** crowded

5. _____ c _____

6. It was a difficult task to *inter* the elephant.
   a. feed **b.** bury **c.** transport **d.** hide

6. _____ b _____

7. My younger brother enjoys movies that involve complex *intrigues*.
   a. schemes **b.** characters **c.** magic **d.** confusion

7. _____ a _____

8. The reporter's *disclosure* was a shock to everyone.
   a. message **b.** secret **c.** story **d.** revelation

8. _____ d _____

9. Lars had a *cache* of marbles in his jacket pocket.
   a. bag **b.** slab **c.** supply **d.** display

9. _____ c _____

10. An English translation of the Italian poetry was *unavailable*.
    a. unobtainable **b.** unknown **c.** undiscovered **d.** unwritten

10. _____ a _____

EXERCISE 4 USING DIFFERENT FORMS OF WORDS

Decide which form of the vocabulary word in parentheses best completes
the sentence. The form given may be correct. Write your answer on the
answer line.

1. Spies avoid behaving _____. *(conspicuous)*

1. _____ conspicuously _____

2. Coral and Stephen found the puzzle _____. *(intrigue)*

2. _____ intriguing _____

3. Rescued miners joined the struggle to _____ those still trapped
   underground. *(unearth)*

3. _____ unearth _____

4. The brilliant, young student spends hours every day in _____ in the
   library. *(secluded)*

4. _____ seclusion _____

5. The emperor's _____ was a solemn affair. *(inter)*

5. _____ interment _____

6. Only students in the photography class are allowed _____ to the
   darkroom. *(accessible)*

6. _____ access _____

7. The investors waited for the chairman to _____ the results of last year's
   financial performance. *(disclosure)*

7. _____ disclose _____

8. Rodney congratulated Jean for her discovery of the _____ of birthday
   presents. *(cache)*

8. _____ cache _____

9. Merchants expected that the _____ of pineapple would continue for
   several days. *(unavailable)*

9. _____ unavailability _____

10. The meaning of my friend's remark was cloaked in _____. *(obscure)*

10. _____ obscurity _____

READING COMPREHENSION

Each numbered sentence in the following passage contains an italicized vocabulary word. After you read the passage, you will complete an exercise.

A RARE CACHE

Fourteen-year-old Martha Henderson had always dreamed of finding buried treasure. One day, to her amazement, her dream came true.

(1) As Martha walked along a *secluded* stretch of Las Tortugas Beach, which was near her house, she immediately noticed and picked up a coin that she assumed to be a quarter. (2) However, this *conspicuous* piece of metal turned out to be a very old Spanish coin.

Martha could not read the writing on the coin. She showed it to her best friend, Consuela Aguilar, who told her that it was Spanish. (3) Furthermore, Consuela knew that it was from seventeenth-century Spain because of the *obscure* image of King Philip V stamped upon it.

(4) The discovery *intrigued* the two girls, and they decided to return to the beach the following day to see if they could find any more "pieces of eight." They set off, along with Martha's dog, Prince, down a long, narrow path. (5) The path led to the part of the beach that was least *accessible* to the public and passed through a thick grove of palm trees, where the girls decided to stop for a while.

Prince, after doing some exploring on his own, drank from a nearby water hole. (6) Noticing the dog, Consuela remarked that fresh water was usually *unavailable* so close to the ocean. She suggested that perhaps a well had been dug there long ago.

Martha agreed and ventured further into the palm grove to explore it, inching her way through the thick, matted beach grass. Suddenly she yelled to Consuela to join her. The tangled grasses concealed the ruins of a Spanish camp. Nothing significant appeared on the surface: some large stones, an old metal cup, and a piece of what seemed to have once been a candlestick.

(7) Modest as it was, the find encouraged the two girls to try to *unearth* other objects. With great effort they moved some of the large stones and uncovered a deep stone-lined pit. Their anticipation building, Martha and Consuela explored the pit by raking the bottom with long sticks of driftwood from the beach.

Unexpectedly, the girls heard the clattering of what sounded like a great many coins. Martha scrambled to the bottom of the pit. (8) To her amazement she discovered hundreds of coins that had been *interred* there. (9) The girls realized that the rare *cache* must have been hidden there more than two centuries before.

Amazed at their good fortune, Martha and Consuela filled their pockets with as many coins as they could carry, covered over the pit, and returned home with Prince. (10) That very afternoon the girls decided to make a *disclosure* of their discovery and turned over the treasure of Las Tortugas to the local museum.

Each of the following statements corresponds to a numbered sentence in the passage. Each statement contains a blank and is followed by four answer choices. Decide which choice fits best in the blank. The word or phrase that you choose must express roughly the same meaning as the italicized word in the passage. Write the letter of your choice on the answer line.

1. Martha walked along a(n) _____ stretch of beach.
   a. central   **b.** pretty   **c.** isolated   **d.** sparkling

   1. _____ c

2. The _____ piece of metal was actually an old Spanish coin.
   a. noticeable   **b.** colorful   **c.** valuable   **d.** dull

   2. _____ a

3. An _____ image of King Philip V was stamped on the coin.
   a. unusual   **b.** apparent   **c.** indistinct   **d.** imperial

   3. _____ c

4. The discovery _____ the two girls.
   a. fascinated   **b.** bored   **c.** pleased   **d.** scared

   4. _____ a

5. A part of the beach could not be _____ by the public.
   a. used frequently   **c.** occupied
   b. considered safe   **d.** easily reached

   5. _____ d

6. Fresh water was usually _____ close to the ocean.
   a. not pure   **c.** not obtainable
   b. expensive   **d.** refreshing

   6. _____ c

7. The two girls tried to _____ other objects.
   a. bury   **b.** find   **c.** stake out   **d.** dig up

   7. _____ d

8. Coins had been _____ in the pit.
   a. buried   **b.** found   **c.** hidden   **d.** placed

   8. _____ a

9. The _____ had been placed there two hundred years before.
   a. Spanish camp   **c.** hidden stockpile
   b. stones for the pit   **d.** tangled grass covering

   9. _____ c

10. The girls made an immediate _____ of their find.
    a. revelation   **b.** secret   **c.** claim   **d.** controversy

    10. _____ a

Directions   On the answer line, write the vocabulary word or a form of it that completes each analogy.

See page 119 for some strategies to use with analogies.

1. Delineate is to duties as _____ is to boundaries. (*Lesson 25*)

   1. _____ demarcate

2. Shoulder is to highway as _____ is to page. (*Lesson 25*)

   2. _____ margin

3. Trivial is to importance as _____ is to restraint. (*Lesson 26*)

   3. _____ impulsive

4. Magnet is to attract as repellent is to _____. (*Lesson 26*)

   4. _____ repulse

5. _____ is to obtained as conspicuous is to seen. (*Lesson 27*)

   5. _____ Accessible

6. _____ is to obtained as inaccessible is to reached. (*Lesson 27*)

   6. _____ Unavailable

7. _____ is to law as revoke is to privilege. (*Lesson 26*)

   7. _____ Repeal

The **Test** for Lessons 25, 26, and 27 is on page T30.

READING SKILLS

THE PREFIX *IN-*

The prefix *in-* meaning "not" is one of a pair of homographs—separate words that are spelled alike but differ in origin and meaning. (The other prefix *in-* means "in.") The prefix *in-* meaning "not" has three alternative forms that are used according to the first letter of the root. The form *il-* is used before *l;* the form *im-* is used before *b, m,* and *p;* and the form *ir-* is used before *r.* The basic form *in-* is used before all other letters.

Prefix Meaning	Word	Definition
not	incorrect	not correct
	illogical	not logical
	immature	not mature
	irreversible	not reversible

To determine the meaning of an unfamiliar word beginning with *in-,* use the following procedure. First, substitute the meaning of the prefix for the prefix itself. Then think of possible definitions for the entire word. Remember that *in-* may mean "in" rather than "not," so be sure that your definition makes sense in the context. Finally, check your definition in the dictionary.

EXERCISE USING THE PREFIX *IN-*

Each sentence in this exercise contains an italicized word with the prefix *in-* or one of its alternative forms. *Step 1:* Write your definition of the word. *Step 2:* Write the dictionary definition of the word. Choose the definition that best fits the way the word is used in the sentence. *Step 3:* Write a sentence of your own in which you use the word correctly.

1. The telegram read, "We regret the *inexplicable* actions of our representative in Great Falls."

   Your Definition _Not explainable_____

   Dictionary Definition _Not capable of being explained_____

   Sentence _When all the facts were in, his disappearance was still inexplicable.___

2. The driving instructor told Darlene that a left turn from the right lane was *illegal.*

   Your Definition _Not legal_____

   Dictionary Definition _Prohibited by law_____

   Sentence _Right turns on red lights are not illegal in some states._____

3. The teacher asked the student to recopy the *illegible* paper.

   Your Definition Not legible

   Dictionary Definition Not capable of being deciphered; not readable

   Sentence I misread his note because several words were illegible.

4. The detective's methods were *irregular,* but he always solved his cases.

   Your Definition Not regular

   Dictionary Definition Not standard or uniform, as in shape, size, length, or arrangement

   Sentence Their family eats at irregular times.

5. "Bad manners are *inexcusable,*" said Aunt Sophie.

   Your Definition Not excusable

   Dictionary Definition Impossible to excuse, pardon, or justify

   Sentence I don't agree that Wes's remark was inexcusable.

6. The large oak cabinet was *immovable.*

   Your Definition Not movable

   Dictionary Definition Not capable of being moved

   Sentence The baby soon learned to crawl around immovable objects.

7. Jim used to have an *irrational* fear of cats.

   Your Definition Not rational

   Dictionary Definition Not based on, or guided by, reason

   Sentence Mike's decisions are usually irrational and impulsive—but never wrong.

8. Ben has an unfortunate tendency to drive at *immoderate* speeds; someday he will get into an accident.

   Your Definition Not moderate

   Dictionary Definition Exceeding normal or appropriate bounds; extreme

   Sentence Dina denies that she has an immoderate desire to be elected class president.

9. Just before construction began, the engineer discovered that her calculations were *inaccurate.*

   Your Definition Not accurate

   Dictionary Definition Not accurate; containing errors

   Sentence We were late because Lila's watch was inaccurate.

10. The dense foliage and vines made the rain forest practically *impenetrable.*

    Your Definition Not able to be penetrated

    Dictionary Definition Not capable of being entered or penetrated

    Sentence The wilderness area is impenetrable without a four-wheel-drive vehicle.

The Latin words *ruptus*, meaning "broken," and *fractus*, meaning "shattered," have given us the roots *-rupt-* and *-fract-*, which form the basis of many of our English words. If you *interrupt* a conversation, for example, you break into it. A *fracture*, on the other hand, is a break in bone or cartilage, and something that is *fragile* is easily shattered. All of the words in this lesson are from the roots *-rupt-* and *-fract-*, and they all have something to do with breaking.

<table>
<tr><td>

WORD LIST

abrupt
disrupt
eruption
fractious
fragment
infraction
infringe
refractory
rout
rupture
</td></tr>
</table>

DEFINITIONS

After you have studied the definitions and example for each vocabulary word, write the word on the line to the right.

1. **abrupt** (ə-brŭpt′) *adjective*   **a.** Unexpected; sudden.   **b.** Brief to the point of rudeness; curt; brusque.   **c.** Very steep: *an abrupt hill.* (From the Latin *ab-*, meaning "off," and *ruptus*, meaning "broken")

   Related Words **abruptly** *adverb;* **abruptness** *noun*
   Example   The turn in the road was so *abrupt* that we almost missed the driveway.

   1. _____

2. **disrupt** (dĭs-rŭpt′) *verb*   **a.** To upset the order of; throw into confusion or disorder.   **b.** To interrupt or block progress. (From the Latin *dis-*, meaning "apart," and *ruptus*)

   Related Words **disruption** *noun;* **disruptive** *adjective*
   Example   Alice's laughter *disrupted* the other students' concentration.

   2. _____

3. **eruption** (ĭ-rŭp′shən) *noun*   **a.** A violent emergence from limits or restraint; an explosion or outburst.   **b.** The forcing out or release of a substance, such as lava from a volcano or steam from a geyser. (From the Latin *ex-*, meaning "out," and *ruptus*)

   Related Word   **erupt** *verb*
   Example   In the climax of the play, the main character reacts with an *eruption* of anger.

   3. _____
   See *rupture.*

4. **fractious** (frăk′shəs) *adjective*   **a.** Inclined to make trouble; unruly.
   b. Irritable; cranky. (From the Latin word *fractus,* meaning "shattered")

   Related Word   **fractiousness** *noun*
   Example   The inexperienced rider could not control the *fractious*
                       horse.

5. **fragment** (frăg′mĕnt′) *verb*   To break apart into pieces; separate.
   noun (frăg′mənt)   **a.** A part broken off or detached.   **b.** Something
   incomplete. (From the Latin word *fragmentum,* meaning "a piece
   broken off")

   Related Words   **fragmentary** *adjective;* **fragmentation** *noun*
   Example   The glass bowl was *fragmented* by rough handling in
                       the mail.

6. **infraction** (ĭn-frăk′shən) *noun*   A violation of a law or rule. (From the
   Latin word *infractus,* meaning "destroyed")

   Example   The sergeant would not tolerate even minor *infractions* of
                       the uniform code.

7. **infringe** (ĭn-frĭnj′) *verb*   **a.** To trespass or encroach on.   **b.** To violate or
   go beyond the limits of (a law, for example). (From the Latin word
   infringere, meaning "to break off" or "to shatter")

   Related Word   **infringement** *noun*
   Example   By building the fence, the Flanagans accidentally
                       infringed on their neighbor's property.

8. **refractory** (rĭ-frăk′tə-rē) *adjective*   **a.** Stubborn; obstinate; unmanageable.
   b. Difficult to melt, shape, or work with.   **c.** Not responsive to medical
   treatment. (From the Latin word *refractus,* meaning "broken up")

   Related Word   **refractorily** *adverb*
   Example   Mules have the reputation of being *refractory* animals.

9. **rout** (rout) *verb*   **a.** To drive or force out.   **b.** To defeat overwhelmingly.
   noun   A defeat or disorderly retreat. (From the Latin word *ruptio,*
   meaning "the act of breaking")

   Example   Jason had the pleasure of seeing his opponent *routed* at
                       the polls.

10. **rupture** (rŭp′chər) *noun*   A break or split.   *verb*   **a.** To break open;
    burst.   **b.** To break off.   **c.** To undergo or suffer a break. (From the Latin
    word *ruptus*)

    Example   The *rupture* in the water line caused a minor flood.

4. _____
See *refractory.*

5. _____

6. _____
See *infringe.*

7. _____
USAGE NOTE:
Infringement and *infraction*
can be used interchange-
ably, but *infringement* can
also suggest the *gradual*
intrusion on someone's
property or rights.

8. _____
USAGE NOTE: A *refrac-
tory* person is stubborn. A
fractious person is one
likely to make trouble.

9. _____

10. _____
MEMORY CUE: An *erup-
tion* of lava might follow a
rupture in a volcano.

EXERCISE I COMPLETING DEFINITIONS

On the answer line, write the word from the vocabulary list that best completes each definition.

1. Someone who causes trouble or tends to be irritable is _____.

2. To trespass on or go beyond limits is to _____.

3. A statement that is sudden or curt is _____.

4. To drive out or to defeat is to _____.

5. To be stubborn is to be _____.

6. To break apart into pieces is to _____.

7. The breaking of a rule is a(n) _____.

8. A violent outburst or explosion is a(n) _____.

9. To upset the order of something is to _____ it.

10. A break or split is a(n) _____.

1. _____ fractious
2. _____ infringe
3. _____ abrupt
4. _____ rout
5. _____ refractory
6. _____ fragment
7. _____ infraction
8. _____ eruption
9. _____ disrupt
10. _____ rupture

EXERCISE 2 USING WORDS CORRECTLY

Decide whether the italicized vocabulary word has been used correctly in the sentence. On the answer line, write *Correct* for correct use and *Incorrect* for incorrect use.

1. Medical research has succeeded in *routing* many infectious diseases such as smallpox.

2. The doctor set Ted's *fractious* arm and placed it in a cast.

3. Mary *infringed* the hem of her skirt with green thread.

4. The pottery vase was *fragmented* in the dishwasher.

5. With an *abrupt* nod, the professor ended our conversation.

6. Oil leaked slowly from a hidden *rupture* in the tank.

7. The principal rewarded Barney for his *infraction* of school rules.

8. Jennifer wished to *disrupt* the band during her favorite song.

9. The *refractory* dog was increasingly difficult to control.

10. The children hid the *eruption* of the plate in the cupboard.

1. _____ Correct
2. _____ Incorrect
3. _____ Incorrect
4. _____ Correct
5. _____ Correct
6. _____ Correct
7. _____ Incorrect
8. _____ Incorrect
9. _____ Correct
10. _____ Incorrect

EXERCISE 3 CHOOSING THE BEST WORD

Decide which vocabulary word or related form best completes the sentence, and write the letter of your choice on the answer line.

1. Brian _____ the quiet classroom with a loud sneeze.
   a. routed   **b.** infringed   **c.** disrupted   **d.** erupted

1. _____ c

2. Carlo hit the brakes when the car ahead made a(n) _____ stop.
   a. abrupt   **b.** fragmented   **c.** refractory   **d.** fractious

2. _____ a

3. Do not allow aggressive people to _____ on your rights.
   a. rout **b.** rupture **c.** disrupt **d.** infringe

3. _____d_____

4. Engineers searched furiously for the _____ in the oil pipeline.
   a. infringement **b.** infraction **c.** rupture **d.** rout

4. _____c_____

5. Not wishing to go to bed, the toddler became _____.
   a. routed **b.** refractory **c.** fragmented **d.** abrupt

5. _____b_____

6. The china doll _____ into tiny pieces when it hit the floor.
   a. fragmented **b.** fractious **c.** infringed **d.** disrupted

6. _____a_____

7. The explosion caused a(n) _____ of water.
   a. infraction **b.** eruption **c.** fragment **d.** infringement

7. _____b_____

8. The _____ youths were asked to leave the theater.
   a. fragmented **b.** routed **c.** abrupt **d.** fractious

8. _____d_____

9. The fire _____ shoppers from the store.
   a. routed **b.** fragmented **c.** ruptured **d.** infringed

9. _____a_____

10. Although Johnny was guilty of a(n) _____ of camp rules, he was not punished because he saved his friend's life in the process.
    a. eruption **b.** refractory **c.** infraction **d.** rupture

10. _____c_____

EXERCISE 4 USING DIFFERENT FORMS OF WORDS

Decide which form of the vocabulary word in parentheses best completes the sentence. The form given may be correct. Write your answer on the answer line.

1. Small annoyances occasionally cause Chris to _____ in anger. *(eruption)*

1. _____erupt_____

2. Greta never realized that reading Felice's diary was an _____ on her privacy. *(infringe)*

2. ____infringement____

3. Fortunately, Dana's parents rushed him to the hospital before his appendix _____. *(rupture)*

3. _____ruptured_____

4. For her _____ of the dormitory rules, Sharon had to appear before the student court. *(infraction)*

4. _____infraction_____

5. The song ended so _____ that Michelle thought her tape player was broken. *(abrupt)*

5. _____abruptly_____

6. Marjorie's friends had not expected such _____ from her. *(fractious)*

6. ____fractiousness____

7. In a surprising victory, the home team _____ the visiting team, which had been heavily favored. *(rout)*

7. _____routed_____

8. Archaeologists put together the pieces of the _____ tablet and attempted to read it. *(fragmented)*

8. _____fragmented_____

9. Four-year-old Jeremy was a _____ influence on the other children. *(disrupt)*

9. _____disruptive_____

10. Jane insisted _____ that she sit in the front seat. *(refractory)*

10. _____refractorily_____

READING COMPREHENSION

Each numbered sentence in the following passage contains an italicized vocabulary word or related form. After you read the passage, you will complete the exercise.

NELLIE BLY: DARING WOMAN JOURNALIST

Elizabeth Cochrane Seaman (1867–1922), the first American woman reporter to achieve international fame, was a pioneer in opening doors for women journalists. The only daughter of a judge, Elizabeth was encouraged to study law—a career not generally open to women at that time. (1) Judge Cochrane's death in 1884 brought an *abrupt* end to her career plans, however. (2) Her older brothers refused to allow her to *disrupt* their lives with what they considered to be ridiculous ideas.

Instead of law, Elizabeth began a career in journalism at the age of eighteen. (3) One day, as she was reading the *Pittsburgh Dispatch,* she *erupted* in anger over an editorial about women in the workplace. (4) Furious with the editor for his *infringement* on the right of women to be employed, she wrote him an indignant letter. The editor was so impressed with her writing style that he wanted to hire her as a reporter. (5) Elizabeth knew that her *refractory,* old-fashioned brothers would not approve of her working as a journalist. When the editor suggested that she use a pen name to protect her identity, Elizabeth chose "Nellie Bly," the familiar Stephen Foster song title.

(6) Nellie Bly concentrated first on exposing the terrible conditions under which people

worked—the long hours, the *fragmentation* of families, and the starvation wages. Although her articles did not make cheerful reading, circulation of the newspaper boomed.

After two years of working, Nellie Bly was less inclined to allow her brothers to dictate her life. She decided to move to New York. (7) Although the *rupture* with her family was painful, she was ready for a change.

New York newspaper editors were totally against hiring women as reporters. Nellie could not even get an interview. Finally she decided that she would not leave the office of Joseph Pulitzer, owner of *The World,* until she had spoken to him. (8) Told repeatedly of the crazy woman camped out all day in the reception area,

Pulitzer, in a *fractious* mood, finally agreed to see her. He gave her three minutes to prove to him that she was a reporter with original ideas. Recalling that people had referred to her all day as "the crazy lady," she told Pulitzer that she wanted to get herself committed to the city mental asylum in order to write the inside story of conditions there. Pulitzer hired her immediately.

As a result of her exposé, "Behind Asylum Bars," Nellie Bly became famous overnight. (9) She unfolded tales of inhuman treatment and countless *infractions* of sound medical practice. Because of her efforts, conditions for inmates were improved.

In 1889 Nellie Bly decided to break the record of Jules Verne's imaginary hero Phileas Fogg in *Around the World in Eighty Days.* The editor and staff of *The World* refused to support her plan at first because they worried about what could happen to an unchaperoned woman on such a trip. (10) By threatening to make the trip anyway and write about it for a rival paper, Nellie completely *routed* their resistance. She became the best-known and most-loved newspaper reporter when she outdid Fogg's fictional time by setting a record of seventy-two days, six hours, and eleven minutes.

Each of the following statements corresponds to a numbered sentence in the passage. Each statement contains a blank and is followed by four answer choices. Decide which choice fits best in the blank. The word or phrase that you choose must express roughly the same meaning as the italicized word in the passage. Write the letter of your choice on the answer line.

1. Her father's death brought a(n) _____ end to her career plans.
   a. sudden   **b.** unhappy   **c.** favorable   **d.** independent

   1. _____ a

2. Elizabeth's older brothers refused to allow her to _____ their lives.
   a. ruin   **c.** upset the order of
   b. manipulate   **d.** take advantage of

   2. _____ c

3. Elizabeth _____ in anger about an editorial in the *Pittsburgh Dispatch*.
   a. wrote   **b.** exploded   **c.** restrained herself   **d.** acted

   3. _____ b

4. Elizabeth was furious with the editor for his _____ the rights of women.
   a. encroachment on   **c.** attitudes toward
   b. decisions about   **d.** goals for

   4. _____ a

5. Elizabeth knew that a newspaper job would cause problems with her _____ brothers.
   a. younger   **b.** dreadful   **c.** practical   **d.** stubborn

   5. _____ d

6. Nellie Bly exposed the terrible conditions of workers, such as the _____ of families and low wages.
   a. employment   **b.** abuse   **c.** breakdown   **d.** intolerance

   6. _____ c

7. Nellie decided to move to New York even though the _____ with her family was painful.
   a. relationship   **b.** break   **c.** argument   **d.** obligation

   7. _____ b

8. Joseph Pulitzer was in a(n) _____ mood when he agreed to see her.
   a. irritable   **b.** famous   **c.** curious   **d.** innocent

   8. _____ a

9. Nellie unfolded tales of countless _____ medical practice.
   a. horrors of   **c.** experiments in
   b. mistakes in   **d.** violations of

   9. _____ d

10. She _____ the staff's resistence by threatening to make the trip anyway.
    a. encouraged   **b.** defeated   **c.** ignored   **d.** predicted

    10. _____ b

Suppose you have a creative idea for a disaster movie that you want to sell to a movie studio. Write a plot outline that describes a catastrophe, such as a hurricane or an earthquake. Invent the characters, explaining what happens to them and how they cope with the disaster. Use five of the vocabulary words from this lesson and underline them.

The **Bonus activity** for Lessons 27 and 28 is on page T32.

29

At first glance the words *harm* and *criticism* may seem rather negative. These words, however, can also be viewed in a positive light. Positive criticism can lead a person to correct a fault. An effective tennis instructor, for example, constructively criticizes a student's playing techniques. In addition, people must understand why something is harmful if they are to protect themselves from it. To warn a child about fire can certainly protect that child from harm. In this lesson you will learn how to use words about harm and criticism to your advantage.

WORD LIST

admonish
alienate
censure
denounce
detriment
imperil
incapacitate
injurious
malign
scoff

DEFINITIONS

After you have studied the definitions and example for each vocabulary word, write the word on the line to the right.

1. **admonish** (ăd-mŏn′ĭsh) *verb*   **a.** To criticize for a fault in a kind but serious way.   **b.** To advise, warn, urge, or caution. (From the Latin words *ad*, meaning "to," and *monere*, meaning "to warn")

   Related Word   **admonition** *noun*
   Example   Mrs. Robbins *admonished* her son for riding his tricycle in the street.

1. _____
   See *denounce*.

2. **alienate** (al′yə-nāt′) *verb*   **a.** To cause to become unfriendly or indifferent.   **b.** To remove or disassociate oneself from other people. (From the Latin word *alius*, meaning "other")

   Related Word   **alienation** *noun*
   Example   Jack's constant arguing *alienated* him from his friends.

2. _____

3. **censure** (sĕn′shər) *noun*   An expression of blame or disapproval. *verb*   To criticize severely or blame. (From the Latin word *censura*, meaning "severe judgment")

   Example   Linda *censured* her younger brother for breaking her camera.

3. _____

4. **denounce** (dĭ-nouns′) *verb*   **a.** To express very strong disapproval of; condemn openly.   **b.** To accuse formally. (From the Latin word *denuntiare*, meaning "to announce" or "to warn")

   Related Word   **denunciation** *noun*
   Example   The politician *denounced* her opponent's tax proposal.

4. _____
   USAGE NOTE: To *denounce* is to criticize in a way that implies rejection. To *admonish* is to criticize in a kindly way.

5. **detriment** (dĕt′rə-mənt) *noun*   **a.** Damage, harm, or loss.   **b.** Something that causes damage, harm, or loss. (From the Latin *de-*, meaning "away," and *terere*, meaning "to rub")

  Related Word   **detrimental** *adjective*
  Example   Little or no rainfall can be a serious *detriment* to a farm community.

5. _____

6. **imperil** (ĭm-pĕr′əl) *verb*   To put in danger.

  Example   The frequent use of pesticides *imperiled* the freshwater supply.

6. _____

7. **incapacitate** (ĭn′kə-păs′ĭ-tāt′) *verb*   To deprive of power, strength, or ability; disable.

  Related Words   **incapacitation** *noun;* **incapacity** *noun*
  Example   The ice skater's sprained ankle *incapacitated* him for several weeks.

7. _____

8. **injurious** (ĭn-jŏŏr′ē-əs) *adjective*   **a.** Causing injury or damage; harmful.
  b. Slanderous; libelous.

  Related Words   **injuriousness** *noun;* **injury** *noun*
  Example   Parents teach their children not to eat or drink anything that is *injurious* to their health.

8. _____

9. **malign** (mə-līn′) *verb*   To speak evil of; tell lies about.   *adjective*   Evil in nature or influence. (From the Latin word *malus*, meaning "bad")

  Example   Carrie *maligned* her former best friend to anyone who would listen.

9. _____
See *scoff.*

10. **scoff** (skŏf) *verb*   To make fun of or mock.   *noun*   An expression of mockery or scorn. (From the Middle English word *scof*, meaning "mockery")

  Related Word   **scoffingly** *adverb*
  Example   Years ago people *scoffed* at "horseless carriages," or early automobiles.

10. _____
USAGE NOTE: To *scoff* is to make fun of mildly. To *malign* is to criticize in an evil way.

EXERCISE I COMPLETING DEFINITIONS

On the answer line, write the word from the vocabulary list that best completes each definition.

1. To _____ a person is to show disapproval of him or her.

2. Something that causes injury or damage is _____.

3. If you _____ at someone, you mock that person.

4. An action that causes harm can be a _____.

5. To disable or deprive of strength is to _____.

6. If you criticize someone gently, you _____ that person.

7. To speak evil of or to lie about is to _____.

8. When you place yourself in danger, you _____ yourself.

9. To cause someone to become unfriendly toward you is to _____ that person.

10. To condemn openly or express strong disapproval of is to _____.

1. _____ censure _____
2. _____ injurious _____
3. _____ scoff _____
4. _____ detriment _____
5. _____ incapacitate _____
6. _____ admonish _____
7. _____ malign _____
8. _____ imperil _____
9. _____ alienate _____
10. _____ denounce _____

EXERCISE 2 USING WORDS CORRECTLY

Decide whether the italicized vocabulary word has been used correctly in the sentence. On the answer line, write *Correct* for correct use and *Incorrect* for incorrect use.

1. Carl *scoffed* at his younger brother's frightened reaction to thunder.

2. Because Brigetta was *incapacitated*, she was able to go skiing.

3. Hank *maligned* the bowling pins, forcing Ralph to reset them.

4. Reading in a dimly lit room can be a *detriment* to your eyesight.

5. The more people you *alienate*, the more friends you will have.

6. When the plant outgrew its pot, Laura *censured* it.

7. Swimming in freezing water can be *injurious* to your health.

8. Smiling, the theater usher *admonished* the girls to stop talking.

9. Charles *denounced* the club for inviting only athletes to become members.

10. Charlene *imperiled* her dog Hector by walking him on a leash.

1. _____ Correct _____
2. _____ Incorrect _____
3. _____ Incorrect _____
4. _____ Correct _____
5. _____ Incorrect _____
6. _____ Incorrect _____
7. _____ Correct _____
8. _____ Correct _____
9. _____ Correct _____
10. _____ Incorrect _____

EXERCISE 3 CHOOSING THE BEST DEFINITION

For each italicized vocabulary word or related form in the following sentences, write the letter of the best definition on the answer line.

1. Joyce *censured* the hotel management for the burned dinner.
   a. complimented **b.** blamed **c.** forgave **d.** sued

2. A severe headache *incapacitated* Joseph for the morning.
   a. disabled **b.** annoyed **c.** cheered **d.** soothed

1. _____ b _____
2. _____ a _____

3. Rudi *admonished* his sister for wandering away from the campsite.   3. _____d_____
   a. encouraged   **b.** laughed at   **c.** praised   **d.** criticized

4. The sewage is *detrimental* to the quality of the water in the river.   4. _____c_____
   a. measurable   **b.** necessary   **c.** harmful   **d.** explainable

5. Janet *scoffed* at her friend's idea for a science project.   5. _____a_____
   a. made fun of   **c.** complimented
   b. identified with   **d.** tuned out

6. The sea captain refused to *imperil* the lives of her passengers by taking the   6. _____c_____
   dangerous route.
   a. add excitement to   **c.** endanger
   b. identify with   **d.** save

7. Doreen *alienated* many of her classmates when she bragged about her trip   7. _____b_____
   to Europe.
   a. pleased   **c.** brought closer
   b. made unfriendly   **d.** cheered up

8. A medical treatment that helped some patients was *injurious* to others.   8. _____d_____
   a. unpleasant   **b.** fair   **c.** soothing   **d.** harmful

9. Gilbert *denounced* the class president's suggestion.   9. _____d_____
   a. approved   **b.** waited for   **c.** reversed   **d.** condemned

10. The former follower *maligned* the unpopular leader.   10. _____a_____
    a. said evil things about   **c.** willingly deserted
    b. plotted against   **d.** greatly assisted

EXERCISE 4   USING DIFFERENT FORMS OF WORDS

Each sentence contains an italicized vocabulary word in a form that does not
fit the sentence. On the answer line, write the form of that word that does fit
the sentence.

1. The lifeguard said that swimmers going anywhere near the severe   1. __imperiling__
   undertow were *imperil* their lives.

2. Marlene risked the *alienate* of her friends by never listening to what   2. __alienation__
   they said.

3. Ricardo minimized the seriousness of his arm *injurious*.   3. __injury__

4. The manager had a bad habit of *censure* players in public.   4. __censuring__

5. Barry's fall down the icy steps resulted in a month's *incapacitate*.   5. __incapacitation__

6. A stern look was the only *admonish* Julie needed to clean up her room.   6. __admonition__

7. At last night's meeting, the town gossip *malign* just about everyone in   7. __maligned__
   the community.

8. Lenore's sudden *denounce* of the club shocked everyone.   8. __denunciation__

9. Rick pointed *scoff* at his brother's new haircut.   9. __scoffingly__

10. Not wearing seat belts could be *detriment* to your health.   10. __detrimental__

READING COMPREHENSION

Each numbered sentence in the following passage contains an italicized vocabulary word or related form. After you read the passage, you will complete an exercise.

ELIZABETH CADY STANTON: EARLY WOMEN'S RIGHTS LEADER

During her long lifetime, Elizabeth Cady Stanton (1815–1902) had a distinguished career as a writer, campaigner, and speaker for the early women's rights movement. Although Mrs. Stanton did not live long enough to see the women's suffrage amendment pass, she helped greatly to stir public consciousness so that women were finally given the right to vote in 1920.

Her keen awareness of women's problems began early. As a child growing up in Johnstown, New York, Elizabeth spent time in her father's law office and was deeply influenced by the moving stories she happened to hear from women seeking legal help. (1) Desperate women described how their husbands had *maligned* them before taking away their property and their children. The current laws supported these unfair actions.

Elizabeth's father was by no means a champion of women's rights. After Elizabeth's only brother died, Daniel Cady turned sadly to the eleven-year-old Elizabeth and said, "Oh, my daughter, I wish you were a boy!" (2) This *admonition* was a challenge to Elizabeth, who already rebelled against the idea that women were mentally and legally inferior to men. (3) Elizabeth did not, however, let this statement *alienate* her from her father. Instead, she decided to prove to him that daughters were as valuable as sons.

As a student Elizabeth was intelligent and resourceful. (4) While her schoolmates *scoffed* at her determination to do well in subjects that were considered unfeminine, Elizabeth mastered mathematics and the classics.

After college Elizabeth took an active role in the antislavery movement. While attending anti-slavery meetings, Elizabeth met her future husband, Henry Brewster Stanton. (5) Stanton was a journalist and reformer who *denounced* the institution of slavery. Elizabeth and Stanton were married on May 10, 1840.

Immediately after the ceremony, Mrs. Stanton accompanied her husband to London, where he was a delegate to the World Anti-Slavery Convention. There she protested the exclusion of women delegates from the convention. (6) Convention leaders *censured* women who wished to participate, with remarks like "Turn out the women!"

This experience strengthened Mrs. Stanton's motivation to improve the status of women. She and another protester, Lucretia Mott, a Quaker minister, promised themselves that they would organize and hold the very first women's rights convention. This dream did not become a reality until eight years later.

In the intervening years, Mrs. Stanton worked for women's rights by circulating petitions for a married women's property bill and by speaking before the New York legislature on the subject. (7) Mrs. Stanton told her audiences that marriage often *incapacitated* women, causing them to submit to laws in which they had had no choice. (8) Marriage, she maintained, was financially *detrimental* to women, since their husbands owned and controlled all property and money. Because of Mrs Stanton's efforts, the New York legislature in 1848 passed a law guaranteeing married women the right to hold real estate in their own name after marriage.

With this success in mind, Mrs. Stanton and Mrs. Mott organized and held the first women's rights convention, in Seneca Falls, New York, on July 19, 1848. (9) For the occasion Mrs. Stanton created a "Declaration of Sentiments," a strong written reaction to the *injurious* treatment that she felt women had suffered.

Mrs. Stanton surprised the convention delegates by introducing a resolution that stated that women must gain the right to vote. (10) There were some who thought that Mrs. Stanton was going too far, that her "daring" demand to gain the vote might *imperil* the overall aims of the movement. However, Elizabeth Cady Stanton's unexpected resolution was to become the rallying point for generations of women as they later campaigned for the right to vote.

Each of the following statements corresponds to a numbered sentence in the passage. Each statement contains a blank and is followed by four answer choices. Decide which choice fits best in the blank. The word or phrase that you choose must express roughly the same meaning as the italicized word in the passage. Write the letter of your choice on the answer line.

1. It was not unusual for husbands to _____ their wives.
   a. tolerate
   b. speak ill of
   c. take action against
   d. question

1. _____ **b**

2. Elizabeth saw her father's _____ as a challenge.
   a. cruel remark
   b. insightful statement
   c. supportive comment
   d. gentle criticism

2. _____ **d**

3. She did not become _____ her father after his comment.
   a. indifferent to
   b. informed by
   c. impressed by
   d. obedient to

3. _____ **a**

4. The other students _____ her desire to do well in school.
   a. praised   b. questioned   c. mocked   d. admired

4. _____ **c**

5. Henry Brewster Stanton _____ the institution of slavery.
   a. struggled against
   b. openly supported
   c. campaigned for
   d. expressed strong disapproval of

5. _____ **d**

6. Antislavery convention leaders _____ women who tried to participate.
   a. strongly endorsed
   b. gently scolded
   c. severely criticized
   d. reacted favorably to

6. _____ **c**

7. Mrs. Stanton felt that marriage could easily _____ women.
   a. disable   b. benefit   c. demoralize   d. destroy

7. _____ **a**

8. She added that marriage could also prove financially _____ to women.
   a. necessary   b. harmful   c. beneficial   d. boring

8. _____ **b**

9. Mrs. Stanton felt that many women had received _____ treatment.
   a. illegal   b. fair   c. critical   d. harmful

9. _____ **d**

10. Some women hoped that Mrs. Stanton's resolution would not _____ the goals of the movement.
    a. enrich   b. gamble with   c. endanger   d. protect

10. _____ **c**

Directions On the answer line, write the vocabulary word or a form of it that completes each analogy.

See page 119 for some strategies to use with analogies.

1. Deliberate is to slow as _____ is to sudden. (*Lesson 28*)

1. _____ **abrupt**

2. Geyser is to gush as volcano is to _____. (*Lesson 28*)

2. _____ **erupt**

3. _____ is to unruly as refractory is to stubborn. (*Lesson 28*)

3. _____ **Fractious**

4. _____ is to condemn as censure is to blame. (*Lesson 29*)

4. _____ **Denounce**

5. Compliment is to praise as scold is to _____. (*Lesson 29*)

5. _____ **admonish**

6. Trespass is to property as _____ is to law. (*Lesson 28*)

6. _____ **infringe**

Whether we volunteer our time to an organization, contribute money to a favorite charity, or simply help a friend complete a task, we perform kind acts on a daily basis. Some people give help out of a sense of duty or obligation; others act kindly in the hope of reward. Regardless of the motive, the result of kindness is the same: the acceptance by others of needed support or assistance. The words in this lesson will enable you to express your thoughts and observations about kindness.

WORD LIST

altruistic
benefactor
beneficial
benevolent
benign
bountiful
gratify
humanitarian
indulge
philanthropic

DEFINITIONS

After you have studied the definitions and example for each vocabulary word, write the word on the line to the right.

1. **altruistic** (ăl′ trōō-ĭs′tĭk) *adjective*   Unselfishly concerned with or devoted to the welfare of others. (From the Latin word *alter*, meaning "other")

    Related Words altruism *noun;* **altruistically** *adverb*
    Example   Andrew Carnegie's *altruistic* beliefs inspired him to donate money for the libraries of the United States.

1. _____

2. **benefactor** (bĕn′ə-făk′ tər) *noun*   One who helps another person in need; one who gives income or property to an institution. (From the Latin phrase *bene facere*, meaning "to do well")

    Related Word **benefaction** *noun*
    Example   In the novel *Great Expectations*, Pip wonders who his *benefactor* is.

2. _____
See *humanitarian.*

3. **beneficial** (bĕn′ ə-fĭsh′əl) *adjective*   Helpful; advantageous; promoting a favorable result. (From the Latin phrase *bene facere*, meaning "to do well")

    Related Words **beneficiary** *noun;* **benefit** *noun;* **benefit** *verb*
    Example   Sunshine and rain are *beneficial* to crops.

3. _____

4. **benevolent** (bə-nĕv′ə-lənt) *adjective*   Characterized by or expressing good will or kindness. (From the Latin words *bene*, meaning "well," and *volens*, meaning "wishing")

    Related Words **benevolence** *noun;* **benevolently** *adverb*
    Example   The Red Cross is a *benevolent* organization that helps victims of fires, floods, and other disasters.

4. _____

5. **benign** (bĭ-nīn') *adjective* **a.** Kind and gently; mild and favorable. **b.** Not seriously harmful. (From the Latin word *benignus*, meaning "kind")

5. _____

   Related Word   benignly *adverb*
   Example   Caroline's *benign* manner makes her an excellent dolphin trainer.

6. **bountiful** (boun'tə-fəl) *adjective* **a.** Plentiful; abundant. **b.** Giving generously. (From the Latin word *bonitas*, meaning "goodness")

6. _____

   Related Words   bountifully *adverb;* **bounty** *noun*
   Example   The family's *bountiful* contribution was used to feed and clothe the refugees.

7. **gratify** (grăt'ə-fī') *verb*   To please or satisfy. (From the Latin word *gratificari*, meaning "to do a favor")

7. _____

   Related Word   gratification *noun*
   Example   The results of the canned-food drive *gratified* the entire committee.

8. **humanitarian** (hyo͞o-măn'ĭ-târ'ē-ən) *noun*   A person concerned with helping to improve human welfare and promote social reform. *adjective*   Relating to the desire to promote human welfare and social reform: *humanitarian contributions.*

8. _____
   USAGE NOTE: A *humanitarian* promotes the welfare of people in general. A *benefactor* helps one person or one institution.

   Related Word   humanitarian *noun*
   Example   Helen Keller is considered a great *humanitarian* because of her work in establishing educational programs for blind and deaf people.

9. **indulge** (ĭn-dŭlj') *verb* **a.** To yield to the desires or wishes of; pamper. **b.** To allow oneself some special pleasure.   **c.** To engage or take part in: *to indulge in a sport.* (From the Latin word *indulgere*, meaning "to be kind")

9. _____

   Related Words   indulgence *noun;* **indulgent** *adjective*
   Example   Mother *indulges* in afternoon naps on Sundays.

10. **philanthropic** (fĭl'ən-thrŏp'ĭk) *adjective*   Relating to the effort to help other people, such as by making donations of money, property, or work; charitable. (From the Greek words *philos*, meaning "loving," and *anthropos*, meaning "person")

10. _____

   Related Words   philanthropically *adverb;* **philanthropist** *noun;* **philanthropy** *noun*
   Example   Most people did not know of Mr. Johnson's *philanthropic* activity until after his death.

EXERCISE I WRITING CORRECT WORDS

On the answer line, write the word from the vocabulary list that fits
each definition.

1. A person who improves human welfare and promotes social reform

2. To please or satisfy

3. Gentle; not seriously harmful

4. One who helps a person in need

5. Characterized by good will or kindness

6. To yield to the desires or wishes of; allow oneself some special pleasure

7. Relating to the effort to help other people through donations or work;
charitable

8. Plentiful; giving generously

9. Helpful; promoting a favorable result

10. Unselfishly concerned with the welfare of others.

1. ____humanitarian____

2. ____gratify____

3. ____benign____

4. ____benefactor____

5. ____benevolent____

6. ____indulge____

7. ____philanthropic____

8. ____bountiful____

9. ____beneficial____

10. ____altruistic____

EXERCISE 2 USING WORDS CORRECTLY

Each of the following statements contains an italicized vocabulary word.
Decide whether the sentence is true or false, and write *True* or *False* on the
answer line.

1. A *humanitarian* treats others badly.

2. An action performed out of spite is *altruistic*.

3. A compliment on a hand-knitted sweater would *gratify* the knitter.

4. Someone who won a large amount of money in a lottery might *indulge* in
a new camera.

5. Clear weather and brisk winds were *beneficial* to sailors on sailing ships.

6. Children would be likely to run in fear from a *benign* dog.

7. A *philanthropic* contribution is usually accepted with gratitude.

8. A *benevolent* person would be generous toward other people.

9. A nation with a *bountiful* supply of food would have food shortages.

10. A person's *benefactor* would take money away from him or her.

1. ____False____

2. ____False____

3. ____True____

4. ____True____

5. ____True____

6. ____False____

7. ____True____

8. ____True____

9. ____False____

10. ____False____

EXERCISE 3 CHOOSING THE BEST WORD

Decide which vocabulary word or related form best completes the sentence,
and write the letter of your choice on the answer line.

1. Christie is a _____ child who tries to help all injured animals.
   a. gratifying **b.** beneficial **c.** benevolent **d.** bountiful

1. ____c____

2. Although the store has run out of shelled walnuts, it has a(n) _____ supply of almonds.
   a. bountiful   **b.** indulged   **c.** philanthropic   **d.** altruistic

2. _____ **a** _____

3. In the winter I _____ by sitting in front of the fireplace and watching old movies on television.
   a. am bountiful   **c.** am benign
   b. act philanthropically   **d.** indulge myself

3. _____ **d** _____

4. "I am _____ by your request for my stew recipe," said the chef.
   a. gratified   **b.** indulged   **c.** benign   **d.** altruistic

4. _____ **a** _____

5. The weather was so _____ when we left home that we did not consider taking umbrellas.
   a. bountiful   **b.** humanitarian   **c.** altruistic   **d.** benign

5. _____ **d** _____

6. The magazine article about Delores Smythe, a local _____, failed to describe her work with the community garden.
   a. benefit   **b.** humanitarian   **c.** bounty   **d.** benevolence

6. _____ **b** _____

7. Milk and milk products _____ for both young children and the elderly.
   a. are benevolent   **c.** are beneficial
   b. seem altruistic   **d.** are bountiful

7. _____ **c** _____

8. _____ is necessary to keep private colleges and universities operating.
   a. Philanthropy   **b.** Bounty   **c.** Gratification   **d.** Indulgence

8. _____ **a** _____

9. Their _____ led the Morrisons to set aside several acres of their farm as a camp for disabled children.
   a. bounty   **b.** benefactor   **c.** indulgence   **d.** altruism

9. _____ **d** _____

10. For years Beth searched for the _____ who had paid for her music lessons.
    a. altruism   **b.** bounty   **c.** benefactor   **d.** humanitarian

10. _____ **c** _____

EXERCISE 4   USING DIFFERENT FORMS OF WORDS

Each sentence contains an italicized vocabulary word in a form that does not fit the sentence. On the answer line, write the form of the word that does fit the sentence.

1. Without the *benefactor* provided by the wealthy stranger, Lee could not have gone to medical school.

1. _____ **benefaction** _____

2. The Sammarcos' *humanitarian* was appreciated by the entire community.

2. _____ **humanitarianism** _____

3. The hungry travelers marveled at the *bountiful* in their hosts' kitchen.

3. _____ **bounty** _____

4. The parents were more *indulge* with their youngest child than with the others.

4. _____ **indulgent** _____

5. *Benevolent* brings rich rewards.

5. _____ **Benevolence** _____

6. The teacher smiled *benign* at the new student standing nervously at the door.

6. _____ **benignly** _____

7. The woman rewarded her nephew for his *altruistic*.

7. _____ **altruism** _____

8. The voice coach's praise brought Jane *gratify*.

8. _____ **gratification** _____

9. The famous *philanthropic* contributed a large sum of money for the new wing of the hospital.

9. _____**philanthropist**_____

10. The primary *beneficial* listed in Mr. McLeod's will was his wife.

10. _____**beneficiary**_____

READING COMPREHENSION

Each numbered sentence in the following passage contains an italicized vocabulary word or related form. After you read the passage, you will complete an exercise.

ALBERT SCHWEITZER: DOCTOR AND HUMANITARIAN

(1) Dr. Albert Schweitzer (1875–1965) was one of the most *altruistic* men of all time. (2) He is remembered and respected as an outstanding *humanitarian* who gave up promising careers in his native Germany to help the people who needed him.

Before he had reached the age of thirty, Dr. Schweitzer was already a well-known philosopher, minister, musician, and writer. (3) His accomplishments in any one of these fields would have *gratified* most people. (4) Although he could have *indulged* himself with comfortable living, Dr. Schweitzer decided instead to serve humanity.

(5) After completing medical school, the *benign* doctor went to Africa in 1913. (6) As a medical missionary, he was ready to put his *philanthropic* dream into action. (7) In French Equatorial Africa, he became the *benefactor* of thousands of people who were without medical attention. Operating under primitive conditions, he fought leprosy, sleeping sickness, and other tropical diseases. (8) He used the *bountiful* donations from his former parishioners, as well as money he had earned from his organ concerts in Germany and France, to finance a modern hospital at Lambaréné. (9) When this *benevolent* man won the Nobel Peace Prize in 1952, he even contributed his prize of thirty-three thousand dollars to the hospital fund.

(10) Dr. Albert Schweitzer is remembered not only for the *benefits* he brought to Africans but also as a symbol. Believing that all people deserve respect, he appreciated the preciousness of life and hated violence. His happiness made him feel a duty to help others. In doing so, he became an example to the world of what kindness in thought and action could accomplish.

Kindness   **197**

READING COMPREHENSION EXERCISE

Each of the following statements corresponds to a numbered sentence in the passage. Each statement contains a blank and is followed by four answer choices. Decide which choice fits best in the blank. The word or phrase that you choose must express roughly the same meaning as the italicized word in the passage. Write the letter of your choice on the answer line.

1. Dr. Albert Schweitzer was one of the most _____ men of all time.
   a. active
   b. unselfishly devoted
   c. clearly honest
   d. talented

   1. ___b___

2. He is remembered and respected as an outstanding _____.
   a. healer of the sick
   b. adviser to governments
   c. entertainer
   d. contributor to others' welfare

   2. ___d___

3. Schweitzer's accomplishments in any one of his careers would have _____ most people.
   a. satisfied   b. annoyed   c. challenged   d. disappointed

   3. ___a___

4. Dr. Schweitzer could have _____ comfortable living.
   a. taught himself
   b. hoped for
   c. given up
   d. pampered himself with

   4. ___d___

5. The _____ doctor went to Africa in 1913.
   a. old   b. talented   c. kind   d. musical

   5. ___c___

6. Schweitzer wanted to put his _____ dream into action.
   a. charitable   b. lifelong   c. impossible   d. realistic

   6. ___a___

7. He became the _____ thousands of people in French Equatorial Africa.
   a. traveler to
   b. helper of
   c. consultant to
   d. organist for

   7. ___b___

8. He used the _____ donations from his former parishioners to build a modern hospital.
   a. small   b. property   c. tax-free   d. generous

   8. ___d___

9. When this _____ man won the Nobel Peace Prize, he contributed his prize money to the hospital fund.
   a. persistent   b. brilliant   c. kind   d. unusual

   9. ___c___

10. Dr. Schweitzer is remembered for the _____ he brought to Africans.
    a. advantages
    b. dramatic cures
    c. knowledge
    d. machinery

    10. ___a___

WRITING ASSIGNMENT

Think of a situation in which a person demonstrated kindness. The situation might have been one that you took part in, or it might have been an event that you witnessed or read about. Write a paragraph in which you narrate the incident, focusing on what happened and what the outcome was. Use at least five of the words from this lesson in your narrative paragraph and underline them.

The **Bonus activity** for Lessons 29 and 30 is on page T33.
The **Test** for Lessons 28, 29, and 30 is on page T34.

READING SKILLS

THE SUFFIXES -ION AND -NESS

A **suffix** is a group of letters added to the end of a root. (A root is the part of a word that contains its basic meaning. A root can also be a complete word.) Some of the words in this book, such as *dissection* and *momentousness*, end with suffixes *-ion* and *-ness*. The suffix *-ion* changes a verb or adjective into a noun. The suffix *-ness* changes an adjective into a noun. Each of these suffixes has one meaning.

Suffix Meaning	Word	Definition
-ion; action, process, or state	correction (correct + *-ion*)	act or process of correcting
	confusion (confuse + *-ion*)	state of being confused
-ness: state or condition	gloominess (gloomy + *-ness*)	state of being gloomy
	softness (soft + *-ness*)	condition of being soft

The spelling of the roots to which *-ion* and *-ness* are added sometimes changes. In the examples above, the final *e* of *confuse* is dropped when *-ion* is added. When *-ness* is added to *gloomy,* the *y* changes to *i.*

To determine the meanings of words ending with *-ion* or *-ness,* follow these steps. First, substitute the meaning of the suffix for the suffix itself. Second, think of possible definitions for the entire word. Third, check each definition in a dictionary.

EXERCISE USING THE SUFFIXES -ION AND -NESS

Each sentence in this exercise contains an italicized verb or adjective. *Step 1:* Form a noun by adding *-ion* or *-ness* to the italicized word. Write the resulting word. *Step 2:* Write your definition of the noun. Use a dictionary to check your definition and spelling of the word. *Step 3:* Write a sentence of your own in which you use the noun correctly.

1. The police officer had to stay *alert* during night duty.

    Noun Form alertness

    Definition The state of being attentive or aware

    Sentence Your alertness affects your performance on tests.

2. Wash your knee so that dirt won't *infect* the bruise.

   Noun Form infection

   Definition The state of being contaminated with germs

   Sentence Enrique's ear infection cleared up within a week.

3. Our city *possesses* the finest public library in the state.

   Noun Form possession

   Definition The state of having or owning

   Sentence The thieves were arrested for the possession of stolen goods.

4. A pilot light *ignites* the gas burner in the water heater.

   Noun Form ignition

   Definition The act or process of starting a fire

   Sentence Ignition of the rocket engines is done by an automatic system.

5. Liz claims that my room is *sloppy*, but I say it just looks lived in.

   Noun Form sloppiness

   Definition A messy condition

   Sentence The sergeant would not tolerate sloppiness in her barracks.

6. His *meek* appearance belied his crafty mind.

   Noun Form meekness

   Definition The state of being patient, humble, or mild

   Sentence With great meekness, he endured his brother's bullying.

7. The author *revised* his book to bring it up to date.

   Noun Form revision

   Definition The act of revising

   Sentence Revision is an important part of the process of writing.

8. The old shack by the railroad station is *mean* and shabby.

   Noun Form meanness

   Definition The state or condition of being poor, common, or low in quality

   Sentence The meanness of the houses was outweighed by the warmth of the people who lived in them.

9. The *harsh* north wind caused Monica's nose to turn bright red.

   Noun Form harshness

   Definition The condition of being severe

   Sentence The harshness of the desert did not stop the prospectors.

CONTENTS

USING BONUS ACTIVITIES AND TESTS

For your convenience, the lesson **Tests** and **Bonus** activities that accompany *Vocabulary for Achievement*, Second Course, are available as reproducible masters in this section. Answers are printed in color on the front of each reproducible master for ease in locating.

This section also contains recordkeeping charts that may be reproduced for each of your classes. These will help you to keep track of student progress on **lesson exercises, Bonus** activities, **Tests,** and **skill features.**

TESTS

There are ten multiple-choice tests, each covering three consecutive lessons. This format ensures that students can demonstrate proficiency with a wider set of vocabulary words than is found in a single lesson.

Test formats resemble those of the lesson exercises. Each test is divided into two parts of fifteen items each, allowing for the testing of all words in the three lessons. Part A focuses on recognizing and recalling definitions, while Part B emphasizes placing words within the context of sentences or discriminating among a choice of synonyms.

BONUSES

Fifteen Bonus activities, each covering two consecutive lessons, offer students further opportunities for reinforcement and enrichment. These activities consist of crossword puzzles, word searches, sentence completions, scrambled words, and other word-game formats. Depending on classroom needs, use these activities as added practice, as reviews of already-mastered words, or as extra-credit assignments.

FOR ACHIEVEMENT

SECOND COURSE

Class Period _____

	Lesson 1 Exercises	Lesson 2 Exercises	Bonus: Lessons 1 & 2	Lesson 3 Exercises	Test: Lessons 1, 2, 3	Skill Lesson	Lesson 4 Exercises	Bonus: Lessons 3 & 4	Lesson 5 Exercises	Lesson 6 Exercises	Bonus: Lessons 5 & 6	Test: Lessons 4, 5, 6	Skill Lesson	Lesson 7 Exercises	Lesson 8 Exercises	Bonus: Lessons 7 & 8	Lesson 9 Exercises	Test: Lessons 7, 8, 9	Skill Lesson	Lesson 10 Exercises	Bonus: Lessons 9 & 10	Lesson 11 Exercises	Lesson 12 Exercises	Bonus: Lessons 11 & 12	Test: Lessons 10, 11, 12	Skill Lesson	Lesson 13 Exercises	Lesson 14 Exercises	Bonus: Lessons 13 & 14	Lesson 15 Exercises	Test: Lessons 13, 14, 15	Skill Lesson
1.																																
2.																																
3.																																
4.																																
5.																																
6.																																
7.																																
8.																																
9.																																
10.																																
11.																																
12.																																
13.																																
14.																																
15.																																
16.																																
17.																																
18.																																
19.																																
20.																																
21.																																
22.																																
23.																																
24.																																
25.																																
26.																																
27.																																
28.																																
29.																																
30.																																
31.																																
32.																																
33.																																
34.																																
35.																																

	Lesson 16 Exercises	Bonus: Lessons 15 & 16	Lesson 17 Exercises	Lesson 18 Exercises	Bonus: Lessons 17 & 18	Test: Lessons 16, 17, 18	Skill Lesson	Lesson 19 Exercises	Lesson 20 Exercises	Bonus: Lessons 19 & 20	Lesson 21 Exercises	Test: Lessons 19, 20, 21	Skill Lesson	Lesson 22 Exercises	Bonus: Lessons 21 & 22	Lesson 23 Exercises	Lesson 24 Exercises	Bonus: Lessons 23 & 24	Test: Lessons 22, 23, 24	Skill Lesson	Lesson 25 Exercises	Lesson 26 Exercises	Bonus: Lessons 25 & 26	Lesson 27 Exercises	Test: Lessons 25, 26, 27	Skill Lesson	Lesson 28 Exercises	Bonus: Lessons 27 & 28	Lesson 29 Exercises	Lesson 30 Exercises	Bonus: Lessons 29 & 30	Test: Lessons 28, 29, 30	Skill Lesson
1.																																	
2.																																	
3.																																	
4.																																	
5.																																	
6.																																	
7.																																	
8.																																	
9.																																	
10.																																	
11.																																	
12.																																	
13.																																	
14.																																	
15.																																	
16.																																	
17.																																	
18.																																	
19.																																	
20.																																	
21.																																	
22.																																	
23.																																	
24.																																	
25.																																	
26.																																	
27.																																	
28.																																	
29.																																	
30.																																	
31.																																	
32.																																	
33.																																	
34.																																	
35.																																	

BONUS LESSONS I AND 2

(pages 1–12)

Use the clues to complete the crossword puzzle.

The crossword grid contains the following answers:

- 1 Across / grid: ARTICULATE
- 6 Across: ISLAND
- 8 Across: ACCENT
- 9 Across: LATITUDE
- 11 Across: VERTICAL
- 12 Across: BASIC
- 14: D
- 16 Across: QUAGMIRE
- 17 Across: ENUNCIATE
- 19 Across: EMPHASIZE
- 20 Across: STATUS
- Down words include: IMAGINARY, INTELLIGIBLE, TERRESTRIAL, CLIFF, DICTION, PENINSULA, PEER, DIALECT, VIEW, ENVELOP, TOPSCAPE

Across

1. Describes a clear and effective speaker

6. Life on a(n) _____ may be *insular*.

8. People from other countries may speak English with a foreign _____.

9. Indicated on a map by horizontal lines

11. Distance east or west of Greenwich is indicated by _____ lines.

12. Synonym for *fundamental*

16. Muddy land, or an entanglement

17. To pronounce in a clear manner

19. Synonym for *stress*

20. From a Latin word meaning "position" or "standing"

Down

2. Having to do with the earth or land

3. Synonym for *precipice*

4. Understandable

5. A *meridian* is a(n) _____ circle.

7. The choice and use of words in speaking and writing

10. Almost an island

13. An equal in age, class, or rank

14. The version of a language that is spoken in a country or region

15. A *panorama* is a wide-ranging _____.

18. *Topography* charts the '_____' of the land.

BONUS LESSONS 1 AND 2

(pages 1–12)

Use the clues to complete the crossword puzzle.

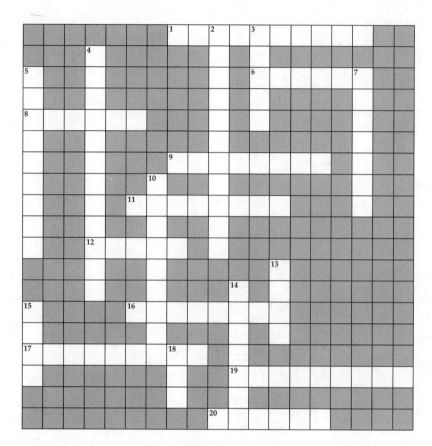

Across

1. Describes a clear and effective speaker

6. Life on a(n) _____ may be *insular.*

8. People from other countries may speak English with a foreign _____ .

9. Indicated on a map by horizontal lines

11. Distance east or west of Greenwich is indicated by _____ lines.

12. Synonym for *fundamental*

16. Muddy land, or an entanglement

17. To pronounce in a clear manner

19. Synonym for *stress*

20. From a Latin word meaning "position" or "standing"

Down

2. Having to do with the earth or land

3. Synonym for *precipice*

4. Understandable

5. A *meridian* is a(n) _____ circle.

7. The choice and use of words in speaking and writing

10. Almost an island

13. An equal in age, class, or rank

14. The version of a language that is spoken in a country or region

15. A *panorama* is a wide-ranging _____ .

18. *Topography* charts the '_____' of the land.

TEST LESSONS 1, 2, AND 3

(pages 1–18)

PART A CHOOSING THE BEST DEFINITION

On the answer line, write the letter of the best definition of the italicized word.

1. Not many two-year-olds can engage in *intelligible* conversation.
   a. scholarly   **b.** understandable   **c.** adult   **d.** literary

   1. _____ **b**

2. The movie star was greeted by a *throng* of admirers.
   a. crowd   **b.** scarcity   **c.** couple   **d.** unruly mob

   2. _____ **a**

3. Recording the *topography* of a mountainous region can be difficult.
   a. physical features   **b.** snowfall   **c.** customs   **d.** plant life

   3. _____ **a**

4. Citizens of Grenchen, Switzerland, speak a *dialect* of German.
   a. unrelated form   **c.** regional version
   b. few words   **d.** elevated style

   4. _____ **c**

5. One of Dale's *miscellaneous* talents is wood carving.
   a. varied   **b.** promising   **c.** obvious   **d.** expert

   5. _____ **a**

6. The Fourth of July celebration will include a *panorama* of the United States' struggle for independence.
   a. overview   **b.** criticism   **c.** definition   **d.** record

   6. _____ **a**

7. Arthur denied having a New England *accent.*
   a. regional pronunciation   **c.** sense of humor
   b. prejudice   **d.** philosophy

   7. _____ **a**

8. The *inductees* to the Hall of Fame will soon be announced.
   a. perfect examples   **c.** visitors
   b. new members   **d.** employees

   8. _____ **b**

9. Troy is studying *terrestrial* and aquatic life forms.
   a. ancient   **b.** strange   **c.** land   **d.** winged

   9. _____ **c**

10. Carmen learned the *fundamental* moves of the chess pieces.
    a. limited   **b.** complicated   **c.** basic   **d.** many

    10. _____ **c**

11. The *consensus* of the committee was to delay voting on the bond issue.
    a. decision   **b.** intent   **c.** agreement   **d.** desire

    11. _____ **c**

12. There is no *meridian* that does not pass through water at some point.
    a. imaginary circle   **c.** geographical point
    b. time zone   **d.** border of a country

    12. _____ **a**

13. Connie gave an *articulate* speech about robots.
    a. fascinating   **b.** scientific   **c.** long   **d.** clearly expressed

    13. _____ **d**

14. Ants quickly *congregated* around the dropped sandwich.
    a. scurried   **b.** swallowed up   **c.** danced   **d.** gathered

    14. _____ **d**

15. The ground surrounding the barn has turned into a *quagmire.*
    a. maze   **b.** muddy land   **c.** pond   **d.** fertile ground

    15. _____ **b**

TEST LESSONS 1, 2, AND 3

(pages 1–18)

PART A CHOOSING THE BEST DEFINITION

On the answer line, write the letter of the best definition of the italicized word.

1. Not many two-year-olds can engage in *intelligible* conversation.
   a. scholarly   **b.** understandable   **c.** adult   **d.** literary

   1. _____

2. The movie star was greeted by a *throng* of admirers.
   a. crowd   **b.** scarcity   **c.** couple   **d.** unruly mob

   2. _____

3. Recording the *topography* of a mountainous region can be difficult.
   a. physical features   **b.** snowfall   **c.** customs   **d.** plant life

   3. _____

4. Citizens of Grenchen, Switzerland, speak a *dialect* of German.
   a. unrelated form   **c.** regional version
   b. few words   **d.** elevated style

   4. _____

5. One of Dale's *miscellaneous* talents is wood carving.
   a. varied   **b.** promising   **c.** obvious   **d.** expert

   5. _____

6. The Fourth of July celebration will include a *panorama* of the United States' struggle for independence.
   a. overview   **b.** criticism   **c.** definition   **d.** record

   6. _____

7. Arthur denied having a New England *accent*.
   a. regional pronunciation   **c.** sense of humor
   b. prejudice   **d.** philosophy

   7. _____

8. The *inductees* to the Hall of Fame will soon be announced.
   a. perfect examples   **c.** visitors
   b. new members   **d.** employees

   8. _____

9. Troy is studying *terrestrial* and aquatic life forms.
   a. ancient   **b.** strange   **c.** land   **d.** winged

   9. _____

10. Carmen learned the *fundamental* moves of the chess pieces.
    a. limited   **b.** complicated   **c.** basic   **d.** many

    10. _____

11. The *consensus* of the committee was to delay voting on the bond issue.
    a. decision   **b.** intent   **c.** agreement   **d.** desire

    11. _____

12. There is no *meridian* that does not pass through water at some point.
    a. imaginary circle   **c.** geographical point
    b. time zone   **d.** border of a country

    12. _____

13. Connie gave an *articulate* speech about robots.
    a. fascinating   **b.** scientific   **c.** long   **d.** clearly expressed

    13. _____

14. Ants quickly *congregated* around the dropped sandwich.
    a. scurried   **b.** swallowed up   **c.** danced   **d.** gathered

    14. _____

15. The ground surrounding the barn has turned into a *quagmire*.
    a. maze   **b.** muddy land   **c.** pond   **d.** fertile ground

    15. _____

TEST LESSONS 1, 2, AND 3

PART B CHOOSING THE BEST WORD

On the answer line, write the letter of the word that best expresses the meaning of the italicized word or phrase.

16. Sal joined a conservation *alliance of people with a common cause.*
    a. coalition   **b.** throng   **c.** accomplice   **d.** meridian

16. _____a_____

17. Mr. Juarez *emphasized when speaking* our need for recreation areas.
    a. enunciated   **b.** accented   **c.** stressed   **d.** articulated

17. _____c_____

18. The fishing boat radioed its location as 115° *the distance west of Greenwich, England.*
    a. latitude   **b.** longitude   **c.** peninsula   **d.** topography

18. _____b_____

19. New Year's Eve celebrations are *public* rituals in many cities.
    a. intelligible   **b.** communal   **c.** fundamental   **d.** insular

19. _____b_____

20. Classical Greek actors, who wore masks, had to *pronounce clearly* their words when performing.
    a. enunciate   **b.** complement   **c.** accent   **d.** accompany

20. _____a_____

21. Certain breeds of sheep and goats can easily climb *steep cliffs.*
    a. precipices   **b.** peninsulas   **c.** meridians   **d.** quagmires

21. _____a_____

22. This striped tie *adds to the effect of* my suit.
    a. complements   **b.** accompanies   **c.** enunciates   **d.** articulates

22. _____a_____

23. Lucinda wrote a report on the *position in society* that women had in Renaissance England.
    a. diction   **b.** stress   **c.** latitude   **d.** status

23. _____d_____

24. This unique location is an island at high tide and a *strip of land with water on three sides* at low tide.
    a. consensus   **b.** longitude   **c.** peninsula   **d.** meridian

24. _____c_____

25. Francesca asked Paco to be her *musician who plays along with a performer* while she danced a flamenco.
    a. peer   **b.** complement   **c.** accomplice   **d.** accompanist

25. _____d_____

26. The class analyzed the *choice and use of words* in the poem.
    a. topography   **b.** diction   **c.** accent   **d.** congregation

26. _____b_____

27. Do you have the *freedom from usual restraints* to determine the hour at which you go to bed?
    a. longitude   **b.** latitude   **c.** status   **d.** consensus

27. _____b_____

28. Who was Jeff's *helper in breaking the law?*
    a. accompanist   **b.** complement   **c.** peer   **d.** accomplice

28. _____d_____

29. The Constitution provides an accused person with the right to be tried by a jury made up of his or her *equals in age, class, or rank.*
    a. accompanists   **b.** throngs   **c.** peers   **d.** accomplices

29. _____c_____

30. Alison went to St. John to study *pertaining to island* weather patterns.
    a. miscellaneous   **b.** fundamental   **c.** communal   **d.** insular

30. _____d_____

TEST LESSONS 1, 2, AND 3

PART B CHOOSING THE BEST WORD

On the answer line, write the letter of the word that best expresses the meaning of the italicized word or phrase.

16. Sal joined a conservation *alliance of people with a common cause.*
    a. coalition   **b.** throng   **c.** accomplice   **d.** meridian

16. _____

17. Mr. Juarez *emphasized when speaking* our need for recreation areas.
    a. enunciated   **b.** accented   **c.** stressed   **d.** articulated

17. _____

18. The fishing boat radioed its location as 115° *the distance west of Greenwich, England.*
    a. latitude   **b.** longitude   **c.** peninsula   **d.** topography

18. _____

19. New Year's Eve celebrations are *public* rituals in many cities.
    a. intelligible   **b.** communal   **c.** fundamental   **d.** insular

19. _____

20. Classical Greek actors, who wore masks, had to *pronounce clearly* their words when performing.
    a. enunciate   **b.** complement   **c.** accent   **d.** accompany

20. _____

21. Certain breeds of sheep and goats can easily climb *steep cliffs.*
    a. precipices   **b.** peninsulas   **c.** meridians   **d.** quagmires

21. _____

22. This striped tie *adds to the effect of* my suit.
    a. complements   **b.** accompanies   **c.** enunciates   **d.** articulates

22. _____

23. Lucinda wrote a report on the *position in society* that women had in Renaissance England.
    a. diction   **b.** stress   **c.** latitude   **d.** status

23. _____

24. This unique location is an island at high tide and a *strip of land with water on three sides* at low tide.
    a. consensus   **b.** longitude   **c.** peninsula   **d.** meridian

24. _____

25. Francesca asked Paco to be her *musician who plays along with a performer* while she danced a flamenco.
    a. peer   **b.** complement   **c.** accomplice   **d.** accompanist

25. _____

26. The class analyzed the *choice and use of words* in the poem.
    a. topography   **b.** diction   **c.** accent   **d.** congregation

26. _____

27. Do you have the *freedom from usual restraints* to determine the hour at which you go to bed?
    a. longitude   **b.** latitude   **c.** status   **d.** consensus

27. _____

28. Who was Jeff's *helper in breaking the law?*
    a. accompanist   **b.** complement   **c.** peer   **d.** accomplice

28. _____

29. The Constitution provides an accused person with the right to be tried by a jury made up of his or her *equals in age, class, or rank.*
    a. accompanists   **b.** throngs   **c.** peers   **d.** accomplices

29. _____

30. Alison went to St. John to study *pertaining to island* weather patterns.
    a. miscellaneous   **b.** fundamental   **c.** communal   **d.** insular

30. _____

BONUS LESSONS 3 AND 4

(pages 13–18, 21–26)

Use the following clues to identify the words, and write the words on the lines to the right. Then circle each word in the word-search box below. The words may overlap and may read in any direction.

1. Made up of a variety of different elements   (13 letters)
2. *Communal* comes from the Latin word meaning "_____."   (6 letters)
3. A *complement* is something that _____.   (9 letters)
4. A *matriarch* belongs to the _____ gender.   (6 letters)
5. General agreement among the members of a group   (9 letters)
6. An *accomplice* helps another person break a(n) _____.   (3 letters)
7. *Maternal* refers to a(n) _____.   (6 letters)
8. An *accompanist* is a(n) _____.   (8 letters)
9. A *descendant* is a(n) _____ of a certain family.   (9 letters)
10. To come together in a crowd   (10 letters)
11. A male leader of a family   (9 letters)
12. Refers to a line of descent from a common ancestor   (7 letters)
13. A *coalition* is a(n) _____ of those sharing a cause.   (8 letters)
14. A crowd   (6 letters)
15. Future generations   (9 letters)

1. **miscellaneous**
2. **common**
3. **completes**
4. **female**
5. **consensus**
6. **law**
7. **mother**
8. **musician**
9. **offspring**
10. **congregate**
11. **patriarch**
12. **lineage**
13. **alliance**
14. **throng**
15. **posterity**

Challenge

Locate and circle the five additional vocabulary words in the word-search box.

generation
inductee
inheritance
parental
sibling

```
C O N M I S C E L L A N E O U S S
G R E G A T E C O M M O N A T U E
A C E C O M P L S E N S U G S S T
C L T P A T R I A R C H R N E N E
E A A N N A I C I S U M E L C O L
C T G E G A E N I L Y S G E N I P
N N E T N H G R E G N N A N A T M
A E R M O T H E R O I C E W T A O
I R G P R A E N C L T E A L I R C
L A N C H N S E B N S L U S R E O
L P O S T E R I T Y F A F S E N I
A E C D U C S T E H E M R O H E T
N C E P A I N D U C T E E T N G R
I A R C G N I R P S F F O H I M A
```

BONUS LESSONS 3 AND 4

(pages 13–18, 21–26)

Use the following clues to identify the words, and write the words on the lines to the right. Then circle each word in the word-search box below. The words may overlap and may read in any direction.

1. Made up of a variety of different elements   (13 letters)

2. *Communal* comes from the Latin word meaning "_____."   (6 letters)

3. A *complement* is something that _____.   (9 letters)

4. A *matriarch* belongs to the _____ gender.   (6 letters)

5. General agreement among the members of a group   (9 letters)

6. An *accomplice* helps another person break a(n) _____.   (3 letters)

7. *Maternal* refers to a(n) _____.   (6 letters)

8. An *accompanist* is a(n) _____.   (8 letters)

9. A *descendant* is a(n) _____ of a certain family.   (9 letters)

10. To come together in a crowd   (10 letters)

11. A male leader of a family   (9 letters)

12. Refers to a line of descent from a common ancestor   (7 letters)

13. A *coalition* is a(n) _____ of those sharing a cause.   (8 letters)

14. A crowd   (6 letters)

15. Future generations   (9 letters)

1. _____
2. _____
3. _____
4. _____
5. _____
6. _____
7. _____
8. _____
9. _____
10. _____
11. _____
12. _____
13. _____
14. _____
15. _____

```
C O N M I S C E L L A N E O U S S
G R E G A T E C O M M O N A T U E
A C E C O M P L S E N S U G S S T
C L T P A T R I A R C H R N E N E
E A A N N A I C I S U M E L C O L
C T G E G A E N I L Y S G E N I P
N N E T N H G R E G N N A N A T M
A E R M O T H E R O I C E W T A O
I R G P R A E N C L T E A L I R C
L A N C H N S E B N S L U S R E O
L P O S T E R I T Y F A F S E N I
A E C D U C S T E H E M R O H E T
N C E P A I N D U C T E E T N G R
I A R C G N I R P S F F O H I M A
```

Challenge

Locate and circle the five additional vocabulary words in the word-search box.

_____

BONUS LESSONS 5 AND 6

(pages 27–38)

Use the clues to complete the crossword puzzle.

```
                              ¹F                    ²G
                    ³O R I G I N              ⁴G E N T R Y
                       R                         N
                    ⁵D E S O L ⁶A T E            E
                       T        N                R
                          ⁷C O N G E N I A L
                                O                C
                 ⁸D           Y
              ⁹R E G E N E R A T E
                 S           D
        ¹⁰B      C                ¹¹M
          L    ¹²D E G ¹³E N E R A T E
        ¹⁴K I N D    N   X        L        ¹⁵A
          T        D   U      ¹⁶D E F I A N T
       ¹⁷F  H      A   B                    C
        R  ¹⁸D E S P O N D E N T            E
        I          T   R                    S
        E          S  ¹⁹A N G U I S H       T
        N          N                        R
       ²⁰D I S E N C H A N T      ²¹W O R R Y
```

Across

3. Synonym for *genesis*

4. People of high social position

5. Lonely and sad

7. Sociable

9. Revive, or replace by growing new tissue

12. To deteriorate

14. One of the meanings of the root *-gen-*

16. A _____ person may resist authority.

18. In low spirits

19. Great physical or mental pain

20. Synonym for *disillusion*

21. Synonym for *distress*

Down

1. *Primogeniture* is the condition of being the _____-born child in a family.

2. Often less expensive than brand-name products

6. Synonym for *disgruntled*

8. *Progeny*

10. Lighthearted

11. *Gender* refers to both _____ and female.

13. Full of enthusiasm

15. *Genealogy*

17. *Amicable* comes from a Latin word meaning "_____."

BONUS LESSONS 5 AND 6

(pages 27–38)

Use the clues to complete the crossword puzzle.

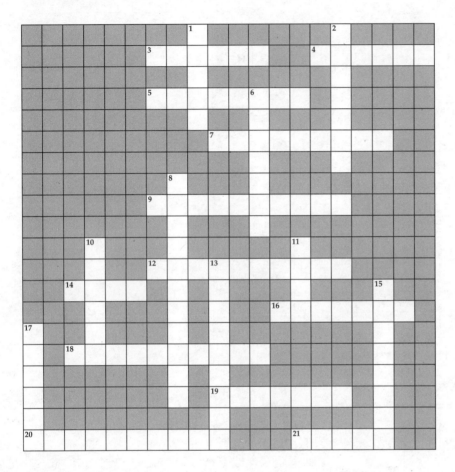

Across

3. Synonym for *genesis*
4. People of high social position
5. Lonely and sad
7. Sociable
9. Revive, or replace by growing new tissue
12. To deteriorate
14. One of the meanings of the root *-gen-*
16. A _____ person may resist authority.
18. In low spirits
19. Great physical or mental pain
20. Synonym for *disillusion*
21. Synonym for *distress*

Down

1. *Primogeniture* is the condition of being the _____-born child in a family.
2. Often less expensive than brand-name products
6. Synonym for *disgruntled*
8. *Progeny*
10. Lighthearted
11. *Gender* refers to both _____ and female.
13. Full of enthusiasm
15. *Genealogy*
17. *Amicable* comes from a Latin word meaning "_____."

TEST LESSONS 4, 5, AND 6

(pages 21–38)

PART A COMPLETING THE DEFINITION

On the answer line, write the letter of the word or phrase that correctly completes each sentence.

1. A *sibling* is a(n) _____.
   a. ancestor   **b.** utensil   **c.** cousin   **d.** brother or sister

   1. _____ d

2. If Sheila is researching her *genealogy,* she is working on her _____.
   a. needlepoint   **b.** ancestry   **c.** career   **d.** special project

   2. _____ b

3. Anything that _____ can be described as *parental.*
   a. includes men and women   **c.** applies to a mother or father
   b. pertains to birth   **d.** is cautious

   3. _____ c

4. Someone who feels *despondent* is _____.
   a. lucky   **b.** successful   **c.** wicked   **d.** dejected

   4. _____ d

5. *Generic* products are _____.
   a. general   **b.** specific   **c.** store-bought   **d.** handmade

   5. _____ a

6. A *matriarch* is a _____.
   a. type of butterfly   **c.** tool used to bale hay
   b. female leader of a family   **d.** type of Greek column

   6. _____ b

7. A member of the *gentry* _____.
   a. is a peasant   **c.** is a person of high social standing
   b. lives in the country   **d.** is involved in business

   7. _____ c

8. *Primogeniture* refers to _____.
   a. the first-born child   **c.** the color of hair and eyes
   b. groups of ancestors   **d.** the ability to dance

   8. _____ a

9. Something _____ is called an *inheritance.*
   a. received after the owner dies   **c.** sacrificed for another
   b. tax deductible   **d.** donated to charity

   9. _____ a

10. If you are *disillusioned,* you feel _____.
    a. cheated   **b.** surrounded   **c.** disenchanted   **d.** foolish

    10. _____ c

11. *Gender* refers to _____ categories of objects or people.
    a. age   **b.** strength   **c.** sex   **d.** origin

    11. _____ c

12. Tracing one's *lineage* involves tracing _____.
    a. ancestors   **b.** shapes   **c.** nationalities   **d.** personal progress

    12. _____ a

13. A person who feels _____ is in *distress.*
    a. energetic   **b.** eager   **c.** inquisitive   **d.** anxious

    13. _____ d

14. When we refer to the _____ of something, we refer to its *genesis.*
    a. complexity   **b.** origin   **c.** movement   **d.** strength

    14. _____ b

15. If offspring from a common ancestor are _____, they are called a *generation.*
    a. at odds with each other   **c.** restricted in number
    b. still living   **d.** at the same level of descent

    15. _____ d

TEST LESSONS 4, 5, AND 6

(pages 21–38)

PART A COMPLETING THE DEFINITION

On the answer line, write the letter of the word or phrase that correctly completes each sentence.

1. A *sibling* is a(n) _____.
   a. ancestor   **b.** utensil   **c.** cousin   **d.** brother or sister

   1. _____

2. If Sheila is researching her *genealogy,* she is working on her _____.
   a. needlepoint   **b.** ancestry   **c.** career   **d.** special project

   2. _____

3. Anything that _____ can be described as *parental.*
   a. includes men and women   **c.** applies to a mother or father
   b. pertains to birth   **d.** is cautious

   3. _____

4. Someone who feels *despondent* is _____.
   a. lucky   **b.** successful   **c.** wicked   **d.** dejected

   4. _____

5. *Generic* products are _____.
   a. general   **b.** specific   **c.** store-bought   **d.** handmade

   5. _____

6. A *matriarch* is a _____.
   a. type of butterfly   **c.** tool used to bale hay
   b. female leader of a family   **d.** type of Greek column

   6. _____

7. A member of the *gentry* _____.
   a. is a peasant   **c.** is a person of high social standing
   b. lives in the country   **d.** is involved in business

   7. _____

8. *Primogeniture* refers to _____.
   a. the first-born child   **c.** the color of hair and eyes
   b. groups of ancestors   **d.** the ability to dance

   8. _____

9. Something _____ is called an *inheritance.*
   a. received after the owner dies   **c.** sacrificed for another
   b. tax deductible   **d.** donated to charity

   9. _____

10. If you are *disillusioned,* you feel _____.
    a. cheated   **b.** surrounded   **c.** disenchanted   **d.** foolish

    10. _____

11. *Gender* refers to _____ categories of objects or people.
    a. age   **b.** strength   **c.** sex   **d.** origin

    11. _____

12. Tracing one's *lineage* involves tracing _____.
    a. ancestors   **b.** shapes   **c.** nationalities   **d.** personal progress

    12. _____

13. A person who feels _____ is in *distress.*
    a. energetic   **b.** eager   **c.** inquisitive   **d.** anxious

    13. _____

14. When we refer to the _____ of something, we refer to its *genesis.*
    a. complexity   **b.** origin   **c.** movement   **d.** strength

    14. _____

15. If offspring from a common ancestor are _____, they are called a *generation.*
    a. at odds with each other   **c.** restricted in number
    b. still living   **d.** at the same level of descent

    15. _____

TEST LESSONS 4, 5, AND 6

PART B IDENTIFYING SYNONYMS

On the answer line, write the letter of the word or phrase that has the meaning that is the same as that of the capitalized vocabulary word.

16. DESOLATE:
    a. guilty   **b.** respectful   **c.** helpful   **d.** lonely

16. _____d_____

17. ANGUISH:
    a. joy   **b.** suffering   **c.** confusion   **d.** satisfaction

17. _____b_____

18. AMICABLE:
    a. friendly   **b.** shy   **c.** curious   **d.** sensitive

18. _____a_____

19. PARTRIARCH:
    a. coach   **c.** boss
    b. president   **d.** male leader of a family

19. _____d_____

20. REGENERATE:
    a. deteriorate   **b.** manipulate   **c.** illuminate   **d.** revive

20. _____d_____

21. BLITHE:
    a. sorrowful   **b.** bitter   **c.** cheerful   **d.** limited

21. _____c_____

22. DESCENDANT:
    a. lawyer   **b.** son-in-law   **c.** underling   **d.** offspring

22. _____d_____

23. DEGENERATE:
    a. deteriorate   **b.** volunteer   **c.** propel   **d.** ignore

23. _____a_____

24. DISGRUNTLED:
    a. agreeable   **b.** cross   **c.** respectful   **d.** tired

24. _____b_____

25. MATERNAL:
    a. kindly   **b.** instructive   **c.** motherly   **d.** long-lived

25. _____c_____

26. PROGENY:
    a. descendants   **b.** families   **c.** liquids   **d.** colleagues

26. _____a_____

27. EXUBERANT:
    a. wrinkled   **b.** noisy   **c.** enthusiastic   **d.** listless

27. _____c_____

28. POSTERITY:
    a. future generations   **c.** predecessors
    b. hosts   **d.** previous neighbors

28. _____a_____

29. CONGENIAL:
    a. foolish   **b.** shameless   **c.** talkative   **d.** sociable

29. _____d_____

30. DEFIANT:
    a. yielding   **b.** resistant   **c.** destructive   **d.** loud

30. _____b_____

TEST LESSONS 4, 5, AND 6

PART B IDENTIFYING SYNONYMS

On the answer line, write the letter of the word or phrase that has the
meaning that is the same as that of the capitalized vocabulary word.

16. DESOLATE:
    a. guilty   b. respectful   c. helpful   d. lonely

16. _____

17. ANGUISH:
    a. joy   b. suffering   c. confusion   d. satisfaction

17. _____

18. AMICABLE:
    a. friendly   b. shy   c. curious   d. sensitive

18. _____

19. PARTRIARCH:
    a. coach   c. boss
    b. president   d. male leader of a family

19. _____

20. REGENERATE:
    a. deteriorate   b. manipulate   c. illuminate   d. revive

20. _____

21. BLITHE:
    a. sorrowful   b. bitter   c. cheerful   d. limited

21. _____

22. DESCENDANT:
    a. lawyer   b. son-in-law   c. underling   d. offspring

22. _____

23. DEGENERATE:
    a. deteriorate   b. volunteer   c. propel   d. ignore

23. _____

24. DISGRUNTLED:
    a. agreeable   b. cross   c. respectful   d. tired

24. _____

25. MATERNAL:
    a. kindly   b. instructive   c. motherly   d. long-lived

25. _____

26. PROGENY
    a. descendants   b. families   c. liquids   d. colleagues

26. _____

27. EXUBERANT:
    a. wrinkled   b. noisy   c. enthusiastic   d. listless

27. _____

28. POSTERITY:
    a. future generations   c. predecessors
    b. hosts   d. previous neighbors

28. _____

29. CONGENIAL:
    a. foolish   b. shameless   c. talkative   d. sociable

29. _____

30. DEFIANT:
    a. yielding   b. resistant   c. destructive   d. loud

30. _____

BONUS LESSONS 7 AND 8

(pages 41–52)

Use the clues to spell out the words on the answer blanks. Then identify the mystery person at the bottom of the page by writing the numbered letters on the lines with the corresponding numbers.

1. A *conflagration* is a large and destructive _____.

1. F I R E
   13

2. Brass is a(n) _____ of zinc and copper.

2. A L L O Y
       14

3. The _____ arts include karate and judo.

3. M A R T I A L
             5

4. A hearty, vigorous person is _____.

4. R O B U S T
     3

5. Having unlimited power or authority

5. O M N I P O T E N T
   4   9

6. Ships cannot enter a harbor when there is a(n) _____.

6. B L O C K A D E
   16   8

7. The process of cutting apart and examining internal structure

7. D I S S E C T I O N
         6

8. The planets are _____ bodies.

8. C E L E S T I A L
       7

9. To clot

9. C O A G U L A T E
             15

10. Firm, steadfast, or loyal

10. S T A U N C H
              10

11. Opposite of timid or fearful

11. V A L I A N T
    11

12. To soak thoroughly

12. S A T U R A T E
                12

13. Firmness of character or purpose

13. S T A B I L I T Y
      1

14. *Distilling* a liquid makes it _____.

14. P U R E
    17

15. To resist by force

15. W I T H S T A N D
          2

T H O M A S   E D I S O N,   I N V E N T O R
1 2 3 4 5 6   7 8 9 6 3 10   9 10 11 7 10 1 3 12

O F   T H E   L I G H T   B U L B
3 13   1 2 7   14 9 15 2 1   16 17 14 16

BONUS LESSONS 7 AND 8

(pages 41–52)

Use the clues to spell out the words on the answer blanks. Then identify the mystery person at the bottom of the page by writing the numbered letters on the lines with the corresponding numbers.

1. A *conflagration* is a large and destructive _____ .

1. __ __ __ __
   13

2. Brass is a(n) _____ of zinc and copper.

2. __ __ __ __ __
   14

3. The _____ arts include karate and judo.

3. __ __ __ __ __ __ __
   5

4. A hearty, vigorous person is _____ .

4. __ __ __ __ __ __
   3

5. Having unlimited power or authority

5. __ __ __ __ __ __ __ __ __
   4   9

6. Ships cannot enter a harbor when there is a(n) _____ .

6. __ __ __ __ __ __ __ __
   16   8

7. The process of cutting apart and examining internal structure

7. __ __ __ __ __ __ __ __ __
   6

8. The planets are _____ bodies.

8. __ __ __ __ __ __ __
   7

9. To clot

9. __ __ __ __ __ __ __ __
   15

10. Firm, steadfast, or loyal

10. __ __ __ __ __ __ __
    10

11. Opposite of timid or fearful

11. __ __ __ __ __ __ __
    11

12. To soak thoroughly

12. __ __ __ __ __ __ __
    12

13. Firmness of character or purpose

13. __ __ __ __ __ __ __ __
    1

14. *Distilling* a liquid makes it _____ .

14. __ __ __ __
    17

15. To resist by force

15. __ __ __ __ __ __ __
    2

__ __ __ __ __ __   __ __ __ __ __ __ ,   __ __ __ __ __ __ __ __
1 2 3 4 5 6   7 8 9 6 3 10   9 10 11 7 10 1 3 12

__ __   __ __ __   __ __ __ __ __   __ __ __ __
3 13   1 2 7   14 9 15 2 1   16 17 14 16

TEST LESSONS 7, 8, AND 9

(pages 41–58)

PART A CHOOSING THE BEST DEFINITION

On the answer line, write the letter of the best definition of the italicized word.

1. Marian made sure that no *combustible* substances were near the furnace.
   a. inflammable   **b.** ancient   **c.** poisonous   **d.** fireproof

   1. _____ a

2. The ancient Greek gods were considered *omnipotent.*
   a. make-believe   **b.** clever   **c.** all-knowing   **d.** all-powerful

   2. _____ d

3. Anne Frank wrote her diary while hiding in a secret *annex.*
   a. added building   **b.** storage area   **c.** passage   **d.** dungeon

   3. _____ a

4. The human body uses vitamin K to help blood *coagulate.*
   a. use oxygen   **b.** clot   **c.** flow   **d.** appear red

   4. _____ b

5. Although its form can be altered, physical matter is *indestructible.*
   a. poorly organized   **c.** not capable of being eliminated
   b. easily saved   **d.** the product of heat and light

   5. _____ c

6. Talented *masons* completed the exterior of the cathedral.
   a. woodworkers   **c.** stone workers
   b. architects   **d.** mural painters

   6. _____ c

7. Ancient mariners depended on *celestial* navigation to chart their courses.
   a. referring to instruments   **c.** common-sense
   b. related to the sky   **d.** symbolic

   7. _____ b

8. The border guards removed the *blockade* and let us pass through.
   a. obstruction   **b.** traffic   **c.** old restriction   **d.** flag

   8. _____ a

9. The Old Manse was the *abode* of Nathaniel Hawthorne.
   a. birthplace   **b.** publisher   **c.** home   **d.** garden

   9. _____ c

10. Pumice is a *buoyant* type of rock produced by volcanic activity.
    a. delicate   **b.** superior   **c.** artificial   **d.** capable of floating

    10. _____ d

11. Although he has turned ninety, Doctor Orwell is still *robust.*
    a. reliable   **b.** strong and healthy   **c.** dedicated   **d.** pleasant

    11. _____ b

12. The Erechtheum is a magnificent *edifice* on the Acropolis.
    a. statue   **b.** playing field   **c.** large building   **d.** cavern

    12. _____ c

13. The weightless environment of space is ideal for producing certain *alloys* that cannot be made on earth.
    a. combinations of metals   **c.** chemical solutions
    b. crystals   **d.** forms of life

    13. _____ a

14. Okinawa is the home of karate, the most famous of all *martial* arts.
    a. military   **b.** oriental   **c.** punishing   **d.** peaceful

    14. _____ a

15. It took many years to *excavate* the ruins of ancient Carthage.
    a. investigate   **b.** uncover   **c.** predict   **d.** conceal

    15. _____ b

TEST LESSONS 7, 8, AND 9

(pages 41–58)

PART A CHOOSING THE BEST DEFINITION

On the answer line, write the letter of the best definition of the italicized word.

1. Marian made sure that no *combustible* substances were near the furnace.   1. _____
   a. inflammable   **b.** ancient   **c.** poisonous   **d.** fireproof

2. The ancient Greek gods were considered *omnipotent*.   2. _____
   a. make-believe   **b.** clever   **c.** all-knowing   **d.** all-powerful

3. Anne Frank wrote her diary while hiding in a secret *annex*.   3. _____
   a. added building   **b.** storage area   **c.** passage   **d.** dungeon

4. The human body uses vitamin K to help blood *coagulate*.   4. _____
   a. use oxygen   **b.** clot   **c.** flow   **d.** appear red

5. Although its form can be altered, physical matter is *indestructible*.   5. _____
   a. poorly organized   **c.** not capable of being eliminated
   b. easily saved   **d.** the product of heat and light

6. Talented *masons* completed the exterior of the cathedral.   6. _____
   a. woodworkers   **c.** stone workers
   b. architects   **d.** mural painters

7. Ancient mariners depended on *celestial* navigation to chart their courses.   7. _____
   a. referring to instruments   **c.** common-sense
   b. related to the sky   **d.** symbolic

8. The border guards removed the *blockade* and let us pass through.   8. _____
   a. obstruction   **b.** traffic   **c.** old restriction   **d.** flag

9. The Old Manse was the *abode* of Nathaniel Hawthorne.   9. _____
   a. birthplace   **b.** publisher   **c.** home   **d.** garden

10. Pumice is a *buoyant* type of rock produced by volcanic activity.   10. _____
    a. delicate   **b.** superior   **c.** artificial   **d.** capable of floating

11. Although he has turned ninety, Doctor Orwell is still *robust*.   11. _____
    a. reliable   **b.** strong and healthy   **c.** dedicated   **d.** pleasant

12. The Erechtheum is a magnificent *edifice* on the Acropolis.   12. _____
    a. statue   **b.** playing field   **c.** large building   **d.** cavern

13. The weightless environment of space is ideal for producing certain *alloys*   13. _____
    that cannot be made on earth.
    a. combinations of metals   **c.** chemical solutions
    b. crystals   **d.** forms of life

14. Okinawa is the home of karate, the most famous of all *martial* arts.   14. _____
    a. military   **b.** oriental   **c.** punishing   **d.** peaceful

15. It took many years to *excavate* the ruins of ancient Carthage.   15. _____
    a. investigate   **b.** uncover   **c.** predict   **d.** conceal

TEST LESSONS 7, 8, AND 9

PART B CHOOSING THE BEST WORD

On the answer line, write the letter of the word that best completes the sentence.

16. The Spartans made a _____ effort to protect their homeland.
    a. celestial   **b.** valiant   **c.** stable   **d.** buoyant

    16. _____ b

17. When you _____ sea water, you separate the water from the salt.
    a. excavate   **b.** prefabricate   **c.** saturate   **d.** distill

    17. _____ d

18. The sun shining through the _____ cast crisscrossed shadows.
    a. trellis   **b.** rotunda   **c.** turret   **d.** edifice

    18. _____ a

19. Many temples in Egypt have _____ the ravages of time.
    a. distilled   **b.** saturated   **c.** withstood   **d.** coagulated

    19. _____ c

20. We watched the _____ of the frog to learn about its digestive system.
    a. dissection   **b.** blockade   **c.** annex   **d.** rotunda

    20. _____ a

21. Thomas Jefferson liked the round design of the Pantheon so well that he used the _____ as the central feature of Monticello.
    a. abode   **b.** alloy   **c.** annex   **d.** rotunda

    21. _____ d

22. The security of a nation depends on the _____ of its leadership.
    a. alloy   **b.** stability   **c.** conflagration   **d.** abode

    22. _____ b

23. Nero played his violin by firelight during the _____ of Rome.
    a. stability   **b.** blockade   **c.** dissection   **d.** conflagration

    23. _____ d

24. Randall Jarrell wrote a sad poem about a man who died in the _____ of a World War II airplane.
    a. rotunda   **b.** blockade   **c.** turret   **d.** conflagration

    24. _____ c

25. The way to stop the Greek hero Achilles was to hit the only _____ spot on his body—his heel.
    a. celestial   **b.** omnipotent   **c.** vulnerable   **d.** indestructible

    25. _____ c

26. The paramedic _____ the bandages with antiseptic.
    a. saturated   **b.** prefabricated   **c.** coagulated   **d.** distilled

    26. _____ a

27. The company _____ tool sheds that you can easily assemble.
    a. excavates   **b.** prefabricates   **c.** withstands   **d.** distills

    27. _____ b

28. An early civil rights leader, John Brown was a _____ advocate of universal freedom.
    a. vulnerable   **b.** staunch   **c.** martial   **d.** coagulated

    28. _____ b

29. The science of _____ has improved greatly since satellites began taking pictures of our atmosphere.
    a. conflagration   **b.** stability   **c.** dissection   **d.** meteorology

    29. _____ d

30. The photoelectric cells on some satellites are aimed toward the sun in order to convert _____ energy into electrical energy.
    a. solar   **b.** omnipotent   **c.** distilled   **d.** indestructible

    30. _____ a

TEST LESSONS 7, 8, AND 9

PART B CHOOSING THE BEST WORD

On the answer line, write the letter of the word that best completes the sentence.

16. The Spartans made a _____ effort to protect their homeland.
    a. celestial   b. valiant   c. stable   d. buoyant

    16. _____

17. When you _____ sea water, you separate the water from the salt.
    a. excavate   b. prefabricate   c. saturate   d. distill

    17. _____

18. The sun shining through the _____ cast crisscrossed shadows.
    a. trellis   b. rotunda   c. turret   d. edifice

    18. _____

19. Many temples in Egypt have _____ the ravages of time.
    a. distilled   b. saturated   c. withstood   d. coagulated

    19. _____

20. We watched the _____ of the frog to learn about its digestive system.
    a. dissection   b. blockade   c. annex   d. rotunda

    20. _____

21. Thomas Jefferson liked the round design of the Pantheon so well that he used the _____ as the central feature of Monticello.
    a. abode   b. alloy   c. annex   d. rotunda

    21. _____

22. The security of a nation depends on the _____ of its leadership.
    a. alloy   b. stability   c. conflagration   d. abode

    22. _____

23. Nero played his violin by firelight during the _____ of Rome.
    a. stability   b. blockade   c. dissection   d. conflagration

    23. _____

24. Randall Jarrell wrote a sad poem about a man who died in the _____ of a World War II airplane.
    a. rotunda   b. blockade   c. turret   d. conflagration

    24. _____

25. The way to stop the Greek hero Achilles was to hit the only _____ spot on his body—his heel.
    a. celestial   b. omnipotent   c. vulnerable   d. indestructible

    25. _____

26. The paramedic _____ the bandages with antiseptic.
    a. saturated   b. prefabricated   c. coagulated   d. distilled

    26. _____

27. The company _____ tool sheds that you can easily assemble.
    a. excavates   b. prefabricates   c. withstands   d. distills

    27. _____

28. An early civil rights leader, John Brown was a _____ advocate of universal freedom.
    a. vulnerable   b. staunch   c. martial   d. coagulated

    28. _____

29. The science of _____ has improved greatly since satellites began taking pictures of our atmosphere.
    a. conflagration   b. stability   c. dissection   d. meteorology

    29. _____

30. The photoelectric cells on some satellites are aimed toward the sun in order to convert _____ energy into electrical energy.
    a. solar   b. omnipotent   c. distilled   d. indestructible

    30. _____

BONUS LESSONS 9 AND 10

(pages 53–58, 61–66)

Unscramble the letters of each italicized vocabulary word, and write the word on the answer line to the right.

1. The *utrdona* had a circular stained-glass window.
2. A(n) *nxean* is located close to the original structure.
3. Today we would consider it a(n) *uiaaettdqn* practice to churn butter by hand.
4. A *eeaainnntcr* has lived one hundred years or longer.
5. Although Maureen is just a *llgfdgnei* cook, she attempts some difficult recipes.
6. George Washington and Thomas Jefferson were *pryrmncooeat* political leaders.
7. The first step in building the house was the *oncvxtaaei* of the basement.
8. A *rosla* heating system depends upon the sun for energy.
9. Climbing roses and clematis grew on the *slerilt* that bordered the garage.
10. The poet lived in a pleasant *oeadb* by the sea.
11. In spite of his age, Geoffrey is often guilty of *lupeier* behavior.
12. The storm destroyed many *tcnaesn* spring flowers.
13. That railing is so *iarfl* that it may give way if you lean on it.
14. Good nutrition and medical care increase your *ivylgntoe*.
15. Colorful banners flew above the *seuttrr* of the castle.
16. Buckingham Palace in England is an impressive *iieefcd* that attracts thousands of tourists every year.
17. Since people are living longer, doctors have become more interested in the field of *ytlroooengg*.
18. The welcoming committee treated the *baveerenl* statesman with great respect.
19. The city planners hired a *oansm* to add a brick front to the courthouse.
20. The *dcerapefiatrb* doghouse took only minutes to assemble.

1. _____rotunda_____
2. _____annex_____
3. _____antiquated_____
4. _____centenarian_____
5. _____fledgling_____
6. _____contemporary_____
7. _____excavation_____
8. _____solar_____
9. _____trellis_____
10. _____abode_____
11. _____puerile_____
12. _____nascent_____
13. _____frail_____
14. _____longevity_____
15. _____turrets_____
16. _____edifice_____
17. _____gerontology_____
18. _____venerable_____
19. _____mason_____
20. _____prefabricated_____

BONUS LESSONS 9 AND 10

(pages 53–58, 61–66)

Unscramble the letters of each italicized vocabulary word, and write the word on the answer line to the right.

1. The *utrdona* had a circular stained-glass window.
1. _____

2. A(n) *nxean* is located close to the original structure.
2. _____

3. Today we would consider it a(n) *uiaaettdqn* practice to churn butter by hand.
3. _____

4. A *eeaainnntcr* has lived one hundred years or longer.
4. _____

5. Although Maureen is just a *llgfdgnei* cook, she attempts some difficult recipes.
5. _____

6. George Washington and Thomas Jefferson were *pryrmncooeat* political leaders.
6. _____

7. The first step in building the house was the *oncvxtaaei* of the basement.
7. _____

8. A *rosla* heating system depends upon the sun for energy.
8. _____

9. Climbing roses and clematis grew on the *slerilt* that bordered the garage.
9. _____

10. The poet lived in a pleasant *oeadb* by the sea.
10. _____

11. In spite of his age, Geoffrey is often guilty of *lupeier* behavior.
11. _____

12. The storm destroyed many *tcnaesn* spring flowers.
12. _____

13. That railing is so *iarfl* that it may give way if you lean on it.
13. _____

14. Good nutrition and medical care increase your *ivylgntoe*.
14. _____

15. Colorful banners flew above the *seuttrr* of the castle.
15. _____

16. Buckingham Palace in England is an impressive *iieefcd* that attracts thousands of tourists every year.
16. _____

17. Since people are living longer, doctors have become more interested in the field of *ytlroooengg*.
17. _____

18. The welcoming committee treated the *baveerenl* statesman with great respect.
18. _____

19. The city planners hired a *oansm* to add a brick front to the courthouse.
19. _____

20. The *dcerapefiatrb* doghouse took only minutes to assemble.
20. _____

BONUS LESSONS 11 AND 12

(pages 67–78)

Use the following clues to identify the words, and write the words on the lines to the right. Then circle each word in the word-search box below. The words may overlap and may read in any direction.

1. An *aqueduct* carries _____ from a distant source.   (5 letters)

2. Sherlock Holmes could _____ the solution to crimes.   (6 letters)

3. The Latin root *-duce-* means "to _____."   (4 letters)

4. Synonym for *incessant*   (8 letters)

5. A *subsequent* action _____ a former one.   (7 letters)

6. A(n) _____ conclusion is accepted ahead of time.   (8 letters)

7. *Reduction* involves making something _____.   (7 letters)

8. Synonym for *belated*   (5 letters)

9. A(n) _____ baby is born earlier than expected.   (9 letters)

10. A *viaduct* carries a(n) _____ over a wide valley.   (4 letters)

11. Synonym for *induce*   (8 letters)

12. A *conduit* is a(n) _____ that transports fluids.   (4 letters)

13. The vacation provided a welcome _____ from their jobs.   (7 letters)

14. *Simultaneous* events occur at the _____ time.   (4 letters)

15. The art museum has guides who _____ visitor tours.   (7 letters)

1. _____ water _____
2. _____ deduce _____
3. _____ lead _____
4. _____ constant _____
5. _____ follows _____
6. _____ foregone _____
7. _____ smaller _____
8. _____ tardy _____
9. _____ premature _____
10. _____ road _____
11. _____ persuade _____
12. _____ pipe _____
13. _____ respite _____
14. _____ same _____
15. _____ conduct _____

```
P R O D U C T I V I T Y D U C T L R U
C I N D U C T I O N E C U D E D E E
M R P D C A T I O N M E D I S L U B R
A E C E D A U S R E P S T A L N T S U
T M E A D U R A T I O N L A W L E R T
M I T D A D L E T A G S M B E A L A A
T E I D E N L N S U B S S E O U T E M
N T P T L L A V E I D E M N M E C E E
S E S Q U T E N C E M D U O F O U R R
G O E N S C O N C A T E M G P O D R P
R E R N S P I T S U B D U E C O N D U
I T O I D U C E A Q U Y D R A T O E V
I C A C C I C S H E R L R O A D C R E
M A T C O N C S W O L L O F S U B D L
```

Challenge

Locate and circle the five additional vocabulary words in the word-search box.

_____

duration
induction
medieval
productivity
subdue

NAME _____ DATE _____

BONUS LESSONS 11 AND 12

(pages 67–78)

Use the following clues to identify the words, and write the words on the lines to the right. Then circle each word in the word-search box below. The words may overlap and may read in any direction.

1. An *aqueduct* carries _____ from a distant source.   (5 letters)
2. Sherlock Holmes could _____ the solution to crimes.   (6 letters)
3. The Latin root *-duce-* means "to _____."   (4 letters)
4. Synonym for *incessant*   (8 letters)
5. A *subsequent* action _____ a former one.   (7 letters)
6. A(n) _____ conclusion is accepted ahead of time.   (8 letters)
7. *Reduction* involves making something _____.   (7 letters)
8. Synonym for *belated*   (5 letters)
9. A(n) _____ baby is born earlier than expected.   (9 letters)
10. A *viaduct* carries a(n) _____ over a wide valley.   (4 letters)
11. Synonym for *induce*   (8 letters)
12. A *conduit* is a(n) _____ that transports fluids.   (4 letters)
13. The vacation provided a welcome _____ from their jobs.   (7 letters)
14. *Simultaneous* events occur at the _____ time.   (4 letters)
15. The art museum has guides who _____ visitor tours.   (7 letters)

1. _____
2. _____
3. _____
4. _____
5. _____
6. _____
7. _____
8. _____
9. _____
10. _____
11. _____
12. _____
13. _____
14. _____
15. _____

```
P R O D U C T I V I T Y D U C T L R U
C I N D U C T I O N E C U D E D E D E
M R P D C A T I O N M E D I S L U B R
A E C E D A U S R E P S T A L N T S U
T M E A D U R A T I O N L A W L E R T
M I T D A D L E T A G S M B E A L A A
T E I D E N L N S U B S S E O U T E M
N T P T L L A V E I D E M N M E C E E
S E S Q U T E N C E M D U O F O U R R
G O E N S C O N C A T E M G P O D R P
R E R N S P I T S U B D U E C O N D U
I T O I D U C E A Q U Y D R A T O E V
I C A C C I C S H E R L R O A D C R E
M A T C O N C S W O L L O F S U B D L
```

Challenge

Locate and circle the five additional vocabulary words in the word-search box.

_____

T12

Copyright © Great Source

TEST LESSONS 10, 11, AND 12

(pages 61–78)

PART A COMPLETING THE DEFINITION

On the answer line, write the letter of the word or phrase that correctly completes each sentence.

1. *Reduction* is a process of _____.
   a. removing irritants   **c.** twisting things
   b. making something smaller   **d.** multiplication
   1. _____b_____

2. The study of _____ is called *gerontology*.
   a. castles   **b.** classical music   **c.** aging   **d.** ancient ruins
   2. _____c_____

3. A *premature* celebration is one that occurs _____.
   a. too soon   **b.** periodically   **c.** abruptly   **d.** conveniently
   3. _____a_____

4. The act of _____ is called *induction*.
   a. conducting business   **c.** formally placing someone in office
   b. surrendering   **d.** leading others
   4. _____c_____

5. An object's *longevity* is its _____.
   a. depth   **b.** price   **c.** composition   **d.** length of life
   5. _____d_____

6. Things that are _____ are said to be *medieval*.
   a. forbidden   **c.** old before their time
   b. characteristic of the Middle Ages   **d.** made of cast iron
   6. _____b_____

7. When you *subdue* something, you _____ it.
   a. ignore   **b.** control   **c.** sell   **d.** visit
   7. _____b_____

8. Something that is *nascent* is _____.
   a. emerging   **b.** already accomplished   **c.** breathing   **d.** destroyed
   8. _____a_____

9. A *respite* is a(n) _____.
   a. authority   **b.** resolution   **c.** rest period   **d.** difficult task
   9. _____c_____

10. *Productivity* is an abundance of _____.
    a. ideas   **b.** output   **c.** resources   **d.** concentration
    10. _____b_____

11. Something that is _____ is *puerile*.
    a. childish   **b.** delicate   **c.** very easy   **d.** innovative
    11. _____a_____

12. *Simultaneous* events _____.
    a. happened long ago   **c.** occur at different times
    b. have importance   **d.** occur at the same time
    12. _____d_____

13. A *viaduct* is a series of _____.
    a. vaccination   **c.** arches carrying a road
    b. copper pipes   **d.** competitive games
    13. _____c_____

14. Something is *venerable* if it is _____.
    a. valuable   **b.** easily broken   **c.** borrowed   **d.** worthy of respect
    14. _____d_____

15. _____ events are said to be *subsequent*.
    a. Frustrating   **b.** Succeeding   **c.** Exciting   **d.** Uncertain
    15. _____b_____

TEST LESSONS 10, 11, AND 12

(pages 61–78)

PART A COMPLETING THE DEFINITION

On the answer line, write the letter of the word or phrase that correctly completes each sentence.

1. *Reduction* is a process of _____.
   a. removing irritants   c. twisting things
   b. making something smaller   d. multiplication

   1. _____

2. The study of _____ is called *gerontology.*
   a. castles   b. classical music   c. aging   d. ancient ruins

   2. _____

3. A *premature* celebration is one that occurs _____.
   a. too soon   b. periodically   c. abruptly   d. conveniently

   3. _____

4. The act of _____ is called *induction.*
   a. conducting business   c. formally placing someone in office
   b. surrendering   d. leading others

   4. _____

5. An object's *longevity* is its _____.
   a. depth   b. price   c. composition   d. length of life

   5. _____

6. Things that are _____ are said to be *medieval.*
   a. forbidden   c. old before their time
   b. characteristic of the Middle Ages   d. made of cast iron

   6. _____

7. When you *subdue* something, you _____ it.
   a. ignore   b. control   c. sell   d. visit

   7. _____

8. Something that is *nascent* is _____.
   a. emerging   b. already accomplished   c. breathing   d. destroyed

   8. _____

9. A *respite* is a(n) _____.
   a. authority   b. resolution   c. rest period   d. difficult task

   9. _____

10. *Productivity* is an abundance of _____.
    a. ideas   b. output   c. resources   d. concentration

    10. _____

11. Something that is _____ is *puerile.*
    a. childish   b. delicate   c. very easy   d. innovative

    11. _____

12. *Simultaneous* events _____.
    a. happened long ago   c. occur at different times
    b. have importance   d. occur at the same time

    12. _____

13. A *viaduct* is a series of _____.
    a. vaccination   c. arches carrying a road
    b. copper pipes   d. competitive games

    13. _____

14. Something is *venerable* if it is _____.
    a. valuable   b. easily broken   c. borrowed   d. worthy of respect

    14. _____

15. _____ events are said to be *subsequent.*
    a. Frustrating   b. Succeeding   c. Exciting   d. Uncertain

    15. _____

TEST LESSONS 10, 11, AND 12

PART B CHOOSING THE BEST WORD

On the answer line, write the letter of the word that best expresses the meaning of the italicized word or phrase.

16. A well-preserved *channel that carries water from a distant source* runs through Segovia.
    a. aqueduct   **b.** centenarian   **c.** fledgling   **d.** viaduct

    16. _____a_____

17. Mrs. Gutierrez is one of several *persons who live 100 years or more* in our town.
    a. durations   **b.** fledglings   **c.** conduits   **d.** centenarians

    17. _____d_____

18. The *constant* howl of the puppy unnerved Jared.
    a. puerile   **b.** incessant   **c.** belated   **d.** nascent

    18. _____b_____

19. Gold is an excellent metal for *acting as a medium through which travels* electricity.
    a. deducing   **b.** conducting   **c.** subduing   **d.** inducing

    19. _____b_____

20. Though she was new at her job, Candy didn't like being called a *young and inexperienced person*.
    a. contemporary   **b.** centenarian   **c.** fledgling   **d.** conduit

    20. _____c_____

21. The possibility of failure in this endeavor was a *previously accepted* conclusion.
    a. incessant   **b.** contemporary   **c.** foregone   **d.** belated

    21. _____c_____

22. The Toltecs built *channels for carrying water* between their buildings.
    a. conduits   **b.** viaducts   **c.** centenarians   **d.** contemporaries

    22. _____a_____

23. Richard moved into a house with an *outmoded* heating system.
    a. contemporary   **b.** foregone   **c.** belated   **d.** antiquated

    23. _____d_____

24. This offer will *come to an end* in thirty days.
    a. conduct   **b.** expire   **c.** deduce   **d.** subdue

    24. _____b_____

25. One can *conclude by logical reasoning* that Gerald is upset.
    a. conduct   **b.** induce   **c.** expire   **d.** deduce

    25. _____d_____

26. Egg shells are very *flimsy*.
    a. frail   **b.** antiquated   **c.** puerile   **d.** nascent

    26. _____a_____

27. Salina used Max's car for the *existing period of time* of his visit.
    a. duration   **b.** respite   **c.** induction   **d.** longevity

    27. _____a_____

28. Paul thought of a way to *influence* his brothers to sing at the party.
    a. deduce   **b.** expire   **c.** induce   **d.** subdue

    28. _____c_____

29. Aleta particularly enjoys *modern* American literature.
    a. premature   **b.** contemporary   **c.** foregone   **d.** subsequent

    29. _____b_____

30. "Please accept my *tardy* apology," said Ben.
    a. belated   **b.** contemporary   **c.** foregone   **d.** frail

    30. _____a_____

TEST LESSONS 10, 11, AND 12

PART B CHOOSING THE BEST WORD

On the answer line, write the letter of the word that best expresses the meaning of the italicized word or phrase.

16. A well-preserved *channel that carries water from a distant source* runs through Segovia.
    a. aqueduct   **b.** centenarian   **c.** fledgling   **d.** viaduct

    16. _____

17. Mrs. Gutierrez is one of several *persons who live 100 years or more* in our town.
    a. durations   **b.** fledglings   **c.** conduits   **d.** centenarians

    17. _____

18. The *constant* howl of the puppy unnerved Jared.
    a. puerile   **b.** incessant   **c.** belated   **d.** nascent

    18. _____

19. Gold is an excellent metal for *acting as a medium through which travels* electricity.
    a. deducing   **b.** conducting   **c.** subduing   **d.** inducing

    19. _____

20. Though she was new at her job, Candy didn't like being called a *young and inexperienced person.*
    a. contemporary **b.** centenarian   **c.** fledgling   **d.** conduit

    20. _____

21. The possibility of failure in this endeavor was a *previously accepted* conclusion.
    a. incessant   **b.** contemporary **c.** foregone   **d.** belated

    21. _____

22. The Toltecs built *channels for carrying water* between their buildings.
    a. conduits   **b.** viaducts   **c.** centenarians **d.** contemporaries

    22. _____

23. Richard moved into a house with an *outmoded* heating system.
    a. contemporary **b.** foregone   **c.** belated   **d.** antiquated

    23. _____

24. This offer will *come to an end* in thirty days.
    a. conduct   **b.** expire   **c.** deduce   **d.** subdue

    24. _____

25. One can *conclude by logical reasoning* that Gerald is upset.
    a. conduct   **b.** induce   **c.** expire   **d.** deduce

    25. _____

26. Egg shells are very *flimsy.*
    a. frail   **b.** antiquated   **c.** puerile   **d.** nascent

    26. _____

27. Salina used Max's car for the *existing period of time* of his visit.
    a. duration   **b.** respite   **c.** induction   **d.** longevity

    27. _____

28. Paul thought of a way to *influence* his brothers to sing at the party.
    a. deduce   **b.** expire   **c.** induce   **d.** subdue

    28. _____

29. Aleta particularly enjoys *modern* American literature.
    a. premature   **b.** contemporary **c.** foregone   **d.** subsequent

    29. _____

30. "Please accept my *tardy* apology," said Ben.
    a. belated   **b.** contemporary **c.** foregone   **d.** frail

    30. _____

BONUS LESSONS 13 AND 14

(pages 81–92)

Use the clues to complete the crossword puzzle.

The completed crossword grid contains the following answers:

- 1 Across: INTERCEDE
- 2 Down: CONTRADICT
- 3 Across: STRENGTHEN
- 4 Down: RETRUFURBISH
- 5 Down: DELIVERANCE
- 6 Down: SKIRMISH
- 7 Across: HAGGLE
- 7 Down: HOLY
- 8 Across: ATTACK
- 9 Down: ARGUMENT
- 10 Across: PACIFY
- 11 Across: ABET
- 12 Across: OFFSET
- 12 Down: OPPONENT
- 13 Down: SPEED
- 14 Down: DEADLOCK
- 15 Across: CONTROVERSY
- 16 Down: STRIFE
- 17 Across: ENNOBLE
- 18 Across: AGREEMENT

Across

1. To plead for another person
3. Synonym for *reinforce*
7. To argue in an attempt to come to terms
8. *Aggression* is a bold, unprovoked _____.
10. Derived from the Latin word meaning "peace"
11. To encourage or assist in doing something wrong
12. To compensate for or counteract
15. A dispute between opposing sides
17. To add to the honor of
18. *Discord* is a lack of _____.

Down

2. To express the opposite of
4. Renew or repair
5. When people are in danger, they hope for _____.
6. A minor battle
7. A *sanctuary* is a(n) _____ place.
9. To *embroil* is to involve in a(n) _____.
12. Synonym for *adversary*
13. To *expedite* a matter is to _____ its progress.
14. Synonym for *stalemate*
16. Bitter conflict

BONUS LESSONS 13 AND 14

(pages 81–92)

Use the clues to complete the crossword puzzle.

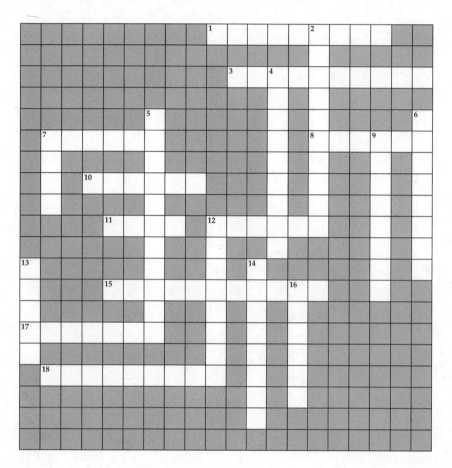

Across

1. To plead for another person

3. Synonym for *reinforce*

7. To argue in an attempt to come to terms

8. *Aggression* is a bold, unprovoked _____.

10. Derived from the Latin word meaning "peace"

11. To encourage or assist in doing something wrong

12. To compensate for or counteract

15. A dispute between opposing sides

17. To add to the honor of

18. *Discord* is a lack of _____.

Down

2. To express the opposite of

4. Renew or repair

5. When people are in danger, they hope for _____.

6. A minor battle

7. A *sanctuary* is a(n) _____ place.

9. To *embroil* is to involve in a(n) _____.

12. Synonym for *adversary*

13. To *expedite* a matter is to _____ its progress.

14. Synonym for *stalemate*

16. Bitter conflict

TEST LESSONS 13, 14, AND 15

(pages 81–98)

PART A CHOOSING THE BEST DEFINITION

On the answer line, write the letter of the best definition of the italicized word.

1. Spain won the *deliverance* of Granada from the Moors.
   a. liberation   **b.** return   **c.** recognition   **d.** control
   1. _____ a _____

2. No one has yet been able to *disclaim* the merits of my plan.
   a. verify   **b.** comprehend   **c.** employ   **d.** reject as untrue
   2. _____ d _____

3. There is natural *aggression* between baboons and lions.
   a. friendly feeling   **c.** tendency to be shy
   b. hostile behavior   **d.** barrier
   3. _____ b _____

4. Chase asked his father to *intercede* with his teachers on his behalf.
   a. bargain   **b.** prophesy   **c.** plead   **d.** debate
   4. _____ c _____

5. Mother's work is *evocative* of that of some impressionist painters.
   a. a duplicate   **c.** a demonstration
   b. tending to call to mind   **d.** little-known proof
   5. _____ b _____

6. The accident *embroiled* the motorists in a heated argument.
   a. surrounded   **b.** subdued   **c.** united   **d.** involved
   6. _____ d _____

7. The Panthers *offset* their scoreless first half with a dramatic comeback.
   a. explained   **b.** changed   **c.** displayed   **d.** made up for
   7. _____ d _____

8. Venus often *invoked* the aid of Cupid.
   a. rewarded   **c.** called upon
   b. recommended   **d.** argued against
   8. _____ c _____

9. Philip likes to *haggle* with car dealers over their prices.
   a. bargain   **b.** bemoan   **c.** joke   **d.** juggle
   9. _____ a _____

10. Ellen's plans for *refurbishing* the old trunk were unrealistic.
    a. selling   **b.** repainting   **c.** dismantling   **d.** renewing
    10. _____ d _____

11. Before pursuing a *vocation*, Patrick interviewed people in a variety of professions.
    a. residence   **b.** tutor   **c.** occupation   **d.** trip
    11. _____ c _____

12. If preseason exhibitions can be considered *skirmishes*, postseason tournaments must be viewed as wars.
    a. tests of skill   **c.** peaceful confrontations
    b. minor battles   **d.** demonstrations of courage
    12. _____ b _____

13. A university should be considered a *sanctuary* for knowledge.
    a. training camp   **b.** safe place   **c.** distributor   **d.** supporter
    13. _____ b _____

14. Mrs. George will *vouch* that I deliver her newspaper on time.
    a. claim   **b.** verify   **c.** complain   **d.** explain
    14. _____ b _____

15. City officials reached a *stalemate* in their negotiations.
    a. deadlock   **b.** agreement   **c.** limitation   **d.** awkward stage
    15. _____ a _____

TEST LESSONS 13, 14, AND 15

(pages 81–98)

PART A CHOOSING THE BEST DEFINITION

On the answer line, write the letter of the best definition of the italicized word.

1. Spain won the *deliverance* of Granada from the Moors.
   a. liberation   **b.** return   **c.** recognition   **d.** control

   1. _____

2. No one has yet been able to *disclaim* the merits of my plan.
   a. verify   **b.** comprehend   **c.** employ   **d.** reject as untrue

   2. _____

3. There is natural *aggression* between baboons and lions.
   a. friendly feeling   **c.** tendency to be shy
   b. hostile behavior   **d.** barrier

   3. _____

4. Chase asked his father to *intercede* with his teachers on his behalf.
   a. bargain   **b.** prophesy   **c.** plead   **d.** debate

   4. _____

5. Mother's work is *evocative* of that of some impressionist painters.
   a. a duplicate   **c.** a demonstration
   b. tending to call to mind   **d.** little-known proof

   5. _____

6. The accident *embroiled* the motorists in a heated argument.
   a. surrounded   **b.** subdued   **c.** united   **d.** involved

   6. _____

7. The Panthers *offset* their scoreless first half with a dramatic comeback.
   a. explained   **b.** changed   **c.** displayed   **d.** made up for

   7. _____

8. Venus often *invoked* the aid of Cupid.
   a. rewarded   **c.** called upon
   b. recommended   **d.** argued against

   8. _____

9. Philip likes to *haggle* with car dealers over their prices.
   a. bargain   **b.** bemoan   **c.** joke   **d.** juggle

   9. _____

10. Ellen's plans for *refurbishing* the old trunk were unrealistic.
    a. selling   **b.** repainting   **c.** dismantling   **d.** renewing

    10. _____

11. Before pursuing a *vocation*, Patrick interviewed people in a variety of professions.
    a. residence   **b.** tutor   **c.** occupation   **d.** trip

    11. _____

12. If preseason exhibitions can be considered *skirmishes*, postseason tournaments must be viewed as wars.
    a. tests of skill   **c.** peaceful confrontations
    b. minor battles   **d.** demonstrations of courage

    12. _____

13. A university should be considered a *sanctuary* for knowledge.
    a. training camp   **b.** safe place   **c.** distributor   **d.** supporter

    13. _____

14. Mrs. George will *vouch* that I deliver her newspaper on time.
    a. claim   **b.** verify   **c.** complain   **d.** explain

    14. _____

15. City officials reached a *stalemate* in their negotiations.
    a. deadlock   **b.** agreement   **c.** limitation   **d.** awkward stage

    15. _____

TEST LESSONS 13, 14, AND 15

PART B IDENTIFYING SYNONYMS

On the answer line, write the letter of the word or phrase that has the meaning that is the same as that of the capitalized vocabulary word.

16. CONTROVERSY:
    a. limitation   b. agreement   c. dispute   d. instrument

16. _____c_____

17. ABET:
    a. hinder   b. aid   c. promise   d. protect

17. _____b_____

18. CLAMOR:
    a. silence   b. friction   c. innocence   d. noise

18. _____d_____

19. ADVERSARY:
    a. enemy   b. partner   c. habit   d. relative

19. _____a_____

20. ENNOBLE:
    a. degrade   b. disguise   c. decide   d. promote

20. _____d_____

21. CLAIMANT:
    a. one who asserts a right   c. suspicious participant
    b. one who searches for gold   d. artful producer

21. _____a_____

22. CONTRADICT:
    a. explain   b. oppose   c. inform   d. believe

22. _____b_____

23. EXPEDIATE:
    a. hasten   b. decide   c. improve   d. prevent

23. _____a_____

24. DECLAIM:
    a. give up   c. announce calmly
    b. prohibit   d. speak forcefully

24. _____d_____

25. DISCORD:
    a. extension   b. harmony   c. disagreement   d. formation

25. _____c_____

26. PACIFY:
    a. dampen   b. agitate   c. calm   d. alter

26. _____c_____

27. RECLAIM:
    a. enhance   b. recover   c. permit   d. lose

27. _____b_____

28. STRIFE:
    a. humor   b. conflict   c. virtue   d. peace

28. _____b_____

29. REINFORCE:
    a. ascend   b. support   c. weaken   d. calculate

29. _____b_____

30. REVOKE:
    a. summon   b. operate   c. validate   d. cancel

30. _____d_____

TEST LESSONS 13, 14, AND 15

PART B IDENTIFYING SYNONYMS

On the answer line, write the letter of the word or phrase that has the meaning that is the same as that of the capitalized vocabulary word.

16. CONTROVERSY:
    a. limitation   **b.** agreement   **c.** dispute   **d.** instrument

    16. _____

17. ABET:
    a. hinder   **b.** aid   **c.** promise   **d.** protect

    17. _____

18. CLAMOR:
    a. silence   **b.** friction   **c.** innocence   **d.** noise

    18. _____

19. ADVERSARY:
    a. enemy   **b.** partner   **c.** habit   **d.** relative

    19. _____

20. ENNOBLE:
    a. degrade   **b.** disguise   **c.** decide   **d.** promote

    20. _____

21. CLAIMANT:
    a. one who asserts a right   **c.** suspicious participant
    b. one who searches for gold   **d.** artful producer

    21. _____

22. CONTRADICT:
    a. explain   **b.** oppose   **c.** inform   **d.** believe

    22. _____

23. EXPEDIATE:
    a. hasten   **b.** decide   **c.** improve   **d.** prevent

    23. _____

24. DECLAIM:
    a. give up   **c.** announce calmly
    b. prohibit   **d.** speak forcefully

    24. _____

25. DISCORD:
    a. extension   **b.** harmony   **c.** disagreement   **d.** formation

    25. _____

26. PACIFY:
    a. dampen   **b.** agitate   **c.** calm   **d.** alter

    26. _____

27. RECLAIM:
    a. enhance   **b.** recover   **c.** permit   **d.** lose

    27. _____

28. STRIFE:
    a. humor   **b.** conflict   **c.** virtue   **d.** peace

    28. _____

29. REINFORCE:
    a. ascend   **b.** support   **c.** weaken   **d.** calculate

    29. _____

30. REVOKE:
    a. summon   **b.** operate   **c.** validate   **d.** cancel

    30. _____

BONUS LESSONS 15 AND 16

(pages 93–98, 101–106)

Choose a vocabulary word from the box to complete each of the following sentences. You may need to change the form of some of the words to fit correctly in the sentence. Use each word only once, and write your answer on the answer line to the right.

anarchy	declaim	impeach	revoke
authoritarian	delegate	inaugurate	Spartan
claimant	disclaim	invoke	tyrant
clamor	dominion	liberal	vocation
conservative	evocative	reclaim	vouch

1. The ____ of the crowd increased as the home team scored a touchdown.

2. After working as a volunteer at the health clinic, Alice decided that medicine was her true ____.

3. The ____ politicians were unwilling to support hasty changes in the law.

4. After the leader of the government died, the country experienced a temporary state of ____.

5. The new president of the small nation was ____ at a special ceremony.

6. During the California Gold Rush, there were many ____ for the same piece of land.

7. The early Romans often ____ Jupiter to assure victory against their enemies.

8. Before the marathon the athlete maintained a(n) ____ routine of practice and rest.

9. Tarcher is a(n) ____ coach who allows no violations of his training rules.

10. President Andrew Johnson suffered disgrace when he was ____ by the House of Representatives in 1868.

11. The suspect ____ any connection with the robbery.

12. Eating homemade bread like his grandmother's was a(n) ____ experience for Ned.

13. Mohandas Gandhi ____ for the independence of India.

14. The ____ forbade all storekeepers to conduct business without his permission.

15. The ____ to the United Nations delivered a stirring address about world hunger.

1. _____clamor_____

2. _____vocation_____

3. _____conservative_____

4. _____anarchy_____

5. _____inaugurated_____

6. _____claimants_____

7. _____invoked_____

8. _____Spartan_____

9. _____authoritarian_____

10. _____impeached_____

11. _____disclaimed_____

12. _____evocative_____

13. _____declaimed_____

14. _____tyrant_____

15. _____delegate_____

BONUS LESSONS 15 AND 16

(pages 93–98, 101–106)

Choose a vocabulary word from the box to complete each of the following sentences. You may need to change the form of some of the words to fit correctly in the sentence. Use each word only once, and write your answer on the answer line to the right.

anarchy	declaim	impeach	revoke
authoritarian	delegate	inaugurate	Spartan
claimant	disclaim	invoke	tyrant
clamor	dominion	liberal	vocation
conservative	evocative	reclaim	vouch

1. The _____ of the crowd increased as the home team scored a touchdown.   1. _____

2. After working as a volunteer at the health clinic, Alice decided that medicine was her true _____ .   2. _____

3. The _____ politicians were unwilling to support hasty changes in the law.   3. _____

4. After the leader of the government died, the country experienced a temporary state of _____ .   4. _____

5. The new president of the small nation was _____ at a special ceremony.   5. _____

6. During the California Gold Rush, there were many _____ for the same piece of land.   6. _____

7. The early Romans often _____ Jupiter to assure victory against their enemies.   7. _____

8. Before the marathon the athlete maintained a(n) _____ routine of practice and rest.   8. _____

9. Tarcher is a(n) _____ coach who allows no violations of his training rules.   9. _____

10. President Andrew Johnson suffered disgrace when he was _____ by the House of Representatives in 1868.   10. _____

11. The suspect _____ any connection with the robbery.   11. _____

12. Eating homemade bread like his grandmother's was a(n) _____ experience for Ned.   12. _____

13. Mohandas Gandhi _____ for the independence of India.   13. _____

14. The _____ forbade all storekeepers to conduct business without his permission.   14. _____

15. The _____ to the United Nations delivered a stirring address about world hunger.   15. _____

BONUS LESSONS 17 AND 18

(pages 107–118)

Use the clues to spell out the words on the answer blanks. Then identify the mystery person at the bottom of the page by writing the numbered letters on the lines with the corresponding numbers.

1. __A__ __R__ __S__ __O__ __N__ comes from a Latin word meaning "to burn."

(3)

2. Criminals try to __C__ __O__ __U__ __N__ __T__ __E__ __R__ __F__ __E__ __I__ __T__ money.

(1)

3. In French, a "false step" is a(n) __F__ __A__ __U__ __X__ __P__ __A__ __S__.

(14)

4. Murder or burglary is considered a(n) __F__ __E__ __L__ __O__ __N__ __Y__.

(7)

5. Leaving her wallet at home was a(n) __B__ __L__ __U__ __N__ __D__ __E__ __R__ that Hannah never made again.

(11)

6. To *repent* is to show __R__ __E__ __G__ __R__ __E__ __T__ for what one has done.

(6)

7. Airlines have taken precautions to prevent planes from being seized by

__H__ __I__ __J__ __A__ __C__ __K__ __E__ __R__ __S__.

(2)

8. Fingerprints may __I__ __N__ __C__ __R__ __I__ __M__ __A__ __T__ __E__ a suspect.

(4)

9. To value too highly is to __O__ __V__ __E__ __R__ __E__ __S__ __T__ __I__ __M__ __A__ __T__ __E__.

(9)

10. A politician who takes bribes is __C__ __O__ __R__ __R__ __U__ __P__ __T__.

(8)

11. A large audience may __F__ __L__ __U__ __S__ __T__ __E__ __R__ an inexperienced speaker.

(10)

12. If you __M__ __I__ __S__ __I__ __N__ __T__ __E__ __R__ __P__ __R__ __E__ __T__ a statement, you draw wrong

(12)

conclusions about it.

13. __C__ __O__ __N__ __F__ __U__ __S__ __E__ is a synonym for *bewilder*.

(5)

14. __F__ __A__ __L__ __L__ __I__ __B__ __L__ __E__ means "capable of making errors."

(13)

__C__ __H__ __R__ __I__ __S__ __T__ __O__ __P__ __H__ __E__ __R__ __C__ __O__ __L__ __U__ __M__ __B__ __U__ __S__,

1 2 3 4 5 6 7 8 2 9 3   1 7 10 11 12 13 11 5

__E__ __X__ __P__ __L__ __O__ __R__ __E__ __R__

9 14 8 10 7 3 9 3

BONUS LESSONS 17 AND 18

(pages 107–118)

Use the clues to spell out the words on the answer blanks. Then identify the mystery person at the bottom of the page by writing the numbered letters on the lines with the corresponding numbers.

1. ___ ___ ___ ___ ___ comes from a Latin word meaning "to burn."
      3

2. Criminals try to ___ ___ ___ ___ ___ ___ ___ ___ ___ ___ ___ money.
           1

3. In French, a "false step" is a(n) ___ ___ ___ ___   ___ ___ ___.
                      14

4. Murder or burglary is considered a(n) ___ ___ ___ ___ ___.
               7

5. Leaving her wallet at home was a(n) ___ ___ ___ ___ ___ ___ ___ that Hannah never made again.
                 11

6. To *repent* is to show ___ ___ ___ ___ ___ ___ for what one has done.
             6

7. Airlines have taken precautions to prevent planes from being seized by

  ___ ___ ___ ___ ___ ___ ___ ___.
  2

8. Fingerprints may ___ ___ ___ ___ ___ ___ ___ ___ ___ a suspect.
        4

9. To value too highly is to ___ ___ ___ ___ ___ ___ ___ ___ ___ ___ ___.
            9

10. A politician who takes bribes is ___ ___ ___ ___ ___ ___ ___.
               8

11. A large audience may ___ ___ ___ ___ ___ ___ an inexperienced speaker.
           10

12. If you ___ ___ ___ ___ ___ ___ ___ ___ ___ ___ ___ a statement, you draw wrong
     12

  conclusions about it.

13. ___ ___ ___ ___ ___ ___ ___ is a synonym for *bewilder*.
         5

14. ___ ___ ___ ___ ___ ___ ___ ___ means "capable of making errors."
          13

___ ___ ___ ___ ___ ___ ___ ___ ___ ___ ___   ___ ___ ___ ___ ___ ___ ___ ___ ,
 1 2 3 4 5 6 7 8 2 9 3   1 7 10 11 12 13 11 5

___ ___ ___ ___ ___ ___ ___
 9 14 8 10 7 3 9 3

TEST LESSONS 16, 17, AND 18

(pages 101–118)

PART A COMPLETING THE DEFINITION

On the answer line, write the letter of the word or phrase that correctly completes each sentence.

1. If a moving vehicle has been *hijacked,* it has been _____.
   a. damaged   **b.** seized   **c.** rented   **d.** towed

   1. _____**b**_____

2. To *misinterpret* something is to _____ it.
   a. translate   **b.** comply with   **c.** misunderstand   **d.** simplify

   2. _____**c**_____

3. A *conservative* attitude is _____.
   a. traditional   **b.** silly   **c.** generous   **d.** modest

   3. _____**a**_____

4. Someone who has committed a *felony* is responsible for _____.
   a. an act of devotion   **c.** charitable contributions
   b. a minor offense   **d.** a serious crime

   4. _____**d**_____

5. If you _____ someone, you have *flustered* him or her.
   a. confuse   **b.** amuse   **c.** ignore   **d.** laugh at

   5. _____**a**_____

6. *Anarchy* is a state of _____.
   a. happiness   **b.** disorder   **c.** indecision   **d.** harmony

   6. _____**b**_____

7. One who *swindles* others _____ them.
   a. entertains   **b.** compliments   **c.** cheats   **d.** interacts with

   7. _____**c**_____

8. If you are guilty of a *faux pas,* you have made a(n) _____.
   a. investment   **b.** social error   **c.** close friend   **d.** change

   8. _____**b**_____

9. To have *dominion* over something is to _____ it.
   a. be nervous about   **b.** have power over   **c.** ignore   **d.** deny

   9. _____**b**_____

10. When you *repent* you _____.
    a. show regret   **b.** protect others   **c.** hurry   **d.** argue

    10. _____**a**_____

11. If you *miscalculate* something, you _____ it.
    a. comprehend   **b.** locate   **c.** voluntarily donate   **d.** incorrectly estimate

    11. _____**d**_____

12. An *authoritarian* person _____
    a. is an expert   **c.** expects strict obedience
    b. charms others   **d.** is a talented performer

    12. _____**c**_____

13. To *incriminate* someone is to _____.
    a. clear the person's reputation
    b. recommend the person for promotion
    c. involve the person in a crime
    d. shock the person

    13. _____**c**_____

14. If you *overestimate* something, you _____.
    a. rate it too highly   **b.** notice it   **c.** waste it   **d.** lose it

    14. _____**a**_____

15. A *delegate* is a(n) _____.
    a. wanderer   **b.** official   **c.** philosopher   **d.** representative

    15. _____**d**_____

TEST LESSONS 16, 17, AND 18

(pages 101–118)

PART A COMPLETING THE DEFINITION

On the answer line, write the letter of the word or phrase that correctly completes each sentence.

1. If a moving vehicle has been *hijacked,* it has been _____.
   a. damaged   **b.** seized   **c.** rented   **d.** towed

   1. _____

2. To *misinterpret* something is to _____ it.
   a. translate   **b.** comply with   **c.** misunderstand   **d.** simplify

   2. _____

3. A *conservative* attitude is _____.
   a. traditional   **b.** silly   **c.** generous   **d.** modest

   3. _____

4. Someone who has committed a *felony* is responsible for _____.
   a. an act of devotion   **c.** charitable contributions
   b. a minor offense   **d.** a serious crime

   4. _____

5. If you _____ someone, you have *flustered* him or her.
   a. confuse   **b.** amuse   **c.** ignore   **d.** laugh at

   5. _____

6. *Anarchy* is a state of _____.
   a. happiness   **b.** disorder   **c.** indecision   **d.** harmony

   6. _____

7. One who *swindles* others _____ them.
   a. entertains   **b.** compliments   **c.** cheats   **d.** interacts with

   7. _____

8. If you are guilty of a *faux pas,* you have made a(n) _____.
   a. investment   **b.** social error   **c.** close friend   **d.** change

   8. _____

9. To have *dominion* over something is to _____ it.
   a. be nervous about   **b.** have power over   **c.** ignore   **d.** deny

   9. _____

10. When you *repent* you _____.
    a. show regret   **b.** protect others   **c.** hurry   **d.** argue

    10. _____

11. If you *miscalculate* something, you _____ it.
    a. comprehend   **b.** locate   **c.** voluntarily donate   **d.** incorrectly estimate

    11. _____

12. An *authoritarian* person _____
    a. is an expert   **c.** expects strict obedience
    b. charms others   **d.** is a talented performer

    12. _____

13. To *incriminate* someone is to _____.
    a. clear the person's reputation
    b. recommend the person for promotion
    c. involve the person in a crime
    d. shock the person

    13. _____

14. If you *overestimate* something, you _____.
    a. rate it too highly   **b.** notice it   **c.** waste it   **d.** lose it

    14. _____

15. A *delegate* is a(n) _____.
    a. wanderer   **b.** official   **c.** philosopher   **d.** representative

    15. _____

TEST LESSONS 16, 17, AND 18

PART B CHOOSING THE BEST WORD

On the answer line, write the letter of the word that best expresses the meaning of the italicized word or phrase.

16. The poem "The Charge of the Light Brigade" tells of men who suffered because someone had *made a serious mistake*.
    a. repented   **b.** flustered   **c.** misinterpreted   **d.** blundered

16. _____d_____

17. The cause of the blaze was *the crime of deliberately setting fires*.
    a. a faux pas   **b.** a felony   **c.** arson   **d.** anarchy

17. _____c_____

18. Private Johnson adjusted to the *simple and self-disciplined* existence of boot camp.
    a. Spartan   **b.** conservative   **c.** corrupt   **d.** authoritarian

18. _____a_____

19. The lawyer proved that the testimony was *false*.
    a. erroneous   **b.** misinterpreted   **c.** bewildering   **d.** conservative

19. _____a_____

20. Uriah Heep, the *immoral* acquaintance of David Copperfield, was imprisoned.
    a. Spartan   **b.** tyrannical   **c.** corrupt   **d.** fallible

20. _____c_____

21. The senate agreed not to *accuse of unacceptable conduct in office* the governor.
    a. impeach   **b.** acquit   **c.** incriminate   **d.** bewilder

21. _____a_____

22. The engineers admitted that they were *capable of making an error*.
    a. corrupt   **b.** fallible   **c.** amiss   **d.** counterfeit

22. _____b_____

23. The defendant was *freed from formal accusation of wrongdoing*.
    a. bewildered   **b.** impeached   **c.** incriminated   **d.** acquitted

23. _____d_____

24. Anne sprinkled her cereal with a *generous in amount* helping of raisins.
    a. fallible   **b.** liberal   **c.** conservative   **d.** Spartan

24. _____b_____

25. Nico realized that something was *out of proper order*.
    a. amiss   **b.** authoritarian   **c.** liberal   **d.** corrupt

25. _____a_____

26. "Who is the *person guilty of an offense* who ate all the popcorn?" asked Dad.
    a. delegate   **b.** culprit   **c.** Spartan   **d.** tyrant

26. _____b_____

27. Pisistratus was an *oppressor* who controlled Athens during the sixth century B.C.
    a. culprit   **b.** delegate   **c.** tyrant   **d.** Spartan

27. _____c_____

28. Alice was *befuddled* by the actions of the White Rabbit.
    a. conservative   **b.** bewildered   **c.** flustered   **d.** corrupt

28. _____b_____

29. The police discovered two rooms of *dishonestly copied* designer clothes.
    a. fallible   **b.** corrupt   **c.** hijacked   **d.** counterfeit

29. _____d_____

30. The alliance between the countries *initiated* an era of prosperity.
    a. incriminated   **b.** bewildered   **c.** inaugurated   **d.** impeached

30. _____c_____

TEST LESSONS 16, 17, AND 18

PART B CHOOSING THE BEST WORD

On the answer line, write the letter of the word that best expresses the meaning of the italicized word or phrase.

16. The poem "The Charge of the Light Brigade" tells of men who suffered because someone had *made a serious mistake.*
    a. repented   **b.** flustered   **c.** misinterpreted   **d.** blundered

    16. _____

17. The cause of the blaze was *the crime of deliberately setting fires.*
    a. a faux pas   **b.** a felony   **c.** arson   **d.** anarchy

    17. _____

18. Private Johnson adjusted to the *simple and self-disciplined* existence of boot camp.
    a. Spartan   **b.** conservative   **c.** corrupt   **d.** authoritarian

    18. _____

19. The lawyer proved that the testimony was *false.*
    a. erroneous   **b.** misinterpreted   **c.** bewildering   **d.** conservative

    19. _____

20. Uriah Heep, the *immoral* acquaintance of David Copperfield, was imprisoned.
    a. Spartan   **b.** tyrannical   **c.** corrupt   **d.** fallible

    20. _____

21. The senate agreed not to *accuse of unacceptable conduct in office* the governor.
    a. impeach   **b.** acquit   **c.** incriminate   **d.** bewilder

    21. _____

22. The engineers admitted that they were *capable of making an error.*
    a. corrupt   **b.** fallible   **c.** amiss   **d.** counterfeit

    22. _____

23. The defendant was *freed from formal accusation of wrongdoing.*
    a. bewildered   **b.** impeached   **c.** incriminated   **d.** acquitted

    23. _____

24. Anne sprinkled her cereal with a *generous in amount* helping of raisins.
    a. fallible   **b.** liberal   **c.** conservative   **d.** Spartan

    24. _____

25. Nico realized that something was *out of proper order.*
    a. amiss   **b.** authoritarian   **c.** liberal   **d.** corrupt

    25. _____

26. "Who is the *person guilty of an offense* who ate all the popcorn?" asked Dad.
    a. delegate   **b.** culprit   **c.** Spartan   **d.** tyrant

    26. _____

27. Pisistratus was an *oppressor* who controlled Athens during the sixth century B.C.
    a. culprit   **b.** delegate   **c.** tyrant   **d.** Spartan

    27. _____

28. Alice was *befuddled* by the actions of the White Rabbit.
    a. conservative   **b.** bewildered   **c.** flustered   **d.** corrupt

    28. _____

29. The police discovered two rooms of *dishonestly copied* designer clothes.
    a. fallible   **b.** corrupt   **c.** hijacked   **d.** counterfeit

    29. _____

30. The alliance between the countries *initiated* an era of prosperity.
    a. incriminated   **b.** bewildered   **c.** inaugurated   **d.** impeached

    30. _____

BONUS LESSONS 19 AND 20

(pages 121–132)

Use the clues to complete the crossword puzzle.

A crossword puzzle grid with the following filled answers:

- 1 Across / 2 Down area: MOMENTOUS
- 3 Down: G
- 4 Across: IMMODERATE
- 2 Down: OUTRAGEOUS
- 5 Down: GLUT
- 6 Down: PROFUSE
- 7 Down: FOREMOST
- 8 Across: SMALL
- 9 Down: STATUS
- 10 Across: PROMINENCE
- 11 Across: ROAD
- 12 Down: INCLINE
- 13 Down: EMINENCE
- 12 Across / 13: INDISPENSABLE
- 14 Down: ESSENTIAL
- 15 Across: SPENDTHRIFT
- 16 Across: SURFACE
- 17 Down: DEEPLY
- 18 Across: PRIORITY
- 19 Across: EMBELLISH
- 20 Across: LAVISH

Across

1. Graduation is this kind of an occasion.

4. Done to an extreme

8. A *petty* complaint is a(n) _____ grievance.

10. The condition of being widely known

11. *Trivial* comes from the Latin word *via*, meaning "_____."

12. Opposite of unnecessary

15. One who spends money foolishly

16. A *superficial* wound exists only on the _____.

18. Primary importance

19. To make beautiful with decoration

20. From the Old French word *lavasse*, meaning "downpour"

Down

2. Shocking

3. To *exceed* is to _____ beyond reasonable limits.

5. An excess of goods may _____ the market.

6. Abundant

7. A *paramount* idea is of _____ importance.

9. To have *prestige* is to possess great _____.

13. The condition of being outstanding in performance or character

14. *Luxurious* items give pleasure but are not _____.

17. *Intense* emotions are _____ felt.

BONUS LESSONS 19 AND 20

(pages 121–132)

Use the clues to complete the crossword puzzle.

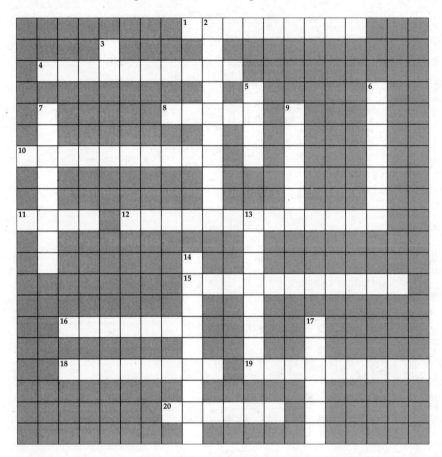

Across

1. Graduation is this kind of an occasion.
4. Done to an extreme
8. A *petty* complaint is a(n) _____ grievance.
10. The condition of being widely known
11. *Trivial* comes from the Latin word *via*, meaning "_____."
12. Opposite of unnecessary
15. One who spends money foolishly
16. A *superficial* wound exists only on the _____.
18. Primary importance
19. To make beautiful with decoration
20. From the Old French word *lavasse*, meaning "downpour"

Down

2. Shocking
3. To *exceed* is to _____ beyond reasonable limits.
5. An excess of goods may _____ the market.
6. Abundant
7. A *paramount* idea is of _____ importance.
9. To have *prestige* is to possess great _____.
13. The condition of being outstanding in performance or character
14. *Luxurious* items give pleasure but are not _____.
17. *Intense* emotions are _____ felt.

TEST LESSONS 19, 20, AND 21

(pages 121–138)

PART A CHOOSING THE BEST DEFINITION

On the answer line, write the letter of the best definition of the italicized word.

1. An *eminent* physician will represent our town at the state convention.
   a. outstanding   **b.** reliable   **c.** kindly   **d.** generous

   1. _____a_____

2. Success in the stock market depends on the proper *discrimination* between risk and sound investment.
   a. relationship   **c.** ability to distinguish
   b. understanding   **d.** ability to guess

   2. _____c_____

3. Robert Browning wrote that "a man's reach should *exceed* his grasp."
   a. be less than   **c.** be greater than
   b. come before   **d.** come after

   3. _____c_____

4. Surviving the winter of 1620–1621 was the American Pilgrims' *paramount* concern.
   a. wishful   **b.** deliberate   **c.** chief   **d.** ever present

   4. _____c_____

5. Jeremy cannot *abide* noise while he studies.
   a. sacrifice   **b.** tolerate   **c.** prevent   **d.** avoid

   5. _____b_____

6. The fans displayed *immoderate* anger over the defeat.
   a. senseless   **b.** little   **c.** contagious   **d.** excessive

   6. _____d_____

7. Mike's *preconceived* notions about sports changed dramatically.
   a. ridiculous   **c.** firm
   b. formed without evidence   **d.** limited in experience

   7. _____b_____

8. Although many British people are *partisans* of the monarchy, some would like to see it replaced.
   a. supporters   **b.** opponents   **c.** rulers   **d.** founders

   8. _____a_____

9. Annie *embellished* her story about the zucchini cake disaster.
   a. published   **b.** wrote   **c.** forgot   **d.** exaggerated

   9. _____d_____

10. The team's *priority* is to stop Number 24 from getting the ball.
    a. job   **b.** responsibility   **c.** main consideration   **d.** strategy

    10. _____c_____

11. Alice did not want to *prejudice* Armando against the movie.
    a. cause someone to be upset   **c.** restrain
    b. cause someone to judge prematurely   **d.** cause someone to miss

    11. _____b_____

12. Dr. Blau's *prestige* increased after the publication of her book.
    a. status   **b.** patients   **c.** finances   **d.** publicity

    12. _____a_____

13. Luke was surprised about the *prominence* of his role in the school play
    a. naturalness   **b.** limits   **c.** difficulty   **d.** conspicuousness

    13. _____d_____

14. Professor Walker is known for her *tolerance* of experimental theories.
    a. encouragement   **b.** agreement   **c.** acceptance   **d.** understanding

    14. _____c_____

15. The film critic gave *lavish* praise to the new adventure film.
    a. undeserved   **b.** little   **c.** generous   **d.** satisfying

    15. _____c_____

TEST LESSONS 19, 20, AND 21

(pages 121–138)

PART A CHOOSING THE BEST DEFINITION

On the answer line, write the letter of the best definition of the italicized word.

1. An *eminent* physician will represent our town at the state convention.
   a. outstanding **b.** reliable **c.** kindly **d.** generous

   1. _____

2. Success in the stock market depends on the proper *discrimination* between risk and sound investment.
   a. relationship **c.** ability to distinguish
   b. understanding **d.** ability to guess

   2. _____

3. Robert Browning wrote that "a man's reach should *exceed* his grasp."
   a. be less than **c.** be greater than
   b. come before **d.** come after

   3. _____

4. Surviving the winter of 1620–1621 was the American Pilgrims' *paramount* concern.
   a. wishful **b.** deliberate **c.** chief **d.** ever present

   4. _____

5. Jeremy cannot *abide* noise while he studies.
   a. sacrifice **b.** tolerate **c.** prevent **d.** avoid

   5. _____

6. The fans displayed *immoderate* anger over the defeat.
   a. senseless **b.** little **c.** contagious **d.** excessive

   6. _____

7. Mike's *preconceived* notions about sports changed dramatically.
   a. ridiculous **c.** firm
   b. formed without evidence **d.** limited in experience

   7. _____

8. Although many British people are *partisans* of the monarchy, some would like to see it replaced.
   a. supporters **b.** opponents **c.** rulers **d.** founders

   8. _____

9. Annie *embellished* her story about the zucchini cake disaster.
   a. published **b.** wrote **c.** forgot **d.** exaggerated

   9. _____

10. The team's *priority* is to stop Number 24 from getting the ball.
    a. job **b.** responsibility **c.** main consideration **d.** strategy

    10. _____

11. Alice did not want to *prejudice* Armando against the movie.
    a. cause someone to be upset **c.** restrain
    b. cause someone to judge prematurely **d.** cause someone to miss

    11. _____

12. Dr. Blau's *prestige* increased after the publication of her book.
    a. status **b.** patients **c.** finances **d.** publicity

    12. _____

13. Luke was surprised about the *prominence* of his role in the school play.
    a. naturalness **b.** limits **c.** difficulty **d.** conspicuousness

    13. _____

14. Professor Walker is known for her *tolerance* of experimental theories.
    a. encouragement **b.** agreement **c.** acceptance **d.** understanding

    14. _____

15. The film critic gave *lavish* praise to the new adventure film.
    a. undeserved **b.** little **c.** generous **d.** satisfying

    15. _____

TEST LESSONS 19, 20, AND 21

PART B IDENTIFYING SYNONYMS

On the answer line, write the letter of the word or phrase that has the same meaning as that of the capitalized word.

16. BIAS:
    a. tape   b. partiality   c. intensity   d. neutrality

17. INDISPENSABLE :
    a. necessary   b. insulting   c. inadequate   d. solid

18. GLUT:
    a. bother   b. harvest   c. reduction   d. oversupply

19. SUPERFICIAL:
    a. rough   b. obvious   c. superb   d. shallow

20. MOMENTOUS:
    a. huge   b. negligible   c. important   d. timely

21. SPENDTHRIFT:
    a. wasteful   b. precise   c. inexpensive   d. miserly

22. OBJECTIVE:
    a. photographic b. emotional   c. false   d. neutral

23. TRIVIAL:
    a. insensitive   b. ordinary   c. profound   d. three-tiered

24. LUXURIOUS:
    a. expensively magnificent   c. uncomfortable
    b. essentially wholesome   d. worshipful

25. AMENABLE:
    a. agreeable   b. uncooperative c. stubborn   d. friendly

26. PETTY:
    a. unattractive b. unmistakable   c. minor   d. confused

27. INTENSE:
    a. subdued   b. forceful   c. lazy   d. musical

28. FORBEARANCE:
    a. descendants   b. apology   c. patience   d. accuracy

29. OUTRAGEOUS:
    a. shocking   b. hasty   c. angry   d. privileged

30. PROFUSE:
    a. threatening   b. abundant   c. supreme   d. proper

16. ____b____

17. ____a____

18. ____d____

19. ____d____

20. ____c____

21. ____a____

22. ____d____

23. ____b____

24. ____a____

25. ____a____

26. ____c____

27. ____b____

28. ____c____

29. ____a____

30. ____b____

TEST LESSONS 19, 20, AND 21

PART B IDENTIFYING SYNONYMS

On the answer line, write the letter of the word or phrase that has the same meaning as that of the capitalized word.

16. BIAS:
    a. tape   b. partiality   c. intensity   d. neutrality

16. _____

17. INDISPENSABLE :
    a. necessary   b. insulting   c. inadequate   d. solid

17. _____

18. GLUT:
    a. bother   b. harvest   c. reduction   d. oversupply

18. _____

19. SUPERFICIAL:
    a. rough   b. obvious   c. superb   d. shallow

19. _____

20. MOMENTOUS:
    a. huge   b. negligible   c. important   d. timely

20. _____

21. SPENDTHRIFT:
    a. wasteful   b. precise   c. inexpensive   d. miserly

21. _____

22. OBJECTIVE:
    a. photographic b. emotional   c. false   d. neutral

22. _____

23. TRIVIAL:
    a. insensitive   b. ordinary   c. profound   d. three-tiered

23. _____

24. LUXURIOUS:
    a. expensively magnificent   c. uncomfortable
    b. essentially wholesome   d. worshipful

24. _____

25. AMENABLE:
    a. agreeable   b. uncooperative c. stubborn   d. friendly

25. _____

26. PETTY:
    a. unattractive b. unmistakable   c. minor   d. confused

26. _____

27. INTENSE:
    a. subdued   b. forceful   c. lazy   d. musical

27. _____

28. FORBEARANCE:
    a. descendants   b. apology   c. patience   d. accuracy

28. _____

29. OUTRAGEOUS:
    a. shocking   b. hasty   c. angry   d. privileged

29. _____

30. PROFUSE:
    a. threatening   b. abundant   c. supreme   d. proper

30. _____

BONUS LESSONS 21 AND 22

(pages 133–138, 141–146)

Use the following clues to identify the words, and write the words on the lines to the right. Then circle each word in the word-search box below. The words may overlap and may read in any direction.

1. *Tolerance* involves _____ for the opinions of others. (7 letters)

2. Synonym for *administer* (6 letters)

3. *Concoct* comes from the Latin word meaning "to _____." (4 letters)

4. Synonym for *render* (4 letters)

5. An undertaking is a(n) _____. (4 letters)

6. You can expect an *amenable* person to _____. (9 letters)

7. *Preconceived* opinions are formed _____ knowing the facts. (6 letters)

8. Synonym for *forbearance* (8 letters)

9. To *reactivate* is to make active _____. (5 letters)

10. An attempt to accomplish something (8 letters)

11. *Animate* comes from a Latin word meaning "_____." (4 letters)

12. Federal laws prevent _____ on the basis of race, creed, age, or sex. (14 letters)

13. To form or arrange in the mind (6 letters)

14. This prevents one from judging situations fairly. (4 letters)

15. A strong supporter of a party or cause (8 letters)

1. ___respect___
2. ___direct___
3. ___cook___
4. ___give___
5. ___task___
6. ___cooperate___
7. ___before___
8. ___patience___
9. ___again___
10. ___endeavor___
11. ___soul___
12. ___discrimination___
13. ___devise___
14. ___bias___
15. ___partisan___

Challenge

Locate and circle the five additional vocabulary words in the word-search box.

abide
execute
implement
objective
prejudice

```
A D M I N A N I M A C O N C O D E V I
T C E R I D I S C R I M I N A T I O N
E O S N D E A V O K E C I D U J E R P
X O I O M P L E O M E T N R E A C L U
E P R E U N D O E R U N A D B E R T A
C E K I N L C G A B I B S I A I C I R
S R O B J E C T I V E C I R I M A N O
A A C I M P L E M E N T M A T I S V
F T R B E A R R O X B J R E C T I E A
O E P A R T O I E S K S A T A A N S E
R P C O N F E C I V E D P J G U D I D
E G I V E D U A M E D I B A I N I V N
T L R B C T C E P S E R I S T E R E E
O W A N E O B J E E C N E I T A P D T
```

BONUS LESSONS 21 AND 22

(pages 133–138, 141–146)

Use the following clues to identify the words, and write the words on the lines to the right. Then circle each word in the word-search box below. The words may overlap and may read in any direction.

1. *Tolerance* involves _____ for the opinions of others.   (7 letters)

2. Synonym for *administer*   (6 letters)

3. *Concoct* comes from the Latin word meaning "to _____."   (4 letters)

4. Synonym for *render*   (4 letters)

5. An undertaking is a(n) _____.   (4 letters)

6. You can expect an *amenable* person to _____.   (9 letters)

7. *Preconceived* opinions are formed _____ knowing the facts.   (6 letters)

8. Synonym for *forbearance*   (8 letters)

9. To *reactivate* is to make active _____.   (5 letters)

10. An attempt to accomplish something   (8 letters)

11. *Animate* comes from a Latin word meaning "_____."   (4 letters)

12. Federal laws prevent _____ on the basis of race, creed, age, or sex.   (14 letters)

13. To form or arrange in the mind   (6 letters)

14. This prevents one from judging situations fairly.   (4 letters)

15. A strong supporter of a party or cause   (8 letters)

1. _____

2. _____

3. _____

4. _____

5. _____

6. _____

7. _____

8. _____

9. _____

10. _____

11. _____

12. _____

13. _____

14. _____

15. _____

```
A  D  M  I  N  A  N  I  M  A  C  O  N  C  O  D  E  V  I
T  C  E  R  I  D  I  S  C  R  I  M  I  N  A  T  I  O  N
E  O  S  N  D  E  A  V  O  K  E  C  I  D  U  J  E  R  P
X  O  I  O  M  P  L  E  O  M  E  T  N  R  E  A  C  L  U
E  P  R  E  U  N  D  O  E  R  U  N  A  D  B  E  R  T  A
C  E  K  I  N  L  C  G  A  B  I  B  S  I  A  I  C  I  R
S  R  O  B  J  E  C  T  I  V  E  C  I  R  I  M  A  N  O
A  A  C  I  I  M  P  L  E  M  E  N  T  M  A  T  I  S  V
F  T  R  B  E  A  R  R  O  X  B  J  R  E  C  T  I  E  A
O  E  P  A  R  T  O  I  E  S  K  S  A  T  A  A  N  S  E
R  P  C  O  N  F  E  C  I  V  E  D  P  J  G  U  D  I  D
E  G  I  V  E  D  U  A  M  E  D  I  B  A  I  N  I  V  N
T  L  R  B  C  T  C  E  P  S  E  R  I  S  T  E  R  E  E
O  W  A  N  E  O  B  J  E  E  C  N  E  I  T  A  P  D  T
```

Challenge

Locate and circle the five additional vocabulary words in the word-search box.

_____

BONUS LESSONS 23 AND 24

(pages 147–158)

Use the clues to complete the crossword puzzle.

							¹P	O	R	T	A	B	L	E		
							L									
				²P	O	R	T	A	G	E						
³I							Y									
N							F									
S			⁴F			U		⁵C	H	A	O	⁶S			⁷S	
U		⁸P	E	A	C	E	F	U	L			P			T	
P			L									E			E	
P		⁹D	I	S	P	¹⁰O	R	T		¹¹P	O	R	T	E	R	
O		Y		E		N				O		D			A	
R		N		L		E		¹²C	A	R	R	Y		¹³C	D	
T		A		Y						T				O	F	
A		M								F				M	A	
¹⁴B	O	I	S	T	E	R	O	U	¹⁵S	O		¹⁶C	O	M	P	O	R	T
L		C							T	L		O		L		
E						¹⁷I	M	P	A	T	I	E	N	T		
						T			T	O		D		A		
						I			I			U		C		
						C			C			C		E		
									T			T		N		
														T		

Across

1. Conveniently moved
2. Necessary when land separates two waterways
5. Great confusion
8. Synonym for *tranquil*
9. To entertain oneself
11. A person employed to carry luggage for travelers
12. The meaning of the Latin root *-port-*
14. Noisy and lacking discipline
16. To _____ oneself in a particular way
17. Synonym for *restive*

Down

1. A *sportive* mood is _____.
3. Intolerable
4. To *purport* is to give the impression, often _____, of being or intending.
6. Synonym for *velocity*
7. Fixed or unchanging
9. From a Greek word meaning "powerful"
10. The meaning of the prefix in *monotonous*
11. A carrying case for papers or photographs
13. Smug
15. Having no motion
16. Synonym for *deportment*

BONUS LESSONS 23 AND 24

(pages 147–158)

Use the clues to complete the crossword puzzle.

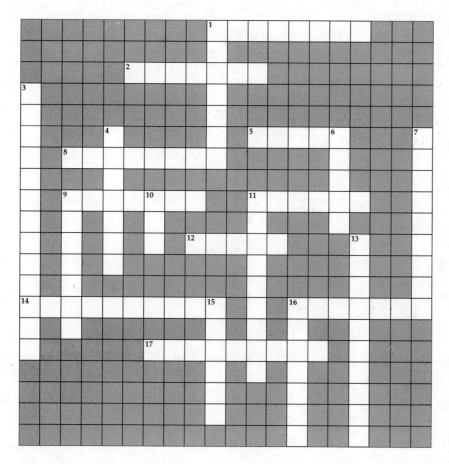

Across

1. Conveniently moved

2. Necessary when land separates two waterways

5. Great confusion

8. Synonym for *tranquil*

9. To entertain oneself

11. A person employed to carry luggage for travelers

12. The meaning of the Latin root *-port-*

14. Noisy and lacking discipline

16. To _____ oneself in a particular way

17. Synonym for *restive*

Down

1. A *sportive* mood is _____.

3. Intolerable

4. To *purport* is to give the impression, often _____, of being or intending.

6. Synonym for *velocity*

7. Fixed or unchanging

9. From a Greek word meaning "powerful"

10. The meaning of the prefix in *monotonous*

11. A carrying case for papers or photographs

13. Smug

15. Having no motion

16. Synonym for *deportment*

TEST LESSONS 22, 23, AND 24

(pages 141–158)

PART A COMPLETING THE DEFINITION

On the answer line, write the letter of the word or phrase that correctly completes each sentence.

1. *Executing* one's duties involves _____ them.
   a. forgetting   **b.** performing   **c.** ignoring   **d.** enduring

2. A *restive* person is _____.
   a. silent   **b.** sleepy   **c.** cheerful   **d.** impatient

3. The carrying of _____ is called *portage*.
   a. heavy objects by animals   **c.** manufactured articles
   b. a boat and supplies over land   **d.** luggage

4. To *reactivate* something is to restore its _____.
   a. reputation   **b.** value   **c.** glamor   **d.** ability to function

5. Anything that is _____ is *static*.
   a. horrifying   **b.** electrical   **c.** exact   **d.** motionless

6. A *porter* _____.
   a. tastes food for a chef   **c.** carries baggage for travelers
   b. moves heavy furniture   **d.** writes articles for newspapers

7. To *implement* something is to _____.
   a. divide it equally   **c.** put it into effect
   b. store it carefully   **d.** reduce it to rubble

8. Someone can be described as *steadfast* when he or she is _____.
   a. loyal   **b.** snobbish   **c.** clever   **d.** poor

9. A *portfolio* is a(n) _____.
   a. stage set   **b.** advertisement   **c.** carrying case   **d.** vehicle

10. An *undertaking* is a _____.
    a. tool   **b.** discovery   **c.** substitute   **d.** task

11. A *tranquil* person feels _____.
    a. agitated   **b.** unhappy   **c.** calm   **d.** seasick

12. *Sportive* applies to something that is _____.
    a. playful   **b.** colorful   **c.** competitive   **d.** repetitive

13. When you *render* aid, you _____ assistance.
    a. question the need for   **b.** provide   **c.** promise   **d.** schedule

14. The *velocity* of an object is its _____.
    a. uniqueness   **b.** speed   **c.** physical dimensions   **d.** sound

15. To *purport* to be something is to _____ having that identity.
    a. profess   **b.** deny   **c.** question   **d.** prefer

1. _____ b
2. _____ d
3. _____ b
4. _____ d
5. _____ d
6. _____ c
7. _____ c
8. _____ a
9. _____ c
10. _____ d
11. _____ c
12. _____ a
13. _____ b
14. _____ b
15. _____ a

TEST LESSONS 22, 23, AND 24

(pages 141–158)

PART A COMPLETING THE DEFINITION

On the answer line, write the letter of the word or phrase that correctly completes each sentence.

1. *Executing* one's duties involves _____ them.
   a. forgetting **b.** performing **c.** ignoring **d.** enduring

   1. _____

2. A *restive* person is _____.
   a. silent **b.** sleepy **c.** cheerful **d.** impatient

   2. _____

3. The carrying of _____ is called *portage*.
   a. heavy objects by animals **c.** manufactured articles
   b. a boat and supplies over land **d.** luggage

   3. _____

4. To *reactivate* something is to restore its _____.
   a. reputation **b.** value **c.** glamor **d.** ability to function

   4. _____

5. Anything that is _____ is *static*.
   a. horrifying **b.** electrical **c.** exact **d.** motionless

   5. _____

6. A *porter* _____.
   a. tastes food for a chef **c.** carries baggage for travelers
   b. moves heavy furniture **d.** writes articles for newspapers

   6. _____

7. To *implement* something is to _____.
   a. divide it equally **c.** put it into effect
   b. store it carefully **d.** reduce it to rubble

   7. _____

8. Someone can be described as *steadfast* when he or she is _____.
   a. loyal **b.** snobbish **c.** clever **d.** poor

   8. _____

9. A *portfolio* is a(n) _____.
   a. stage set **b.** advertisement **c.** carrying case **d.** vehicle

   9. _____

10. An *undertaking* is a _____.
    a. tool **b.** discovery **c.** substitute **d.** task

    10. _____

11. A *tranquil* person feels _____.
    a. agitated **b.** unhappy **c.** calm **d.** seasick

    11. _____

12. *Sportive* applies to something that is _____.
    a. playful **b.** colorful **c.** competitive **d.** repetitive

    12. _____

13. When you *render* aid, you _____ assistance.
    a. question the need for **b.** provide **c.** promise **d.** schedule

    13. _____

14. The *velocity* of an object is its _____.
    a. uniqueness **b.** speed **c.** physical dimensions **d.** sound

    14. _____

15. To *purport* to be something is to _____ having that identity.
    a. profess **b.** deny **c.** question **d.** prefer

    15. _____

TEST LESSONS 22, 23, AND 24

PART B CHOOSING THE BEST WORD

On the answer line, write the letter of the word that best completes the sentence.

16. The advice columnist was unable to _____ a solution to her reader's problem.
    a. execute   **b.** undertake   **c.** implement   **d.** devise

16. _____ d

17. Kevin quit his job after his working conditions had become _____.
    a. insupportable   **b.** animated   **c.** sportive   **d.** restive

17. _____ a

18. Insecure people may see confident individuals as _____.
    a. boisterous   **b.** dynamic   **c.** complacent   **d.** sportive

18. _____ c

19. Shirley made a valiant _____ to save the old theater from demolition.
    a. portage   **b.** undertaking   **c.** endeavor   **d.** deportment

19. _____ c

20. Cafeteria monitors will not tolerate rowdy _____.
    a. concoctions   **b.** velocity   **c.** deportment   **d.** chaos

20. _____ c

21. Ruth was lulled to sleep by the _____ drone of the lawnmower.
    a. static   **b.** monotonous   **c.** complacent   **d.** dynamic

21. _____ b

22. Quiz show contestants are expected to be intelligent and _____.
    a. animated   **b.** reactivated   **c.** restive   **d.** monotonous

22. _____ a

23. If the children promise to _____ themselves well while we're out, we'll bring them a surprise.
    a. concoct   **b.** comport   **c.** animate   **d.** purport

23. _____ b

24. The rules make it clear that no _____ activities are permitted during study hours.
    a. monotonous   **b.** boisterous   **c.** insupportable   **d.** tranquil

24. _____ b

25. This medication must be _____ to the patient at four-hour intervals.
    a. administered   **b.** reactivated   **c.** executed   **d.** concocted

25. _____ a

26. Chelsea picked up the _____ television and carried it into the den.
    a. portable   **b.** dynamic   **c.** static   **d.** monotonous

26. _____ a

27. Robert is a powerful salesman because he has such a _____ personality.
    a. restive   **b.** monotonous   **c.** tranquil   **d.** dynamic

27. _____ d

28. The secret agent _____ an alibi for her absence from the country.
    a. executed   **b.** disported   **c.** concocted   **d.** purported

28. _____ c

29. If young children have the right kind of toys, they can learn to _____ themselves at a very early age.
    a. reactivate   **b.** animate   **c.** render   **d.** disport

29. _____ d

30. The appearance of the cat created _____ among the dogs in the veterinarian's waiting room.
    a. deportment   **b.** static   **c.** chaos   **d.** velocity

30. _____ c

TEST LESSONS 22, 23, AND 24

PART B CHOOSING THE BEST WORD

On the answer line, write the letter of the word that best completes the sentence.

16. The advice columnist was unable to _____ a solution to her reader's problem.
    a. execute   **b.** undertake   **c.** implement   **d.** devise

16. _____

17. Kevin quit his job after his working conditions had become _____.
    a. insupportable   **b.** animated   **c.** sportive   **d.** restive

17. _____

18. Insecure people may see confident individuals as _____.
    a. boisterous   **b.** dynamic   **c.** complacent   **d.** sportive

18. _____

19. Shirley made a valiant _____ to save the old theater from demolition.
    a. portage   **b.** undertaking   **c.** endeavor   **d.** deportment

19. _____

20. Cafeteria monitors will not tolerate rowdy _____.
    a. concoctions   **b.** velocity   **c.** deportment   **d.** chaos

20. _____

21. Ruth was lulled to sleep by the _____ drone of the lawnmower.
    a. static   **b.** monotonous   **c.** complacent   **d.** dynamic

21. _____

22. Quiz show contestants are expected to be intelligent and _____.
    a. animated   **b.** reactivated   **c.** restive   **d.** monotonous

22. _____

23. If the children promise to _____ themselves well while we're out, we'll bring them a surprise.
    a. concoct   **b.** comport   **c.** animate   **d.** purport

23. _____

24. The rules make it clear that no _____ activities are permitted during study hours.
    a. monotonous   **b.** boisterous   **c.** insupportable   **d.** tranquil

24. _____

25. This medication must be _____ to the patient at four-hour intervals.
    a. administered   **b.** reactivated   **c.** executed   **d.** concocted

25. _____

26. Chelsea picked up the _____ television and carried it into the den.
    a. portable   **b.** dynamic   **c.** static   **d.** monotonous

26. _____

27. Robert is a powerful salesman because he has such a _____ personality.
    a. restive   **b.** monotonous   **c.** tranquil   **d.** dynamic

27. _____

28. The secret agent _____ an alibi for her absence from the country.
    a. executed   **b.** disported   **c.** concocted   **d.** purported

28. _____

29. If young children have the right kind of toys, they can learn to _____ themselves at a very early age.
    a. reactivate   **b.** animate   **c.** render   **d.** disport

29. _____

30. The appearance of the cat created _____ among the dogs in the veterinarian's waiting room.
    a. deportment   **b.** static   **c.** chaos   **d.** velocity

30. _____

BONUS LESSONS 25 AND 26

(pages 161–172)

Unscramble the letters of each italicized vocabulary word, and write the word on the answer line to the right.

1. Nobel scientists *mybdoe* the spirit of dedication and hard work.

2. Each of the puppies has a(n) *nitcsdti* personality.

3. The American colonists fought to *eaeprl* England's harsh and restrictive laws.

4. The insect *npllreeet* had little effect on the ravenous mosquitoes.

5. Finishing the race, the runner could feel her heart *stlpaue*.

6. We sometimes forget that the change of seasons is *pmerintenos*.

7. Because of the dense vegetation, *eettnpnrioa* of the jungle was difficult.

8. The students spent a(n) *ttlbsaiusan* portion of their time studying.

9. The townspeople were accustomed to the hourly *lpae* of the church bells.

10. Louise was not a(n) *luievmpsi* shopper, but she could not resist buying another hat.

11. The patient's *nsmooiplcu* to exercise worried the doctor.

12. Compared to Maria's excellent work, Kristen's report was *gnlaaimr*.

13. Bob's sprained hand was definitely *dsedidten*.

14. The odor of the polluted pond *eueldspr* the hikers.

15. In a gentle tone, the child *lldpemei* the cat to jump down from the closet shelf.

16. The burning desert marked the eastern *esiocfnn* of the country.

17. The racing car's incredible speed was due to jet *sluoiopprn*.

18. The artist *eeeatddlni* the arches and columns of the amphitheater in the sketch.

19. The lines of *rcmtneaaoid* showed up clearly on the surveyor's map.

20. A shortage of gasoline *ldploeecm* people to drive less.

1. __embody__
2. __distinct__
3. __repeal__

4. __repellant__
5. __pulsate__
6. __omnipresent__
7. __penetration__
8. __substantial__
9. __peal__
10. __impulsive__

11. __compulsion__
12. __marginal__
13. __distended__
14. __repulsed__
15. __impelled__

16. __confines__
17. __propulsion__
18. __delineated__

19. __demarcation__
20. __compelled__

BONUS LESSONS 25 AND 26

(pages 161–172)

Unscramble the letters of each italicized vocabulary word, and write the word on the answer line to the right.

1. Nobel scientists *mybdoe* the spirit of dedication and hard work.

          1. _____

2. Each of the puppies has a(n) *nitcsdti* personality.

          2. _____

3. The American colonists fought to *eaeprl* England's harsh and restrictive laws.

          3. _____

4. The insect *npllreeet* had little effect on the ravenous mosquitoes.

          4. _____

5. Finishing the race, the runner could feel her heart *stlpaue*.

          5. _____

6. We sometimes forget that the change of seasons is *pmerintenos*.

          6. _____

7. Because of the dense vegetation, *eettnpnrioa* of the jungle was difficult.

          7. _____

8. The students spent a(n) *ttlbsaiusan* portion of their time studying.

          8. _____

9. The townspeople were accustomed to the hourly *lpae* of the church bells.

          9. _____

10. Louise was not a(n) *luievmpsi* shopper, but she could not resist buying another hat.

          10. _____

11. The patient's *nsmooiplcu* to exercise worried the doctor.

          11. _____

12. Compared to Maria's excellent work, Kristen's report was *gnlaaimr*.

          12. _____

13. Bob's sprained hand was definitely *dsedidten*.

          13. _____

14. The odor of the polluted pond *eueldspr* the hikers.

          14. _____

15. In a gentle tone, the child *lldpemei* the cat to jump down from the closet shelf.

          15. _____

16. The burning desert marked the eastern *esiocfnn* of the country.

          16. _____

17. The racing car's incredible speed was due to jet *sluoiopprn*.

          17. _____

18. The artist *eeeatddlni* the arches and columns of the amphitheater in the sketch.

          18. _____

19. The lines of *rcmtneaaoid* showed up clearly on the surveyor's map.

          19. _____

20. A shortage of gasoline *ldploeecm* people to drive less.

          20. _____

TEST LESSONS 25, 26, AND 27

(pages 161–178)

PART A CHOOSING THE BEST DEFINITION

On the answer line, write the letter of the best definition of the italicized word.

1. The *demarcation* of the two properties had never been recorded.
   a. map   **b.** history   **c.** geography   **d.** separation

   1. _____d_____

2. Diane is motivated by a *compulsion* to be the best at whatever she does.
   a. attempt   **b.** reward   **c.** code   **d.** urge

   2. _____d_____

3. Ethan followed the squirrel to its *cache* of nuts.
   a. nest   **b.** gift   **c.** wealth   **d.** hidden supply

   3. _____d_____

4. I got the *distinct* impression that something was bothering Darcie.
   a. unmistakable   **b.** logical   **c.** undefined   **d.** uncomfortable

   4. _____a_____

5. The rhythm of Poe's poem "The Bells" imitates the *peal* of its subject matter.
   a. color   **b.** attractiveness   **c.** ringing   **d.** shape

   5. _____c_____

6. A famous quotation from *Julius Caesar* is "The evil that men do lives after them, /The good is oft *interred* with their bones."
   a. buried   **b.** consumed   **c.** forgotten   **d.** destroyed

   6. _____a_____

7. George Orwell's *1984* describes a society in which there is no privacy, even within the *confines* of one's house.
   a. rooms   **b.** limits   **c.** secrecy   **d.** foundations

   7. _____b_____

8. Rose *impelled* her friends to join her crusade for a litter-free city.
   a. forced   **b.** selected   **c.** honored   **d.** urged

   8. _____d_____

9. The architects made the building *accessible* for the disabled.
   a. illegal   **b.** necessary   **c.** useless   **d.** approachable

   9. _____d_____

10. A balloon *distends* when it is blown up.
    a. breaks   **b.** is destroyed   **c.** expands   **d.** becomes rigid

    10. _____c_____

11. *Billy Budd,* a story by Herman Melville, relates the tragic consequences of a young man's *impulsive* actions.
    a. illegal   **b.** uncalculated   **c.** physical   **d.** ridiculous

    11. _____b_____

12. Paula felt uncomfortably *conspicuous* at the formal dance.
    a. noticeable   **b.** overdressed   **c.** anxious   **d.** ignored

    12. _____a_____

13. The captain of the debate team *delineated* the group's strategy.
    a. described in detail   **c.** improved the quality of
    b. restructured   **d.** eliminated

    13. _____a_____

14. Nothing would *compel* the dog to let go of its bone.
    a. allow   **b.** coax   **c.** force   **d.** exhaust

    14. _____c_____

15. The committee discovered several inaccuracies in the candidates' financial *disclosures*.
    a. records   **c.** business dealings
    b. revelations   **d.** campaign promises

    15. _____b_____

TEST LESSONS 25, 26, AND 27

(pages 161–178)

PART A CHOOSING THE BEST DEFINITION

On the answer line, write the letter of the best definition of the italicized word.

1. The *demarcation* of the two properties had never been recorded.
   a. map   **b.** history   **c.** geography   **d.** separation

   1. _____

2. Diane is motivated by a *compulsion* to be the best at whatever she does.
   a. attempt   **b.** reward   **c.** code   **d.** urge

   2. _____

3. Ethan followed the squirrel to its *cache* of nuts.
   a. nest   **b.** gift   **c.** wealth   **d.** hidden supply

   3. _____

4. I got the *distinct* impression that something was bothering Darcie.
   a. unmistakable   **b.** logical   **c.** undefined   **d.** uncomfortable

   4. _____

5. The rhythm of Poe's poem "The Bells" imitates the *peal* of its subject matter.
   a. color   **b.** attractiveness   **c.** ringing   **d.** shape

   5. _____

6. A famous quotation from *Julius Caesar* is "The evil that men do lives after them, /The good is oft *interred* with their bones."
   a. buried   **b.** consumed   **c.** forgotten   **d.** destroyed

   6. _____

7. George Orwell's *1984* describes a society in which there is no privacy, even within the *confines* of one's house.
   a. rooms   **b.** limits   **c.** secrecy   **d.** foundations

   7. _____

8. Rose *impelled* her friends to join her crusade for a litter-free city.
   a. forced   **b.** selected   **c.** honored   **d.** urged

   8. _____

9. The architects made the building *accessible* for the disabled.
   a. illegal   **b.** necessary   **c.** useless   **d.** approachable

   9. _____

10. A balloon *distends* when it is blown up.
    a. breaks   **b.** is destroyed   **c.** expands   **d.** becomes rigid

    10. _____

11. *Billy Budd*, a story by Herman Melville, relates the tragic consequences of a young man's *impulsive* actions.
    a. illegal   **b.** uncalculated   **c.** physical   **d.** ridiculous

    11. _____

12. Paula felt uncomfortably *conspicuous* at the formal dance.
    a. noticeable   **b.** overdressed   **c.** anxious   **d.** ignored

    12. _____

13. The captain of the debate team *delineated* the group's strategy.
    a. described in detail   **c.** improved the quality of
    b. restructured   **d.** eliminated

    13. _____

14. Nothing would *compel* the dog to let go of its bone.
    a. allow   **b.** coax   **c.** force   **d.** exhaust

    14. _____

15. The committee discovered several inaccuracies in the candidates' financial *disclosures*.
    a. records   **c.** business dealings
    b. revelations   **d.** campaign promises

    15. _____

TEST LESSONS 25, 26, AND 27

PART B CHOOSING THE BEST WORD

On the answer line, write the letter of the word that best expresses the meaning of the italicized word or phrase.

16. No one recognized the speaker's *uncommon* reference to Robert Frost's poem "Once by the Pacific."
    a. obscure   **b.** marginal   **c.** impulsive   **d.** omnipresent

    16. _____a_____

17. The town council voted to *withdraw officially* certain useless bylaws.
    a. inter   **b.** repulse   **c.** repeal   **d.** delineate

    17. _____c_____

18. Roger's qualifications for the job are *barely acceptable*.
    a. obscure   **b.** marginal   **c.** substantial   **d.** unavailable

    18. _____b_____

19. Erik just read a mystery novel about international *secret plots*.
    a. penetration   **b.** intrigue   **c.** compulsion   **d.** disclosure

    19. _____b_____

20. Technicians checked the *process of pushing forward* system of the space shuttle for today's lift off.
    a. repellent   **b.** demarcation   **c.** compulsion   **d.** propulsion

    20. _____d_____

21. A *considerable* portion of Wendy's first paycheck went to taxes.
    a. substantial   **b.** conspicuous   **c.** distinct   **d.** marginal

    21. _____a_____

22. During excavation for the office building, a construction worker *dug up* an old chest.
    a. embodied   **b.** unearthed   **c.** interred   **d.** delineated

    22. _____b_____

23. Alana could feel the blood *throb* at her temples.
    a. pulsate   **b.** penetrate   **c.** distend   **d.** impel

    23. _____a_____

24. Greek sculpture *gives concrete form to* the classical concepts of balance and proportion.
    a. repulses   **b.** compels   **c.** delineates   **d.** embodies

    24. _____d_____

25. The barber will be *not at hand* for appointments next week.
    a. unavailable   **b.** omnipresent   **c.** conspicuous   **d.** marginal

    25. _____a_____

26. Bigotry is *causing disgust* to most people.
    a. substantial   **b.** obscure   **c.** repellent   **d.** marginal

    26. _____c_____

27. A camera crew recorded the scientist's *act of entering* of the ancient crypt.
    a. disclosure   **b.** intrigue   **c.** penetration   **d.** demarcation

    27. _____c_____

28. Jan found her brother studying in an *isolated* corner of the library.
    a. marginal   **b.** obscure   **c.** secluded   **d.** conspicuous

    28. _____c_____

29. "If we're to win this game, we must *drive back* the next goal-line surge," the coach emphasized.
    a. repeal   **b.** repulse   **c.** penetrate   **d.** pulsate

    29. _____b_____

30. At the carnival the feeling of excitement was *in existence everywhere at the same time*.
    a. omnipresent   **b.** substantial   **c.** distinct   **d.** repellent

    30. _____a_____

TEST LESSONS 25, 26, AND 27

PART B CHOOSING THE BEST WORD

On the answer line, write the letter of the word that best expresses the meaning of the italicized word or phrase.

16. No one recognized the speaker's *uncommon* reference to Robert Frost's poem "Once by the Pacific."
    a. obscure   **b.** marginal   **c.** impulsive   **d.** omnipresent

    16. _____

17. The town council voted to *withdraw officially* certain useless bylaws.
    a. inter   **b.** repulse   **c.** repeal   **d.** delineate

    17. _____

18. Roger's qualifications for the job are *barely acceptable*.
    a. obscure   **b.** marginal   **c.** substantial   **d.** unavailable

    18. _____

19. Erik just read a mystery novel about international *secret plots*.
    a. penetration   **b.** intrigue   **c.** compulsion   **d.** disclosure

    19. _____

20. Technicians checked the *process of pushing forward* system of the space shuttle for today's lift off.
    a. repellent   **b.** demarcation   **c.** compulsion   **d.** propulsion

    20. _____

21. A *considerable* portion of Wendy's first paycheck went to taxes.
    a. substantial   **b.** conspicuous   **c.** distinct   **d.** marginal

    21. _____

22. During excavation for the office building, a construction worker *dug up* an old chest.
    a. embodied   **b.** unearthed   **c.** interred   **d.** delineated

    22. _____

23. Alana could feel the blood *throb* at her temples.
    a. pulsate   **b.** penetrate   **c.** distend   **d.** impel

    23. _____

24. Greek sculpture *gives concrete form to* the classical concepts of balance and proportion.
    a. repulses   **b.** compels   **c.** delineates   **d.** embodies

    24. _____

25. The barber will be *not at hand* for appointments next week.
    a. unavailable   **b.** omnipresent   **c.** conspicuous   **d.** marginal

    25. _____

26. Bigotry is *causing disgust* to most people.
    a. substantial   **b.** obscure   **c.** repellent   **d.** marginal

    26. _____

27. A camera crew recorded the scientist's *act of entering* of the ancient crypt.
    a. disclosure   **b.** intrigue   **c.** penetration   **d.** demarcation

    27. _____

28. Jan found her brother studying in an *isolated* corner of the library.
    a. marginal   **b.** obscure   **c.** secluded   **d.** conspicuous

    28. _____

29. "If we're to win this game, we must *drive back* the next goal-line surge," the coach emphasized.
    a. repeal   **b.** repulse   **c.** penetrate   **d.** pulsate

    29. _____

30. At the carnival the feeling of excitement was *in existence everywhere at the same time*.
    a. omnipresent   **b.** substantial   **c.** distinct   **d.** repellent

    30. _____

BONUS LESSONS 27 AND 28

(pages 173–178, 181–186)

Use the clues to complete the crossword puzzle.

			¹C												
²U		³F	R	A	G	M	E	N	T						
N			C												
A			H	⁴S		⁵D									
V		⁶E	R	U	P	T	I	O	N		⁷R				
A			D		G			⁸U	N	R	U	L	Y		
⁹I	¹⁰O	L	A	T	E	D					P				
L	B			¹¹E	A	R	T	H	¹³F	R	¹⁴A	C	T	U	S
A	S		¹⁵P	N		E			C		U				
B	C		L	F					C		S				
L	U		O	R					E						
E	¹⁶R	O	U	T		¹⁷L	A	W		¹⁸S	P	L	I	T	
	E			A		C	¹⁹D		S						
				T		²⁰I	N	F	R	I	N	G	E		
		²¹O	B	V	I	O	U	S		B					
				R		R				L					
				Y		U				E					
						P									
		²²R	E	V	E	L	A	T	I	O	N				

Across

3. An incomplete part

6. A volcanic _____

8. Synonym for *fractious*

9. A *secluded* location is _____.

11. *Inter* comes from the Latin word *terra*, meaning "_____."

13. Latin word meaning "shattered"

16. To drive out or force out

17. An *infraction* is a violation of the _____.

18. Synonym for *rupture*

20. A person should not _____ upon the rights of others.

21. Synonym for *conspicuous*

22. A *disclosure* is a(n) _____.

Down

1. A hidden supply or reserve

2. Not at hand

4. An *abrupt* ending is a(n) _____ conclusion.

5. To *unearth* is to _____ up from underground.

7. Latin word meaning "broken"

10. Not well known or not easily found

12. Stubborn or unmanageable

14. Easily approached, obtained, or reached

15. An *intrigue* is a scheme or secret _____.

19. To throw into confusion or disorder

BONUS LESSONS 27 AND 28

(pages 173–178, 181–186)

Use the clues to complete the crossword puzzle.

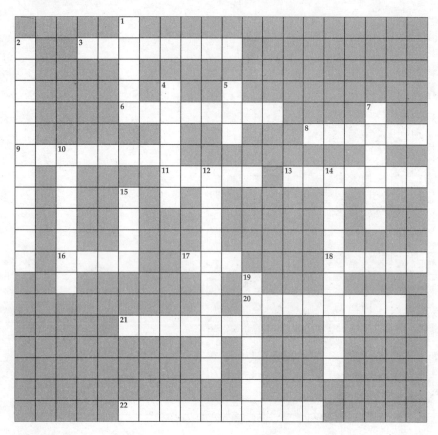

Across

3. An incomplete part

6. A volcanic _____

8. Synonym for *fractious*

9. A *secluded* location is _____.

11. *Inter* comes from the Latin word *terra*, meaning "_____."

13. Latin word meaning "shattered"

16. To drive out or force out

17. An *infraction* is a violation of the _____.

18. Synonym for *rupture*

20. A person should not _____ upon the rights of others.

21. Synonym for *conspicuous*

22. A *disclosure* is a(n) _____.

Down

1. A hidden supply or reserve

2. Not at hand

4. An *abrupt* ending is a(n) _____ conclusion.

5. To *unearth* is to _____ up from underground.

7. Latin word meaning "broken"

10. Not well known or not easily found

12. Stubborn or unmanageable

14. Easily approached, obtained, or reached

15. An *intrigue* is a scheme or secret _____.

19. To throw into confusion or disorder

BONUS LESSONS 29 AND 30

(pages 187–198)

Use the clues to complete the crossword puzzle.

```
 1H    2A                                      3P
4W E L L           5D        6S                 L
   L     T      7I N C A P A C I T A T E        E
   P     R    8A        N        O              N
   U     A  L        G        F        9C    T   10I
 11C R I T I C I Z E     F     12B E N I G N
   S     E          R        N     F     D
   T     N                   S     U     U
 13D I S A P P R O V A L     U     L     L
   C     T            14G     R        G
 15B E N E F A C T O R     E
   E                  A
16H U M A N I T A R I A N   T
   E                  I
17H A R M F U L          F
      I             Y
      C
18D E T R I M E N T
      A
 19M A L I G N
```

Across

4. *Benevolent* comes from the Latin word *bene*, meaning "_____."

7. What an ankle injury could do to you.

11. If you *admonish* someone, you _____ that person in a kind, but serious, way.

12. Not especially harmful

13. To *denounce* is to express very strong _____.

15. One who helps another person in need

16. One who promotes social reform

17. Synonym for *injurious*

18. Something that causes damage, harm, or loss

19. To speak evil of

Down

1. *Philanthropic* pertains to the effort to _____ others.

2. From the Latin word *alter*, meaning "other"

3. Synonym for *bountiful*

5. To *imperil* involves putting something in _____.

6. To make fun of

8. To cause to become unfriendly

9. Disapproval or blame

10. To pamper

14. To please or satisfy

15. Something that promotes a favorable result is _____.

BONUS LESSONS 29 AND 30

(pages 187–198)

Use the clues to complete the crossword puzzle.

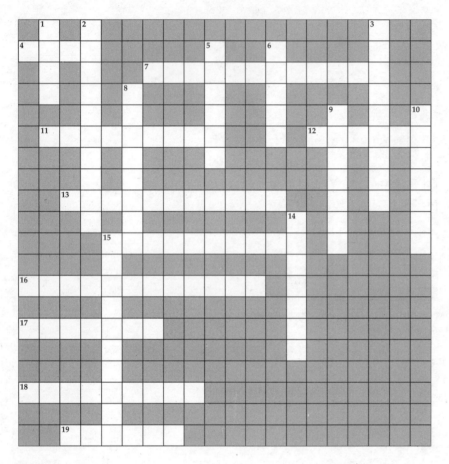

Across

4. *Benevolent* comes from the Latin word *bene*, meaning "_____."

7. What an ankle injury could do to you.

11. If you *admonish* someone, you _____ that person in a kind, but serious, way.

12. Not especially harmful

13. To *denounce* is to express very strong _____.

15. One who helps another person in need

16. One who promotes social reform

17. Synonym for *injurious*

18. Something that causes damage, harm, or loss

19. To speak evil of

Down

1. *Philanthropic* pertains to the effort to _____ others.

2. From the Latin word *alter*, meaning "other"

3. Synonym for *bountiful*

5. To *imperil* involves putting something in _____.

6. To make fun of

8. To cause to become unfriendly

9. Disapproval or blame

10. To pamper

14. To please or satisfy

15. Something that promotes a favorable result is _____.

T33

TEST LESSONS 28, 29, AND 30

(pages 181–198)

PART A COMPLETING THE DEFINITION

On the answer line, write the letter of the word or phrase that correctly completes each sentence.

1. When you *censure* someone, you _____ him or her.
   a. pay   **b.** trust   **c.** voluntarily help   **d.** severely criticize

   1. _____d_____

2. An *incapacitated* person is _____.
   a. disabled   **b.** mistaken   **c.** recommended   **d.** successful

   2. _____a_____

3. Anything that can _____ is said to be *injurious*.
   a. be decided by a jury   **c.** revive dying plants
   b. cause harm or damage   **d.** make a person stronger

   3. _____b_____

4. When you study *eruptions* in science, you learn about _____.
   a. rocks   **b.** the ocean   **c.** climate   **d.** explosions

   4. _____d_____

5. A *benefactor* is one who _____.
   a. helps others   **b.** is friendly   **c.** works hard   **d.** complains

   5. _____a_____

6. An *infraction* is a _____.
   a. major argument   **c.** minor concern
   b. violation of a law   **d.** perceptive observation

   6. _____b_____

7. If you *indulge* a child, you _____ him or her.
   a. confuse   **b.** punish   **c.** teach   **d.** pamper

   7. _____d_____

8. A *fractious* person is _____.
   a. practical   **b.** shy   **c.** irritable   **d.** well liked

   8. _____c_____

9. *Philanthropic* impulses are _____.
   a. unobserved   **b.** deceitful   **c.** astonishing   **d.** charitable

   9. _____d_____

10. Drivers who *infringe* the traffic laws _____ them.
    a. ignore   **b.** depend on   **c.** violate   **d.** enforce

    10. _____c_____

11. *Altruistic* people are _____.
    a. habitually late   **c.** unselfishly concerned about others
    b. dedicated   **d.** entertaining

    11. _____c_____

12. A *rout* is a _____.
    a. defeat   **b.** highway   **c.** weakness   **d.** refusal

    12. _____a_____

13. If you *scoff* at something, you _____ it.
    a. study   **b.** mock   **c.** ignore   **d.** cherish

    13. _____b_____

14. When a water or gas pipe *ruptures*, it _____.
    a. freezes   **b.** shrinks   **c.** breaks   **d.** becomes rusted

    14. _____c_____

15. *Humanitarian* contributions _____.
    a. help to improve human welfare   **c.** develop hidden talents
    b. inform others   **d.** prevent jealousy

    15. _____a_____

T34

TEST LESSONS 28, 29, AND 30

(pages 181–198)

PART A COMPLETING THE DEFINITION

On the answer line, write the letter of the word or phrase that correctly completes each sentence.

1. When you *censure* someone, you _____ him or her.
   a. pay   **b.** trust   **c.** voluntarily help   **d.** severely criticize

   1. _____

2. An *incapacitated* person is _____.
   a. disabled   **b.** mistaken   **c.** recommended **d.** successful

   2. _____

3. Anything that can _____ is said to be *injurious*.
   a. be decided by a jury   **c.** revive dying plants
   b. cause harm or damage   **d.** make a person stronger

   3. _____

4. When you study *eruptions* in science, you learn about _____.
   a. rocks   **b.** the ocean   **c.** climate   **d.** explosions

   4. _____

5. A *benefactor* is one who _____.
   a. helps others   **b.** is friendly   **c.** works hard   **d.** complains

   5. _____

6. An *infraction* is a _____.
   a. major argument   **c.** minor concern
   b. violation of a law   **d.** perceptive observation

   6. _____

7. If you *indulge* a child, you _____ him or her.
   a. confuse   **b.** punish   **c.** teach   **d.** pamper

   7. _____

8. A *fractious* person is _____.
   a. practical   **b.** shy   **c.** irritable   **d.** well liked

   8. _____

9. *Philanthropic* impulses are _____.
   a. unobserved   **b.** deceitful   **c.** astonishing   **d.** charitable

   9. _____

10. Drivers who *infringe* the traffic laws _____ them.
    a. ignore   **b.** depend on   **c.** violate   **d.** enforce

    10. _____

11. *Altruistic* people are _____.
    a. habitually late   **c.** unselfishly concerned about others
    b. dedicated   **d.** entertaining

    11. _____

12. A *rout* is a _____.
    a. defeat   **b.** highway   **c.** weakness   **d.** refusal

    12. _____

13. If you *scoff* at something, you _____ it.
    a. study   **b.** mock   **c.** ignore   **d.** cherish

    13. _____

14. When a water or gas pipe *ruptures*, it _____.
    a. freezes   **b.** shrinks   **c.** breaks   **d.** becomes rusted

    14. _____

15. *Humanitarian* contributions _____.
    a. help to improve human welfare   **c.** develop hidden talents
    b. inform others   **d.** prevent jealousy

    15. _____

T34

TEST LESSONS 28, 29, AND 30

PART B IDENTIFYING SYNONYMS

On the answer line, write the letter of the word or phrase that has the same meaning as that of the capitalized word.

16. BENEFICIAL:
    a. abnormal   **b.** harmful   **c.** advantageous   **d.** unnecessary

17. ABRUPT:
    a. sudden   **b.** rude   **c.** gradual   **d.** upset

18. DENOUNCE:
    a. arrive   **b.** combine   **c.** excel   **d.** condemn

19. BENIGN:
    a. kind   **b.** harsh   **c.** ancient   **d.** direct

20. MALIGN:
    a. praise moderately   **c.** speak evil of
    b. please   **d.** plan carefully

21. ALIENATE:
    a. frighten   **b.** befriend   **c.** disassociate   **d.** measure

22. BOUNTIFUL:
    a. large   **b.** scarce   **c.** festive   **d.** plentiful

23. FRAGMENT:
    a. separate   **b.** unify   **c.** torment   **d.** reduce

24. ADMONISH:
    a. baffle   **b.** warn   **c.** compliment   **d.** surprise

25. GRATIFY:
    a. smooth   **b.** satisfy   **c.** accept   **d.** displease

26. REFRACTORY:
    a. unresponsive   **b.** unmanageable   **c.** transparent   **d.** sloppy

27. DETRIMENT:
    a. damage   **b.** condiment   **c.** benefit   **d.** necessity

28. BENEVOLENT:
    a. lazy   **b.** kind   **c.** mean   **d.** dishonest

29. DISRUPT:
    a. hasten   **b.** organize   **c.** demand   **d.** hinder

30. IMPERIL:
    a. decorate   **b.** protect   **c.** endanger   **d.** neglect

16. ___c___
17. ___a___
18. ___d___
19. ___a___
20. ___c___
21. ___c___
22. ___d___
23. ___a___
24. ___b___
25. ___b___
26. ___b___
27. ___a___
28. ___b___
29. ___d___
30. ___c___

TEST LESSONS 28, 29, AND 30

PART B IDENTIFYING SYNONYMS

On the answer line, write the letter of the word or phrase that has the same meaning as that of the capitalized word.

16. BENEFICIAL:
    a. abnormal   **b.** harmful   **c.** advantageous   **d.** unnecessary

    16. _____

17. ABRUPT:
    a. sudden   **b.** rude   **c.** gradual   **d.** upset

    17. _____

18. DENOUNCE:
    a. arrive   **b.** combine   **c.** excel   **d.** condemn

    18. _____

19. BENIGN:
    a. kind   **b.** harsh   **c.** ancient   **d.** direct

    19. _____

20. MALIGN:
    a. praise moderately   **c.** speak evil of
    b. please   **d.** plan carefully

    20. _____

21. ALIENATE:
    a. frighten   **b.** befriend   **c.** disassociate   **d.** measure

    21. _____

22. BOUNTIFUL:
    a. large   **b.** scarce   **c.** festive   **d.** plentiful

    22. _____

23. FRAGMENT:
    a. separate   **b.** unify   **c.** torment   **d.** reduce

    23. _____

24. ADMONISH:
    a. baffle   **b.** warn   **c.** compliment   **d.** surprise

    24. _____

25. GRATIFY:
    a. smooth   **b.** satisfy   **c.** accept   **d.** displease

    25. _____

26. REFRACTORY:
    a. unresponsive   **b.** unmanageable   **c.** transparent   **d.** sloppy

    26. _____

27. DETRIMENT:
    a. damage   **b.** condiment   **c.** benefit   **d.** necessity

    27. _____

28. BENEVOLENT:
    a. lazy   **b.** kind   **c.** mean   **d.** dishonest

    28. _____

29. DISRUPT:
    a. hasten   **b.** organize   **c.** demand   **d.** hinder

    29. _____

30. IMPERIL:
    a. decorate   **b.** protect   **c.** endanger   **d.** neglect

    30. _____